ANTIMICROBIAL
CHEMOTHERAPY

ANTIMICROBIAL CHEMOTHERAPY

Edited by

DAVID GREENWOOD

University Hospital, Queen's Medical Centre
Nottingham

OXFORD   NEW YORK   TOKYO
OXFORD UNIVERSITY PRESS
1989

Oxford University Press, Walton Street, Oxford OX2 6DP

Oxford New York Toronto
Delhi Bombay Calcutta Madras Karachi
Petaling Jaya Singapore Hong Kong Tokyo
Nairobi Dar es Salaam Cape Town
Melbourne Auckland

and associated companies in
Berlin Ibadan

Oxford is a trade mark of Oxford University Press

Published in the United States
by Oxford University Press, New York

First edition published by Ballière Tindall, 1983
Second edition published by Oxford University Press, 1989

British Library Cataloguing in Publication Data
Antimicrobial chemotherapy.—2nd ed.
1. Medicine. Drug therapy. Antimicrobials
I. Greenwood, David
615. '329
ISBN 0-19-261817-2
ISBN 0-19-261894-6

Library of Congress Cataloging in Publication Data
Antimicrobial chemotherapy / edited by David Greenwood.—2nd ed.
Bibliography Includes index.
1. Anti-infective agents. 2. Communicable diseases—Chemotherapy.
I. Greenwood, David, 1935-   .
[DNLM: 1. Anti-Infective Agents—therapeutic use. QV 250 A629]
RM267.A55 1989 616.9'0461—dc20 89-9348
ISBN 0-19-261817-2 ISBN 0-19-261894-6 (pbk.)

Set by Downdell Limited, Oxford
Printed in Great Britain by
Courier International Ltd
Tiptree, Essex

Preface to the second edition

The years since the appearance of the first edition of this book in 1983 have been dominated by the emergence of the Acquired Immune Deficiency Syndrome (AIDS) and by an increasing public awareness of problems of infection in general.

The 1980s have also seen significant advances in the development of antimicrobial agents, notably in antibacterial compounds, among which fluoroquinolones and novel β-lactam antibiotics have been prominent; it is pleasing to note that there have also been important advances in the less abundant fields of antiviral and anthelminthic agents.

These and other developments have been fully considered in preparing this new edition. Each chapter has been thoroughly revised, and in some cases rewritten. Two of the original chapters, *Other Antibacterial and Antifungal Agents* and *Skin, Soft-tissue, and Skeletal Infections* have been split to render them less cumbersome, and the chapter on *Paediatric Prescribing* has been extended to include the other extreme of age.

We have once more elected to omit details of dosage regimens from the book for two reasons: firstly, because practices vary considerably from country to country and it is hoped that the book will have international relevance; secondly, because such information is normally already easily available to the prescriber. In the UK, the *British National Formulary*, which is updated every six months and issued free to all practising doctors, is an invaluable source of information on formulations, dosages, side-effects, and price of all types of prescription drug.

Despite the continued proliferation of antimicrobial agents, infection is here to stay and all doctors, in whatever field they practise, need to understand the fundamental principles of the treatment of infection. The sinister implications of the AIDS pandemic, with its attendant opportunistic infections, many of which present new and unfamiliar therapeutic dilemmas, make it more important than ever that medical students and young doctors should acquire a firm grasp of the principles underlying the use of antimicrobial drugs.

The primary intent of this book continues to be to instil good prescribing habits in trainee doctors; but we have also continued to bear in mind the needs of other health-care groups, including nurses, pharmacists, medical laboratory scientific officers, and the staff of pharmaceutical companies, who need to understand the properties of antimicrobial agents and their use.

Reviews of the first edition were gratifyingly enthusiastic and we hope that we have gone some way towards fulfilling the purposes for which the book was written. We believe that we have been able fully to maintain the quality of the text in this new edition, but we of course welcome any constructive suggestions that readers might have for further improvements in subsequent editions.

Three of our previous authors, P. W. Greaves, A. D. Macrae, and F. O'Grady have retired from the burdens of authorship; although their topics have been taken over by other members of the team, much of their original text has been retained and this we gratefully acknowledge. We are also grateful to Richard Edwards, Carol Webster, and George Sharp for help with the preparation of material and photography; to Patricia Blake, Linda Bowering, Margaret Thompson, and Cherry Webb for secretarial help; and to the staff of Oxford University Press who have undertaken the publication of this new edition.

January 1989   D.G.

Preface to the first edition

Antimicrobial agents are among the most commonly prescribed of all drugs. An enormous profusion of them (often bearing confusingly similar names) is available to the practitioner and they continue to proliferate. They vary immensely in potency, spectrum of activity, and toxicity as well as in their pharmacokinetic behaviour in the patient. Moreover, they come in all shapes, sizes, and formulations. Two or more may be mixed in a single preparation; even alone they are frequently administered with other drugs with which they may interact.

Given this huge diversity, it is perhaps not surprising that a number of surveys have revealed that antimicrobial drugs are often prescribed inappropriately, irrationally, and inefficiently. The cost of such wasteful prescribing in terms of unnecessary adverse reactions in the patient, or simply in terms of cash, can only be guessed at.

A thorough knowledge of the properties of antimicrobial agents should be part of every doctor's stock-in-trade. It is puzzling to find, therefore, that the subject of antimicrobial chemotherapy seldom occupies a prominent place in the medical student's curriculum. It is particularly surprising that no introductory textbook devoted to the basic principles of antimicrobial therapy exists. In general, the student is expected to glean his information on antimicrobial agents from specialized textbooks of microbiology, pharmacology, or infectious disease.

Books abound that tabulate dosages, treatment regimens, and minimum inhibitory concentration values of antimicrobial drugs, or deal in depth with their chemistry and mechanism of action; some of these books are extremely good and are recommended to the student for reference at the end of the present volume.

However, our aims have been more modest: we have specifically avoided unnecessary attention to chemistry, inhibitory concentrations, and dosages. Instead, we have concentrated on introducing the student to the general properties of antibiotics; to the role of the microbiology laboratory; and to the basic principles underlying the choice of treatment. The question of how much microbiological and clinical background to include has exercised us considerably. In the event we have tried to err on the side of generosity, especially in those areas where the student's knowledge might be anticipated to be shaky. However, it must be stressed that this is not a textbook of microbiology or infectious disease, and students who feel that their background knowledge is lacking are advised to supplement their reading appropriately.

Our use of two terms needs clarification: 'antibiotic' and 'microbe'. *Antibiotic* strictly refers to antimicrobial substances produced by micro-organisms. However, except in the Historical Introduction, where the distinction has some relevance, we have sometimes used the word more loosely to include those synthetic drugs that may be used systemically to treat microbial disease. Use of the word *microbe* has been arbitrarily extended to include helminths (worms); while it may be difficult to view a 5-m tapeworm as a microbe, the study of such beasts falls within the province of the microbiologist and treatment of such infections within the scope of chemotherapy.

The basic framework of this book is taken from the formal didactic component of a 6-week course that is offered to students at Nottingham during their third year, which at this Medical School is a specialized 'honours' year. We have been gratified to find that the course has proved extremely popular and has been explicitly commended by the students as being of practical value in their subsequent clinical studies.

We strongly believe that there is a need for a book of this description in Medical Schools, and it is at the trainee doctor that this work is primarily aimed. We hope that it will have relevance beyond the shores of this country and we have been particularly concerned to try to remember the needs of the less developed nations.

No book can be all things to all men, but it has not escaped our attention that a book pitched at the introductory level we have aimed at might also serve to fill a gap for groups other than medical students who are required in their training to have a basic knowledge of the properties and uses of antimicrobial drugs. Such groups would include trainee nurses, pharmacists, and medical laboratory scientific officers (particularly those specializing in microbiology) as well as those often-forgotten employees of the pharmaceutical houses who develop, test, manufacture, and sell most of the agents with which this book is concerned. Nor would the book be out of place in the hands of the newly qualified houseman, who may feel that his crowded curriculum has left him little time to study the principles of chemotherapy that he is now expected to practise daily.

It is our sincere hope that this book will respond to the needs of all these groups of people.

November, 1982   D.G.

Contents

Contributors

R. G. Finch, FRCP, MRC PATH
Consultant Physician, City Hospital, Nottingham;
Senior Lecturer in Microbial Diseases,
University of Nottingham Medical School;
Honorary Consultant Microbiologist, Public Health Laboratory Service

D. Greenwood, DSC, MRC PATH
Professor of Antimicrobial Science,
University of Nottingham Medical School;
Honorary Microbiologist, Public Health Laboratory Service

P. Ispahani, DIP BACT, DCP, FRC PATH
Consultant Microbiologist,
Public Health Laboratory, Nottingham

M. J. Lewis, MD, DIP BACT
Director, Public Health Laboratory, Nottingham;
Senior Lecturer in Microbiology, University of Nottingham Medical School

R. C. B. Slack, MA, MRC PATH, D OBST RCOG
Senior Lecturer in Microbiology, University of Nottingham Medical School;
Honorary Consultant Microbiologist, Public Health Laboratory Service

Historical introduction

Although the 'antibiotic revolution' can be accurately dated to the early 1940s when Howard Florey and his colleagues in Oxford seized upon Alexander Fleming's penicillin and turned it into a major therapeutic compound and Selman Waksman in the United States began his systematic pursuit of antibiotics from soil micro-organisms, the quest for chemotherapeutic agents active against pathogenic microbes began much earlier. Indeed, hopes of discovering specific antimicrobial drugs were kindled almost as soon as the microbial enemy was definitively identified by Louis Pasteur, Robert Koch and others during the second half of the nineteenth century. By the end of the century, Paul Ehrlich, often called the 'Father of chemotherapy', had started the work which was to put the quest on a sound scientific footing.

Of course, man's search for effective remedies is as old as mankind itself, but before the aetiological agents of infectious disease were identified and made amenable to laboratory investigation, progress had to rely entirely on the vagaries of chance and empirical observation.

Not surprisingly, therefore, mankind's earliest therapeutic successes against infecting organisms came in the form of plant extracts that expelled worms visible to the naked eye. Examples of such herbal anthelminthics known since antiquity include extract of male fern (*Dryopteris filix-mas*), an effective vermifuge for tapeworms; santonin (obtained from the seedheads of *Artemesia cina*; wormseed) and oil of chenopodium (*Chenopodium ambrosioides*; American wormseed), both of which may be used to expel intestinal roundworms.

Observations that natural substances controlled the spectacular symptoms of certain diseases no doubt led to the initial recognition of two other ancient remedies: quinine, obtained from the bark of the cinchona tree, and emetine, an alkaloid obtained from ipecacuanha root. Curiously, both these compounds originated in South America (from where they were introduced into European medicine in the seventeenth century), both are active against protozoa (the parasites of malaria and amoebic dysentery respectively) and both have survived into present-day use.

So far as antibacterial remedies were concerned, even less had been achieved when Ehrlich began his work: mercury had been used for the treatment of syphilis since the sixteenth century (giving rise to the aphorism 'one night with Venus—a lifetime with Mercury') and chaulmoogra oil from the seeds of various species of *Hydnocarpus* had been used since ancient times in India for the treatment of leprosy. Apart from these, the only antibacterial compounds known were a few antiseptics, chiefly phenolic substances and mercury salts, which were far too toxic for systemic use. Right at the end of the nineteenth century hexamine, a compound which spontaneously decomposes in acid conditions to release formaldehyde, was described as being useful in urinary tract infection.

THE FOUNDATIONS OF MODERN CHEMOTHERAPY

Oddly, in view of later developments, the foundations of twentieth century chemotherapy were built on a search for antiprotozoal agents, since it was to the newly discovered parasites of malaria and African sleeping-sickness (trypanosomiasis) that Paul Ehrlich first turned his attention. Ehrlich reasoned that since these parasites could be differentiated from the tissues of infected patients by various dyes in the laboratory, such substances might display a preferential affinity for the parasites in the body as well. In a phrase, such dyes might exhibit *selective toxicity*.

Early tests of this hypothesis employed the aniline dyes methylene blue and trypan red. Neither compound proved to be of much value, but the idea was pursued by the French workers, F. Mesnil and M. Nicolle, who found two related dyes, trypan blue and afridol violet, had some useful effects in trypanosomiasis of animals. Interest in dyes as chemotherapeutic agents continued, and was later to pay off in several directions (see below); however, Ehrlich was deflected from the study of dyes and turned to arsenicals.

ARSENICALS

The event that caught Ehrlich's interest appears to have been a report of the work of H. W. Thomas and A. Breinl from the Liverpool School of Tropical Medicine, who in 1905 demonstrated that an arsenical compound, atoxyl, protected mice from infection with trypanosomes. Arsenicals, in common with other metallic compounds had been used in medicine at least since the time of the sixteenth-century Swiss physician,

Paracelsus (Theophrastus, Bombastus von Hohenheim). Atoxyl itself had been described 40 years before its antitrypanosomal activity was investigated.

Despite its name, atoxyl was anything but atoxic and Ehrlich, together with his Japanese assistant Sahachiro Hata and his chemist Alfred Bertheim, set about trying to modify the molecule to produce derivatives with a better *therapeutic index*: the ratio of the toxic to the effective dose. As the work developed, the spirochaetes of syphilis, relapsing fever and chicken spirillosis were included in the screening programme. Success came in 1909, when the 606th derivative of atoxyl that Ehrlich's team tested was shown to cure animals infected with each of the three spirochaetes and, equally importantly, to display an acceptable therapeutic index. Compound 606, later known as arsphenamine and marketed as Salvarsan, was the first really efficacious antibacterial agent, although its activity was restricted to spirochaetes, which are scarcely typical bacteria. An improved derivative, neo-arsphenamine (Neosalvarsan), was produced in Ehrlich's laboratory in 1912.

Interest in arsenicals and other metals was also pursued elsewhere. Hopes of finding a drug to replace atoxyl for the treatment of trypanosomiasis remained alive and a variety of arsenicals were tried, of which tryparsamide and (much later) melarsoprol (Mel B) have emerged as drugs of value. In some other parasitic diseases of the tropics, another ancient metallic remedy, tartar emetic (potassium antimony tartrate) was discovered to exhibit useful activity. Tartar emetic was a familiar nostrum of Victorian medicine; its chief value was judged to lie in its emetic properties. However, Ehrlich's success with arsenicals and their use in trypanosomiasis prompted doctors working in the tropics to try other metallic compounds empirically in previously untreatable conditions. This led to the discovery of the efficacy of tartar emetic in two very different tropical diseases: kala azar (a protozoal disease of the reticuloendothelial system) and bilharzia (a worm infection of the blood). Antimonials are still used for the treatment of kala azar, but safer drugs have been developed with which to treat bilharzia.

DYES

Paul Ehrlich's optimistic hope of exploiting the differential affinities of dyes therapeutically, came to nothing. However, the idea was to bear fruit eventually in a wide variety of therapeutically useful antimicrobial compounds which, though uncoloured themselves, were derived, directly or indirectly, from dyes.

Suramin

The most direct link with Ehrlich's ideas is provided by suramin (Germanin), a colourless derivative of trypan blue developed by scientists of the Bayer organization in Germany. Like tartar emetic, suramin has proved useful in two quite unrelated parasitic diseases, in this case trypanosomiasis and onchocerciasis (a worm disease of the skin).

Antimalarials

By a remarkable coincidence, the very discovery of aniline dyes was sparked off by an antimalarial compound, since it was during an investigation into the possible synthesis of quinine from coal tar in 1856 that the 19-year-old William Perkin, a student at the Royal College of Chemistry, stumbled upon mauve purple, the first aniline dye.

The progression from dye to antimalarial was finally accomplished indirectly through attempts, again by scientists at Bayer, to improve the activity of Ehrlich's methylene blue. Modification of the dye produced nothing of value, but information gained on the effects of various substitutions prompted the chemists to try similar substitutions on other heterocyclic compounds. In this way the 8-aminoquinoline drug, plasmoquine, and the acridine derivative, mepacrine, were produced. In their turn these compounds led to the synthesis of primaquine (another 8-aminoquinoline) and the 4-aminoquinoline, chloroquine, which are used today.

Sulphonamides

The German obsession with dyes also paid off with the discovery of the first broad-spectrum antibacterial agents, the sulphonamides. In the event, the discovery came about by another of those happy accidents with which the history of chemotherapy is littered. In 1932, Gerhard Domagk, a bacteriologist working in the laboratories of the Bayer wing of the I. G. Farbenindustrie consortium, tested a number of dyes synthesized by his colleagues, Fritz Mietzsch and Josef Klarer, in experimental streptococcal infection in mice. Remarkably, mice treated with one such dye, prontosil red, survived the otherwise fatal infection. However, when prontosil was tested against streptococci *in vitro* it was found to have no antibacterial activity whatsoever. This paradox was explained when it was discovered by the Tréfouëls and their colleagues in France, that in the experimental animal the dye was split into two components, one of which was sulphanilamide, a colourless compound hitherto unsuspected of possessing any antimicrobial activity.

Table 1. Some of the chemotherapeutic agents (and the indications for their use) that predate the first therapeutic use of penicillin in 1941

	extract of male fern	: tapeworm
	santonin	: intestinal roundworm
	oil of chenopodium	: intestinal roundworm
Pre-1890	cinchona bark (quinine) *	: malaria
	ipecacuanha root (emetine) *	: amoebic dysentery
	mercury	: syphilis
	chaulmoogra oil	: leprosy

Arsenicals and antimonials

1905 atoxyl	: trypanosomiasis
1909 arsphenamine	: syphilis
1912 neoarsphenamine: syphilis
1912 tartar emetic	: leishmaniasis
1917 tartar emetic	: schistosomiasis
1919 tryparsamide *	: trypanosomiasis

Dyes and dye derivatives

1891 methylene blue: malaria
1904 trypan red	: trypanosomiasis
1906 trypan blue	: trypanosomiasis
1906 afridol violet	: trypanosomiasis
1920 suramin *	: trypanosomiasis
1927 plasmoquine	: malaria
1932 mepacrine *	: malaria (etc.)
1932 prontosil red	: bacteria
1934 chloroquine *†	: malaria

Other substances

1895 hexamine *	: urinary infection
1899 pyocyanase	: bacteria (topically)
1925 tetrachloroethylene *: hookworm
1939 tyrothricin *	: bacteria (topically)

* Still in use. (N.B. mepacrine is no longer in regular use as an antimalarial, but is still used as a second-line drug in the treatment of giardiasis and tapeworm infection. Prontosil is no longer used, but has given rise to the large sulphonamide family).
† Chloroquine was discovered in 1934, but not used in malaria until 1945.

Sulphanilamide was already well known to the chemist and since the compound lay in the public domain, Bayer were unable to protect the discovery by patent. Naturally, many other firms seized the opportunity to market the drug, so that by 1940, sulphanilamide itself was available under at least 33 different trade names and a start had been made on producing the numerous sulphonamide derivatives that are now available.

Such was the situation when penicillin appeared on the scene as a potential therapeutic agent in 1940 (see Table 1).

ANTIBIOTICS

Penicillins and cephalosporins

When Howard Florey and his team at the Sir William Dunn School of Pathology in Oxford first took an interest in penicillin, the concept of antibiosis and its therapeutic potential was not new. In fact, the observation that organisms, including fungi, sometimes produced substances capable of preventing the growth of others was as old as bacteriology itself. One antibiotic substance, pyocyanase, produced by the bacterium *Pseudomonas aeruginosa*, had actually been used therapeutically by instillation into wounds, at the turn of the century.

Thus, when Alexander Fleming returned from holiday to his laboratory in St. Mary's Hospital to make his famous observation on an old contaminated culture plate of staphylococci, he was merely one in a long line of workers who had noticed similar phenomena. However, it was Fleming's observation that was to spark off the events that led to the development of penicillin as the first non-toxic antibiotic in the strict sense of the term.

The actual circumstances of Fleming's discovery have become interwoven with myth and legend. Attempts to reproduce the phenomenon have led to the conclusion that the lysis of staphylococci in the area surrounding a contaminant *Penicillium* colony on Fleming's original plate, could only have arisen by an extraordinary concatenation of accidental events.

Although Fleming was hopeful about the possible therapeutic value of his discovery, his attempts to exploit it were fairly half-hearted and eventually foundered on a failure to purify and concentrate the substance. It was left to Ernst Chain, a German biochemist who had sought refuge in England from Nazi persecution, and who had been set the task by Florey of investigating naturally occurring antibacterial substances (including lysozyme, another of Fleming's discoveries) to obtain a crude, but stable extract of penicillin. It was with these crude extracts, which were subsequently shown to contain less than 1 per cent pure penicillin, that the first therapeutic experiments were performed in mice and men. In view of the impurity of the substances used, it is indeed fortunate that problems of serious toxicity were not encountered in these early trials.

Further development of penicillin was beyond the means of wartime Britain, and Florey visited the USA in 1941 with his assistant, Norman Heatley, to enlist the support of the American authorities and drug firms. Once Florey had convinced them of the potential of penicillin, progress was rapid and by the end of the Second World War, bulk production of penicillin was in progress and the drug was beginning to become readily available.

The discovery of the first of the cephalosporins (sister compounds to the penicillins, which share many features of structure and activity) is, in its way, equally extraordinary.

Between 1945 and 1948, Giuseppe Brotzu, former Rector of the University of Cagliari, Sardinia, investigated the microbial flora of a sewage outflow in the hope of discovering naturally occurring antibiotic substances. One of the organisms recovered from the sewage was a *Cephalosporium* mould which displayed striking inhibitory activity against several bacterial species, including *Salmonella typhi*, the causative organism of typhoid, that were beyond the reach of penicillin at that time. Brotzu carried out some preliminary bacteriological and clinical studies, and obtained some encouraging results. However, he lacked the facilities to progress the compound further, and through a British acquaintance the mould was sent to the Sir William Dunn School in Oxford.

The first thing to be discovered by the Oxford scientists was that Brotzu's mould produced two antibiotics, which they called cephalosporin P and cephalosporin N, because the former inhibited Gram-positive organisms (e.g. staphylococci and streptococci) while the later was active against Gram-negative organisms (e.g. *Escherichia coli* and *S. typhi*). As chance would have it, it turned out that neither of these substances was a cephalosporin in the sense that the term is used today: cephalosporin P proved to be an antibiotic with a steroid-like structure; cephalosporin N turned out to be a penicillin (adicillin). The forerunner of the cephalosporins now in use, cephalosporin C, was detected later as a minor component on fractionation of cephalosporin N.

Antibiotics from soil

The development of penicillin, cephalosporin C, and, subsequently, their numerous derivatives, represents only one branch of the antibiotic story. The other main route to present day antibiotics came through an investigation into antimicrobial substances produced by micro-organisms in soil. The chief moving spirit in this investigation was Selman A. Waksman, an emigré from the Russian Ukraine, who had taken up the study of soil microbiology in the USA as a young man. In 1940, Waksman initiated a systematic search for non-toxic antibiotics produced by soil micro-organisms, notably actinomycetes, a group that includes the *Streptomyces* spp. which were to yield many therapeutically useful compounds. Waksman was probably influenced in his decision to undertake this study by the then recent discovery by an ex-pupil, René Dubos, of the antibiotic complex, tyrothricin in culture filtrates of *Bacillus brevis*.

Waksman's first discoveries were, like Dubos's tyrothricin, too toxic for systemic use, although they included actinomycin, a compound later used in cancer chemotherapy. The first real breakthrough came in 1943 with the discovery of streptomycin, the first aminoglycoside antibiotic, which was found to have a spectrum of activity that neatly complemented penicillin by inhibiting many Gram-negative bacilli and—very importantly at that time—*Mycobacterium tuberculosis*.

The appearance of streptomycin triggered a more general hunt for naturally occurring antibiotics and when the pharmaceutical houses joined in the chase, soil samples by the hundred thousand from all over the world were screened for antibiotic-producing micro-organisms. Thousands of antibiotic substances were discovered and rediscovered by this means and, although most failed preliminary toxicity tests, by the mid-1950s representatives of most of the major families of antibiotics, including aminoglycosides, chloramphenicol, tetracyclines, and macrolides, had been discovered. Indeed, it is possible to argue that, by 1960, practically all the antibacterial agents required by medicine were known.

FURTHER DEVELOPMENTS

Since 1960 only a very few truly novel antibiotic substances have been discovered, although in the past few years a surprising number of naturally occurring substances displaying fundamental molecular variations on the penicillin structure have emerged.

A more fruitful line of approach has been to modify existing agents chemically in an attempt to derive compounds with enhanced properties. This has been most successful in the penicillin and cephalosporin field, where numerous semi-synthetic derivatives are now available.

Chemists and microbiologists have been active, too, in exploiting the antibacterial potential of non-antibiotic substances, although only a very small number have been devised by premeditated attack on known biochemical pathways. In fact, of antimicrobial drugs presently used therapeutically, only the diaminopyrimidines, trimethoprim, and pyrimethamine, really fall into that category. Others, including the nitrofurans, the imidazoles, quinolones (and related compounds of the nalidixic acid type in which there has been a marked resurgence of interest in the 1980s) as well as several antituberculous drugs, have emerged through an indefinable mixture of serendipity, biochemical know-how, inspired hunch, and luck.

THE SCOPE OF ANTIMICROBIAL CHEMOTHERAPY

Without question, the appearance in the late 1930s and early 1940s of potent, non-toxic chemotherapeutic agents selectively active against bacteria, revolutionized the treatment of infection. Indeed, the discovery of these first 'miracle drugs'—sulphonamides, penicillin, and strepto-mycin—was sanguinely declared by some to herald the disappearance of bacterial infection as a disease entity of any importance. With 40 years' hindsight and hundreds of new agents at our disposal, we are now able to take a more dispassionate view of the benefits and limitations of anti-microbial therapy.

Many things have happened to modify our views of the capabilities of antimicrobial drugs, but four things stand out particularly.

1. Bacteria have displayed a truly amazing versatility in terms of their ability to avoid, withstand or repel the antibiotic onslaught.

2. The pattern of bacterial disease, particularly hospital-acquired infection, has altered considerably, most significantly in the wake of new operation procedures, instrumentation techniques, and treatment regimens which severely compromise the patient's own capacity to withstand infection.

3. The use of antibiotics often disturbs the delicate bacterial ecology of the body, allowing the proliferation of resistant species and some-times initiating new infections that are worse than the one originally treated.

4. It turns out that no antibacterial drug is entirely free from toxic side-effects so that use of any of these agents has its attendant risks.

Finally, it should not be forgotten that most therapeutic triumphs have been restricted to the treatment of bacterial disease. Those numerous infections caused by viruses, protozoa, helminths, and fungi are, with some notable exceptions, less amenable to chemotherapy. Indeed, many of these non-bacterial infections are only treatable by toxic agents of restricted potency, and a few lie beyond the scope of systemic therapy altogether.

Part I

General properties of
antimicrobial agents

1

Inhibitors of bacterial cell wall synthesis

The essence of antimicrobial chemotherapy is *selective toxicity*—to kill or inhibit the microbe without harming the patient. So far as bacteria are concerned, a prime target for such attack is the cell wall, since practically all bacteria (with the exception of mycoplasmas) possess a cell wall and mammalian cells lack this feature.

Not all bacterial cell walls are the same. Indeed, of the many species that have been investigated, no two have been found to be identical. However, in general they conform to two basic patterns which may readily be distinguished by that most familiar of all microbiological techniques, the Gram stain.

The cell walls of Gram-positive and Gram-negative bacteria differ in many fundamental respects, but both groups possess a cross-linked chain of peptidoglycan (also called mucopeptide, or murein) and cell wall active antibiotics act by interfering with the biosynthesis of this structure. Peptidoglycan consists of a backbone of alternating *N*-acetylglucosamine (NAG) and *N*-acetylmuramic acid (NAMA) units. The NAMA molecules are substituted with short peptides made up of five amino acids which cross-link (via an interpeptide bridge composed of further amino acids in most Gram-positive organisms) to give the peptidoglycan its characteristic rigidity.

In Gram-positive organisms the peptidoglycan is thick (*c*. 30 nm), tightly cross-linked and interspersed with polysugarphosphate residues (teichoic acids) some of which may have a lipophilic tail buried in the cell membrane (lipoteichoic acids). Gram-negative bacteria, in contrast, have a relatively thin peptidoglycan layer (2-3 nm) which is loosely cross-linked. External to the Gram-negative peptidoglycan is a membrane-like structure, composed chiefly of lipopolysaccharide and lipoprotein, which renders the cell impermeable to many antibiotics.

CELL WALL SYNTHESIS

The bacterial peptidoglycan in both Gram-positive and Gram-negative organisms is assembled from units of NAG, initially linked to uridine-diphosphate (UDP). UDP-NAMA units are manufactured from UDP-NAG by the addition of a lactic acid moiety derived from phosphoenolpyruvate. The NAMA then receives, one by one, three amino acids which are usually L-alanine, D-glutamic acid and either L-lysine (in Gram-positive organisms) or *meso*-diaminopimelic acid (in Gram-negative organisms). Meanwhile, two D-alanine residues, produced from L-alanine by an enzyme called alanine racemase, are joined together by another enzyme, D-alanine synthetase. The linked unit, D-ala-D-ala is added to the tripeptide side-chain of NAMA and the NAMA-pentapeptide thus formed is passed to a lipid carrier in the cell membrane. Here a UDP-NAG unit transfers its NAG to the NAMA-pentapeptide and any amino acids needed for interpeptide bridges are added to the L-lysine of the pentapeptide side-chain. The whole building block is now transferred to the end of the growing peptidoglycan chain of the existing cell wall, where the final cross-linking reaction takes place. The process is illustrated in outline in Fig. 1.1.

Antibiotics which interfere with this process of cell wall synthesis include bacitracin, fosfomycin, cycloserine, vancomycin, and β-lactam agents.

BACITRACIN

Bacitracin is one of a group of antibiotics, also including gramicidin and tyrocidine, which exhibit a cyclic structure made up of about ten amino acids. Bacitracin itself (actually a mixture of three closely related compounds, bacitracin A, B, and C, of which bacitracin A is the major component) was first obtained from a strain of *Bacillus subtilis* grown from the infected wound of a 7-year-old girl called Margaret Tracy, in whose honour the antibiotic was named.

Bacitracin and the related cyclic peptides are fairly potent anti-bacterial agents although the spectrum of activity is virtually restricted to Gram-positive organisms. They have proved too toxic for systemic use and their usage is nowadays restricted to topical preparations or, in the case of bacitracin itself, as a growth promotant in animal feedstuffs. Bacitracin also finds a place in microbiology laboratories in the presumptive identification of *Streptococcus pyogenes*, which is exquisitely susceptible to its action.

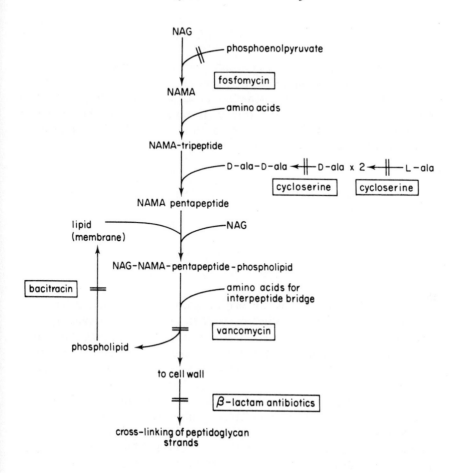

Fig. 1.1. Simplified scheme of bacterial cell wall synthesis showing site of action of cell wall active antibiotics.

The antibacterial activity of bacitracin appears to reside in its ability to prevent regeneration of the lipid carrier in the cell membrane, which is left in an unusable phosphorylated form (Fig. 1.1). Gramicidin and tyrocidine have a different mechanism of action, interfering with the integrity of the cell membrane.

FOSFOMYCIN

Fosfomycin (formerly known as phosphonomycin) is a naturally occurring antibiotic originally obtained from a species of *Streptomyces* isolated in Spain. Structurally, it is the simplest of all antibiotics (Fig. 1.2). The molecule inhibits the pyruvyl transferase enzyme which brings about the condensation of phosphoenolpyruvate and N-acetylglucosamine in the formation of N-acetylmuramic acid (Fig. 1.1).

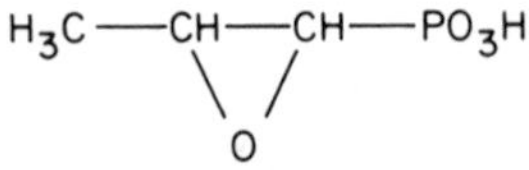

$$H_3C - CH - CH - PO_3H_2$$

Fig. 1.2. Structure of fosfomycin.

Although fosfomycin has not been marketed in the UK, it has been extensively used in many other parts of the world. It is reputedly non-toxic and efficacious, and the ready emergence of bacterial resistance that is observed *in vitro* does not appear to have been a major problem in treatment. The activity of fosfomycin covers a fairly broad spectrum, although Gram-positive cocci are rather less susceptible than Gram-negative rods. The precise level of activity is a matter of dispute, since the in vitro activity can be manipulated by altering the test medium: the presence of glucose-6-phosphate potentiates the activity, whereas glucose and phosphate individually have an adverse effect. The potentiating effect of glucose-6-phosphate appears to be due to the fact that fosfomycin can enter bacteria by an active transport process that is inducible by glucose-6-phosphate, but not by fosfomycin itself.

Fosfomycin is formulated as the sodium salt for parenteral use, but this is unsuitable for oral administration. The calcium salt, which has been widely used for oral therapy, is rather poorly and erratically absorbed, and is likely to be superseded by the trometamol salt, which is highly soluble, well absorbed, and excreted in high concentration in urine.

CYCLOSERINE

Cycloserine bears a structural resemblance to the D-isomer of alanine. Because of this cycloserine interferes with alanine racemase (the enzyme that converts the natural form, L-alanine, to D-alanine) and also blocks the synthetase enzyme used to link two D-ala molecules together before they are inserted into the cell wall (Fig. 1.1).

Cycloserine has broad-spectrum, but rather feeble antibacterial activity and has not found much use. Its chief attraction lies in its activity against *Mycobacterium tuberculosis*, but even against this important pathogen cycloserine is used only as a second-line drug, mainly because of toxicity problems.

VANCOMYCIN

Vancomycin is a complex heterocyclic molecule consisting of a heptapeptide backbone to which are attached glucose and a novel aminosugar, vancosamine; hence, this and related agents are known collectively as *glycopeptides*. Glycopeptides are too bulky to penetrate the external membrane of Gram-negative bacteria, so the spectrum of activity is generally restricted to Gram-positive organisms. Acquired resistance appears to be very uncommon.

Vancomycin exhibits good activity against staphylococci and other Gram-positive cocci. It has been particularly favoured for the treatment of bacterial endocarditis in patients hypersensitive to penicillin and for infections caused by staphylococci that are resistant to methicillin and other β-lactam antibiotics. Vancomycin is also useful in the treatment of antibiotic-associated diarrhoea caused by toxigenic strains of *Clostridium difficile* (see Chapter 22).

Vancomycin has been available for many years, but early preparations contained impurities that gave the drug a reputation for toxicity. New, highly purified preparations are said to be much safer, but renal and ototoxicity still occur and the drug has to be administered by slow intravenous infusion.

A new glycopeptide, teicoplanin, which is a naturally-occurring mixture of several closely-related compounds has a spectrum of activity similar to that of vancomycin, although some coagulase-negative staphylococci are less susceptible to teicoplanin. Unlike vancomycin, teicoplanin can be administered by intramuscular injection; it also has a much longer plasma half-life.

PENICILLINS AND CEPHALOSPORINS
(β-LACTAM ANTIBIOTICS)

The penicillins and cephalosporins are closely related families of compounds which share the structural feature of a β-lactam ring (Fig. 1.3); such compounds are collectively known as β-lactam antibiotics. The

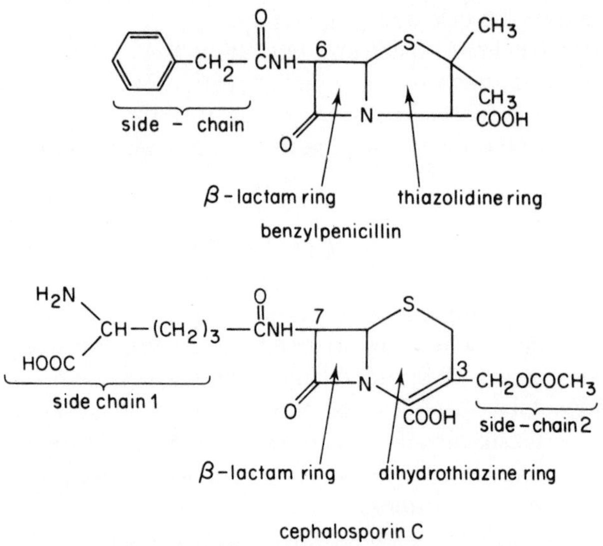

Fig. 1.3. Structures of benzylpenicillin and cephalosporin C, forerunners of the penicillin and cephalosporin groups, respectively. The fused ring systems and the side-chains which offer the possibility of modifications introduced in semi-synthetic derivatives are indicated.

β-lactam ring is the Achilles' heel of this group of antibiotics, because many bacteria possess enzymes (β-lactamases; see Chapter 12) capable of breaking open the ring and rendering the molecule antibacterially inactive.

In the penicillins the β-lactam ring is fused to a five-membered thiazolidine ring, whereas the cephalosporins display a fused β-lactam/dihydrothiazine ring structure.

The original penicillin used in therapy, benzylpenicillin, contains a phenylacetamido side-chain at the 6-position of the fused ring system (Fig. 1.3). Early attempts to modify this structure relied on presenting the *Penicillium* mould used to produce penicillin with different side-chain precursors during the manufacturing process. Later a method was discovered of removing the acyl side-chain of benzylpenicillin to liberate the penicillin nucleus, 6-aminopenicillanic acid (6-APA). Various chemical groupings could then be added to 6-APA according to the ingenuity of the chemist and a large number of compounds, collectively called *semi-synthetic penicillins*, have been prepared in this way.

Semi-synthetic cephalosporins can be prepared from cephalosporin C (Fig. 1.3) in an analogous way, the nucleus remaining after removal of the side-chain being, in this case, 7-aminocephalosporanic acid. However, the extra carbon atom in the cephalosporin ring system offers the possibility of additional modifications at the C3 position and alterations at either end of the molecule may profoundly affect the antibacterial activity. Cephalosporin C itself and some of its semi-synthetic derivatives (including cephalothin, cephapirin, cephacetrile, and cefotaxime) bear an acetoxymethyl group at the C3 position. Cephalosporins exhibiting this feature are slowly metabolized in the body by liver enzymes which deacetylate the molecule to produce the corresponding hydroxymethyl cephalosporin. In general, the antibacterial activity of these derivatives is inferior to that of the parent compound and they may also display different pharmacokinetic behaviour.

Penicillins

The original preparations of penicillin were found on analysis to be mixtures of four closely related compounds which were called penicillin F, G, K, and X. Benzylpenicillin (penicillin G) was chosen for further development because it exhibited the most attractive properties and because a manufacturing process was developed in which *Penicillium chrysogenum* was persuaded to produce benzylpenicillin almost exclusively.

Benzylpenicillin revolutionized the treatment of many potentially lethal bacterial infections, particularly those caused by the pyogenic cocci like scarlet fever, puerperal sepsis, bacterial endocarditis, pneumococcal pneumonia, staphylococcal sepsis, meningococcal meningitis, and gonorrhoea. The overwhelming importance of benzylpenicillin as a major breakthrough in therapy may be gauged from the fact that it remains today the treatment of choice for all these diseases. However, resistance has eroded the value of benzylpenicillin. Nearly all staphylococci and many strains of gonococci are now resistant, and there are disturbing reports from various parts of the world of an increasing prevalence of penicillin-resistant pneumococci, and even meningococci.

Despite its attractive properties benzylpenicillin is less than the perfect antimicrobial agent: it exhibits a restricted antibacterial spectrum; it causes hypersensitivity reactions in a small proportion of persons to whom it is given; it is broken down by gastric acidity when administered orally; it is eliminated from the body at a spectacular rate by the kidneys and it is hydrolysed by β-lactamases produced by many bacteria including staphylococci.

Subsequent developments in β-lactam agents have all been aimed at overcoming these inherent disabilities whilst retaining the attractive properties of benzylpenicillin: high intrinsic activity and lack of toxicity.

Acid stability

The first major success in improving the pharmacological properties of penicillin was achieved with phenoxymethylpenicillin (penicillin V). This compound has very similar properties to benzylpenicillin, but is acid stable and, thus, achieves better and more reliable serum levels when given orally, at the expense of some intrinsic antibacterial activity.

Prolongation of serum levels

Four approaches have been tried in order to maintain effective levels of penicillin in the body. One, the blockbuster approach, is simply to give enormous doses of this non-toxic drug. The second, the slow-release approach, is to mix penicillin with oily or waxy excipients; these preparation are injected intramuscularly, where they act as depots from which penicillin is slowly liberated. The third approach is a variant of this in which insoluble derivatives of penicillin are prepared. Three such 'long-acting' penicillins are still in common use: procaine penicillin, benethamine penicillin, and benzathine penicillin. The latter will maintain low levels of penicillin in the blood for many days. The fourth manoeuvre, the competitive approach, is to administer probenecid orally at the same time as the penicillin. Probenecid competes for sites of active tubular secretion in the kidney, slowing down the elimination of penicillin.

Extension of spectrum

The first success with extending the spectrum of benzylpenicillin to encompass Gram-negative bacilli was achieved by adding an amino group to the side-chain to form ampicillin. Ampicillin is slightly less active than benzylpenicillin against Gram-positive cocci and is equally susceptible to staphylococcal β-lactamase. However, it displays much improved activity against some enterobacteria, including *Escherichia coli*, *Salmonella* spp. and *Shigella* spp. as well as against *Haemophilus influenzae*. It is not particularly well absorbed when given orally, but absorption can be improved by esterifying the molecule to form so-called *pro-drugs* which are split by non-specific tissue esterases in the intestinal mucosa to release ampicillin during absorption. Examples of esterified pro-drugs include pivampicillin, bacampicillin, and talampicillin. Improved absorption has also been achieved by minor modifications to the molecule to produce amoxycillin, hetacillin, and ciclacillin.

A peculiar change of spectrum was brought about by altering the form of the linkage at the 6-position of the penicillanic acid nucleus to amidino $(N - CH = N)$ instead of acyl $(CO - NH)$. The only penicillin of this type to become available, mecillinam (known as amdinocillin in the United States), is extremely active against ampicillin-sensitive enterobacteria and further extends the ampicillin spectrum to embrace some of the more resistant Gram-negative rods. However, mecillinam displays no useful activity against Gram-positive cocci. Mecillinam is poorly absorbed when given orally, but a pro-drug form, pivmecillinam, is available for oral administration.

None of the agents so far mentioned has any activity against *Pseudomonas aeruginosa*, an important opportunist pathogen in burns, cystic fibrosis and immunocompromised patients. Activity is, however, demonstrated by carbenicillin, another simple derivative of benzylpenicillin which bears a carboxyl substituent instead of the amino group of ampicillin. The antipseudomonal activity of carbenicillin is not particularly good, but this has since been improved upon by ticarcillin, the thienyl variant of carbenicillin and by a group of *N*-acyl substituted ureido derivatives of ampicillin which include azlocillin, mezlocillin, piperacillin, and apalcillin. All these antipseudomonal penicillins must be administered by injection, but two esterified pro-drugs of carbenicillin have been produced: carfecillin and carindacillin.

β-Lactamase-stable penicillins

By the end of the 1950s 80 per cent of staphylococci isolated in hospitals were resistant to benzylpenicillin because of their ability to produce penicillinase (*β*-lactamase). The rise to prominence of these resistant organisms, which often gave rise to serious cross-infection problems, stimulated research into derivatives which were insusceptible to *β*-lactamase hydrolysis. Success was achieved with nafcillin, methicillin and the isoxazolylpenicillins—oxacillin, cloxacillin, dicloxacillin, and flucloxacillin. All except methicillin can be given orally. The isoxazolylpenicillins are all highly bound to serum protein in the body (see Chapter 16), but this does not seem to affect their therapeutic efficacy; fluxcloxacillin achieves higher serum levels than the others and is probably to be preferred in therapy.

A form of resistance to penicillinase-stable penicillins may be encountered in staphylococci, which is not caused by inactivating enzymes, but by alterations in the penicillin target. Such strains may fully display the resistance phenotype only under abnormal laboratory conditions (at a reduced growth temperature or in the presence of high salt concentrations) and for this reason the therapeutic relevance of the resistance has been disputed. However, resistant staphylococci of this kind undoubtedly do cause therapeutic problems. Indeed, some strains of *Staphylococcus aureus* which are not only resistant to methicillin (and all other *β*-lactam agents), but also to gentamicin and many other antibiotics—thus known as multiresistant *Staph. aureus* or MRSA—have become endemic in some units where they cause persistent problems.

Cephalosporins

Cephalosporin C was originally detected as a minor component of a mixture of antibiotics produced by a *Cephalosporium* mould. Such a substance could easily have been dismissed, but it was pursued because it exhibited the attractive properties of activity against Gram-negative bacilli and stability to staphylococcal penicillinase. In the event cephalosporin C has given rise to a large family of compounds which continues to expand.

Cephalosporin C itself was never marketed since two more active derivatives quickly became available: cephalothin, which has been widely used in the USA and cephaloridine, which was favoured in the UK, but has since been withdrawn. Both suffer from disadvantages. Cephalothin is somewhat the less active of the two and is metabolized in the body to the even less active desacetyl compound. Cephaloridine, on the other hand, has the distinction of being the first β-lactam antibiotic to display serious toxicity—nephrotoxicity—when given in high doses. Use of both these compounds quickly established the fact that cephalosporins were less likely to cause hypersensitivity reactions than were their penicillin cousins. Only about 5–10 per cent of persons known to be hypersensitive to penicillins react to cephalosporins as well.

Further development of the cephalosporins produced cephalexin, a compound which is considerably less active than cephalothin or cephaloridine, particularly in terms of its bactericidal activity against Gram-negative bacilli, but which displays the attraction of being virtually completely absorbed when given orally. The property of oral absorption is unusual among cephalosporins and most oral derivatives are structurally minor variations on the cephalexin theme. Such compounds include cephradine (the properties of which are practically indistinguishable from those of cephalexin), cefaclor (which is somewhat more active, but less stable) and cefadroxil (which exhibits a modestly extended plasma half-life). Cephaloglycin, cefroxadine, and cefatrizine are similar compounds available in certain countries. The principle of esterification to improve oral absorption has also been applied to cephalosporins. An ester of cefuroxime (see below), cefuroxime axetil, has been marketed in the UK and similar compounds are under development.

Some cephalosporins that have been developed offer no discernible improvement over earlier compounds; cefapirin and cephacetrile (neither of which has been marketed in the UK) come into this category. Others offer modest advantages: cephazolin has improved antibacterial activity and the interesting property of being excreted in fairly high concentration in bile; cephamandole has a modestly expanded spectrum.

More important advances came with the development of cephalosporins exhibiting almost complete stability to enterobacterial β-lactamases. The first of these were cefuroxime and cefoxitin, the latter being one of a group of cephalosporins, collectively called cephamycins, which bear a stabilizing methoxy grouping on the β-lactam ring. Other cephamycins available in some countries include cefotetan, cefbuperazone, and cefmetazole.

These compounds have been somewhat overshadowed by the appearance of cephalosporins that combine almost complete stability to β-lactamases with exceptional intrinsic activity. Cefotaxime was the forerunner of this group of compounds, but others are now available in many countries: ceftizoxime and cefmenoxime are similar to cefotaxime; ceftazidime displays much the best antipseudomonal activity; ceftriaxone possesses a very long plasma half-life; and latamoxef (strictly an oxacephem because it has an oxygen atom in place of sulphur in its ring system) exhibits the best activity against anaerobes. Confusingly, latamoxef is known as moxalactam in the United States and has sometimes been referred to as lamoxactam in the European literature.

Two other cephalosporins need to be mentioned because of their antipseudomonal activity: cefoperazone and cefsulodin. Cefoperazone is a fairly potent broad-spectrum agent, although its activity is rather less than that of cefotaxime and its relatives. Cefsulodin is extraordinary in being virtually inactive against bacteria other than *Ps. aeruginosa*.

A number of cephalosporins, including cephamandole, cefotetan, cefmenoxime, latamoxef, and cefoperazone possess a methyltetrazolethiomethyl side chain at the C-3 position of the molecule. This substituent has been implicated in causing hypoprothrombinaemia in some patients treated with these compounds.

Comparative activities of penicillins and cephalosporins

The comparative antibacterial activities of various penicillins and cephalosporins are summarized in Tables 1.1 and 1.2. In compiling these tables we have avoided giving the conventional minimum inhibitory concentration (MIC) values, since these are very variable depending on the test conditions and, particularly, on the bacterial inoculum used. It should also be noted that antibiotics grouped together because of their similar properties may not display entirely identical antibacterial activity.

OTHER β-LACTAM AGENTS

In addition to penicillins and cephalosporins, a wide variety of other compounds display a β-lactam ring in their structure (Fig. 1.4). The cephamycins and the oxa-cephem, latamoxef, both of which share the general properties of cephalosporins (see above) are examples of such

Table 1.1. Summary of the antibacterial properties of penicillins

Penicillin	Compounds with similar antibacterial properties	Staphylococci		Streptococci	Neisseria	Haemophilus	Enterobacteria		Pseudomonas	Anaerobes
		Activity	Stability*				Activity	Stability*		
Benzyl-penicillin	Procaine- Benethamine- Benzathine-penicillins	Excellent	Poor	Excellent	Excellent	Fair	—No useful activity—			Variable
Phenoxy-methyl-penicillin	Phenethicillin Propicillin	Excellent	Poor	Excellent	Good	Poor	—No useful activity—			Variable
Ampicillin	Amoxycillin Ampicillin-esters Hetacillin Ciclacillin	Good	Poor	Excellent	Excellent	Good	Good	Poor	No useful activity	Variable
Carbeni-cillin	Ticarcillin Azlocillin Mezlocillin Piperacillin Carfecillin Carindacillin	Fair	Poor	Fair	Good	Good	Variable	Variable	Good	Fair
Cloxacillin	Flucloxacillin Oxacillin Dicloxacillin Methicillin Nafcillin	Good	Good	Fair	Fair	Poor	—No useful activity—			Fair
Mecillinam	Pivmecillinam	—No useful activity—		Fair	Poor	Poor	Good	Variable	Poor	Poor

Table 1.2. Summary of the antibacterial properties of cephalosporins

Cephalosporin	Compounds with similar antibacterial properties	Staphylococci Activity	Staphylococci Stability*	Streptococci†	Neisseria	Haemophilus	Enterobacteria Activity	Enterobacteria Stability*	Pseudomonas*	Anaerobes
Cephalothin	Cephaloridine, Cefapirin, Cephacetrile, Cephazolin, Ceftezole	Good	Fair	Fair	Fair	Poor	Variable	Variable	No useful activity	Variable
Cephalexin	Cephradine, Cefaclor, Cefadroxil	Good	Good	Fair	Fair	Poor	Variable	Variable	No useful activity	Poor
Cefuroxime	Cefoxitin, Cephamandole	Good	Good	Good	Good	Good	Good	Good	No useful activity	Fair
Cefoperazone		Good	Good	Fair	Good	Good	Variable	Variable	Good	Fair
Cefsulodin		Poor	Good	Poor	—No useful activity—				Excellent	Poor
Cefotaxime	Ceftizoxime, Ceftazidime, Ceftriaxone, Latamoxef	Good	Good	Excellent	Excellent	Excellent	Excellent	Excellent	Poor‡	Poor

* Stability to β-lactamases of these organisms
† Enterococci are resistant to all cephalosporins.
‡ Ceftazidime is an exception.

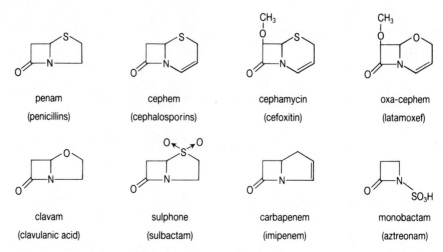

Fig. 1.4. Basic nuclear structures of β-lactam antibiotics currently available (examples in parentheses).

structural variants. Fundamentally different are clavulanic acid, a naturally occurring substance obtained from *Streptomyces clavuligerus*, and sulbactam, a penicillanic acid sulphone. These two compounds have been developed as β-lactamase inhibitors for use in combination with β-lactamase-labile agents with a view to restoring their activity (see Chapter 9).

Among structurally novel compounds that exhibit antibacterial activity in their own right are the carbapenem, imipenem (formerly called N-formimidoyl thienamycin) and aztreonam, the first of a group of compounds collectively known as *monobactams*, which have a β-lactam ring, but no associated fused ring system. Imipenem exhibits the broadest spectrum of all β-lactam antibiotics, with high activity against nearly all Gram-positive and Gram-negative aerobes and anaerobes (but not intracellular bacteria such as chlamydia). Although it is extremely stable to most bacterial β-lactamases, it is readily hydrolysed by a dehydropeptidase located in the mammalian kidney and is administered together with a dehydropeptidase inhibitor, cilastatin. The activity of aztreonam, in contrast, is restricted to aerobic Gram-negative bacteria. These two compounds thus typify two diametrically opposed approaches to the war on pathogenic microbes: blanket eradication and targeted therapy.

The β-lactam family is the largest and most diverse of all antibiotic groups and defies any attempt at rigid classification. A general categorization of β-lactam agents available in various parts of the world is provided in Table 1.3.

MODE OF ACTION OF β-LACTAM AGENTS

A few years ago it could be confidently stated that penicillins and cephalo-sporins act simply by interfering with the cross-linking reaction which gives the bacterial peptidoglycan its final rigidity. Bacterial death was thought to be secondary to this event in that continued growth led to osmotic rupture of cells no longer protected by an intact wall. More recent work has suggested that the situation is a good deal more com-plicated.

The chief complicating observation so far as the mode of action is con-cerned, was that several distinct proteins were discovered in isolated cell membranes which efficiently bound penicillin (so-called penicillin-binding proteins; PBPs). In *Esch. coli*, the best studied species, there are seven of these proteins numbered 1a, 1b, 2, 3, 4, 5, and 6 according to the order in which they are separated by polyacrylamide gel electrophoresis. PBPs 4, 5, and 6 are thought to be unconnected with the antibacterial effect of β-lactam agents. Binding to the remainder has been correlated with the various morphological effects of β-lactam antibiotics. Thus, cephalexin binds almost exclusively to PBP 3 and inhibits the division process only, causing the bacteria to grow as long filaments. The amidinopenicillin, mecillinam, binds preferentially to PBP 2 and causes a generalized effect on the cell wall so that the bacteria gradually assume a spherical shape. Most other β-lactam antibiotics bind to PBPs 1–3 and induce the formation of osmotically fragile, wall-deficient forms (spheroplasts) which typically emerge through cell wall lesions situated at incipient division points. These morphological events are illustrated in Fig. 1.5.

The osmotic theory of the bactericidal effect of β-lactam agents has also undergone some modification in recent years, although it remains valid for Gram-negative bacilli, where cell death can be quantitatively prevented by raising the osmolality of the growth medium. However, in the case of Gram-positive organisms, one of the first events to occur fol-lowing exposure to β-lactam antibiotics is a release of lipoteichoic acid from the cell wall, an event which appears to trigger a generalized autolytic dismantling of the peptidoglycan.

A further complication in Gram-positive organisms is that increasing the concentration of β-lactam antibiotics often results in a reduced bacteri-cidal effect. The mechanism of this optimal dosage effect (known as the *Eagle phenomenon* after its discoverer) is obscure, but may be related to the multiple sites of penicillin action, in that rapid bacteristasis achieved by blocking one cellular function may prevent the lethal events which follow inhibition of another by lower drug levels.

Table 1.3. β-lactam agents in clinical use throughout the world

Benzylpenicillin and its oral and long-acting derivatives		
benzylpenicillin*	azidocillin	procaine penicillin*
phenoxymethylpenicillin*	clometocillin	benzathine penicillin*
phenethicillin	penethamate hydriodide	benethamine penicillin*
penamecillin*	(penethacillin)	clemizole penicillin
propicillin	penimepicycline	hydrabamine penicillin V
Antistaphylococcal penicillins		
methicillin*	nafcillin	diphenicillin
cloxacillin*	oxacillin	(ancillin)
flucloxacillin*	dicloxacillin	
Broad-spectrum penicillins		
ampicillin* ±sulbactam	bacampicillin*	mecillinam*
amoxycillin* ±clavulanate*	pivampicillin*	pivmecillinam*
ciclacillin*	talampicillin*	hetacillin
aspoxicillin	metampicillin	fibracillin
epicillin	lenampicillin	penimocycline
Antipseudomonal β-lactam agents		
carbenicillin*	piperacillin*	carindacillin
ticarcillin* ±clavulanate*	apalcillin	cefoperazone±sulbactam
azlocillin*	sulbenicillin	cefsulodin*
mezlocillin*	carfecillin*	

Oral cephalosporins
cephalexin*   cefadroxil*   pivalexin
cephradine*   cephaloglycin   cefroxadine
cefaclor*   cefatrizine

β-lactamase-susceptible injectable cephalosporins
cephalothin*   cephacetrile   cefazedone
cephaloridine   cefapirin   ceftezole
cefazolin*   ceforanide   cefpimazole
cephamandole*   cefonicid   cefpiramide

β-lactamase-stable β-lactam agents
cefuroxime*   ceftizoxime*   cefotiam
cefoxitin*   ceftriaxone   cefmetazole
cefotaxime*   cefmenoxime   latamoxef*
ceftazidime*   cefotetan   aztreonam*
                                       imipenem*

_____

*On the market in the UK.

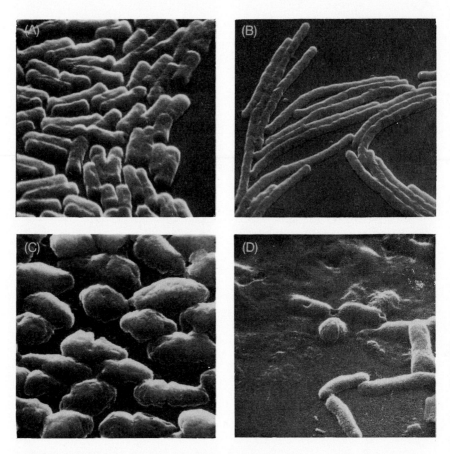

Fig. 1.5. Morphological effects of penicillins and cephalosporins on Gram-negative bacilli (scanning electron micrographs). (A) Normal *Escherichia coli* cells. (B) *Esch. coli* exposed to cephalexin, 32 mg/l, for 1 hour. (C) *Esch. coli* exposed to mecillinam, 10 mg/l, for 2 hours; this effect is peculiar to mecillinam. (D) *Esch. coli* exposed to ampicillin, 64 mg/l, for 1 hour, showing lysed debris, central cell wall lesions, and a spheroplast; higher concentrations of most β-lactam agents cause this effect. [A-C from D. Greenwood and F. O'Grady (1973). *Journal of Infectious Diseases* **128**, 791-4. D from D. Greenwood and F. O'Grady (1969). *Journal of Medical Microbiology* **2**, 435-41.]

In both Gram-positive and Gram-negative bacteria, a proportion of the population survive exposure to concentrations of β-lactam antibiotics lethal for the rest of the culture. These *persisters* are apparently unaffected morphologically. They remain dormant so long as the antibiotic is present and resume growth when it is removed. In addition, some strains of staphylococci and streptococci display *tolerance* to β-lactam antibiotics in that they succumb much more slowly than usual to the lethal action of β-lactam agents. The therapeutic significance, if any, of persisters is unknown, but penicillin-tolerance has been implicated in therapeutic failures in bacterial endocarditis where bactericidal activity is crucial to the success of treatment.

2

Inhibitors of bacterial
protein synthesis

The remarkable process by which proteins are manufactured on the ribosomal conveyor belt according to a blueprint provided by the cell nucleus is so fundamentally important and intrinsically fascinating that no-one who has studied any aspect of modern biology can fail to have encountered it.

For the present purpose it is sufficient to outline the main features of the process. The first step is the formation of an initiation complex, consisting of messenger RNA, transcribed from the appropriate area of a DNA strand, the two ribosomal subunits and methionyl-transfer-RNA (N-formylated in bacteria) which occupies the 'peptidyl donor' site ('P' site) on the larger ribosomal subunit. Aminoacyl-tRNA appropriate to the next codon to be read slots into place in the aminoacyl 'acceptor' site ('A' site) and an enzyme called peptidyl transferase attaches the methionine to the new amino acid with the formation of a peptide bond. The mRNA and the ribosome now move with respect to one another so that the dipeptide is translocated from the A to the P site and the next codon of the mRNA is aligned with the A site in readiness for the next aminoacyl tRNA. The process continues to build up amino acids in the nascent peptide chain according to the order dictated by mRNA until a 'nonsense' codon is encountered which signals chain termination.

Although the general mechanism of protein synthesis is thought to be universal, the process as it occurs in bacterial cells is sufficiently different from mammalian protein synthesis to offer scope for the selective toxicity required of therapeutically useful antimicrobial agents. The chief difference that is exploited involves the actual structure of the ribosomal workshop in both the protein and RNA components. These structural differences are reflected in the sedimentation characteristics of the two types of ribosome when they are subjected to ultracentrifugation analysis. Bacterial ribosomes exhibit a sedimentation coefficient of 70S and dissociate into 50S and 30S subunits; mammalian ribosomes, on the other hand, display an 80S sedimentation coefficient, and are composed of 60S and 40S subunits.

An antibiotic such as puromycin, which as a structural analogue of the terminal aminoacyladenosine common to all tRNAs, is a potent inhibitor of protein synthesis, is of no use therapeutically since its action is non-specific. Puromycin has, however, been widely used by biochemists as a probe for unravelling the secrets of protein synthesis by virtue of its specific action as a cause of premature termination of protein synthesis.

Antibiotics which selectively interfere with protein synthesis on 70S ribosomes include chloramphenicol, the tetracyclines, fusidic acid, erythromycin and other macrolides, the lincosamides, and the amino-glycosides.

CHLORAMPHENICOL

Chloramphenicol was one of the first therapeutically useful antibiotics to appear from systematic screening of *Streptomyces* strains in the wake of the discovery of streptomycin in the 1940s. Although it is a naturally occurring compound the molecular structure is relatively simple (Fig. 2.1) and can readily be synthesized. Attempts to modify the structure of chlor-amphenicol have generally resulted in a marked loss of activity, but thiamphenicol, a compound which possesses a sulphomethyl group in place of the nitro group of chloramphenicol, displays antibacterial activity comparable to chloramphenicol itself. Fluorinated derivatives of chlor-amphenicol and thiamphenicol that exhibit good antibacterial activity and retain activity against chloramphenicol-resistant strains have also been described. Unfortunately, these compounds have not yet been developed for therapeutic use.

Pure chloramphenicol is very insoluble in water and is extremely bitter to the taste. Both these problems have been overcome by pro-drug forms of the antibiotic: chloramphenicol palmitate and stearate to improve palat-ability and chloramphenicol succinate to improve solubility for injection. These compounds have no antibacterial activity *per se*, but serve to release chloramphenicol in the body; they should not be used for laboratory tests of bacterial sensitivity.

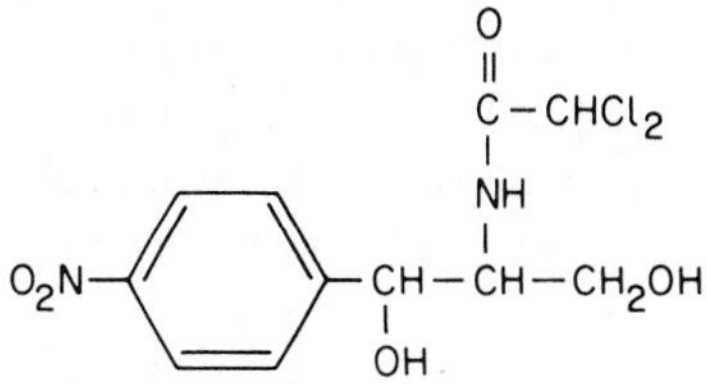

Fig. 2.1. Structure of chloramphenicol.

Chloramphenicol acts by inhibiting the peptidyl transferase reaction—the step at which the peptide bond is formed—on 70S ribosomes. The spectrum of activity embraces most Gram-positive and Gram-negative bacteria, and also extends to chlamydia and rickettsia, those strictly intracellular bacteria that cause a variety of infections, including trachoma, psittacosis, and typhus (Table 2.1). Resistance when it occurs is usually due to bacterial enzymes that acetylate the two hydroxyl groups. The action of chloramphenicol against enterobacteria is purely bacteristatic and this has led to its reputation as a generally bacteristatic drug. However, against many other bacteria, including the Gram-positive cocci, chloramphenicol may display quite potent bactericidal activity. The drug also possesses the important properties of diffusing well into cerebrospinal fluid and of penetrating into cells—a very useful feature in the treatment of diseases such as typhoid, typhus, and other conditions where intracellular bacteria are involved. Resistance to chloramphenicol is generally uncommon, although resistant strains of *Salmonella typhi* have caused serious problems in areas of the world where typhoid is endemic. Strains of *Haemophilus influenzae* that are resistant to chloramphenicol are also being encountered with increasing frequency.

Given all these attractive qualities it is a great pity that chloramphenicol displays one grave drawback: potentially fatal depression of the bone marrow. This side-effect, though extremely rare, has been sufficient to relegate chloramphenicol to the role of a reserve drug for special purposes. Use of thiamphenicol is also commonly associated with toxicity to the bone marrow, but the irreversible effects are said not to occur with this drug. Among conditions for which chloramphenicol is still widely used are typhoid fever and meningitis, including neonatal meningitis when, however, the other potentially fatal side-effect of the antibiotic ('grey baby' syndrome) may follow if the dosage is not properly adjusted.

TETRACYCLINES

The first tetracycline, chlortetracycline (Fig. 2.2) was described in 1948 as a product of *Streptomyces aureofaciens*. Oxytetracycline and tetracycline itself (so-called because it lacks both the chlorine of chlortetracycline and the hydroxyl of oxytetracycline) quickly followed. These, and other members of the group including demeclocycline, doxycycline, and minocycline, are closely related structural variants of the same tetracyclic molecule.

The tetracycline group is among the most broad-spectrum of all antimicrobial agents, displaying good activity against Gram-positive and Gram-negative bacteria, rickettsia, chlamydia, mycoplasma and spirochaetes

Table 2.1. Summary of the antibacterial spectrum of inhibitors of bacterial protein synthesis

Antibiotic	Staphylococci	Streptococci	Neisseria	Haemophilus	Enterobacteria	Pseudomonas	Anaerobes	Rickettsia and chlamydia	Mycoplasma
Chloramphenicol	Good	Good	Good	Good	Good	Poor	Good	Good	Fair
Tetracyclines	Good	Good	Good	Good	Good	Poor	Fair	Good	Good
Fusidic acid	Good	Fair	Good	— No useful activity —			Fair	— No useful activity —	
Erythromycin (and other macrolides)	Good	Good	Good	Good	— No useful activity —		Variable	Fair	Good
Lincomycin (and clindamycin)	Good	Good	— No useful activity —				Good	(Fair)*	Variable
Aminoglycosides	Good	Poor	Fair	Fair	Good	Variable	— No useful activity —		Fair

N.B. It should be noted that individual strains of susceptible species may be resistant to any of these agents.

* Lincomycin, poor; clindamycin, fair.

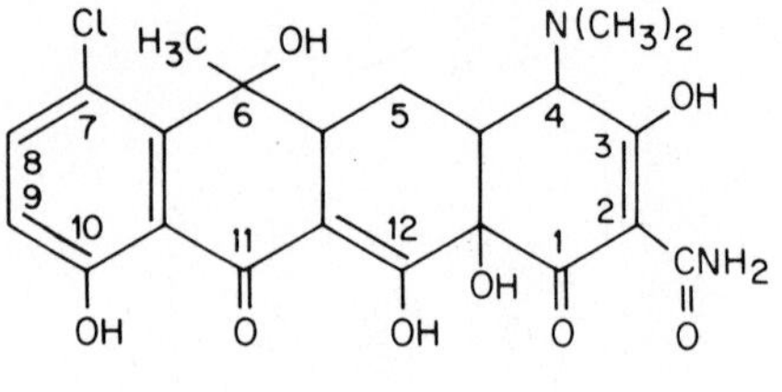

Fig. 2.2. Structure of chlortetracycline.

(Table 2.1). The different tetracyclines do not differ much in their anti-bacterial activity and are distinguished more by their pharmacokinetic behaviour. Doxycycline and minocycline are the most widely used: unlike the others they do not aggravate renal failure so that they can be used in patients suffering renal impairment; they also exhibit marginally better antibacterial activity; and they display sufficiently long serum half-lives to allow them to be given only twice daily.

Susceptible bacteria concentrate tetracyclines by an active transport process. In the cell they interact with the 30S ribosomal subunit and thereby interfere with the binding of aminoacyl-tRNA to the A site on the ribosome. Like chloramphenicol, the tetracyclines are predominantly bacteristatic, but some species may be affected bactericidally. The therapeutic importance of the group as a whole has declined over the years with the upsurge of resistant strains, particularly among enterobacteria and streptococci. The mechanism of the resistance is unusual in that a new protein is produced which appears to prevent uptake of the drug (Chapter 12). There is almost complete cross-resistance between tetracyclines, although minocycline may retain activity against some tetracycline-resistant strains.

Tetracyclines are still widely used for the treatment of respiratory infections, particularly chronic bronchitis and mycoplasma pneumonia, and they are the drugs of choice for rickettsial and chlamydial infections of all types. Their use should be avoided in young children, since they chelate calcium and are deposited in calcifying tissue so that their yellow pigment can permanently discolour growing teeth.

FUSIDIC ACID

Fusidic acid is the only therapeutically useful member of a group of naturally occurring antibiotics that display a steroid-like structure (Fig. 2.3). The antibiotic acts to prevent the translocation step in bacterial protein

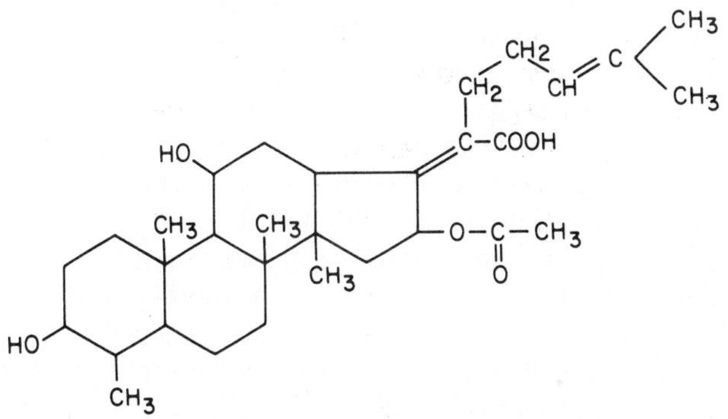

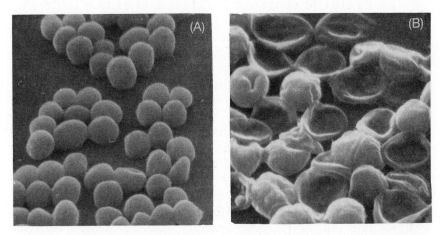

Fig. 2.3. Structure of fusidic acid.

Fig. 2.4. Morphological effects of fusidic acid on *Staph. aureus*. (A) No antibiotic. (B) Bacteria exposed to fusidic acid (2 mg/l) for 3 hours. Similar morphological changes can be demonstrated following exposure of staphylococci to erythromycin and lincomycin.

synthesis by inhibiting one of the substances (factor G) essential for this reaction. As a secondary effect of the inhibition of protein synthesis, susceptible staphylococci collapse (Fig. 2.4), perhaps because cell wall growth becomes unbalanced in the absence of essential enzymes normally provided by the ribosomal factory. This secondary collapse is prevented by penicillins (see Chapter 9).

Fusidic acid is active *in vitro* against Gram-positive and -negative cocci *Mycobacterium tuberculosis*, *Nocardia asteroides*, and many anaerobes; the ribosomes of Gram-negative bacilli are susceptible to the action of the drug, but access is denied by the Gram-negative cell wall. *Staphylococcus aureus* is particularly susceptible to fusidic acid and the compound is usually regarded simply as an antistaphylococcal agent. The antibiotic penetrates well into infected tissues, including bone, and it is favoured by some authorities for the treatment of staphylococcal osteomyelitis. A potential drawback to use of the drug is the presence in any large staphylococcal population, of a small number of fusidic acid-resistant variants which might proliferate during therapy. For this reason, fusidic acid is usually administered together with another antibiotic, often a penicillin. Fusidic acid is usually free from side-effects when given orally. Intravenous administration of the diethanolamine salt is sometimes accompanied by a reversible jaundice.

ERYTHROMYCIN AND OTHER MACROLIDES

Erythromycin is the most important of a group of antibiotics produced by various species of *Streptomyces*. The group shares a similar molecular structure characterized by a large macrocylic lactone ring substituted with some unusual sugars. Members of the group are collectively referred to as *macrolides*. All are thought to act by interfering with the translocation step in bacterial protein synthesis.

Erythromycin base is broken down in the acid conditions of the stomach. To overcome this, enteric-coated tablets, the stearate salt, or esterified pro-drug forms are used for oral administration. Two ester formulations are in general use: the ethylsuccinate and the estolate (the lauryl sulphate salt of the propionyl ester). Erythromycin lactobionate and erythromycin gluceptate are available for intravenous administration. Erythromycin estolate has been generally regarded as the most toxic formulation, because of its propensity to cause reversible cholestatic jaundice. However, this complication can arise with any of the preparations.

Erythromycin was originally discovered at a time when resistance of staphylococci to penicillin was first becoming a serious problem. In the fear that the usefulness of erythromycin might be similarly compromised, the drug tended to be used with circumspection as a reserve antistaphylococcal agent or as a second-line antistreptococcal agent for use in patients hypersensitive to penicillin. Usage of erythromycin has largely continued along these lines and it is perhaps underused in terms of its efficacy and general lack of toxicity. The antibiotic lacks useful activity against enterobacteria or *Pseudomonas aeruginosa*, but is active against *Mycoplasma pneumoniae*. In recent years erythromycin has acquired two new indications for its use: *Campylobacter jejuni* enteritis and *Legionella pneumophila* pneumonia.

Other macrolides that have been used in various parts of the world include oleandomycin (or its better absorbed derivative triacetyloleandomycin), spiramycin, josamycin, and midecamycin. None of them seems to offer much therapeutic advantage over erythromycin. Spiramycin is sometimes used as an alternative to pyrimethamine in infections caused by the protozoan parasite, *Toxoplasma gondii*. It has also been tentatively suggested, on the basis of little evidence, that it might be of value in cryptosporidiosis, a protozoal disease that is highly refractory to anti-microbial therapy.

LINCOSAMIDES

There are only two therapeutically important lincosamides, lincomycin, a naturally occurring product of *Streptomyces lincolnensis*, and clindamycin, a chemically modified derivative (7-chloro-7-deoxylincomycin; Fig. 2.5) which exhibits improved antibacterial activity and is thus generally preferred in therapy.

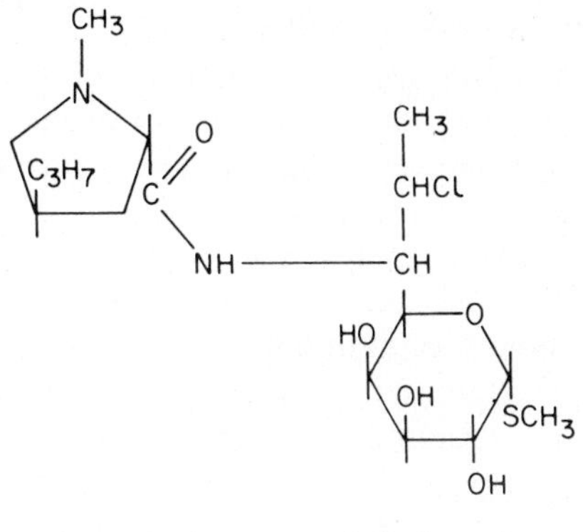

Fig. 2.5. Structure of clindamycin.

Lincosamides interfere with the process of peptide elongation in a way that has not been precisely defined. The ribosomal binding site is probably similar to that of erythromycin, since resistance to erythromycin caused by an inducible methylation of the ribosomal binding site affects lincosamides as well.

Lincomycin and clindamycin possess good antistaphylococcal and anti-streptococcal activity and have also proved therapeutically useful in the treatment of infections due to *Bacteroides fragilis* and some other anaerobes. Enterobacteria and *Ps. aeruginosa* lie outside the spectrum of activity (Table 2.1).

Patients treated with clindamycin (or lincomycin) commonly experience diarrhoea, which may occasionally develop into a potentially fatal pseudo-membranous colitis caused by a clostridial toxin (see Chapter 22). Other antibiotics, notably ampicillin and broad-spectrum cephalosporins, may also cause this side-effect, but the incidence of toxin-associated colitis appears to be somewhat higher following clindamycin therapy than with other agents.

AMINOGLYCOSIDES

The discovery of the first aminoglycoside, streptomycin, in 1943 was a major landmark in the development of therapeutically useful antibiotics, particularly as it extended the sphere of influence of chemotherapy to embrace one of the major microbial scourges—tuberculosis. Later discoveries disclosed the fact that streptomycin was just one of a large family of related antibiotics produced by various species of *Streptomyces* and *Micromonospora*. Those derived from the latter organism, such as gentamicin and sissomicin, are distinguished in their spelling by an 'i' rather than a 'y' in the 'mycin' suffix.

Structurally, most aminoglycosides consist of a linked ring system composed of aminosugars and an aminosubstituted cyclic polyalcohol (aminocyclitol). For this reason the group is sometimes given the cumbersome designation 'aminoglycosidic-aminocyclitol' group. One antibiotic usually included with the group, spectinomycin, contains no amino-glycoside substituent and is properly regarded as a pure aminocyclitol. The aminocyclitol moiety of aminoglycosides usually consists of one of two derivatives of streptamine: streptidine (present in streptomycin and its relatives) or deoxystreptamine (present in most other therapeutically useful aminoglycosides (Fig. 2.6). Deoxystreptamine-containing amino-glycosides can, in their turn, be subdivided into two major groups: the *neomycin group*, and the *kanamycin group*. The aminoglycosides most commonly used in present day medicine, including gentamicin and tobramycin, belong to the kanamycin group. The designation 'kanamycin', 'gentamicin', or 'neomycin' indicates a family of closely related compounds and commercial preparations usually contain a mixture of these. For example, gentamicin, as used therapeutically, is a mixture of three structural variants of the gentamicin C complex (Fig. 2.7).

General properties of aminoglycosides

The aminoglycosides are potent, broad-spectrum bactericidal agents which must be injected for systemic use, since they are very poorly

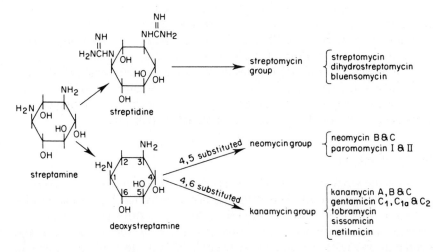

Fig. 2.6. Grouping of therapeutically useful aminoglycosides according to characteristics of the aminocyclitol ring. In most aminoglycosides the aminocyclitol moiety is either streptidine or deoxystreptamine, both derivatives of streptamine. The deoxystreptamine group can be sub-divided into those in which sugar substituents are linked at the 4- and 5-hydroxyls, and those substituted at the 4- and 6-hydroxyl positions.

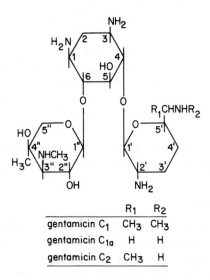

	R_1	R_2
gentamicin C_1	CH_3	CH_3
gentamicin C_{1a}	H	H
gentamicin C_2	CH_3	H

Fig. 2.7. Structure of the gentamicin C complex, showing the ring numbering system and variations in structure of the different gentamicins.

absorbed when administered orally. They lack useful activity against streptococci and anaerobes, but the activity against streptococci can often be improved by using them in conjunction with penicillins, with which they interact synergically (Chapter 7). Some members of the group display important activity against *M. tuberculosis* or *Ps. aeruginosa* (Table 2.2).

As a group the aminoglycosides display considerable toxicity, affecting both the ear and the kidney, and their use may require careful laboratory monitoring (Chapter 8). In the laboratory the activity of aminoglycosides is markedly affected by pH and other variables (Chapter 7).

Mode of action

Most of the work on the mode of action of aminoglycosides has concentrated on streptomycin. This drug has been shown to bind to a particular protein in the 30S ribosomal subunit. Alteration of this protein results in streptomycin resistance, but aminoglycosides of the kanamycin and neomycin groups are generally unaffected. Several effects of the binding of streptomycin and other aminoglycosides have been noted, including a tendency to cause misreading of certain codons of mRNA resulting in the production of defective proteins. It is unlikely that this effect is sufficient to account completely for the antibacterial activity of aminoglycosides and other convincing lines of evidence suggest that the primary site of action lies in the formation of non-functioning initiation complexes. Neither hypothesis satisfactorily explains the potent bactericidal activity of aminoglycosides compared with other inhibitors of protein synthesis. Definitive solutions to these and other paradoxical aspects of amino-glycoside action are still the subject of dispute. One plausible explanation is that the misreading effect, brought about by low concentrations of the antibiotic early in the encounter between bacterium and drug, causes the formation of faulty membrane-associated proteins that render the membrane leaky; this has the dual effect of allowing the loss of essential small molecules and enhanced uptake of more aminoglycoside, which is then sufficient to prevent irreversibly further protein synthesis.

Streptomycin group

Streptomycin itself is the most important member of this group, although various other derivatives, including dihydrostreptomycin and bluenso-mycin have been described. Once a drug of major chemotherapeutic importance, its use has declined with the appearance of other amino-glycosides, although it is still a common component of antituberculosis regimens (see Chapter 26). It has also been widely used together with penicillin in the treatment of streptococcal (in particular enterococcal)

Table 2.2. Summary of the antibacterial spectrum and toxicity of aminoglycosides

Aminoglycoside	Staphylococci	Streptococci	Enterobacteria	*Pseudomonas aeruginosa*	*Mycobacterium tuberculosis*	Relative degrees of	
						ototoxicity	nephrotoxicity
Streptomycin	Good	Poor	Good	Poor	Good	+ + +	±
Kanamycin	Good	Poor	Good	Poor	Good	+ +	+ +
Gentamicin	Good	Fair	Good	Good	Poor	+ +	+ +
Tobramycin	Good	Poor	Good	Good	Poor	+ +	+ +
Sissomicin	Good	Poor	Good	Good	Poor	+ +	+ +
Netilmicin	Good	Poor	Good	Good	Poor	+	+
Amikacin	Good	Poor	Good	Good	Good	+ +	+
Neomycin	Good	Poor	Good	Poor	Fair	+ + +	+ + +

endocarditis, but has largely been displaced by gentamicin for this indication in recent years (see Chapter 23).

Neomycin group

Neomycin is among the most toxic of all aminoglycosides that have been developed for therapeutic use and it is now little used, except in topical preparations; even such usage is discouraged because of the risk of promoting the emergence of bacteria displaying non-specific aminoglycoside resistance. The poor oral absorption has also been exploited in the use of oral neomycin for the treatment of diarrhoea of unproven aetiology, or as a method of sterilizing the gut prior to abdominal surgery. Neither of these procedures is entirely rational: antibiotics are not usually of value in infectious diarrhoea (see Chapter 22) and the inactivity of aminoglycosides against anaerobes ensures that the majority of the gut flora escapes the antibacterial effects of the drug when used prior to bowel surgery. Framycetin, also a common component of topical preparations, is identical to neomycin B.

One aminoglycoside of the neomycin group, paromomycin, is unusual in exhibiting activity against the amoebae causing amoebic dysentery. However, the drug does not appear to offer any advantage over nitro-imidazoles and other drugs in the treatment of this condition.

Kanamycin group

This group includes kanamycin itself, gentamicin, tobramycin, netilmicin, sissomicin, and two semi-synthetic derivatives of kanamycin, amikacin, and dibekacin.

Kanamycin, in the naturally occurring form obtained from the producer organism, is a mixture of three closely related compounds, kanamycin A, B, and C. Pharmaceutical preparations of kanamycin consist almost exclusively of kanamycin A. Kanamycin was the aminoglycoside which ousted streptomycin from its pedestal in the early 1960s. Its spectrum of activity is similar to that of streptomycin (and, like it, includes *M. tuberculosis*), but it retains activity against streptomycin-resistant strains and is less likely to cause vestibular damage.

In its turn kanamycin has been virtually superseded by gentamicin and tobramycin (deoxykanamycin B), which are more active against many enterobacteria and, more importantly, include *Ps. aeruginosa* in their spectrum. This has been a major factor in the popularity of these agents for the 'blind' therapy of serious infection before the results of laboratory tests are known.

The relative merits of gentamicin and tobramycin have been the subject of much debate. Tobramycin appears to be marginally less nephrotoxic and slightly more active against *Ps. aeruginosa*; against other susceptible bacteria, gentamicin probably has the edge.

Other agents of the kanamycin group, including sissomicin (sometimes spelt sisomicin) and dibekacin (dideoxykanamycin B) seem to offer little or no advantage over gentamicin or tobramycin. Netilmicin (*N*-acetyl sissomicin), the latest derivative to come into therapeutic use, is claimed to be less toxic than its predecessors and is more stable to some aminoglycoside-modifying enzymes (see Chapter 12).

Amikacin, a semi-synthetic derivative of kanamycin A in which an α-aminobutyric acid substituent has been added to an amino group on the deoxystreptamine ring, was specifically developed as a compound resistant to aminoglycoside-modifying enzymes. Although it is somewhat less active than gentamicin or tobramycin, higher serum levels are achieved on conventional dosage and the drug has found some use in those units troubled by gentamicin resistance. Strains of bacteria that are resistant to gentamicin by non-enzymic mechanisms are, however, cross-resistant to amikacin and other aminoglycosides.

Spectinomycin

The aminocyclitol antibiotic, spectinomycin, exhibits properties that separate it from the true aminoglycosides. It displays inferior antibacterial activity against most species and generally achieves a bacteristatic, rather than a bactericidal effect. Spectinomycin has, however, found a niche for itself in the treatment of gonorrhoea in patients who are either hypersensitive to penicillin, or infected with gonococci resistant to penicillin.

3

Synthetic antibacterial agents and miscellaneous antibiotics

Various targets other than the cell wall and bacterial ribosome are available for selective attack by chemotherapeutic agents. These include the cell membrane, the processes of nucleic acid synthesis and many essential metabolic activities taking place within the cell cytoplasm. Most of the antibacterial drugs which act at these levels are not antibiotics in the strict sense (i.e. they are synthetic chemicals rather than naturally occurring products of micro-organisms). Some antibacterial agents considered under this heading are largely (in some cases exclusively) restricted to the treatment of urinary infections, although others have wider uses.

URINARY ANTISEPTICS

Hexamine

Hexamine (Fig. 3.1), also known as methenamine, was used in the treatment of urinary tract infection before the turn of the present century. The compound owes its antibacterial activity to the fact that, under mildly acidic conditions, such as commonly exist in urine, it decomposes into formaldehyde (which is non-specifically bactericidal) and ammonia.

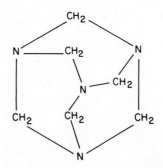

Fig. 3.1. Structure of hexamine.

The activity of hexamine is dependent on urinary pH and the drug is totally ineffective in *Proteus* infections, in which the ability of the organisms to split urea ensures that the urine is alkaline. Hexamine is often administered in the form of salts of organic acids; hexamine hippurate and hexamine mandelate are commonly used. This is done in the dual hope that the organic acid moiety might help to keep urinary pH low and may also contribute some antibacterial activity of its own.

The activity of hexamine and its salts is relatively feeble and unpredictable. With the appearance of much more potent antibacterial agents its importance as a therapeutic agent has been virtually eclipsed. The drug may still have some value in the less demanding role of prophylactic agent for the long-term prevention of infection in those patients prone to recurrent urinary infection.

Nitrofurantoin

A number of nitrofuran derivatives have attracted attention over the years, but only one, nitrofurantoin (Fig. 3.2), has found widespread use, and this is restricted to the treatment of urinary infection. The reason for this restriction is that after oral absorption it is rapidly excreted into urine and the small amount that finds its way into tissues is inactivated there. Nausea is fairly common after administration of nitrofurantoin, but gastrointestinal intolerance is improved with the macrocrystalline formulation.

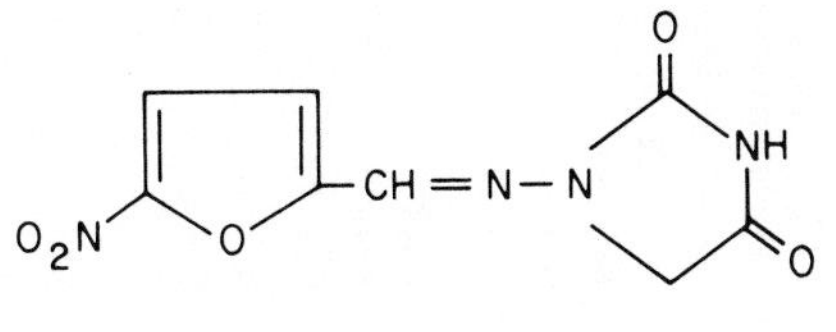

Fig. 3.2. Structure of nitrofurantoin.

Nitrofurantoin is active against most urinary tract pathogens, but *Proteus* spp. and *Pseudomonas aeruginosa* are usually resistant (Table 3.1). The occurrence of resistant strains among susceptible species is uncommon. The activity of nitrofurantoin is affected by pH, acid conditions favouring the activity.

The mode of action of nitrofurantoin has not been precisely elucidated. It appears likely that, as with metronidazole (see below), a reduced form of the drug is produced intracellularly and this interacts with DNA in some way.

Nitrofurans related to nitrofurantoin include nitrofurazone (marketed for topical use and bladder irrigation); nifuratel (used in some countries

Table 3.1. Summary of the antibacterial spectrum of urinary antiseptics

Antibacterial compound	Escherichia coli	Proteus spp.	Other coliforms	Enterococcus (Streptococcus) faecalis	Staphylococci	Pseudomonas aeruginosa
Hexamine (methenamine)	Fair	Poor	Fair	Fair	Fair	Fair
Nitrofurantoin	Good	Poor	Good	Poor	Fair	Poor
Nalidixic acid	Good	Good	Good	Poor	Poor	Poor
Sulphonamides	(Good)	(Good)	(Good)	Poor	(Good)	Poor
Trimethoprim	Good	Good	(Good)	Good	Good	Poor

Brackets indicate that resistant strains are common.

for *Trichomonas vaginalis* infection); furazolidone (an orally non-absorbed compound sometimes used for intestinal infections) and nifurtimox (used in Chagas' disease; see Chapters 5 and 30).

Sulphonamides

When, in the 1930s, a red dye called prontosil was found to cure infections caused by haemolytic streptococci in mice and men, a major breakthrough had been accomplished in the chemotherapy of bacterial infections (see Historical Introduction).

Paradoxically, prontosil was found to be inactive *in vitro*, but it was quickly realized that its activity in the body was due to the liberation of sulphanilamide, an analogue of para-aminobenzoic acid (Fig. 3.3). PABA is an essential metabolite in bacterial folate synthesis. Most bacteria synthesize folic acid and cannot take it up preformed from the environment. Mammalian cells, in contrast, use preformed folate and cannot make their own. Sulphonamides block an early stage in folate synthesis, the condensation of PABA with dihydropteridine to form dihydropteroic acid.

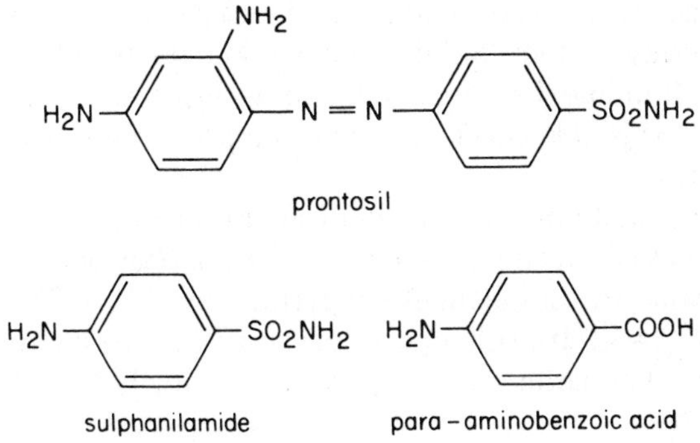

Fig. 3.3. Structures of prontosil, sulphanilamide, and para-aminobenzoic acid.

Chemical modification of the sulphanilamide molecule has resulted in the production of hundreds of different sulphonamides which differ chiefly in their pharmacological properties. Relatively few of them have become established in regular clinical use.

Sulphonamides are broad-spectrum (Table 3.1), predominantly bacteristatic and relatively slow to act: several generations of bacterial growth are needed to deplete the folate pool before inhibition of growth occurs. Resistance emerges readily and bacteria resistant to one sulphonamide are cross-resistant to the others. Sensitivity tests present problems in the laboratory since results critically depend on the composition of the culture medium and the inoculum size (see Chapter 7).

Following the introduction of sulphonamides into clinical medicine, they were extensively and successfully used for a wide variety of infections. The emergence of resistant strains and the appearance of more potent antimicrobial agents has relegated the sulphonamide group to a minor therapeutic role, chiefly as agents for use in uncomplicated urinary infection. Sulphonamides (usually sulphadiazine) also remain useful for the protection of close contacts of cases of meningococcal meningitis, providing the strain of *Neisseria meningitidis* involved is sulphonamide sensitive (Chapter 19).

The majority of sulphonamides are well absorbed when given orally and are chiefly excreted in the urine, partly in an antibacterially inactive acetylated form. The compounds diffuse relatively well into CSF and were successfully used for treating meningitis before resistance became common. Sulphonamides that are poorly absorbed when given orally (including sulphaloxate and sulphaguanidine) have been used for intestinal infections, but are not recommended.

Less soluble sulphonamides (e.g. sulphathiazole and sulphadiazine) are prone to cause renal damage due to the deposition of crystals in the urinary collecting system. Sulphafurazole (known as sulfisoxazole in the USA), sulphadimidine (known as sulfamethazine in the USA), and sulphamethizole lack this side-effect and are to be preferred in the treatment of urinary infection.

Some other sulphonamides in clinical use are distinguished by long plasma half-lives ($T_{1/2}$) and are known as *long-acting sulphonamides*. The most important are sulphamethoxypyridazine ($T_{1/2} = 35$ h); sulphadimethoxine ($T_{1/2} = 40$ h); sulfametopyrazine ($T_{1/2} = 60$ h); and sulfadoxine ($T_{1/2} = 120$ h). The latter two are excreted so slowly that they need only be given weekly.

Trimethoprim

Trimethoprim (Fig. 3.4) is one of the few antibacterial agents to have been developed according to rational biochemical principles. The drug selectively inhibits bacterial dihydrofolate reductase, the enzyme which generates tetrahydrofolate (the active form of the vitamin) from metabolically inactive dihydrofolate. The corresponding mammalian enzyme has a much reduced affinity for trimethoprim and this is the basis of the selective toxicity of the compound.

Since sulphonamides and trimethoprim act at different points in the same metabolic pathway they interact synergically: bacteria are inhibited

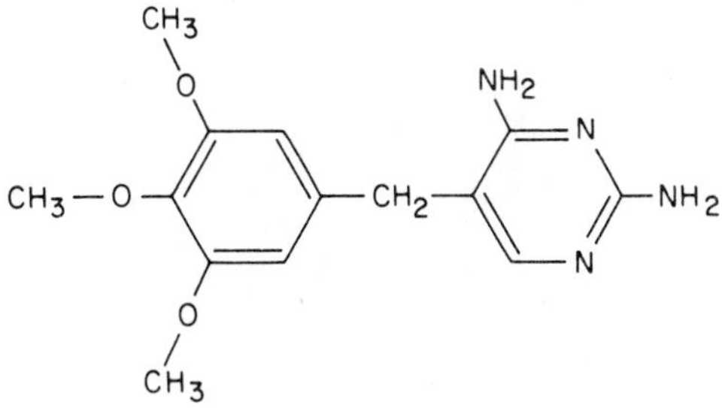

Fig. 3.4. Structure of trimethoprim.

by much lower concentrations of the combination than by either agent alone. For this reason trimethoprim and sulphonamides are often combined in therapeutic formulations although trimethoprim alone is probably as effective and less toxic. The most commonly used combination is trimethoprim and sulphamethoxazole (co-trimoxazole), but combinations of trimethoprim with sulphadiazine (co-trimazine) and sulphamoxole (co-trifamole) are also available.

Trimethoprim is active in low concentration against most common pathogenic bacteria, but *Ps. aeruginosa* is a notable exception (Table 3.1). Resistance is on the increase; up to 30 per cent of urinary isolates have been reported as resistant in some series, but this is not universal experience. The drug is rapidly absorbed from the gut and excreted almost exclusively by the kidneys with a plasma half-life of about 10 hours. Toxic side-effects are uncommon, but residual effects on folate metabolism may cause haematological changes in folate-depleted patients.

The chief use for trimethoprim is in urinary tract infection. The combination with sulphamethoxazole has also been extensively used in many other clinical situations, including chest infection, typhoid fever, and brucellosis.

Compounds related to trimethoprim include tetroxoprim (which exhibits similar properties), the antimalarial agents pyrimethamine and proguanil (Chapters 5 and 30), and the antineoplastic agent, methotrexate.

Quinolones

Nalidixic acid and its early congeners
Nalidixic acid (Fig. 3.5) was the first representative to appear of a family of compounds which share close similarities of structure. Early members of the group, developed in the 1960s and 1970s and available in various

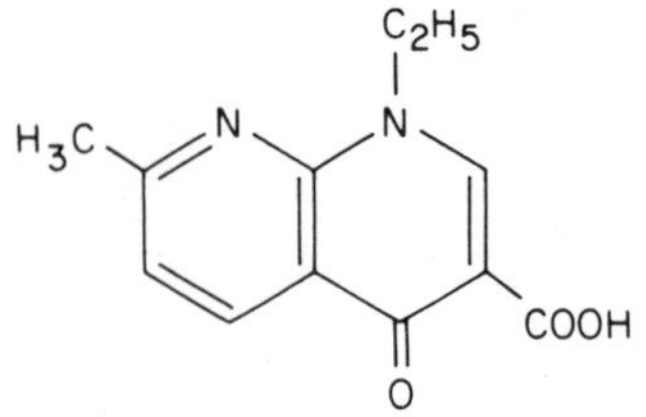

Fig. 3.5. Structure of nalidixic acid.

countries throughout the world, include nalidixic acid, cinoxacin, oxolinic acid, pipemidic acid, piromidic acid, flumequine, and acrosoxacin.

The site of action of these compounds has been pinpointed with unusual precision to a subunit of that remarkable enzyme, DNA gyrase, which unwinds the supercoiled DNA helix prior to replication and transcription.

Nalidixic acid and its congeners are all well absorbed when administered orally and are more-or-less extensively metabolized in the body before being excreted into the urine. Nalidixic acid itself is largely converted to hydroxynalidixic acid (which retains antibacterial activity) and glucuronide conjugates (which do not).

Most Gram-negative bacteria, with the exception of *Ps. aeruginosa*, are susceptible to nalidixic acid, but Gram-positive organisms are usually resistant (Table 3.1). Susceptible bacteria can readily be converted to resistance in the laboratory and the emergence of resistance sometimes causes treatment failure. However, 'wild' strains resistant to nalidixic acid are uncommon, perhaps because resistance, when it occurs, is not spread by plasmids (see Chapter 13). The drug is used only in urinary infection.

The various early congeners of nalidixic acid share similar antibacterial properties; oxolinic acid and flumequine display enhanced activity against enterobacteria *in vitro*, and there is some evidence that resistance does not emerge so readily with cinoxacin as with other compounds of this group. Acrosoxacin exhibits good activity against *Neisseria* and is sometimes used for the treatment of gonorrhoea in patients allergic to penicillin.

Newer quinolones

During the last 10 years, a new series of quinolone derivatives has appeared. These compounds, which are all piperazine-substituted fluoroquinolones, extend the spectrum of nalidixic acid and its early congeners to include Gram-positive cocci and *Ps. aeruginosa*. They also exhibit reasonably good activity *in vitro* against some problem organisms, such as

Chlamydia trachomatis, *Legionella pneumophila*, and *Mycobacterium tuberculosis*, but at the time of writing it is too soon to tell whether this will be translated into reliable clinical efficacy. The activity of the newer quinolones against enterobacteria is considerably better than that of nalidixic acid.

Fluoroquinolones presently available throughout the world include ciprofloxacin (the most active derivative), norfloxacin, enoxacin, ofloxacin, and pefloxacin. Many others are under development. They are usually administered by the oral route, although some, including ciprofloxacin can also be given intravenously. Therapeutic dosages achieve relatively low concentrations in plasma, but the compounds are extremely well distributed in tissues (but not cerebrospinal fluid) and are concentrated within mammalian cells. The major route of excretion is renal, in the form of native compound and various metabolites, some of which retain antibacterial activity. In general, they are less extensively metabolized than nalidixic acid.

Uses of newer quinolones   The extremely broad spectrum of activity of ciprofloxacin and its congeners, and their ease of administration by the oral route make them attractive candidates for 'blind' therapy in hospital and domiciliary practice. The manufacturers have not been slow to promote their widespread use as agents that will cure practically everyone of almost any infection. The truth is less spectacular. While these compounds have undoubted value in many infective conditions, they are not universal panaceas and they should not be used indiscriminately. For example, activity against Gram-positive cocci may be inadequate to cover for pneumococci in chest infection. Moreover, although plasmid-mediated resistance is virtually unknown, alterations in the permeability characteristics of bacteria, or to the DNA gyrase target, may reduce the susceptibility sufficiently to render the drugs therapeutically ineffective. This is a particular worry with organisms like staphylococci, streptococci, and *Ps. aeruginosa*, for which the margin of safety between therapeutically-achievable concentrations and inhibitory activity is not large. Indeed, failures of therapy due to small increments in resistance in these organisms are already well documented.

It should also be remembered that all quinolones, old and new, are liable to cause adverse reactions: rashes and diarrhoea are fairly common with the newer quinolones; photophobia and various non-specific neurological complaints are also sometimes encountered. Since these compounds act on DNA, there is always the fear of teratogenic effects and they are known to affect the deposition of cartilage in experimental animals. For these reasons licensing authorities have cautioned against their use in children, pregnant women, and, sometimes, women of child-bearing age.

MISCELLANEOUS ANTIBACTERIAL AGENTS

Polymyxins

The polymyxins are a family of five compounds (polymyxins A, B, C, D, and E) produced by *Bacillus polymyxa* and related bacteria. Only polymyxins B and E are used therapeutically. Polymyxin E is usually known by its alternative name, colistin.

Structurally, the polymyxins are polypeptides with a long hydrophobic tail. Most of the peptide portion is arranged in a cyclic fashion, reminiscent of bacitracin and the cyclic peptides. The polymyxins act like cationic detergents by binding to the cell membrane and causing the leakage of essential cytoplasmic contents. The effect is not entirely selective, and both polymyxin B and colistin exhibit considerable toxicity.

Derivatives of the polymyxins in which up to five diaminobutyric acid residues are substituted with sulphomethyl groups are better tolerated and more quickly excreted than the parent compounds. These sulphomethyl-polymyxins exhibit diminished antibacterial activity, but the precise loss in activity is difficult to estimate because the substituted compounds spontaneously break down to the more active parent.

The antibacterial spectrum of the polymyxins encompasses most Gram-negative bacteria except *Proteus* spp., but the importance of these antibiotics has hinged on their activity against *Ps. aeruginosa*. With the appearance of antipseudomonal β-lactam agents, aminoglycosides and fluoroquinolones, the polymyxins have virtually fallen into disuse for systemic therapy, although they are still used in some topical preparations.

Novobiocin

Novobiocin is an antibiotic with an idiosyncratic spectrum of activity which has attracted most attention as an antistaphylococcal agent. The molecule displays a complex heterocyclic structure that is unrelated to other antibiotics. The target site of the drug is thought to be the same DNA gyrase enzyme that is inhibited by nalidixic acid, but novobiocin appears to bind to a different enzyme subunit.

Since untoward reactions are common in patients treated with novobiocin, and bacterial resistance develops readily, the drug is little used.

Pristinamycin

This is an antibiotic of the streptogramin family, a group of naturally-occurring compounds that are unusual in that they consist of two structurally dissimilar components which interact synergically. Component A is a polyunsaturated macrolide, distantly related to erythromycin; component B is a cyclic peptide (strictly a hexadepsipeptide). Streptogramins have been mostly used as growth promotors in animal husbandry, but pristinamycin has been used in human medicine, chiefly in France. The spectrum of activity includes Gram-negative and Gram-positive cocci (including methicillin-resistant staphylococci) and *Haemophilus influenzae*, but pristinamycin is best regarded solely as an antistaphylococcal agent.

Nitroimidazoles

As a group, the imidazoles are synthetic antimicrobials which are remarkable in that derivatives are known which between them cover bacteria, fungi, viruses, protozoa, and helminths; in fact, the whole antimicrobial spectrum. Outside the antimicrobial field certain imidazoles have been shown to exhibit radio-sensitizing properties and have attracted attention as adjuncts to radiation therapy for some tumours.

The members of this family of compounds used as antibacterial agents are 5-nitroimidazoles, of which metronidazole (Fig. 3.6) is best known. Related 5-nitroimidazoles include tinidazole, ornidazole, and nimorazole; they have similar properties to metronidazole and will not be considered separately.

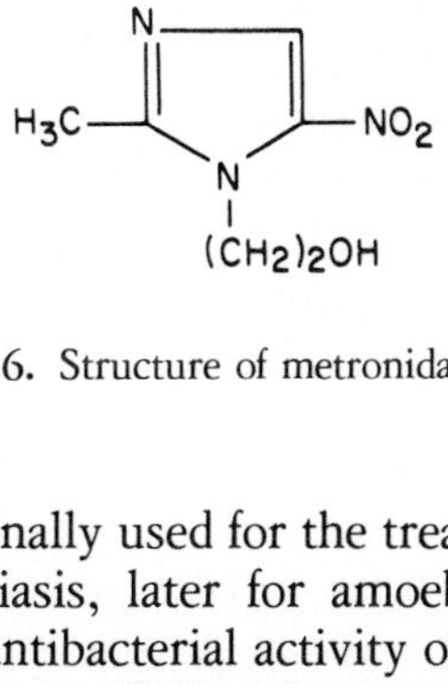

Fig. 3.6. Structure of metronidazole.

Metronidazole was originally used for the treatment of protozoal infections, first for trichomoniasis, later for amoebiasis and giardiasis (see Chapters 5 and 30). The antibacterial activity of the compound was only recognized when a patient suffering from acute ulcerative gingivitis responded spontaneously while receiving metronidazole for a *T. vaginalis* infection. Anaerobic bacteria are commonly incriminated in gingivitis, and it was subsequently shown that metronidazole possessed potent antibacterial activity that was entirely restricted to anaerobes (the protozoa against which the drug is effective are also anaerobes).

Metronidazole is so effective against anaerobic bacteria and resistance is so uncommon, that it is now widely considered the drug of choice for the treatment of anaerobic infections. It is also commonly used as a prophylactic drug in some surgical procedures in which postoperative anaerobic infection is a frequent complication (see Chapter 19).

The basis of the selective activity against anaerobes resides in the fact that the antibacterially active form of the drug is a reduced derivative produced intracellularly at the low redox values attainable by anaerobes, but not by aerobes. The reduced form of metronidazole is thought to act by inducing strand breakage in DNA by a mechanism that has not been precisely determined.

ANTIMYCOBACTERIAL AGENTS

Although one of the earliest antibiotics, streptomycin, possesses very potent activity against *M. tuberculosis*, the development of agents for the treatment of mycobacterial disease has tended to evolve along specialized lines so that many of the drugs used for these infections have little or no use outside the mycobacterial field. Part of the reason for this lies in the fact that mycobacteria are slow-growing intracellular bacteria and are structurally unusual in possessing a waxy coat that is impermeable to many antibacterial agents. Indeed, one useful antituberculous agent, isonicotinylhydrazine (isoniazid) probably acts by interfering with the synthesis of mycolic acid which, unusually among bacteria, is a major component of the wall of *M. tuberculosis*.

The major antimycobacterial drugs, apart from streptomycin and isoniazid, are para-aminosalicylic acid, diaminodiphenyl sulphone (dapsone; a drug used specifically for the treatment of leprosy) rifampicin, pyrazinamide, and ethambutol. The properties of these and other antimycobacterial compounds will be considered in the context of their use in Chapter 26. Rifampicin, however, deserves special mention here because its importance extends beyond the mycobacterial field.

Rifampicin

Rifampicin, known in the USA as rifampin, is a semisynthetic derivative of rifamycin B, one of a group of structurally complex compounds produced by *Streptomyces mediterranei*. The antibiotic interferes with mRNA formation by binding to the β-subunit of the DNA-dependent RNA polymerase that transcribes mRNA from DNA. Mutations in the enzyme subunit occur readily and render the bacteria resistant to rifampicin.

As well as being highly active against the two major mycobacterial scourges of mankind, tuberculosis and leprosy, rifampicin exhibits potent bactericidal activity against a wide range of bacteria, chlamydia, and rickettsia. The compound even displays some antiviral activity *in vitro*, although this is not of any clinical value.

The chief drawback to the use of rifampicin is the frequency with which resistant mutants develop. For this reason, the drug is often used in combination with other agents.

Rifampicin has established itself as such a useful antimycobacterial drug that there has been a move to confine its use to tuberculosis and leprosy on the grounds that more widespread use might inadvertantly encourage the emergence of resistant mycobacterial strains. Critics of this view claim that an agent which possesses exceptionally good antistaphylococcal activity and useful activity against other bacteria is being unnecessarily restricted on unproven and unlikely grounds.

Among other rifamycin derivatives that have been developed are rifapentine, which exhibits an extended half-life, but is otherwise similar to rifampicin, and rifabutin (ansamycin). A good deal of interest has focused on the possibility that these agents might be of therapeutic value in infections caused by mycobacteria of the *avium-intracellulare* group. These mycobacteria are normally low-grade pathogens, but they can cause disseminated disease in patients with cancer or acquired immune deficiency syndrome (AIDS). Unlike other mycobacteria they are commonly resistant to rifampicin and other antituberculous drugs. Rifabutin and rifapentine exhibit good activity *in vitro* against mycobacteria of the *avium-intracellulare* group, but their performance in preliminary clinical studies has been disappointing.

4

Antifungal agents

Fungi may cause benign, but unsightly infection of the skin, nail, or hair (dermatophytosis), relatively trivial infection of mucous membranes (thrush), or systemic infection causing progressive, often fatal disease.

It is common practice to classify medically important fungi into four morphological groups:

1. True yeasts (e.g. *Cryptococcus neoformans*).
2. Yeast-like fungi that produce a pseudomycelium (e.g. *Candida albicans*).
3. Filamentous fungi that produce a true mycelium (e.g. *Aspergillus fumigatus*).
4. Dimorphic fungi that grow as yeasts or filamentous fungi, depending on the cultural conditions (e.g. *Histoplasma capsulatum*).

There is now some evidence that *Pneumocystis carinii*, an organism of uncertain affiliation that is an important opportunist pathogen of patients with AIDS, may be a fungus; if so, it is unclear to which group it belongs. This organism has morphological features resembling some protozoa and it is insusceptible to antifungal agents. Consideration of antimicrobial compounds active against *P. carinii* will be deferred to the next chapter.

Fungi are eukaryotic organisms and antibacterial agents have no effect on them. Specialized antifungal agents must therefore be used. Only a small number of these exist and some are quite toxic. In order to minimize problems of toxicity, superficial lesions are usually treated by topical application, but deep mycoses, which are serious life-threatening infections, need vigorous systemic therapy. The differential activity of the chief antifungal agents in common use is summarized in Table 4.1. Precise assessment of the activity of antifungal agents *in vitro* is beset with methodological difficulties and susceptibility tests are not generally available.

Table 4.1. Summary of the differential activity of antifungal agents against the more common pathogenic fungi

Fungus	Principal diseases caused	Polyenes	Flucytosine	Griseofulvin or tolnaftate	Imidazoles
Yeast					
Cryptococcus neoformans	Meningitis	+	+	–	+
Yeast-like fungus					
Candida albicans	Thrush; Systemic candidiasis	+	+	–	+
Filamentous fungi					
Trichophyton spp.	Infection of skin, nail or hair ('ringworm')	–	–	+	+
Microsporum spp.		–	–	+	+
Epidermophyton floccosum		–	–	+	+
Aspergillus fumigatus	Pulmonary aspergillosis	+	–	–	(+)*
Dimorphic fungi					
Histoplasma capsulatum	Histoplasmosis	+	–	–	+
Coccidioides immitis	Coccidioidomycosis	+	–	–	+
Blastomyces dermatitidis	Blastomycosis	+	–	–	+

+ = Useful activity; − = no useful activity; * = limited activity, itraconazole may be useful.

POLYENES

The polyenes are naturally occurring compounds exhibiting a macrocyclic lactone structure with an extensive conjugated system of double-bonds. The most commonly used members of the group are nystatin and amphotericin B (Fig. 4.1). Related polyenes include candicidin, natamycin (also known as pimaricin) and trichomycin (also known as hachimycin). All of these compounds act by binding to sterols in the fungal cell membrane, thereby interfering with membrane integrity and causing leakage of essential metabolites.

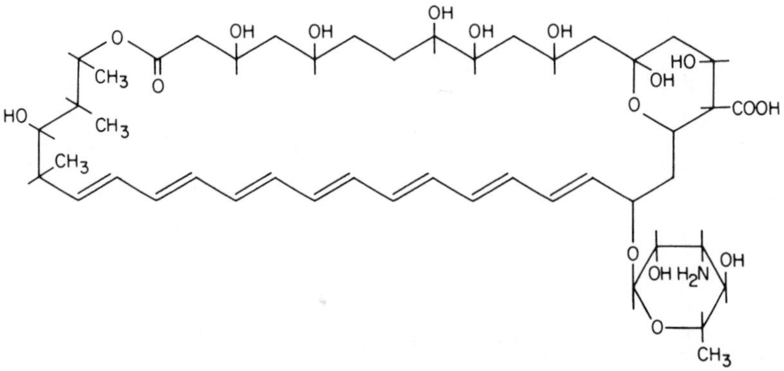

Fig. 4.1. Structure of amphotericin B.

The activity of the polyenes embraces a variety of pathogenic fungi, and yeasts are particularly susceptible. Nystatin has been extensively used for treating candida infections of the mucous membranes. Natamycin and trichomycin display some activity against the protozoon *Trichomonas vaginalis*, and have been used for treating vaginitis in which either *Candida* or *T. vaginalis* may be involved. For systemic fungal infections including those caused by *A. fumigatus* and dimorphic fungi, amphotericin B is used. Toxicity is a major problem in systemic therapy with amphotericin B and the drug needs to be used with care. In an effort to minimize toxicity problems, amphotericin B may be combined with 5-fluorocytosine (see below) and encouraging results have been obtained with this combination in the treatment of systemic yeast infections. Despite its toxicity amphotericin B remains the most important weapon in the antifungal armamentarium.

GRISEOFULVIN

Griseofulvin was the first antifungal antibiotic to be described. Use of the drug is confined to the treatment of dermatophyte infections (fungal infections of the skin, nail, or hair) and griseofulvin is peculiarly suited to this purpose since it exhibits the remarkable property of being deposited in newly formed keratin. The compound is well absorbed when administered orally, particularly if a fine-particle formulation is used.

The mode of action of griseofulvin has not been definitively established, but its activity appears to be directed against the process of mitosis, perhaps by interfering with the microtubules of the mitotic spindle.

TOLNAFTATE

The activity of tolnaftate is also confined to dermatophyte fungi, but unlike griseofulvin, it is used topically. The mode of action is unknown.

BENZOIC ACID

A variety of ointments containing benzoic acid (e.g. Whitfield's ointment: benzoic acid and salicylic acid in an emulsifying base) have been used traditionally for treating dermatophyte infections of the skin. Though old-fashioned and a little messy, they are cheap and effective, and still have a place in treatment.

5-FLUOROCYTOSINE (FLUCYTOSINE)

Flucytosine is a pyrimidine analogue originally developed as an anticancer drug, but found to have considerable activity against yeasts; it has no useful activity against filamentous fungi. The activity of the compound depends on its being converted intracellularly to 5-fluorouracil, which is incorporated into fungal RNA. Resistance develops readily and sometimes emerges during treatment. For this reason flucytosine is often administered together with amphotericin B, an arrangement that has the additional advantage of allowing a lower dose of amphotericin B to be used. It has also been suggested that the amphotericin B, by interfering with the permeability of the fungal membrane, may facilitate entry of flucytosine into the fungal cell.

IMIDAZOLES

The versatility of imidazoles has already been referred to. Several imidazole derivatives display antifungal activity and, in fact, these compounds offer the nearest approximation we have to broad-spectrum antifungal agents. The structure of clotrimazole, the first member of this group to be introduced into clinical medicine, is shown in Fig. 4.2.

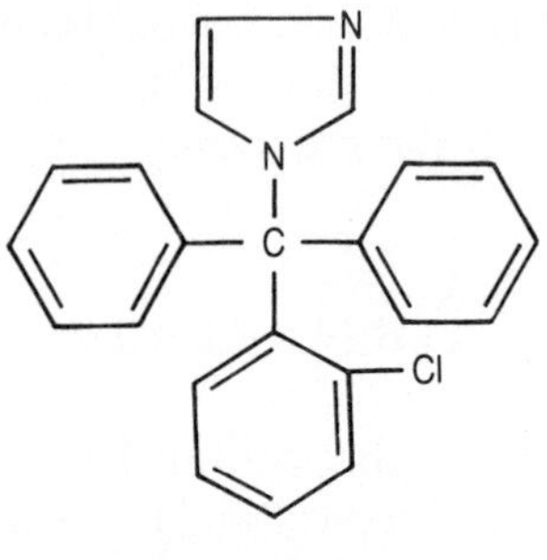

Fig. 4.2. Structure of clotrimazole.

Antifungal imidazoles are most widely used for topical application in superficial fungal infections and as pessaries for use in vaginal candidiasis. Indeed, these are virtually the only useful roles for clotrimazole, miconazole, econazole, isoconazole and sulconazole, all of which have very similar properties and indications. Miconazole is also available as an intravenous preparation for use in deep-seated *Candida* infections, but toxicity has restricted its value. One antifungal imidazole, tioconazole has been marketed as a 28 per cent solution formulated in a nail-penetrating base. The solution is painted on infected nails and is said to be effective alone, or as an adjunct to griseofulvin therapy.

A significant advance in the oral therapy of systemic fungal infections was achieved with the introduction of ketoconazole. This imidazole derivative is well absorbed when given orally and achieves therapeutic concentrations for several hours. However, early enthusiasm for ketoconazole has waned somewhat in the light of clinical experience, especially when it was realized that the drug was occasionally implicated in fatal hepatotoxic reactions. Nevertheless, ketoconazole remains a useful drug in the treatment of systemic mycoses, when the benefits outweigh the risks. It should not be used for trivial dermatophyte infections.

The latest antifungal compounds to appear on the UK market are fluconazole and itraconazole. These agents are strictly triazoles rather than imidazoles. Fluconazole is well absorbed after oral administration and has an extremely long plasma half-life (25 ~ 30 hours), properties that make it suitable for once-daily administration. Fluconazole is claimed to be effective in the single-dose treatment of vaginal thrush. Unlike other antifungal azoles it penetrates well into cerebrospinal fluid and there are preliminary reports of the value of the drug in cryptococcosis in AIDS patients.

None of the azole derivatives so far mentioned displays sufficient activity against *A. fumigatus* to be of therapeutic value in the serious infections that this filamentous fungus sometimes causes in immunocompromised and pneumocompromised patients. However, preliminary clinical studies suggest that the triazole derivative, itraconazole, may be of value in aspergillosis.

The antifungal imidazoles probably act by interfering with the biosynthesis of ergosterol, a component of the fungal cell membrane.

5

Antiprotozoal and anthelminthic agents

Pathogenic protozoa and helminths are among the most important causes of morbidity and mortality in the world. An estimated 700 million people suffer from malaria, filariasis, and schistosomiasis alone, and two-thirds of the world's population lives in conditions where parasitic diseases are unavoidable.

Some parasitic diseases were among the first to be treatable by specific remedies; indeed, cures for malaria, amoebic dysentery, and tapeworm infection have been known for centuries. Nevertheless, the therapeutic armamentarium for parasitic infection remains severely restricted. Many of the antiparasitic drugs that are available leave much to be desired in terms of efficacy and safety, and a few parasitic infections remain for which there is no effective remedy at all.

PROTOZOA

Protozoa are all unicellular organisms. Those of medical importance are conveniently classified into four groups: amoebae, flagellates, sporozoa, and 'others' (Table 5.1).

Amoebae

Seven species of parasitic amoebae may be found in man. Only one, *Entamoeba histolytica*, the causative parasite of amoebic dysentery and amoebic liver abscess, is commonly incriminated in disease. Invasive disease is caused by the motile trophozoite form, but the disease is transmitted by non-motile cysts which represent a more resistant resting phase.

An effective treatment for amoebiasis has been available for many years in the form of emetine, an alkaloid of ipecacuanha. Emetine, whether as the hydrochloride, as the dehydroemetine derivative or as the bismuth iodide complex, all of which are used therapeutically, acts by inhibiting protein synthesis in amoeba.

Table 5.1. Principal pathogenic protozoa infecting man, and the drugs used in treatment

Species	Diseases caused	Useful drugs
Amoebae		
Entamoeba histolytica	Amoebic dysentery	} Metronidazole
	Invasive amoebiasis	etc.
Naegleria fowleri	Meningoencephalitis	?Amphotericin B
Acanthamoeba spp.	Amoebic keratitis	?Propamidine
Flagellates		
Trypanosoma rhodesiense	Sleeping sickness	Melarsoprol
Trypanosoma gambiense		Suramin
		Pentamidine
Trypanosoma cruzi	Chagas' disease	Nifurtimox
Leishmania tropica	Oriental sore	}
Leishmania donovani	Kala-azar	}
Leishmania braziliensis	Espundia	} Sodium stibogluconate
Leishmania mexicana	Chiclero's ulcer	}
Trichomonas vaginalis	Vaginitis	Metronidazole
Giardia lamblia	Diarrhoea	} Metronidazole
	Steatorrhoea	}
Sporozoa		
Plasmodium falciparum	Malignant tertian malaria	}
Plasmodium vivax	Benign tertian malaria	} Chloroquine, etc.
Plasmodium ovale	Benign tertian malaria	} (see Chapter 30)
Plasmodium malariae	Quartan malaria	}
Toxoplasma gondii	Congenital malformation	} Pyrimethamine +
	Ocular toxoplasmosis	} sulphonamide;
	Encephalitis (AIDS)	} Spiramycin
Cryptosporidium spp.	Diarrhoea	None
Others		
Balantidium coli	Diarrhoea	?Diodoquin
Babesia spp.	Babesiosis	?Quinine + clindamycin
Pneumocystis carinii	Pneumonia	Co-trimoxazole
		Pentamidine

Emetine has now largely been replaced by metronidazole, which has proved a very effective and non-toxic substitute in acute amoebiasis and amoebic liver abscess. Other drugs sometimes used in amoebiasis include di-iodohydroxyquinoline (diodoquin), chloroquine, and diloxanide furoate, all of which have the virtue of being cheap. Diloxanide furoate is particularly useful for the elimination of cysts from symptomless excreters.

Two antibiotics, tetracycline and the aminoglycoside paromomycin, have also been found to have some activity against amoebae. Problems in treating the various manifestations of *E. histolytica* infection are discussed in more detail in Chapter 30.

Although *E. histolytica* is, to all intents and purposes, the only parasitic amoeba pathogenic to man, certain species of free-living amoebae (*Naegleria* spp.) occasionally cause primary amoebic meningoencephalitis. The condition is almost invariably fatal and only amphotericin B, an antifungal agent, has shown any useful activity in in-vitro tests. Free-living amoebae of the *Acanthamoeba* group may occasionally be involved in eye infections (amoebic keratitis). Suitable antimicrobial chemotherapy for this condition remains to be defined.

Flagellates

Trypanosomes and leishmania

Most flagellates have a simple life cycle similar to that of the amoebae. One family, the Trypanosomatidae (trypanosomes and leishmania) have a much more complex life cycle involving developmental stages in an insect and their distribution is restricted to those areas where the insect vector is found. In tropical Africa, tsetse flies transmit *Trypanosoma gambiense* and *Trypanosoma rhodesiense*, both of which give rise to 'sleeping sickness', an ultimately fatal infection. The treatment of the various stages of sleeping sickness is dealt with in Chapter 30. Drugs used include organic arsenicals such as tryparsamide and melarsoprol (Mel B) and the non-metallic compounds, pentamidine and suramin.

South American trypanosomiasis, Chagas' disease, is a different disease caused by *Trypanosoma cruzi* and transmitted by reduviid bugs, nick-named 'kissing bugs' because of their predilection for feeding round the mouth of sleeping persons. There is presently no drug of proven efficacy in Chagas' disease, although some modest success has been obtained with the nitrofuran derivative, nifurtimox, and the imidazole, benznidazole.

Leishmania, which are related to the trypanosomes, also cause a variety of clinical conditions and are also transmitted by biting insects, in this case sandflies. Cutaneous leishmaniasis (oriental sore) caused by *Leishmania tropica* is usually self-limiting, but visceral leishmaniasis (kala-azar) in which the reticulo-endothelial system is infected by *Leishmania donovani*, is potentially fatal. Both *L. tropica* and *L. donovani* occur in the Middle East, India, parts of Africa, and the Mediterranean countries. Various *Leishmania* spp. have been incriminated in disease in Central and South America, including *L. braziliensis* (mucocutaneous leishmaniasis, or espundia) and *L. mexicana* (cutaneous leishmaniasis or Chiclero's ulcer).

The only drugs of proven value in leishmaniasis are the pentavalent antimonials, of which sodium stibogluconate and meglumine antimonate are in universal use, and pentamidine.

Other flagellates

Two other flagellates cause disease in man: *Giardia lamblia* (also known as *Giardia intestinalis*) a common cause of diarrhoea, abdominal pain and steatorrhoea, and *Trichomonas vaginalis*, a common cause of vaginitis or, more rarely, urethritis. *G. lamblia* is transmitted in the cyst form, often in infected water; *T. vaginalis* is transmitted venereally. Both of these parasites are susceptible to nitroimidazoles such as metronidazole. Mepacrine (known in the United States as quinacrine) is also efficacious in giardiasis.

Sporozoa

The sporozoa are all parasitic; they have a complex life cycle involving alternate sexual and asexual phases. Two kinds of sporozoa infect man, the malaria parasites and the coccidia.

Malaria parasites

Malaria is, without doubt, the most important of all parasitic diseases. Despite sustained efforts to eradicate the disease it remains the commonest cause of fever in the world and is a major cause of morbidity and mortality among the 800 million persons who live in areas of high endemicity throughout the tropical belt. Four species infect man: *Plasmodium falciparum* is the most dangerous, since primary infections are often rapidly fatal if left untreated. *Plasmodium vivax* and *Plasmodium ovale*, which cause benign tertian malaria, and *Plasmodium malariae*, which causes quartan malaria, rarely kill, but give rise to debilitating infections. The most common species worldwide is *P. falciparum*, which accounts for over 90 per cent of infections in tropical Africa, but in some parts of the world, notably the Indian sub-continent, *P. vivax* is the dominant species.

The malaria parasite is transmitted by the bite of infected female *Anopheles* mosquitoes. The parasites first infect liver cells; after 1-2 weeks the liver parasites mature and infect circulating red blood cells to commence the cycle of erythrocytic schizogony which is responsible for the overt signs of disease. *P. vivax* and *P. ovale* can also set up a cryptic infection in the liver, which may cause relapse of symptoms up to 2 years after the infection is acquired.

A proportion of erythrocytic parasites differentiate into male and female gametocytes, which do not develop further in the mammalian host, but complete the sexual phase of development in the anopheline vector when ingested during a blood meal.

The traditional mainstay of the treatment of malaria was quinine, originally derived from the bark of the cinchona tree in Peru, but during the course of the present century a variety of other effective antimalarials have been developed. These include the 4-aminoquinolines, chloroquine, amodiaquine, and, more recently, mefloquine and halofantrine, all of which kill developing erythrocytic schizonts by a mechanism which remains to be precisely defined. Mepacrine, an acridine dye with a similar structure to chloroquine, is also an effective antimalarial, but is no longer widely used. Pyrimethamine, a dihydrofolate reductase inhibitor related to trimethoprim, exhibits a selectively high affinity for the plasmodial enzyme and has found widespread use as a malaria prophylactic, both alone and in combination with sulfadoxine, a long-acting sulphonamide, or with dapsone, a sulphone used for treating leprosy. Also used for prophylaxis is proguanil (or its analogue, chlorproguanil), a substance that is metabolized in the body to a compound closely related structurally to pyrimethamine and having an identical mode of action.

All the above drugs act solely, or predominantly, on erythrocytic parasites and to eradicate parasites undergoing exoerythrocytic replication in the liver it is necessary to use the 8-aminoquinoline, primaquine, which is selectively active against the liver forms.

The factors governing the choice of antimalarial for treatment and prophylaxis will be discussed in Chapter 30.

Coccidia

Phylogenetically related to the malaria parasites are the coccidia, which share many features of the complex life cycle, but are not transmitted by insect vectors. Several species of coccidia may infect man. *Isospora hominis*, *Isospora belli* and *Cryptosporidium* spp. cause diarrhoea which is usually self-limiting. However, in immunocompromised patients, especially those suffering from AIDS, cryptosporidia (and to a lesser extent *Isospora*) may cause a profuse, intractable diarrhoea for which no suitable antimicrobial therapy has yet been devised. Spiramycin and eflornithine have been used experimentally, but success has been, at best, modest.

The most important human coccidian parasite is *Toxoplasma gondii*. Intrauterine infections with this organism are an important cause of congenital malformations and stillbirth throughout the world. AIDS sufferers may develop toxoplasmal encephalitis, apparently by reactivation of latent infection. Cats often harbour the parasite and liberate the infectious oocysts in their faeces; this probably represents a major reservoir of infection. Pyrimethamine, in combination with a sulphonamide (usually sulphadiazine) is the treatment of choice in toxoplasmosis. Clindamycin and the macrolide antibiotic spiramycin have also been used with some success, especially in combination with pyrimethamine. Spiramycin has been particularly recommended during pregnancy, when antifolates are considered by some to be best avoided.

Other protozoa

Balantidium coli

This is the only ciliate pathogenic to man. It is a rare cause of severe diarrhoea, cosmopolitan in distribution. Treatment of balantidiasis has never been properly defined, but di-iodohydroxyquinoline and tetra-cycline appear to be effective.

Babesia

Although *Babesia* spp., like malaria parasites, infect red blood cells, they are in fact unrelated. They are predominantly animal parasites, occasionally transmitted to man by the bite of ixodid ticks. Recorded European cases have all been in splenectomized patients and have usually been caused by *Babesia divergens*, but infection in previously healthy persons caused by *Babesia microti* has been reported from North America. Most cases of babesiosis have been treated with chloroquine, following a mistaken diagnosis of malaria. However, chloroquine treatment often fails and this is clearly not the drug of choice. What should be used remains to be clarified. Studies in laboratory animals which suggested that primaquine and pentamidine might be effective have not been substantiated in clinical practice. There is anecdotal evidence that the combination of quinine and clindamycin might be effective.

Pneumocystis carinii

This organism is of uncertain taxonomic status and there is, in fact, evidence that it may be a fungus. It used to be found only as a rare cause of interstitial pneumonia in infants, but has lately come into prominence as a respiratory pathogen of immunocompromised individuals, notably those with AIDS in whom it commonly causes a life-threatening pneumonia. Co-trimoxazole and pentamidine are active against the organism, but both carry problems of toxicity, which seem to be increased in patients suffering from AIDS. Direct instillation of nebulized drug into the lung appears to offer a safe and effective mode of administration of pentamidine. In this, as in other uses of pentamidine, the isethionate salt is preferable to the mesylate salt since it is somewhat less prone to cause hypoglycaemia.

HELMINTHS

Helminths are parasitic worms. They often have a complex life-cycle involving a period of development outside the definitive host either in soil or in some intermediate host. Helminths of medical importance fall into three major groups: nematodes (roundworms), trematodes (flukes), and cestodes (tapeworms) (Table 5.2).

Nematodes

Filarial worms

The most important group of nematodes are the filarial worms, which are transmitted by biting insects. Filariae infecting man include *Wuchereria bancrofti*, which causes elephantiasis throughout the tropics, *Onchocerca volvulus*, the cause of 'river blindness' in West Africa and *Loa loa*, the African 'eye worm'. Until recently the only drug of proven value in filariasis was diethylcarbamazine (DEC), a derivative of piperazine. This drug may cause unpleasant side-effects as well as evoking severe reaction to dead filarial larvae (Mazzotti reaction). The mode of action of DEC is completely unknown and is something of a mystery since it appears to have no effect on the viability of microfilariae (the larval forms found in blood or skin) *in vitro*. One possibility is that the drug has a relatively trivial effect on the surface integument of the worms which then succumb to immune clearance mechanisms. This explanation is perfectly feasible since it is known that the worms provoke an immune response, but in the absence of drug, they are able to avoid its consequences.

A major breakthrough in the treatment of onchocerciasis, and possibly other filarial infections, seems to have been achieved with the veterinary anthelminthic, ivermectin. This compound is a derivative of avermectin B_1, one of a family of macrocyclic lactone antibiotics produced by *Streptomyces avermitilis*. It has been extensively used in animals, in which it exhibits the astonishing property of dealing not only with helminthic parasites, but also many of the arthropod ectoparasites that cause problems in animal husbandry. In field trials of human parasitic disease, ivermectin has so far been most widely used in infection with *O. volvulus*. Treatment of this disease has been singularly successful; moreover, use of ivermectin does not seem to be accompanied by the severe side-effects (Mazzotti reaction) associated with the administration of DEC.

Intestinal nematodes

Less important than filariae as causes of clinical disease, but extremely common world-wide, are the intestinal nematodes, which include the

Table 5.2. Prinicipal helminth parasites of man and the drugs used in treatment

Species	Intermediate host	Geographical distribution	Useful drugs
Nematodes			
Wuchereria bancrofti	Mosquitoes	Tropical belt	Diethylcarbamazine,
Loa loa	*Chrysops* spp.	Tropical Africa	(suramin)
Brugia malayi	Mosquitoes	S.E. Asia	
Onchocerca volvulus	*Simulium* spp.	Tropical Africa, Central America	Ivermectin
Dracunculus medinensis	Cyclops (water flea)	Africa, Arabia, India, Pakistan	Niridazole, thiabendazole
Trichinella spiralis	Pig, etc.	Worldwide	?Mebendazole
Ancyclostoma duodenale	None	Tropics and subtropics	
Necator americanus	None	Tropics and subtropics	Mebendazole etc.
Ascaris lumbricoides	None	Worldwide	(see Table 30.1,
Trichuris trichiura	None	Worldwide	Chapter 30)
Strongyloides stercoralis	None	Tropics and subtropics	
Enterobius vermicularis	None	Worldwide	
Trematodes			
Schistosoma mansoni	Snail	Africa; W. Indies; S. America	Praziquantel etc.
Schistosoma haematobium	Snail	Africa	(see Table 30.2,
Schistosoma japonicum	Snail	Far East	Chapter 30)
Fasciola hepatica	Snail/vegetation	Worldwide	Bithionol
Clonorchis sinensis	Snail/fresh-water fish	Far East	
Paragonimus westermani	Snail/crabs, crayfish	Far East	Praziquantel
Fasciolopsis buski	Snail/water chestnut	Far East	
Cestodes			
Echinococcus granulosus	Man, sheep	Worldwide	?Albendazole
Taenia saginata	Cattle	Worldwide	
Taenia solium	Pig	Worldwide	Niclosamide
Hymenolepis nana	None	Worldwide	Praziquantel
Diphyllobotbrium latum	Cyclops/fish	Chiefly Finland	

hookworms, *Ancylostoma duodenale* and *Necator americanus*; the common roundworm, *Ascaris lumbricoides*; the threadworm, *Enterobius vermicularis*; and the whipworm, *Trichuris trichiura*. These are not restricted in distribution to the tropics, but are, with the possible exception of *E. vermicularis*, more common in countries with poor standards of hygiene. Treatment of infection with these and related intestinal worms has traditionally relied on a variety of compounds of variable efficacy, including tetrachloroethylene, piperazine and bephenium. More recently, levamisole and pyrantel pamoate have emerged as useful anthelminthics, but the most convincing advance came with the development of the benzimidazoles, a group of broad-spectrum anthelminthics active against most intestinal roundworms. The benzimidazoles currently available, thiabendazole and mebendazole, have become the drugs of choice for the elimination of intestinal roundworms, but they are rather expensive for widespread use in the poorer countries where they are most needed. The veterinary benzimidazole, albendazole, has also been used with success in human infections. Roundworms other than filariae that invade tissues include *Trichinella spiralis*, now an uncommon cause of human infection, and the Guinea worm, *Dracunculus medinensis*. Anthelminthic therapy is probably unnecessary in either of these infections, but benzimidazoles have some activity against both parasites and the antischistosomal drug niridazole (see below) has been used against Guinea worm.

Larvae of the dog ascarid, *Toxocara canis*, sometimes infect children who come into contact with infected dogs. Thiabendazole and DEC has been used in treatment.

Trematodes

Trematodes (flukes) generally have a complex life cycle involving a stage of development in a snail and a secondary intermediate host as well as in the definitive host in which the mature adult forms develop.

Schistosomes (blood flukes)

The most important trematodes are the schistosomes which cause human infection in many parts of Africa as well as the Far East, the West Indies, and South America. Schistosomes are unusual among flukes in having no secondary intermediate host and infection is acquired when cercaria (the forms released by infected snails) penetrate the skin following exposure to water inhabited by infected snails. Mature adults develop in the portal vessels from where they migrate to the small veins of the rectum (*Schistosoma mansoni* and *Schistosoma japonicum*) or the bladder (*Schistosoma haematobium*). Eggs are then passed through the rectal or bladder mucosa into the faeces or urine.

For many years treatment relied on trivalent antimonials of which sodium (or potassium) antimony tartrate (tartar emetic) was the mainstay. Now at least half a dozen compounds are available that offer advantages over antimonials. These include the nitrothiazole derivative, niridazole; the thiaxanthones, lucanthone and hycanthone; metriphonate, originally developed as an organophosphate insecticide; and the hydroxyquinoline derivatives, oxamniquine and praziquantel. The last-named is the only one that is highly active against all three species of *Schistosoma* that commonly infect man. The use of these compounds is discussed in Chapter 30.

Other flukes

Other important trematodes include *Fasciola hepatica* (liver fluke), *Clonorchis sinensis* (Chinese liver fluke) and *Paragonimus westermani* (lung fluke). *Fasciola hepatica* is predominantly a parasite of sheep and human infection usually follows eating wild watercress gathered near pastures. *Clonorchis sinensis* is acquired from eating uncooked fresh-water fish and is extremely common in parts of the Far East where raw fish is widely eaten. Similarly, *Paragonimus westermani* infection is acquired from eating raw or undercooked crabs and crayfish.

No entirely satisfactory treatment of these fluke infections exists; a halogenated phenol, bithionol, originally used as a skin antiseptic, but later withdrawn because of problems of dermatitis, probably offers the best chance of cure. Evidence is accumulating that praziquantel may be more effective and less toxic than bithionol in fluke infections, but there have been reports of failures of praziquantel therapy in fascioliasis.

Cestodes

Tapeworms usually have a simpler life cycle than flukes, but transmission generally involves an intermediate host.

Hydatid worms

By far the most important tapeworms are *Echinococcus granulosus* and the closely related *Echinococcus multilocularis* (the hydatid worms). These parasites are unusual in that man is an intermediate host, harbouring the larval form in hydatid cysts which arise, usually in the liver, following ingestion of eggs from an infected dog. The internal wall of the hydatid cyst consists of a germinal layer from which 'brood capsules' containing protoscolices develop. Each protoscolex is capable of forming the head of a mature worm when ingested by the definitive host (usually the dog), or to initiate a fresh hydatid cyst within the intermediate host if the mother cyst is ruptured.

Hydatid disease occurs in many countries, including parts of the UK, where sheep and sheepdogs maintain the cycle of infection.

There is no effective chemotherapy for hydatid disease, although claims have been made for success using benzimidazoles, including mebendazole and albendazole. Praziquantel may also be of benefit, but chemotherapy remains an adjunct to surgical removal, which is not without risk due to spillage of viable protoscolices into the peritoneal cavity.

Other tapeworms

Other tapeworms infecting man include *Taenia saginata*, the beef tapeworm; *Taenia solium*, the pork tapeworm (now very rare); *Hymenolepis nana*, the dwarf tapeworm and *Diphyllobothrium latum*, the fish tapeworm. Despite their reputation, none of these well-adapted parasites causes much mischief under normal circumstances, although autoinfection with the larval form of *T. solium* can cause a condition known as cerebral cysticercosis which may respond to treatment with praziquantel given together with steroids. *D. latum* is responsible for a form of pernicious anaemia in Finland, where it is particuarly prevalent, because of competition by the worm for vitamin B_{12}.

The ancient, and effective treatment for tapeworm infection is extract of male fern (*Dryopteris filix-mas*), but this has been replaced first by the acridine dye, mepacrine, and more recently by niclosamide, which is at least 90 per cent effective in all forms of intestinal tapeworm infection. However, niclosamide treatment causes disruption of the worm and is probably best avoided in *T. solium* infection because of the risk of cysticercosis caused by autoinfection with liberated eggs. The new antischistosomal drug, praziquantel, has been shown to exhibit good activity against intestinal tapeworms and offers a useful alternative to niclosamide.

6

Antiviral agents

Viruses are almost as versatile as bacteria in the range of diseases they can cause. Vertebrates, insects, plants, and even bacteria are all open to attack. Some viruses of vertebrates (arboviruses) develop in and are transmitted by mosquitoes or other arthropods; others—rabies is a good example—can infect a wide variety of mammalian hosts. In general, however, viruses are highly specific in their host range.

All viruses are *obligate intracellular parasites*; that is, they replicate only within living cells and cannot usually survive for long outside the host cell. Selectivity usually extends not only to the host, but also to the type of cell within the host, thus giving rise to the characteristic symptoms of various viral diseases. For example, the virus responsible for most cases of acquired immune deficiency syndrome (AIDS), human immunodeficiency virus type 1 (HIV-1), carries a distinctive protein in its outer envelope which binds to a specific surface receptor on certain cells of the immune system.

Intact skin is impermeable to viruses and access to sites within the body can only occur through mucous membranes, damaged skin, insect bites, or direct inoculation. Most viruses that infect man gain entry to the body by adsorption to superficial cells of the mucous membranes of the respiratory and intestinal tracts or of the conjunctivae.

The principal types of virus causing human disease are listed in Table 6.1.

PROPERTIES OF VIRUSES

Viruses are deceptively simple. Some consist of little more than a fragment of nucleic acid protected within a protein coat; others, however, are of remarkable structural complexity considering their minute size.

The protein coat or *capsid* consists of repeating structural units that are generally arranged in helical or cubic symmetry. The nucleic acid core consists of DNA or RNA (never both) and this may be single or double stranded. Some viruses have a lipoprotein outer envelope, which is largely derived from the membrane of the host cell. Sizes range from about 20 nm

Table 6.1. Principal types of virus causing human disease

Family	Examples	Diseases	Mode of transmission
RNA viruses			
Orthomyxoviruses	Influenza A virus	Influenza	Respiratory
Paramyxoviruses	Mumps virus	Mumps	
	Measles virus	Measles	
	Respiratory syncytial virus	Lower respiratory tract infection esp. babies	} Respiratory
	Parainfluenza virus		
Rhabdoviruses	Rabies virus	Rabies	Bite of rabid animals
Arenaviruses	Lassa virus	Lassa fever	?Respiratory/contact rodent reservoir
Togaviruses	Many arboviruses	Yellow fever	Arthropod vectors
	Rubella virus	German measles	Respiratory/congenital
Piconaviruses	Enteroviruses:		
	polio	Meningitis/paralysis	
	echo	} Meningitis	} Faeco-oral
	coxsackie A		
	coxsackie B		
	hepatitis A	Infectious hepatitis	
	Rhinoviruses	Colds	Respiratory
Retroviruses	Human immunodeficiency virus (HIV)	AIDS	Inoculation/sexual
Reoviruses	Rotavirus	Infantile diarrhoea	Faeco-oral

DNA viruses			
Poxviruses	Variola	Smallpox (now eradicated)	Mainly respiratory
	Vaccinia	Smallpox vaccine	Vaccination
	Molluscum contagiosum	Skin disease	Contact
	Orf		Contact with sheep
Herpes viruses	Herpes simplex	Cold sores	Saliva/contact
		Genital herpes	Sexual
	varicella-zoster	Chickenpox	Respiratory
	Cytomegalovirus	Non-specific illness	Close contact/congenital
	Epstein-Barr virus	Glandular fever	Saliva, e.g. kissing
Adenoviruses	Many serotypes	Conjunctivitis/pharyngitis	Respiratory
Papovaviruses	Papillomavirus	Warts	Contact
Hepadnaviruses	Hepatitis B virus	Serum hepatitis	Inoculation/sexual
Parvoviruses	Parvovirus	Erythema infectiosum (fifth disease)	Respiratory

(parvovirus) to 30 nm (poxvirus); consequently, even the biggest viruses fall barely within the limits of resolution of conventional light microscopy and the electron microscope must be used to visualize them.

The nucleic acid of the virus particle provides all the information needed for replication once it is released within the host cell. Uncoating is carried out by cellular proteases and the intruder then takes over biochemical functions within the cell for its own purposes. Once the viral factory is established, complete virus particles (*virions*) are assembled and released, either by destruction of the infected cell or by continuous export through the cell membrane. With certain viruses, the viral genome can become inserted into the chromosome of the host cell and replicate thereafter with the host DNA. This is assumed to occur, for example, with herpes simplex, the virus of 'cold sores', which can be reactivated and cause periodic symptoms. Such a situation is known as *latency*; it may also occur with other viruses of the herpes group, such as varicella-zoster (chickenpox virus) in which reactivation takes the form of the characteristic circumscribed rash of shingles. Some single-stranded RNA viruses, the retroviruses (including HIV) replicate a DNA copy by use of the enzyme *reverse transcriptase*, subsequently forming a duplex strand of DNA which persists in the cell by integration into the host chromosome. Viruses which become integrated in this way have the potential for modifying host cell behaviour and some have been incriminated in initiating malignant changes.

TARGETS FOR ANTIVIRAL DRUGS

All stages of the cycle of viral replication in cells are theoretically open to selective attack. These include:

(1) adsorption to the cell surface;

(2) uptake into the host cell;

(3) uncoating by lysosomal enzymes;

(4) transcription of the viral genome;

(5) synthesis and assembly of new viral components;

(6) release of complete virus.

In the event, the intimate relationship between the virus and its host cell has meant that the design or discovery of compounds that inhibit the virus without harming the host has been beset with considerable problems. Numerous compounds have been described which interfere with various stages in the replicative cycle of viruses, but very few have been found to exhibit sufficient selective toxicity to render them suitable for therapeutic use.

Moreover, antiviral therapy is often at a disadvantage for quite a different reason: in many viral diseases initial infection and spread is commonly asymptomatic and the onset of illness often occurs at the peak of viral multiplication when the host defences—which are usually quite able to deal with the infection unassisted—have been fully mobilized. Consequently, therapeutic intervention, even with active compounds, has little influence on the course of the disease.

Despite these discouraging considerations, a certain amount of success has been achieved in the development of antiviral compounds and a handful of antiviral agents are now in regular use (Table 6.2). Most presently available agents are nucleoside analogues which interfere with viral replication and most clinical progress has been achieved with agents active against viruses of the herpes group.

Table 6.2. Antiviral agents available in the UK (1988)

Compound	Indication	Mode of action	Route of Administration
Acyclovir	Herpes simplex	Nucleoside analogue	Oral; Topical; i.v.
Amantadine	Influenza A	Uncoating/assembly of virus particles	Oral
Ganciclovir	Cytomegalovirus	Nucleoside analogue	i.v.
Idoxuridine	Herpes simplex	Nucleoside analogue	Topical
Inosine pranobex	(Herpes simplex)	Immunomodulator	Oral
Tribavirin	Respiratory syncytial virus	Nucleoside analogue	Nebulizer
Vidarabine	Herpes viruses	Nucleoside analogue	i.v.
Zidovudine	Human immuno-deficiency virus	Nucleoside analogue	Oral

Because of the problems associated with the treatment of acute infection, a great deal of attention has centred on the prevention of viral diseases. Chemotherapeutic agents have only had a relatively small part to play in this strategy. Much the most effective prophylaxis against viral diseases is provided by immunization and highly effective vaccines are available against a wide variety of important viral infections. Indeed, vaccination against smallpox, first popularized by Edward Jenner at the end of the 18th century, has been so spectacularly successful, that it has been possible to eradicate this dreadful disease from the world.

PROPERTIES OF ANTIVIRAL AGENTS

Acyclovir

This is the only antiviral agent presently available that exhibits true selective toxicity. Structurally, it is acycloguanosine (Fig. 6.1); that is, it is an analogue of the purine nucleoside, guanosine, in which the ribose moiety has lost its cyclic configuration and is much modified. In order to achieve their antiviral effect, all nucleoside analogues must first be phosphorylated within the infected cell to the triphosphate form. Acyclovir is unique in that the first phosphorylation step is accomplished by a thymidine kinase enzyme specified by certain herpes viruses, which produce the enzyme as part of their own replicative cycle. Cellular thymidine kinase is much less efficient in producing acyclovir monophosphate. Consequently, the drug is activated only in cells infected with those herpes viruses (herpes simplex and varicella-zoster viruses) that possess the viral thymidine kinase. There have been fears that resistance to acyclovir might arise by the emergence of viral mutants with altered thymidine kinase activity, since such variants arise readily *in vitro*. However, failure of therapy due to resistance to acyclovir seems to be presently uncommon in clinical practice, although some such cases have been documented, especially in immunocompromised patients.

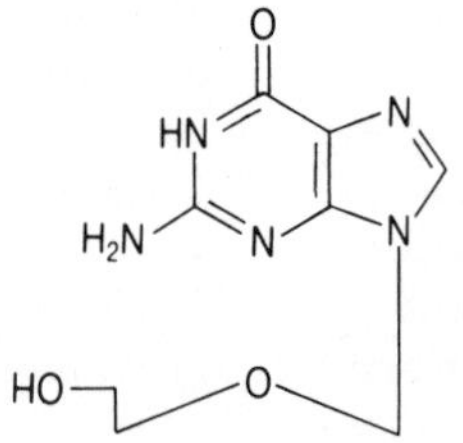

Fig. 6.1. Structure of acyclovir.

Acyclovir has proved useful in severe systemic infections (e.g. encephalitis) with herpes simplex or varicella-zoster, particularly in immunocompromised patients. The drug may indeed be life-saving in these conditions. It has also been used successfully in prophylaxis of those at risk of developing severe herpes virus infections including patients prone to severe recurrent genital herpes. Acyclovir may also reduce the severity of established local lesions to some extent, but the efficacy is not usually very striking and it is doubtful if this expensive drug should be used in relatively mild, self-limiting herpetic eruptions.

Treatment of herpes infection is, of course, not completely curative since the virus is not eliminated and recurrences are not prevented.

A pro-drug form of acyclovir that improves oral absorption, deoxy-acyclovir, is under investigation.

Amantadine and rimantadine

Amantadine (Fig. 6.2) is a tricyclic amine derivative of adamantane, a compound that originally aroused interest because of its symmetrical three-dimensional structure composed entirely of carbon atoms and, thus, related to the crystalline array of natural diamonds. The antiviral activity of amantadine was first described in 1964. Rimantadine is a closely-related substance which has been widely used in the USSR.

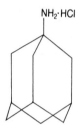

Fig. 6.2. Structure of amantadine.

The activity of both amantadine and rimantadine is restricted to influenza A virus. Other influenza viruses are virtually unaffected at therapeutically achievable concentrations. The compounds are thought to achieve their effect by interfering with the uncoating of the virus, which has an unusually complex envelope, within the infected cell. There is some evidence that the assembly of new virions is also affected.

Amantadine and rimantadine have only a minimal effect on the course of influenza A infection once symptoms develop, but these agents have been successfully used during influenza epidemics for the protection of the elderly, who are at special risk of fatal complications, or of health care workers and other selected groups. Even for these indications, vaccination is now preferred, although chemotherapy may be used in those who escape vaccination programmes.

Amantadine is also licensed in the UK for use in shingles, but this has few advocates. A non-viral use of the compound is as a dopaminergic drug in Parkinson's disease.

Ganciclovir

Known in the earlier literature as dihydroxypropoxymethylguanine (DHPG), this is a close relative of acyclovir and has a similar spectrum of activity. Ganciclovir is, however, much more active against cytomegalovirus. Unfortunately, ganciclovir is also much more toxic than acyclovir, a feature that has been ascribed to the readiness with which it is phosphorylated by cellular thymidine kinase. Because of its toxicity, the use of ganciclovir is restricted to life-threatening cytomegalovirus infection in immunocompromised patients.

Idoxuridine

This is one of the older nucleoside analogues and, like the others, interferes with DNA replication after conversion to the triphosphate form within the cell. Idoxuridine is used for the topical treatment of herpes simplex infections, most commonly in the form of eye drops or ointment for ophthalmic infections. Another halogenated nucleoside analogue, trifluridine, is available for similar indications in some countries.

Inosine pranobex

This compound, also known as isoprinosine and inosiplex, has had a chequered history. It was originally described as an antiviral agent on the strength of its in-vitro activity against influenza A virus. Later, inosine pranobex was shown to exhibit immunopotentiating properties and any antiviral effect achieved *in vivo* may, in fact, be attributable to its effect in bolstering the immune system.

Inosine pranobex is marketed for oral use in the treatment of warts and cold sores, but its efficacy is doubtful and its value in herpes infection certainly less than that of acyclovir. It is contraindicated in patients with a history of gout since the inosine moiety is excreted principally as uric acid.

Tribavirin (ribavirin)

Tribavirin (Fig. 6.3) is the British Approved Name for the substance known elsewhere as ribavirin. It is a triazole compound structurally related to guanosine. Like other nucleoside analogues it has to be activated intracellularly by phosphorylation. In the triphosphate form it inhibits protein synthesis, apparently by interfering with 'cap' formation at the 5′ end of mRNA.

Tribavirin has an unusually broad spectrum of activity, at least *in vitro*,

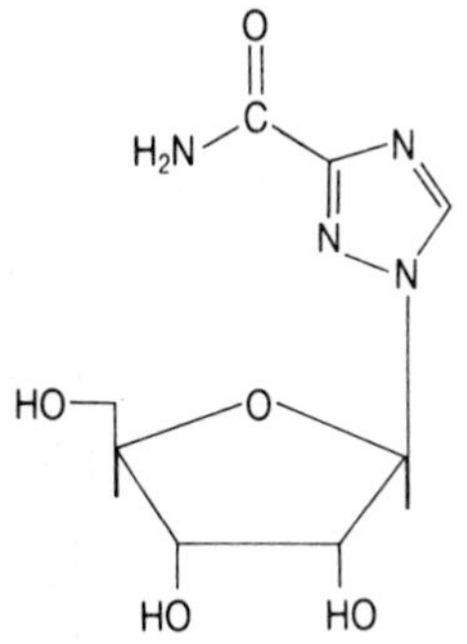

Fig. 6.3. Structure of tribavirin (ribavirin).

chiefly directed against RNA viruses. Its main use is in the treatment of respiratory syncytial virus infections in infants and young children. The compound is administered by inhalation of an aerosolized solution.

In addition, tribavirin has activity against the virus of Lassa fever, but experience is understandably limited. The compound has also been used experimentally in patients with AIDS, but it is too soon to assess any possible benefit.

Vidarabine

This is another purine nucleoside with activity against herpes viruses. It has been used both topically and systemically in severe herpes simplex infections, including herpes encephalitis, for which purpose it has now been largely superseded by acyclovir.

Zidovudine

Zidovudine (azidothymidime; often simply called AZT), is a dideoxy-nucleoside in which the 3′ hydroxyl group of thymidine has been replaced by an azido (N_3) group (Fig. 6.4). Like other nucleoside analogues it is activated by cellular thymidine kinase.

In nucleic acids, the nucleotides are joined by 5′-3′ phosphodiester links; compounds in which the 3′ hydroxyl is modified cannot form the necessary links and chain elongation is prevented during nucleic acid synthesis. Compounds of this type have been widely investigated for anticancer activity, but zidovudine was found to inhibit the reverse transcriptase activity of retroviruses at concentrations considerably less than those needed to interfere with synthesis of host cell DNA. Consequently, the compound was investigated in controlled clinical trials of patients with HIV infection. It was shown partially to restore immune

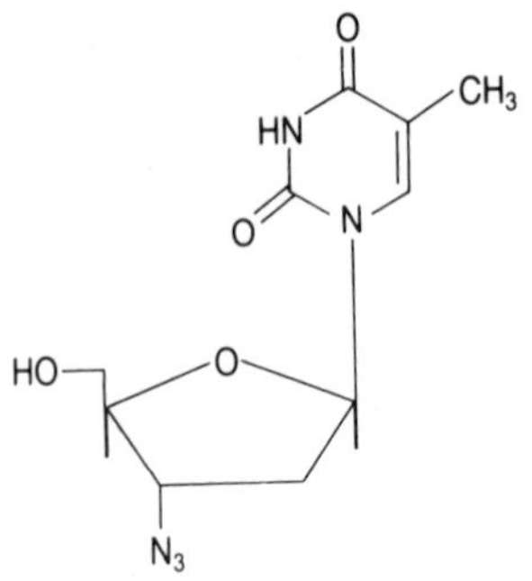

Fig. 6.4. Structure of zidovudine (AZT).

function, to reduce the incidence of opportunistic infection, and to increase survival of patients with AIDS. Adverse reactions, particularly bone marrow depression, were, however, common.

Zidovudine has since been licensed for use in several countries with unusual rapidity. It is clearly of value in AIDS, although it is merely virustatic and not curative. Since HIV is integrated into host cell DNA, it is presumably spread of virus to uninfected lymphocytes that is prevented. Virus recovered from patients treated with zidovudine may exhibit reduced susceptibility in tests *in vitro*. There is some concern that this may eventually limit the usefulness of the drug.

There is some preliminary evidence that the activity of zidovudine may be potentiated by acyclovir, interferon (see below) or other agents, but ribavirin has been reported to antagonize activity, at least *in vitro*. Apparently, ribavirin increases cellular deoxythymidine triphosphate levels and this results in feedback inhibition of thymidine kinase so that zidovudine is not phosphorylated.

Other antiviral agents

Various other antiviral agents have been tried in the past or are under development, while the AIDS pandemic has stimulated renewed interest in the scope of antiviral therapy. Much attention has been paid to nucleoside analogues in an attempt to improve on acyclovir or zidovudine, but a number of novel compounds have also been described. These are mentioned not because they represent major advances in themselves, but because they may point the way to compounds with improved properties.

Methisazone is a thiosemicarbazone which is active against pox viruses. It has been used in the protection of unvaccinated contacts of smallpox and in vaccinia gangrenosa. The world eradication of smallpox has rendered obsolete any value that methisazone might have had.

Enviroxime is a benzimidazole derivative claimed to act against the viruses that cause the common cold. In clinical trial adverse reactions were common and efficacy poor.

Foscarnet, also known as phosphonoformate, is an extremely simple phosphonic acid derivative that exhibits activity against herpesviruses and also inhibits reverse transcriptase activity *in vitro*. It has been used in pilot studies in AIDS with very modest success.

Suramin is an old antiparasitic agent that has been shown to inhibit retroviral reverse transcriptase activity. Clinical trials have been disappointing.

Ampligen

The idea of inducing the endogenous antiviral compound interferon (see below) has some attraction and several naturally-occurring inducers (e.g. helanine and statolon) enjoyed a brief vogue some years ago. These compounds are probably composed largely of fragments of double-stranded RNA and in clinical use they have generally been found to be toxic. Ampligen is a synthetic double-stranded RNA in which base pairs in a region of the helix are mismatched. In this form the polymer appears to retain its ability to induce interferon and other lymphokines, without the side-effects associated with other inducers. Ampligen inhibits HIV *in vitro* and may act synergically with zidovudine and interferon.

Interferon

Interferon was described in 1957 as an antiviral compound in chick embryo cells. It turns out that the activity is associated with a family of species-specific glycosylated proteins produced *in vivo* in response to viral or antigenic challenge. There are three types of human interferon: interferon-α (IFN-α), produced by leucocytes; interferon-β (IFN-β), produced by fibroblasts; and interferon-γ (IFN-γ) (immune interferon) produced by lymphocytes.

Early optimism about the value of interferon in antiviral therapy was dashed by difficulties in producing sufficient quantities and by unexpected toxicity. Interest was revived when interferon-α was shown to exhibit anticancer activity in certain lymphomas and solid tumours. Recombinant interferon, manufactured by techniques of genetic engineering, is now licensed in the UK and elsewhere for use in cancer chemotherapy. Hopes persist that the antiviral activity of these substances might find some clinical use. Interferon-α is presently under investigation for the therapy of genital warts. It has also shown some promise in the treatment of patients with AIDS who develop Kaposi's sarcoma; this effect seems to be a combination of antiviral and antitumour activity.

ANTIVIRAL VACCINES

Viral diseases generally produce long-lasting immunity. Conferment of active immunity by vaccination is appropriate in diseases that may have serious consequences and in which the number of virus serotypes is limited. Vaccination after the event is less effective, but is practised in rabies, a disease which has a long incubation period and which has an inexorably fatal outcome.

Live vaccines

The most effective vaccines contain live suspensions of virus. They may consist of naturally-occurring, or related strains, of reduced virulence, such as those which have been used in smallpox vaccines; more commonly, virulent strains that have been *attenuated* by repeated culture in the laboratory are used. Attenuated live virus vaccines are available against polio, measles, mumps, rubella, and yellow fever.

Live polio vaccine contains all three serotypes and multiple doses are given to ensure that each type can multiply in the gut without interference. Virus may be excreted in low titre and spread to unvaccinated persons. This may be beneficial in ensuring dissemination through the community, but also carries the small risk of reversion to virulence—a fact which probably accounts for the very rare occurrence of polio caused by identifiable vaccine strains.

Measles, mumps, and rubella vaccines are available as a combined live vaccine which is highly effective in reducing the incidence of these diseases.

Inactivated vaccines

Vaccines prepared from virulent strains that are rendered non-viable, usually by treatment with formalin or β-propiolactone, are used when suitable attenuated strains are unavailable, as in influenza or hepatitis B, or when the consequences of reversion to virulence may be catastrophic, as in rabies or, in the view of some authorities, polio. Hepatitis B vaccine used to be prepared from the plasma of human carriers, but genetically engineered vaccines are now available. Influenza vaccines are reviewed annually to reflect the antigenic diversity of strains circulating in the community.

Multiple injections, including booster doses at intervals, are necessary to maintain immunity provided by inactivated vaccines.

Passive immunization

Serum from persons who have recovered from viral diseases will temporarily protect non-immune persons if given in sufficient amount before the virus has a chance to multiply and spread. Extracted globulin is preferred to whole serum because this limits adverse effects that may be caused by other proteins. Immunoglobulin has been used most extensively for the protection of travellers at risk of hepatitis A. The effect is shortlived, at most 3 months.

In practice, globulin from large donor pools is used. These are screened for antibody to common viruses. In special circumstances, specific globulin may be prepared from pooled sera of persons convalescent from a particular disease. This principle has been used to protect immunodeficient persons and neonates against chickenpox by use of varicella-zoster immunoglobulin. Hyperimmune serum obtained by immunization of volunteers has been used as a source of globulin against rabies and hepatitis B.

Immune globulin is effective only when the time of exposure to a virus is known and when it can be given shortly after exposure.

Part II

Laboratory aspects of antimicrobial therapy

7

Antibiotic sensitivity testing

PURPOSE OF SENSITIVITY TESTING

Since therapy of infection normally begins, quite properly, before laboratory results are available, antibiotic sensitivity testing primarily plays a supplementary role in confirming that the organism is susceptible to the agent that is being used. Sometimes it may enable the clinician to change from a toxic to a less toxic agent.

Usually the laboratory report will influence treatment only if the patient is failing to respond. By this time, the laboratory should have succeeded in establishing the sensitivity pattern of the offending organism (if it is bacterial) sufficiently for the clinician to be able to make an informed decision as to how treatment might be modified. Sensitivity testing of non-bacterial pathogens is not usually possible.

In addition to this primary purpose the laboratory also has an important function in recording and storing data on the sensitivity patterns of common pathogens in the hospital and in the community, in order that reliable predictions of their probable sensitivity may be made. Patterns of bacterial sensitivity and resistance vary considerably from place to place and hospitals, or even wards, often have their own particular resistance problems. It is, therefore, important that each hospital keeps its own record of resistance trends.

Finally, sensitivity testing is used to establish the degree and spectrum of in-vitro activity of new antibacterial agents, first of all in the laboratories of the pharmaceutical houses from whence most new developments emanate, but also in diagnostic laboratories where the new agent can be tested against the various types of organism encountered locally.

SENSITIVITY TESTING METHODS

The antibiotic sensitivity of bacteria can be assessed in a variety of ways according to individual preference, the constraints of cost, the nature of the bacterium, the number of strains requiring investigation and the degree of accuracy required. Most methods fall into one of three main categories.

1. *Agar diffusion tests*, in which the antibiotic is allowed to diffuse from a point source, commonly in the form of a filter paper disc (but sometimes as a tablet, well or porous cup), into an agar medium which has been seeded with the test organism.
2. *Broth dilution tests*, in which serial (usually two-fold) dilutions of antibiotic in a suitable fluid medium are inoculated with the test organism. The highest dilution of the antibiotic to inhibit growth after overnight incubation is the *minimum inhibitory concentration* (MIC).
3. *Agar incorporation tests*, which are essentially similar to broth dilution tests except that the antibiotic dilutions are incorporated in an agar medium in a series of Petri dishes. These are spot-inoculated with a number of test organisms, usually by means of a semi-automatic inoculating device.

Agar diffusion tests

Most diagnostic microbiology laboratories test antibiotic sensitivity of bacteria by some form of agar diffusion test in which the organism under investigation is exposed to a diffusion gradient of antibiotic provided by an impregnated disc of filter paper. When the bacterial population reaches a certain critical concentration, no further inhibition of growth can be achieved and the edge of an inhibition zone is formed. Up to six antibiotics can be tested on one culture plate and several firms manufacture specially designed systems involving disc dispensers or multiple discs in order to facilitate this.

Several versions of the disc diffusion test are in use in different countries, but none has achieved universal approval. A highly standardized version of the method using a single high-content disc, the Bauer-Kirby test, is officially sanctioned by the Food and Drug Administration in the USA. This test, if properly performed, enables a highly reproducible determination of sensitivity to be made.

The formation of inhibition zones represents the dynamic interaction between antibiotic diffusion and bacterial growth. Within certain limits the size of the inhibition zone is a measure of the MIC of the antibiotic for the test organism, but for individual strains the relationship between the two may be far from perfect. By examining numerous strains of known MIC, regression analysis can be applied and a characteristic regression equation established for each bacterial species and antibiotic (Fig. 7.1).

Factors affecting disc tests
Many of the factors determining the outcome of disc tests are the same as

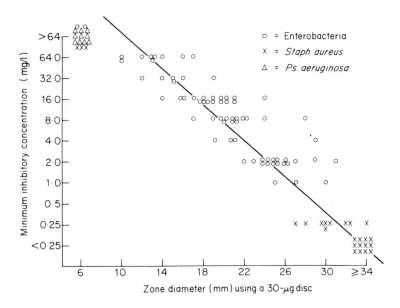

Fig. 7.1. Hypothetical example of correlation of disc diffusion zone sizes and minimum inhibitory concentration (MIC) values. Note that MIC values are plotted on a logarithmic scale and appear in discrete $\log_2$ steps, whereas disc zone sizes are measured on a continuous arithmetic scale. A zone size of 6 mm indicates no zone of inhibition, since this is the diameter of the antibiotic-containing disc. The example shown indicates that most *Staph. aureus* strains are fully susceptible to the antibiotic, but a few strains are fully resistant; all *Ps. aeruginosa* strains are resistant. A very wide spread of susceptibility values is observed with enterobacteria and correlation is less than perfect. It is this group that presents interpretative difficulties.

those encountered in other methods of sensitivity testing (see below: factors affecting sensitivity tests), but some are peculiar to this method.

The size of the inhibition zone may be profoundly influenced by the physico-chemical characteristics of the antibacterial agent such as solubility, ionic charge, and molecular size. Large cyclic peptides, such as the polymyxins, diffuse poorly and produce small zones of inhibition even when highly sensitive organisms are tested against high drug concentrations.

The growth rate of the bacteria will also affect zone sizes, slow-growing organisms giving rise to large zones. A corollary of this is that if cultures are allowed to stand at room temperature prior to incubation at 37°C an overestimate of bacterial susceptibility may be made.

One of the most difficult factors to control adequately is the initial amount of antibiotic in the disc. Commercially available discs usually contain the stated amount of drug within a tolerance of 67–150° per cent: i.e. a disc rated at 30 μg may contain between 20 and 45 μg of drug. If discs are incorrectly stored or used beyond the expiry date, the lower limit may be considerably overstepped. Note that disc content is described in μg per disc, which should not be confused with μg per ml, often used to specify antibacterial potency. In fact, in disc-testing the concentration of antibiotic in μg per ml in the area immediately surrounding the disc can be a much higher value than that of the nominal disc content.

Despite these and other variables, the disc diffusion test is widely used for antibiotic sensitivity tests for reasons of speed, simplicity and cost. When employed under carefully controlled conditions it is capable of producing satisfactory results with the more common rapidly growing pathogens such as *Staphylococcus aureus*, *Pseudomonas aeruginosa* and various enterobacteria; it is less suitable for other more fastidious or slow-growing bacteria such as anaerobes, streptococci, *Haemophilus* spp. and *Neisseria* spp., for which alternative procedures are preferable. *Mycobacterium tuberculosis*, which grows extremely slowly, requires special methods of testing.

Control of disc diffusion tests

Since zone sizes are affected by many variable factors it is essential that all tests include adequate controls. A common, but not very satisfactory method of control is to include a series of plates inoculated with organisms of known sensitivity along with each batch of tests and to measure the size of the inhibition zones produced. This adequately controls culture medium composition (providing the same batch of medium is used for all tests) and incubation conditions, but makes no allowance for variations in disc content or size of the bacterial inoculum.

Disc content is more satisfactorily controlled by Stokes' 'comparative method' in which both test and control organisms are inoculated onto the same culture plate so that a direct comparison of zone size and inoculum density can be made (Fig. 7.2). With this method it is preferable for control and test strains to be of the same species and it is essential that both strains should have similar growth characteristics on the medium used. Critics of the method point to the difficulty of reliably achieving these conditions in routine practice.

Broth dilution tests

Conventional test

Conventional broth dilution tests are expensive in both time and materials and tend to be used when only a few strains of bacteria need to be tested or when an accurate MIC estimation is required. A series of two-fold

Fig. 7.2. Disc sensitivity testing by the Stokes' method, in which inhibition of the test organism by antibiotics is directly compared with that of a similar control organism of known sensitivity. In the example shown, the test organism (*Staph. aureus*) is resistant to penicillin (right-hand disc), but fully sensitive to erythromycin (left-hand disc). (Photograph courtesy of George Sharp and Richard Edwards.)

dilutions of the antibiotic under study is prepared in a suitable broth medium and a standard inoculum of the test strain (commonly 10^5 bacteria) is introduced into each tube. The test is incubated at 37°C overnight and the end-point read as that concentration of antibiotic in which no turbidity can be seen. Uninoculated tubes containing broth plus antibiotic and broth alone act as sterility controls and an antibiotic-free tube inoculated with the test organism serves to indicate that the organism is alive and well in case the end-point is missed. The whole test is controlled by titrating the antibiotic against an organism of known sensitivity, in parallel (Fig. 7.3).

Micro-method

One-millilitre volumes are traditionally used for broth dilution MIC tests, but a micro-method using much smaller volumes in microtitration trays is

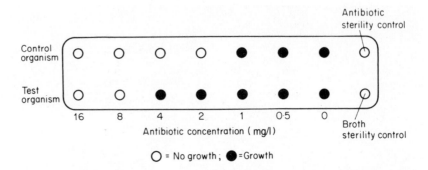

Fig. 7.3. Broth dilution test of antibiotic susceptibility. Two-fold dilutions of antibiotic are inoculated with a known number of organisms and incubated at 37°C overnight. The potency of the antibiotic is checked by titrating it against a control organism of known susceptibility. The minimum inhibitory concentration (MIC) is the highest dilution in which no turbidity develops (2 mg/l for the control organism and 8 mg/l for the test organism in the example shown).

also used. A further convenience is provided by using preprepared trays containing freeze-dried antibiotic. Such trays are available commercially. The antibiotic dilutions are reconstituted with preseeded culture medium and incubated as before.

Determination of MBC

A major advantage claimed for broth dilution procedures is that the *minimum bactericidal concentration* (MBC) of antibiotic for the test strain may additionally be determined if so desired. This is done by subculturing onto solid medium a standard volume of broth from those antibiotic dilutions showing no visible growth after overnight incubation. The number of colonies developing after a further overnight period of incubation is compared with the number originally inoculated. The MBC is arbitrarily defined as the lowest concentration which kills 99.9 per cent of the original inoculum; i.e. the concentration at which there is a thousand-fold reduction in bacterial numbers. Clearly if 10^5 bacteria were inoculated into 1 ml of broth, a 0.1 ml volume subcultured onto solid medium should yield less than 10 colonies if the antibacterial agent is bactericidal.

Killing curves

The MBC is a very crude estimate of bactericidal potency which reveals nothing about the kinetics of bacterial response. It is more satisfactory, but much more laborious, to construct killing curves in which sequential viable counts are carried out at regular intervals after exposure to various concentrations of the drug. This provides information as to the rate of bacterial killing and may detect recovery during the overnight incubation period which would be masked in the overnight end-point. It should be noted that viable counting methods detect colony-forming units, not absolute numbers of bacteria since chains and clumps give rise to single colonies. An antibiotic such as cephalexin, which affects the division process of Gram-negative bacteria, but does not stop them from growing during the first few hours' exposure, will cause the viable count to stop rising even though growth continues.

Agar incorporation tests

In this method the antibiotic dilutions are made in solid agar medium by adding antibiotics to molten agar (at 45 °C) and pouring into Petri dishes. The test strains are inoculated onto the surface of the medium. This is the preferred method when large numbers of strains are to be examined since up to 56 strains (but, more commonly 20–36) can be accommodated on a single conventional 9-cm plate. The inoculum is applied with a suitably designed multipoint inoculator which transfers a small drop of broth culture to each of the desired number of antibiotic-containing plates. A suitable inoculum yields a barely confluent spot of culture after overnight incubation on an antibiotic-free control plate. A series of control strains of known sensitivity are included on each plate.

Break-point tests

By using an appropriate series of antibiotic concentrations, MICs can be estimated by the agar incorporation method. The results are commonly found to be one or two twofold dilutions lower than those obtained by

Table 7.1. Example of antibiotic susceptibility testing using the 'break-point' method

Test organism	Ampicillin concentration			Result
	Plate 1 (nil)	Plate 2 (8 µg/ml)	Plate 3 (64 µg/ml)	
1	Growth	No growth	No growth	Fully sensitive
2	Growth	Growth	No growth	Reduced sensitivity*
3	Growth	Growth	Growth	Fully resistant
4	No growth	No growth	No growth	Void test †

* Susceptible to levels achievable in urine.
† Control failed to grow.

broth dilution. Since accurate MICs are seldom required for routine sensitivity tests the range of dilutions can be considerably reduced by using only one or two preselected 'break-point' concentrations related to agreed cut-off points of sensitivity or resistance (Table 7.1). Like the content of antibiotic discs these break-points are somewhat arbitrary, but are related to levels achievable in serum, tissue or urine during therapy. Inaccuracies introduced in preparing appropriate antibiotic concentration for the break-point method may be minimized by using commercially prepared antibiotic tablets of guaranteed potency which are simply dissolved in the correct volume of molten agar and poured into Petri dishes.

FACTORS AFFECTING SENSITIVITY TESTS

Inoculum size

The most important single factor affecting the result of sensitivity tests is the number of bacteria present in the original inoculum and this must be carefully standardized if reliable and reproducible results are to be obtained. Unfortunately, the therapeutically 'correct' inoculum has never been precisely defined and the inocula usually employed are based on tradition rather than firm evidence. With some antibacterial agents, notably the sulphonamides, antibacterial activity is abolished *in vitro* if dense inocula are used and this clearly does not accord with clinical experience. However, the sulphonamides represent a special case because they achieve their effect only after bacterial growth has continued normally for 2 or 3 hours and it is unwise to assume that dense bacterial populations (such as are frequently present in infection) are generally inappropriate in sensitivity tests.

Composition of culture medium

Culture media used for sensitivity testing must be free of antibiotic antagonists and readily support growth of the bacteria under test. Several formulations of medium suitable for sensitivity testing of a wide range of bacterial pathogens are commercially available. Mueller-Hinton medium has become established for the purpose in the USA, but it is unclear that this has any special properties which single it out as being particularly suitable and other, specially formulated sensitivity test media are usually preferred elsewhere. Media which contain thymidine are unsuitable for testing sulphonamides, but the addition of lysed horse blood to the medium renders it suitable because horse blood contains the enzyme thymidine phosphorylase.

As well as being able to support growth of the major pathogens well, sensitivity test media should be standardized for carbohydrate content, pH, osmolality, and cation content. Excess fermentable carbohydrate will cause a change in pH of the medium during growth which may alter not only the rate of growth of the bacteria, but also the activity of the anti- biotic. The aminoglycosides and erythromycin are much less active in an acid than in an alkaline medium whilst nitrofurantoin is more active at an acid pH. Aminoglycosides may be affected by a number of different constituents of culture media including divalent cations (Ca^{2+} and Mg^{2+}), NaCl, and phosphates. These factors may differentially affect the activity against different species of bacteria so that, for example, the activity of aminoglycosides against *Ps. aeruginosa* is particularly affected by alterations in divalent cations.

Osmolality of culture medium

The bactericidal activity of β-lactam antibiotics, which in general rely on osmotic rupture of the bacterial cell to achieve their lethal effect, is markedly influenced by the osmolality of the growth medium. Species of bacteria which have a naturally low internal osmolality, such as *Proteus mirabilis* and *Haemophilus influenzae*, are predominantly affected bacteri- statically by β-lactam agents unless the osmolality of broth media is artificially reduced to below physiological levels.

Antibiotic formulation

An obvious factor which is sometimes overlooked in sensitivity testing is that the formulation of the antibiotic used must be appropriate. Although the esters of ampicillin, carbenicillin, mecillinam, cefuroxime, and erythromycin are used clinically it should be remembered that these are antibacterially inactive pro-drugs which only release the active parent compound in the body. Similarly, chloramphenicol succinate is inactive *in vitro* and chloramphenicol itself should be used in laboratory tests. It is also preferable to avoid using sulphomethyl derivatives of polymyxins (polymyxin B and colistin) which are much less active *in vitro* than the non-sulphomethylated varieties, although they do spontaneously break down to the more active parent form on incubation.

NEWER METHODS OF SENSITIVITY TESTING

A number of alternative methods of assessing bacterial susceptibility to antibiotics are gradually coming into use in an effort to obtain results more quickly than by traditional procedures. Most rapid of all are the tests which detect resistance to β-lactam antibiotics by the demonstration of β-lactamase activity in the bacteria. Several methods are available which will accomplish this in a few minutes once a bacterial culture is available. However, since a wide range of β-lactamases are encountered to which various β-lactam agents display differential susceptibility the tests are of limited value. They have been widely and successfully used to detect β-lactamase-mediated resistance to penicillin and ampicillin in *Neisseria gonorrhoeae* and *H. influenzae* which is exclusively due at present to one particular variety of β-lactamase (TEM-1, see Chapter 12).

Of wider applicability are those techniques which employ turbidimetry to detect antibacterial activity by comparing the growth of bacteria exposed to antibiotic with a drug-free control over a time span which for fast-growing organisms can be as little as 2 or 3 hours. Several machines have been described which do this with various degrees of sophistication. Turbidimetric results show discrepancies with more traditional methods with certain bacterium/drug combinations and there is controversy about the correct interpretation of these.

Any method which measures bacterial growth or metabolism can theoretically be used to assess the influence of antibacterial agents on the normal course of events and a variety of techniques based on impedance measurements, bioluminescence, chemiluminescence, and microcalorimetry have been described. None of these, at the time of writing, looks like achieving the status of a routine test.

An alternative approach that is gaining in popularity is the use of gene probes that are able to detect DNA sequences associated with resistance traits. These provide a specific and reliable means of detecting antibiotic resistance. However, because of the large array of resistance mechanisms that may be encountered, as well as other technical problems, it is likely to be some time before gene probes can be economically introduced into routine laboratory practice for sensitivity testing.

8

Antibiotic assay

Antibiotic assay means the estimation of antibiotic concentrations in serum, urine, or other body fluids at appropriate times after giving the drug. The indications to assay antimicrobial drugs in biological material in routine practice are few. However, in the development of a new drug, determination of the pharmacokinetic profile in health and disease forms an important part of the evaluation of the agent, and frequent assays in various body fluids are part of this process.

In the management of individual treatment, determination of antibiotic concentration is usually only necessary on two counts: first, with drugs of known toxicity where the adverse effect is dose-related; second, to monitor efficacy when there is a narrow therapeutic range between adequate and toxic levels (Fig. 8.1). Occasionally, it may be useful to check antibiotic levels when there is reason to doubt that treatment is achieving adequate levels, for example in CSF, but this is seldom done.

Some workers advocate a special form of assay in the treatment of certain infections such as bacterial endocarditis, in which it is important to achieve bactericidal levels of drug. In this case a sample of the patient's serum, obtained at a period of time after administration of the antibiotic at which a peak concentration is anticipated, is titrated against the organism responsible for the infection (so-called *back-titration*). Since the object is to establish that a sufficiently high bactericidal titre is maintained it is necessary to measure the bactericidal, not just the bacteristatic end-point.

ASSAY OF AMINOGLYCOSIDES

In practice, aminoglycosides, and gentamicin in particular, are the most commonly assayed antibiotics in hospital laboratories. These drugs are excreted into urine by glomerular filtration. With degrees of renal impairment the usual interval of 8 hours between doses must be lengthened or accumulation will occur, with subsequent manifestation of the unpleasant nephrotoxic and ototoxic side-effects associated with this group of drugs (see Chapter 18). Serum for assay should be taken 1 hour after the dose is given (*peak*) and just before the next injection (*trough*). If the drug is given intravenously there will be rapid equilibration in the vascular

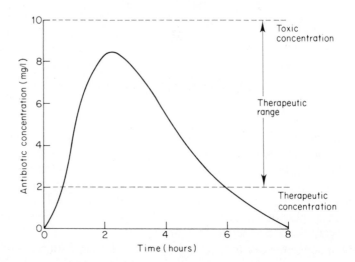

Fig. 8.1. The concept of 'therapeutic range'. An antibiotic administered to a patient at time 0 reaches a peak concentration in plasma and is subsequently eliminated. The therapeutic concentration needed to achieve an antibacterial effect (usually taken as the MIC for the infecting organism) is shown by the lower dashed line; the concentration above which toxic side-effects are known to be commonly encountered is shown by the upper dashed line. The difference between these values is the *therapeutic range*. The *therapeutic index* is the ratio of the toxic concentration to the therapeutic concentration.

compartment and the 1-hour concentration is not a true peak, but if blood is taken at a standard time there will be comparability between assays.

The therapeutic range of gentamicin concentrations in serum is approximately 2-10 mg/l. This depends on the MIC of the infecting organism as well as the toxic concentration. As far as the latter is concerned, it is far from certain that high peak concentrations correlate simply with adverse effects. What may be of more importance is the *area under the curve*, i.e. the total concentration of drug related to time. Thus, relatively minor increases in trough levels, such as occur with minimal renal impairment, may be of more importance than high peaks.

A trough concentration above 2 mg/l is an indication to reduce the dose or to prolong the interval between doses. In most patients with normal renal function the gentamicin trough level is below 1 mg/l and may be undetectable by some assay methods; with a peak concentration above 5 mg/l this can be considered satisfactory. If the peak turns out to be very high, but the trough is below 2 mg/l, there is no cause to alter the dose immediately, but a further assay should be done to check the levels. If the peak is below 5 mg/l and the trough level undetectable, the dose must be increased and the assays repeated.

In patients with stable renal function it is usually necessary to perform only one set of assays (peak and trough) during therapy. Where there are fluctuations in serum creatinine (the indicator of glomerular function that is usually used) it will be necessary to monitor aminoglycoside therapy more closely.

Nomograms

Because of the necessity to start treatment before assay results are available and because of their unavailability in some areas, attempts have been made to construct simple guides to aminoglycoside dosage. The one most widely used in the UK utilizes the sex-related serum creatinine level for the patient's age as a measure of renal function and relates this to body weight to provide a first (*loading*) dose and a subsequent *maintenance* dose appropriate to the individual patient. A nomogram based on such data, originally described by Mawer and his colleagues, is shown in Fig. 8.2. The instructions are those given by our department and the hospital pharmacy and are available on the wards in Nottingham hospitals so that junior doctors may reliably dose patients before assay results are known. The Mawer nomogram was originally devised for gentamicin and can also be used for tobramycin, but not for amikacin or netilmicin which are given in higher doses.

It should be noted that this nomogram does not apply to children or to those undergoing renal dialysis. In both these situations regular monitoring by assay is important. Children may be dosed on a weight basis; although great variations will be found when assaying their serum levels, this method is a useful guide.

Experience has shown that the manufacturers' recommended regimens often give inadequate serum concentrations.

ANTIBIOTIC ASSAY METHODS

Numerous methods have been described to assay various antimicrobial substances. Some compounds, such as β-lactam antibiotics and sulphonamides, lend themselves to chemical assay methods, but these are often insufficiently sensitive to measure the small amounts which may be present in body fluids and in some cases do not discriminate between active compound and inactivate metabolites. More attractive to microbiologists are bacteriological methods which directly quantify antibacterial activity.

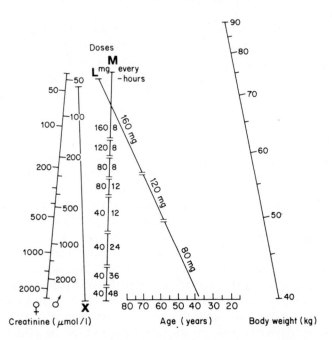

Fig. 8.2. Nomogram for determining a suitable dose regimen for gentamicin. *Instructions* —for patients not receiving dialysis treatment: 1. Join with a straight line the serum creatinine concentration appropriate to the sex on the left hand scale, and the age on the lower scale. Mark the point at which the straight line cuts line X. 2. Join with a straight line the mark on line X and the bodyweight on the right hand scale. Mark the points at which this cuts the dosage lines L and M. 3. The loading dose in milligrams is written against the mark on line L and the maintenance dose against the mark on line M.

The nomogram is designed to give serum concentrations of gentamicin within the range 5-10 mg/l 1 hour after each dose. In patients with renal insufficiency it is essential to perform assays before and after the second or third maintenance dose, as this nomogram is only a guide to treatment. It is desirable in all seriously ill patients to perform at least one early assay to check that the nomogram has given an appropriate schedule for that individual patient.

NB. Patients with any degree of renal impairment are liable to ototoxicity after exposure to gentamicin, especially *if it is given with or after certain other drugs*. Patients who have had an earlier course of gentamicin, or who have had or are having any other aminoglycoside antibiotic, cephalosporin, frusemide, or other potentially nephrotoxic or ototoxic drug, should be treated with particular care—and alternative antibiotics wherever possible. (Adapted from G. E. Mawer *et al.* (1974). *British Journal of Clinical Pharmacology* **1**, 45-50.)

Microbiological assay

The simplest method is to titrate the antibiotic-containing fluid against a known sensitive organism and to compare the result with a parallel titration of a standard solution of the drug in question. The standard solution should be initially prepared in a similar fluid to that of the test (serum, urine, etc.). Although the method has the virtue of simplicity it is not very accurate because test and standard are being compared in a discontinuous series of concentrations and because antibiotic titrations are inherently irreproducible within two-fold limits.

More satisfactory from this point of view, and therefore more widely used, is the agar diffusion method of assay. In this test a sterile punch is used to cut a series of wells in a prearranged pattern in agar contained in a flat-bottomed plate. The agar may be seeded with the test organism prior to its distribution in dishes, so that the bacteria are in the agar, or the surface may be flooded with an appropriately diluted suspension of bacteria and allowed to dry before the wells are cut. The wells are filled with the test fluid (which may be diluted if high levels are anticipated) and a series of standard antibiotic concentrations prepared in the same body fluid as the test.

After overnight incubation at 37°C the diameter of each inhibition zone is carefully measured (Fig. 8.3). A graph of the square of the zone diameter is plotted against the logarithm of the antibiotic concentration for the antibiotic standards. A linear relationship should be obtained if the test is working satisfactorily. The levels of antibiotic in the test fluid can then be determined by reference to the graph (Fig. 8.4).

The organism used in the assay should obviously be chosen for its sensitivity to the antibiotic in question, but should not be so sensitive that huge inhibition zones are produced by therapeutic concentrations. *Bacillus subtilis*, *Sarcinia lutea*, or the Oxford strain of *Staphylococcus aureus* are widely used. For gentamicin assays done by the microbiological method it is commonplace to use a fast-growing organism such as *Klebsiella aerogenes* so that results can be obtained within 4 or 5 hours if required. If a strain of *Klebsiella* is chosen which has a restricted susceptibility pattern, interference with the assay by other antibacterial agents can be minimized. Since the method merely detects antimicrobial activity, antibiotics other than the one being assayed may interfere with the result unless steps are taken to inactivate the other compound, or to use an organism that is resistant to it. It is essential that assay requests made to the laboratory should reveal *all* antimicrobial therapy that the patient is currently receiving.

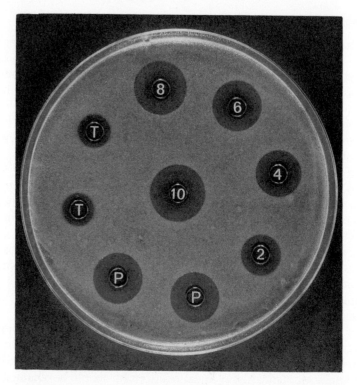

Fig. 8.3. Microbiological assay of antibiotic levels in patient's serum. Wells cut in agar (previously seeded with an indicator organism) are filled with patient's serum, or standard dilutions of antibiotic of known potency. After overnight incubation the zones of inhibition are measured, a graph is drawn from results obtained with the standards (see Fig. 8.4) and the concentration in the patient's serum is read off from the graph. In the example shown, the figures represent the concentrations of the antibiotic standards used; patient's serum was obtained 1 hour after receiving a dose of antibiotic (peak level, P) and immediately before administration of the next dose (trough level, T). (Photograph courtesy of George Sharp and Richard Edwards.)

Non-microbiological assay methods

Apart from chemical assays specifically designed for individual anti-microbial compounds and high-pressure liquid chromatography (see below) most non-microbiological assays have been developed to cope with the demand for the rapid estimation of aminoglycoside levels in serum.

Enzymatic assays

Enzymatic methods utilize the susceptibility of aminoglycosides to specific adenylyl- or acetyl-transferase enzymes. In the presence of one or

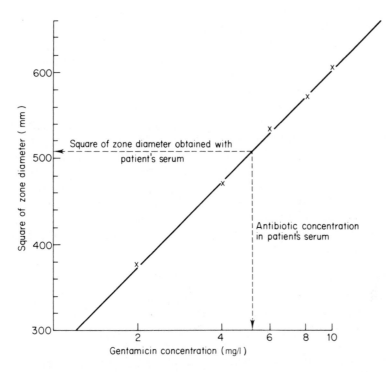

Fig. 8.4. Calibration graph used for estimating concentrations of an antibiotic in patient's serum. Values obtained with standard concentrations of the antibiotic in a test such as that depicted in Fig. 8.3 are plotted as shown. The concentration of antibiotic in the appropriate test sample can then be read off by reference to the graph. In the example shown, the patient's serum produced an inhibition zone measuring 22.5 mm in diameter (zone squared = 506 mm) indicating an antibiotic concentration of 5.1 mg/l. (Graph, based on an assay of gentamicin in serum, kindly provided by Anthony Cowlishaw.)

other of these enzymes, radio-labelled adenyl or acetyl groups can be transferred from ATP or acetyl coenzyme A to any gentamicin present in the sample. After removing unreacted ATP or acetyl CoA, the radio-activity is measured in a scintillation counter. The method is specific, rapid, and accurate, but expensive.

Immunoassay

Various kinds of immunoassay have been described. In all of them antibody against gentamicin, prepared in rabbits, is allowed to react with the patient's serum where it combines with any gentamicin that is present. A known amount of radio-, fluorescein-, or enzyme-labelled gentamicin is then added to the mixture and reacts with any remaining antibody. The radioactivity, fluorescence or enzyme activity is measured and the loss, compared to a control value, is proportional to the amount of gentamicin in the serum. The reagents for this test must be highly standardized and a scintillation counter, fluorimeter or spectrophotometer is required to read the result. As with transferase methods, immunoassay is rapid and precise, but expensive on reagents and equipment. These methods are available as diagnostic kits. A commercially available polarization fluoro-immunoassay system has now virtually replaced old-fashioned micro-biological methods for the assay of aminoglycosides in most laboratories in the UK and other parts of the world where the cost is not prohibitive. In addition to those available for the assay of gentamicin, tobramycin, and amikacin, kits have also been developed for the assay of vancomycin (which also has a relatively narrow therapeutic range) and chloramphenicol, for which monitoring of plasma and CSF levels may be needed in the treatment of neonates.

High-pressure liquid chromatography (HPLC)

This is a development of traditional chromatographic procedures which have been used in biochemistry laboratories for many years. Compounds are separated according to their differential retention times as they are passed under pressure through a special column containing particles which delay the test substance to a greater or lesser degree depending on small variations in surface charge. By manipulating the conditions of the fluid (*mobile phase*) in which the test material is dissolved, the system can be made highly selective. Substances which have a characteristic ultra-violet (UV) absorption spectrum can be detected rapidly and quantitatively by continuously monitoring the outflow of the chromatographic column spectrophotometrically, using UV light at the appropriate wavelength. Compounds which do not absorb UV can usually be detected in other ways, often by chemically treating the sample to form a fluorescent derivative. This must be done for aminoglycosides and this, together with the extraction procedure needed to remove proteins and other interfering substances from serum samples, makes the method cumbersome for routine use even in those laboratories where the necessary equipment is available.

However, HPLC is an extremely useful and versatile method for the assay of many antibiotics and it is widely used in pharmacokinetic studies. It has the great advantage that it can discriminate between very closely related compounds and can therefore be used to detect not only native antibiotic, but also any derivatives that may be produced in the body, which may display modified pharmacological, toxicological, or antibacterial properties.

9

Antibiotic interactions

When the antimicrobial activity of combinations of antibiotics is studied, several results are possible.

1. The combined effect may be greater than that which either agent alone could achieve—a small increase is generally due to simple additive effects, larger increases may indicate true *synergy*.

2. The overall effect may be reduced, in which case the combination is *antagonistic*.

3. Each compound may ignore the presence of the other and the more active compound prevails. In this case the compounds are said to show *indifference*.

SYNERGY

Antimicrobial synergy, implying the beneficial interaction between two drugs exceeding simple additive effects, may take several forms (Table 9.1). One compound may potentiate the activity of the other at a biochemical level; one may assist the other to penetrate into the bacterial cell; one may protect the other from destruction; or the two compounds may act on separate sections of the bacterial population.

Table 9.1. Types of antimicrobial synergy

Type	Mechanism	Drugs
Biochemical interaction	Sequential blockade Complementation	Trimethoprim-sulphonamides Mecillinam-cephalexin
Enhancement of permeability	Cell wall Cell membrane	β-lactam antibiotics Polymyxins
Protection	Enzyme inhibition	Clavulanic acid-amoxycillin
Differential population effects	Suppression of resistance	Antituberculosis drugs

Biochemical synergy

The clearest example of biochemical synergy is provided by the combination of trimethoprim and sulphonamides which is most commonly used clinically as co-trimoxazole. Sulphonamides and diaminopyrimidines like trimethoprim interfere with sequential stages in bacterial folate synthesis. Sulphonamides cut off the folate supply at source, while trimethoprim stops regeneration of the biologically active form of the vitamin (tetrahydrofolate), which is oxidized in the course of helping in the manufacture of thymidylic acid for nucleic acid synthesis. The complete shutting off of folate activity can be accomplished by concentrations of sulphonamides and trimethoprim which alone are ineffective or only feebly inhibitory.

Another type of double blockade occurs with the β-lactam antibiotics, mecillinam, and cephalexin. These two agents induce distinct and characteristic morphological changes in susceptible Gram-negative bacilli, but together complement one another to elicit the spheroplast response which most other β-lactam agents evoke (cf Fig. 1.4). The explanation of this is that mecillinam binds to a particular protein in the bacterial envelope which has the effect of causing generalized surface changes in the cell wall. Cephalexin binds to a different protein which is involved in bacterial division; the bacteria continue to grow, but fail to divide. When both processes are inhibited simultaneously, a region of cell wall weakness develops at the potential cleavage site as the bacteria grow and a wall-deficient spheroplast starts to emerge at the incipient division point. Because the spheroplast is osmotically fragile it normally bursts unless osmotic protection is given, and the combination of mecillinam and cephalexin is consequently much more rapidly bactericidal than are the individual compounds. It is important to remember that mecillinam and cephalexin are unusual members of the β-lactam family, most of which do not exhibit this form of synergy simply because they are able alone to attack both the sites that mecillinam and cephalexin individually affect.

Enhancement of permeability

Many bacteria are antibiotic resistant, not because their intracellular target site is insusceptible to the drug, but because the cell manages to keep out the noxious agent. For example, the protein-synthesizing machinery of *Escherichia coli* is as susceptible to erythromycin as that of *Staphylococcus aureus*, but the drug penetrates the *Esch. coli* cell only with difficulty.

Those antibiotics which act at the level of the cell wall (e.g. β-lactam agents) or the cell membrane (e.g. polymyxins) may interfere with the cells' ability to exclude another agent. The most familiar example of this is provided by the interaction of penicillins and aminoglycosides acting against enterococci. Streptococci in general are resistant to aminoglycosides and the resistance is associated with failure of the drug to penetrate the cell wall. Penicillin alone, in sufficient concentration, kills enterococci relatively slowly and *persisters* survive prolonged exposure. In the presence of penicillins and aminoglycosides the rate of killing is much increased and persisters are also killed. Studies with radio-active streptomycin have shown that this is associated with an increase in uptake of the aminoglycoside.

β-Lactam antibiotics and aminoglycosides act synergically against other species of bacteria, but the effect is not usually so dramatic as in the case of enterococci. Many other examples of synergy involving β-lactam antibiotics or polymyxins exist.

Protection

The resistance of bacteria to β-lactam antibiotics is generally due to bacterial enzymes (β-lactamases) which destroy the drug. This mode of resistance suggests the possibility, mooted many years ago, of using an enzyme inhibitor to allow the enzyme-labile drug to achieve its effect unscathed. Various attempts have been made over the years to make use of this notion, usually by using penicillins like cloxacillin and nafcillin (which are β-lactamase stable, but have no useful activity against Gram-negative bacilli) in combination with ampicillin in an attempt to overcome the resistance of some Gram-negative bacilli. Unfortunately, success achieved with these combinations was limited because of the wide variety of β-lactamases produced by Gram-negative rods, not all of which are inhibited by β-lactamase-stable penicillins. More recently, potent broad-spectrum enzyme inhibitors have been developed which offer better prospects of success. One of the most active of these is the novel naturally-occurring β-lactam compound, clavulanic acid, which, in combination with amoxycillin or ticarcillin is available therapeutically as the 'Augmentin' and 'Timentin' formulations.

Oral formulations of clavulanic acid and amoxycillin are well absorbed, but an interesting possibility which is being actively considered for sulbactam, a β-lactamase inhibitor that is poorly absorbed when given orally, is that it might be joined as a linked ester to ampicillin to produce a so-called *mutual pro-drug*. This manoeuvre is intended to improve the oral absorption of both compounds in a similar manner to the various esters of ampicillin; as in the case of ampicillin pro-drugs (see Chapter 1), mutual pro-drugs are separated by tissue esterases as they are absorbed.

Although resistance to non-β-lactam antibiotics, including aminoglycosides and chloramphenicol, may be mediated by enzymic mechanisms, the protection principle has not yet been applied outside the β-lactam field.

Differential population effects

Where spontaneous mutation to resistance occurs with a high degree of frequency, two or more antibiotics may be used together mutually to prevent the emergence of resistance. If the frequency of resistance is one in every million bacteria (1 in 10^6) and if resistance is unlinked, the probability of double resistance occurring in a single bacterium is one in a million million (1 in 10^{12}). If three drugs are involved, the probability becomes 1 in 10^{18}. In order to contemplate this astronomical figure it might be useful to consider that this is equivalent to one triple mutant occurring in a solid mass of bacteria weighing 1000 kg.

All the major anti-tuberculosis drugs suffer from mutational resistance problems and the mutual prevention of resistance principle has been widely and successfully used for many years in the chemotherapy of tuberculosis.

ANTAGONISM

In the same way that two antibacterial compounds can operate in a mutually beneficial way, they can sometimes interfere with each other's activity.

Antagonism of bactericidal activity

The form of antagonism which has received most attention is that occurring between predominantly bacteristatic agents, such as tetracycline and chloramphenicol, and those bactericidal agents (pre-eminently, β-lactam antibiotics) which rely on cell growth to achieve their lethal effect. Clearly, if bacterial growth is rapidly halted, the bactericidal activity of such agents will be abolished.

Mutual antagonism

In most cases antagonism operates in one direction only: one substance interferes with another, but is itself unaffected. This means that if the interfering substance is the more active of a pair, its dominance will prevail and any antagonism will be undetectable.

An exception to the general one-way rule is provided by fusidic acid and some penicillins which when combined exhibit mutual antagonism against certain strains of staphylococci. Both fusidic acid and penicillin are usually bactericidal to *Staph. aureus*, but against some strains substantially less killing is observed with the combination than with either agent alone. What apparently happens is that fusidic acid prevents the growth of those cells that it does not kill and, as already stated, penicillins are unable to kill non-growing bacteria. Cell death mediated by fusidic acid is accompanied by collapse of the bacteria, suggesting a secondary effect on the bacterial cell wall following the primary inhibition of protein synthesis—perhaps because the autolytic/synthetic balance which occurs in normal wall growth is upset by the non-production of essential enzymes. Penicillin in some way prevents this secondary effect on the bacterial cell wall and thus interferes with the bactericidal action of fusidic acid. It is probable that a similar interaction occurs between penicillins and other inhibitors of protein synthesis in *Staph. aureus*.

Despite the mutual antagonism that can be demonstrated in the test tube, there is little evidence that this form of interaction has any therapeutic relevance, presumably because pharmacokinetic differences between the agents and therapeutic dosage schedules are excluded from laboratory tests.

Chemical interactions

Occasionally two drugs may interact chemically. Thus, in mixtures of relatively high concentrations of carbenicillin and gentamicin, the gentamicin is slowly inactivated. Subsequent study has shown that this interaction occurs between various penicillins and aminoglycosides and is a chemical reaction between the β-lactam ring of the penicillin and amino groups of the aminoglycoside, so that both compounds are, in fact, inactivated. This interaction probably has no significance at the concentrations achieved therapeutically, but penicillins and aminoglycosides should not be mixed together in intravenous infusions.

Dissociated resistance

An unusual form of antagonism is mediated by erythromycin in those erythromycin-resistant staphylococci that owe their resistance to an inducible methylation reaction occurring at the ribosomal binding site (see Chapter 12). Erythromycin is the specific inducer of the enzyme causing this reaction and lincosamides and macrolides other than erythromycin do not trigger the effect. Consequently, erythromycin can antagonize these compounds by inducing resistance to them.

The phenomenon is readily shown by disc testing of staphylococci

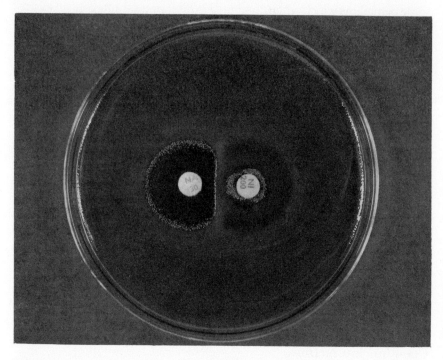

Fig. 9.1. Antagonism of nalidixic acid (NA 30) by nitrofurantoin (NI 200). (Photograph courtesy of George Sharp and Richard Edwards.)

displaying dissociated resistance. A very similar reduction of the inhibition zone produced by nalidixic acid and other quinolones can be caused by nitrofurantoin in some enterobacteria (Fig. 9.1), but in this case the mechanism of the antagonism is unknown.

METHODS FOR DEMONSTRATING ANTIBIOTIC INTERACTIONS

Chessboard titration

The most popular method used to detect antimicrobial interactions is the chessboard or checkerboard titration test in which two drugs are cross-titrated against each other (Fig. 9.2). After incubation a so-called *isobologram* is constructed by plotting the inhibition of growth observed at each drug concentration on an arithmetic scale. The line of *additivity* joins the MICs of the individual drugs acting alone; a deviation of this line

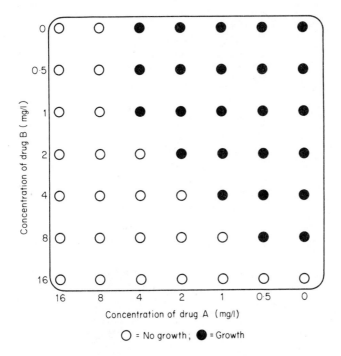

Fig. 9.2. Chessboard titration of two drugs. The example shows synergy: the MIC of drug A alone is 8 mg/l and that of B is 16 mg/l; in combination 2 mg A plus 4 mg B per litre inhibits growth of the test organism.

towards the axes of the graph suggests synergy; a deviation away from the axes is often taken to indicate antagonism, although indifference may also produce this result (Fig. 9.3). Alternatively, the summation of the *fractional inhibitory concentrations* (ΣFIC) can be calculated: if drugs A and B alone each inhibit growth at a concentration of 4 mg/l and the combination of the two inhibits growth in a mixture containing 1 mg of each drug per l, then the ΣFIC $= \frac{1}{4} + \frac{1}{4} = \frac{1}{2}$. A ΣFIC of 1 clearly indicates simple additivity. Theoretically, a ΣFIC below 1 should indicate synergy, but in practice partial antibacterial effects below the MIC often cause apparent deviations from additivity when true synergy is absent. It is probably wise to ignore results which indicate less than a four-fold reduction in the MIC of at least one of the components.

It is not often sufficiently appreciated that chessboard titrations will only detect certain types of interaction. Those interactions in which it is bactericidal activity which is being potentiated or suppressed cannot usually be adequately investigated by this means. Such interactions can

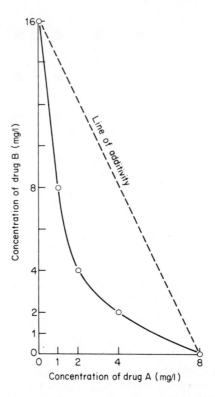

Fig. 9.3. Isobologram drawn from data presented in Fig. 9.2. The lowest concentrations of the two drugs to inhibit growth (alone and in combination) are plotted. Because the two drugs interact synergically, the resultant isobologram deviates from the line of additivity towards the axes of the graph. If the two drugs had displayed antagonism, the line would have deviated above the line of additivity. Note that, although the drugs are tested in $\log_2$ concentration steps, the results are plotted on an arithmetic scale.

usually be demonstrated effectively only by carrying out viable counts at intervals and constructing killing curves. Bactericidal end-points can be measured in chessboard titrations, but this is usually unsatisfactory since it is often the rate of killing which is affected.

Agar diffusion tests

Antimicrobial synergy and antagonism can often be demonstrated in agar diffusion tests as shown in Fig. 9.1 for nalidixic acid and nitrofurantoin. When this method is employed, it is common to use two strips of anti-biotic-impregnated filter paper instead of discs, which are then laid at right angles on the inoculated agar plate. Increase or reduction in inhibition can be seen at the junction of the two strips. Various transfer techniques have been devised to assess bactericidal activity in this type of test. Agar diffusion techniques offer a visually satisfying method of demonstrating antibiotic interactions, but are insufficiently quantitative for most purposes.

THERAPEUTIC RELEVANCE OF ANTIBIOTIC INTERACTIONS

Demonstration of synergy or antagonism *in vitro* by no means guarantees that the interaction will have any relevance in treatment. Pharmacokinetic differences between agents may, for example, dictate that the compounds do not meet in the body in a ratio which has been shown to interact in the laboratory. Even when interacting compounds are carefully chosen to ensure comparable pharmacokinetics, crucial factors militating against the interaction may be overlooked. The synergy between trimethoprim and sulphonamides is so striking when tested in chessboard titrations, that the possibility of using trimethoprim alone was scarcely considered for many years. It is now clear that, in most clinical situations, trimethoprim alone is equally effective. In urinary tract infection, the major indication for co-trimoxazole therapy, the concentration of trimethoprim achieved in urine is so far above the MIC that the slower-acting sulphonamide gets no opportunity to act. In other therapeutic situations, where lower concentrations are involved, differential partition of trimethoprim and sulphonamides into intra- and extracellular compartments may prevent their interaction.

In fact, only a few antimicrobial interactions have been proven to have therapeutic relevance. These include: the interaction between penicillin and aminoglycosides in enterococcal endocarditis; the avoidance of resistance by triple therapy in tuberculosis; the protection of β-lactam agents by clavulanic acid and the antagonism between tetracycline and penicillin in pneumococcal meningitis.

Important interactions between antimicrobial agents and other pharmaceutical preparations are considered in Chapter 18.

10

Use of the laboratory

This book is about antimicrobial therapy and is not intended as a treatise on clinical laboratory microbiology. However, basic microbiological principles must be understood in order to appreciate the scope and limitations of laboratory control of antimicrobial therapy in the individual patient, and the object of this chapter is to fill in a little of this background.

There is still more art to the science of microbiology than to other branches of clinical pathology. There is, for example, more scope for singular methods of processing specimens and for individual interpretation of results in examining a specimen of sputum than in measuring plasma urea. Very often the methods used depend on the experience and preferences of the individual microbiologist. In some countries attempts have been made to bring about more standardization of microbiological methods (in particular antibiotic susceptibility testing), but standardization does not guarantee that the correct result is always obtained!

SPECIMEN COLLECTION

Clinical laboratories rely on the quality of the specimens they receive; none more so than microbiology departments where the 'result' of culture may depend on the degree of care observed in taking the specimen. A single extraneous bacterium introduced into a blood culture during collection may contaminate the culture, resulting in a false positive result. This is one of the many slips that can totally alter laboratory results and may, on occasion, be detrimental to the patient.

A few of the more common problems are listed.

1. *Inappropriate specimen*: saliva is submitted instead of sputum; a superficial skin swab is taken instead of a swab of pus (a specimen of pus in a sterile bottle is always preferable to a swab when possible).

2. *Inadequate specimen*: the specimen may be too small (especially fluids for culture for tubercle bacilli); rectal swabs are no substitute for faeces.

3. *Wrong timing*: specimens taken after the start of chemotherapy, when the causative organism may no longer be demonstrable, or

after the patient has recovered—it is not uncommon for the laboratory to receive rock-hard faeces from patients with 'diarrhoea'.

4. *Wrong container*: blood for culture put in a plain (sometimes unsterile) bottle instead of the correct culture fluid; biopsies put into bactericidal fixatives.

5. *Clerical errors*: incorrect labelling; incomplete or misleading information on request forms.

SPECIMEN TRANSPORT

Not only must the specimen be collected properly, but it must also be received in the laboratory in good condition. Prompt transport to the laboratory is essential. Material submitted for culture is alive; any delay in reaching the optimal cultural conditions will result in loss of viability. With fastidious organisms such as gonococci or viruses this may result in failure to isolate the organism. The converse problem—overgrowth of pathogens by fast-growing commensals—also commonly occurs during the period between collection of the specimen and processing in the laboratory.

The ideal would be to eliminate transport problems by inoculating appropriate culture media at the bedside and incubating them immediately. This may be achieved in special units with laboratories attached, but is not practicable in most situations. An exception is blood culture where the counsel of perfection should apply.

The nearest approach to 'culture in transit' that has been widely adopted is the dip-culture method for culture of urine. For swabs, most laboratories recommend a form of suspended animation in which the specimen is placed in a special transport medium comprising soft buffered agar containing charcoal to inactivate any toxic substances.

Specimens from potential medical emergencies, such as bacterial meningitis or malaria, should be delivered to the laboratory immediately (and it should not be below the dignity of a doctor to do this!) and brought to the attention of a senior member of the laboratory staff.

SPECIMEN PROCESSING

The flow diagram (Fig. 10.1) outlines the three main steps which occur for every bacteriological request: microscopy, culture, identification and sensitivity testing. Even with the most rapidly growing bacteria and with improved methods, results of culture and sensitivity often take 48 hours.

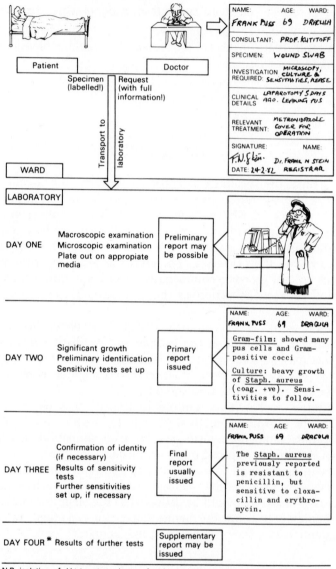

NAME:	AGE:	WARD:
FRANK PUSS	69	DRACULA

CONSULTANT: PROF. KUTITOFF

SPECIMEN: WOUND SWAB

INVESTIGATION REQUIRED: MICROSCOPY, CULTURE & SENSITIVITIES, PLEASE

CLINICAL DETAILS: LAPAROTOMY 5 DAYS AGO. LEAKING PUS

RELEVANT TREATMENT: METRONIDAZOLE COVER FOR OPERATION

SIGNATURE: F.N.Stein. NAME: Dr. FRANK N STEIN

DATE: 24·2·92 REGISTRAR

Patient — Specimen (labelled!) — Request (with full information!) — **Doctor**

Transport to laboratory

WARD

LABORATORY

DAY ONE
Macroscopic examination
Microscopic examination
Plate out on appropiate media
→ Preliminary report may be possible

DAY TWO
Significant growth
Preliminary identification
Sensitivity tests set up
→ Primary report issued

NAME:	AGE:	WARD:
FRANK PUSS	69	DRACULA

Gram–film: showed many pus cells and Gram-positive cocci

Culture: heavy growth of Staph. aureus (coag. +ve). Sensitivities to follow.

DAY THREE
Confirmation of identity (if necessary)
Results of sensitivity tests
Further sensitivities set up, if necessary
→ Final report usually issued

NAME:	AGE:	WARD:
FRANK PUSS	69	DRACULA

The Staph. aureus previously reported is resistant to penicillin, but sensitive to cloxacillin and erythromycin.

DAY FOUR * Results of further tests
→ Supplementary report may be issued

*N.B. isolation of *M.tuberculosis* viruses, fungi, unusual organisms and special tests may take longer

Fig. 10.1. Flow diagram showing the various steps between obtaining a specimen from a patient and the issue of the final report. Note the importance of the period before the specimen arrives in the laboratory: unless the specimen is properly taken and transported it may be useless and unless the request card is properly completed, wrong tests may be done.

This may be further delayed if there is a mixture of organisms or if slow-growing pathogens, such as *Mycobacterium tuberculosis* or viruses, are involved. Not all micro-organisms are readily cultivable and a report of 'Sterile' or 'No growth' does not definitively mean that the specimen contained no organisms, but that the laboratory was unable to isolate any from the specimen.

Because of the inevitable delay in obtaining culture results there is a need to inform clinicians of really important findings before the complete results are known. Microscopical findings are usually available on the same day as the specimen is received and in urgent cases can be reported within 1 hour or less. For example, a Gram-film of CSF can be done very quickly and may give the physician a reliable guide to primary therapy (which may be life-saving) while waiting for cultural confirmation of the result. Similarly, positive blood cultures and other findings serious to the individual patient or his immediate contacts are usually telephoned directly to the doctor. Where the antibiotic sensitivity is predictable (e.g. *Streptococcus pyogenes* is always sensitive to penicillin) this advice may be given with the initial report. With many bacteria the report 'sensitivity to follow' is all that can be imparted before sensitivity testing, although a 'best guess' based on known patterns of resistance in the hospital or community may be suggested.

SIGNIFICANT ISOLATIONS

Although many diseases have a well-defined microbial aetiology, the information obtained about patients and the data accrued from the laboratory examination of their specimens are often too sparse to form a complete opinion as to the microbial cause in an individual case. Most patients with infection survive and many improve so rapidly that the significance of microbes isolated is never known. Thus, although we know from historical and epidemiological evidence that *Str. pyogenes* causes tonsillitis and is involved in the aetiology of rheumatic fever, when an individual patient presents with joint pains following a sore throat we cannot be absolutely sure that the *Str. pyogenes* in his throat is the cause of his illness, since we know, also on epidemiological evidence, that these bacteria are carried normally in the pharynx of about 5 per cent of the community, and sore throat is often due to other causes. In such situations, additional information (such as raised antistreptolysin O antibodies in the serum in this case) may be needed in order to establish a causal relationship.

The greatest difficulty is encountered with specimens from areas of the body which have a resident microbial flora which may sometimes assume a pathogenic role. Isolations from respiratory sources are often the most difficult to interpret. Demonstration of *M. tuberculosis* is always a significant finding and even in the absence of clinical disease the patient must be further examined and treated. This organism, a recognized cause of tuberculosis from the time of Koch, is a true human pathogen and is high on anyone's list of 'wanted bacteria'. On the other hand *Candida albicans* would often be thought of as a harmless commensal, although it can cause serious disease in immunocompromised patients. The ability of some organisms to strike whilst the host defences are down has given these the title *opportunist* pathogens. However, merely by looking at cultures of these opportunists, it is impossible to say in a particular case whether or not they are adopting a pathogenic role and laboratory personnel have to make an informed guess as to their significance based on ancillary findings (e.g. presence or absence of pus; numbers of organisms isolated) and clinical information provided on the request card. If the latter is absent, non-contributory or misleading, as it frequently is, the report may be valueless.

In the absence of adequate guidance, the laboratory can adopt one of two approaches: report any microbe isolated regardless of any possible significance or report only common pathogens and dismiss all the others as 'normal flora'.

The importance of this to ultimate laboratory control of antimicrobial therapy is that if the isolate is not considered 'significant', no further work, including sensitivity tests, will be carried out. The corollary is that many sensitivities may be tested and reported on organisms that have no role in the patient's disease. This occurs more commonly than is usually admitted. Many patients receive potentially toxic antimicrobials because commensal bacteria isolated from a badly taken specimen were considered significant and sensitivity tests reported. Sometimes a great deal of effort and expense is put into treating colonizing organisms which are merely filling a vacuum left by the normal flora and which would quietly disappear if antimicrobial chemotherapy were withheld.

WHAT THE LABORATORY REPORTS

The final report reaching the clinician must be self-explanatory, even dogmatic. It is not practicable, or desirable, to test each organism isolated against all antibiotics. What usually happens is that a restricted range of antimicrobials is tested against isolates considered significant with a different selection for Gram-positive and Gram-negative bacteria. Primary testing can often be restricted to a few old and well-tried agents that are perfectly adequate for most common infections (Table 10.1). More ex-

Table 10.1. Examples of a restricted range of antimicrobial agents selected for primary sensitivity testing of some common pathogens

Organism	Antimicrobial agents tested
Staphylococcus aureus	Benzylpenicillin
	Cloxacillin (methicillin)
	Erythromycin
Streptococcus pyogenes	Benzylpenicillin
(and other streptococci)	Erythromycin
Anaerobes	Benzylpenicillin
	Clindamycin
	Metronidazole
Escherichia coli	Ampicillin (amoxycillin)
(and other enterobacteria)	Trimethoprim
	Cephalosporins*
	Gentamicin
Pseudomonas aeruginosa	Azlocillin (ticarcillin)
	Gentamicin (tobramycin)
Urinary isolates †	Ampicillin (amoxycillin)
	Trimethoprim
	Sulphonamides
	Nalidixic acid
	Nitrofurantoin

* A representative of the earlier cephalosporins, such as cephaloridine, is usually chosen for primary testing.
† Fosfomycin might usefully be included in those countries in which it is available.

tensive testing, particularly of expensive, broad-spectrum agents, should be reserved for resistant isolates or to bacteria from patients with serious infections that are presenting problems of management. Usually, only two or three of the sensitivities tested are reported even if more are performed. Restricted reporting has the important function of reinforcing local antibiotic policies and of discouraging clinicians from using inappropriate agents. Additional tests carried out, but not reported, are often useful if the patient fails to respond to the chosen agent or is hypersensitive to it.

Most infections are caused by a single organism, often a well-known pathogen. In these cases there is usually no problem in deciding what to test and report. However, some specimens (e.g. those from abdominal wounds) are often infected with mixtures of organisms and each must be individually identified and tested against appropriate antimicrobials.

The choice of antibiotic tested varies with the site of infection and the pharmacological properties of the drug. Some agents, such as nitrofurantoin and nalidixic acid, only achieve therapeutic concentrations in urine and are of no value in other infections. Information about the individual patient may alter drug testing; if the patient is allergic to penicillins alternatives will be sought; in pregnancy, sulphonamides and trimethoprim should be avoided if possible because of the risk of folate deficiency; tetracyclines should not be used in young children due to deposition in teeth. These limitations of sensitivity testing can only be taken into account by the laboratory if the appropriate information is given on the request card.

Restrictions imposed by the large number of available antibiotics may be approached in various ways. Some groups of agents, such as sulphonamides or tetracyclines, are so similar in terms of their antibacterial spectrum that only one representative of each needs to be tested. With other drugs where there is differential susceptibility of bacteria to different members of the group, such a decision is less easy. An organism sensitive to cephaloridine, one of the earliest cephalosporins, is also usually sensitive to all subsequent members of that group and this is often used as a screen for cephalosporin-sensitive bacteria. However, the converse is not true; an organism resistant to cephaloridine may be sensitive to later cephalosporins and a definitive statement in this regard can only be made by testing the appropriate compound.

INTERPRETING SENSITIVITY REPORTS

The report to the clinician shown in Fig. 10.1 tells him that *Staphylococcus aureus* is the likely causative organism of the wound infection and that penicillin would be inappropriate, but that erythromycin or cloxacillin would be useful. The statement 'this organism is resistant to penicillin' means that penicillin would not influence the outcome. The infection may well improve due to host defences or to adequate drainage of pus, but since penicillin-resistant staphylococci are invariably β-lactamase producers any penicillin which reached the wound would be rapidly destroyed. Such a statement is based on sound laboratory and clinical evidence. On the other hand, with bacteria of relatively low-level resistance (i.e. where disc testing shows inhibition of growth which is less than that produced using a sensitive control organism) the statement of resistance is more difficult to determine and depends on such factors as site of infection and drug penetration. The laboratory will try to weigh up the evidence and score the result as *sensitive* or *resistant*, or may play safe by using the rather unsatisfactory phrase *reduced sensitivity*.

The statement 'this organism is sensitive to cloxacillin' implies that use of this antibiotic (or a related β-lactamase-stable penicillin) would influence the outcome. This is more difficult to support than a statement about resistance. Treatment with the antibiotic may elicit little response in the patient because insufficient drug may have penetrated into a large collection of pus. More importantly (although unlikely in the present example, since *Staph. aureus* is commonly incriminated in infected wounds) the wrong organism may have been tested. One crucial limitation of the report to the clinician is that the innocent bystander was picked from a collection of bacteria isolated.

Assuming the correct organism and antimicrobials were tested and the results as good as possible in the laboratory, there is still a large gap between saying the isolate is sensitive and saying that the patient will recover from the infection. Many of the host factors influencing the outcome will be described in Chapter 15.

CONCLUSION

The use of the laboratory requires a brain at both ends: thought in the request and in the collection of specimens and thought in the processing of the specimens and in the production of the end report in the laboratory. The final synthesis of interpretation and action based on the report depends on cooperation between clinicians and microbiologists, so that each knows what the other requires. Microbiological expertise is available in most centres to advise on antimicrobial therapy and it is in the interests of the patients to use it. Many laboratories have virology departments and many of the points on specimen collection also apply to virus investigations. When in doubt, the laboratory should be consulted. For unusual diseases and problem cases it is often possible to seek help from specialized units such as tropical hospitals and institutes. In some countries reference laboratories are available which provide expertise in particular areas. In the UK many of these operate under the aegis of the Public Health Laboratory Service at Colindale. Worldwide, the Centers for Disease Control (CDC) Atlanta, Georgia, USA, offer a service for the diagnosis and therapy of unusual infectious diseases.

Part III

Resistance to antimicrobial agents

11

The problem of resistance

Introduction of clinically effective antimicrobial agents has regularly been followed by the rapid emergence of strains of bacteria resistant to them. This has seriously reduced the therapeutic value of many important antibiotics, and has also been a major stimulus to the pharmaceutical industry in its constant search for newer and more effective antibacterial drugs.

The first systematic observations of acquired drug resistance were made by Paul Ehrlich between 1902 and 1909. Ehrlich was studying the experimental treatment of mice infected with trypanosomes, using azo dyes, organic arsenicals, and triphenylmethane derivatives. He soon detected the emergence of strains of trypanosomes resistant to each of these groups of agents, and recognized that although trypanosomes resistant to, say, one azo dye were also resistant to other similar dyes, resistance was restricted to chemicals of the same general kind, that is, strains which became resistant to azo dyes during treatment with one of these agents remained sensitive to organic arsenicals and to triphenylmethanes.

The introduction of sulphonamides into clinical practice in 1935 marked the beginning not only of the effective treatment of bacterial infections, but also of bacterial drug resistance as a practical clinical problem. Within a very few years sulphonamide-resistant strains of originally sensitive bacteria were common. *Neisseria gonorrhoeae* is an outstanding example. In 1938 almost all strains were sensitive to sulphonamides. By 1948 less than 20 per cent of clinical isolates were still sensitive and sulphonamides were no longer regularly used in the treatment of gonorrhoea. A similar, although less dramatic, increase in sulphonamide resistance was found with haemolytic streptococci, pneumococci, coliform bacilli, and many other bacteria.

Antibiotics brought similar problems. The extent has varied from one antibiotic to another and with different bacteria. For example, when penicillin came into use in 1941, rather less than 1 per cent of all strains of *Staphylococcus aureus* were already resistant to its action. By 1946, under the selective pressure of the use of this antibiotic, the proportion of penicillin-resistant strains found in hospitals had risen to 14 per cent. A year later, 38 per cent were resistant and today resistance is found in more than 90 per cent of all strains of *Staph. aureus*. In contrast, over the same period, an equally important pathogen, *Streptococcus pyogenes*, has remained uniformly sensitive to penicillin.

Why these marked differences occur is not entirely clear. Part of the explanation is undoubtedly the fact that strains of staphylococci capable of destroying penicillin existed before penicillin became available, whereas no such strains of streptococci have been found. However, there is no guarantee that resistance will not emerge in *Str. pyogenes*. For many years *Str. pneumoniae* strains were regarded as invariably highly sensitive to penicillin, but occasional strains of penicillin-resistant pneumococci are now being isolated in many countries, and in some places they have become quite common. The importance of this has been further under-lined by the appearance and rapid spread of strains of *N. gonorrhoeae* capable of destroying penicillin. At one time this species was also univer-sally susceptible to penicillin, although the original degree of exquisite susceptibility did decline somewhat over the years. Aquisition of the necessary genetic information for high-level resistance apparently occurred in gonococci as a rare transfer event (see Chapter 13) and rapid dissemination was ensured by the particularly efficient mode of spread of this organism. So far, the closely related *Neisseria meningitidis* remains penicillin sensitive.

However, the possession of the genetic capacity for resistance in a species does not always explain its prevalence. Although about 90 per cent of all strains of *Staph. aureus* are now penicillin-resistant, the same has not happened to sulphonamide or ampicillin resistance in *Escherichia coli* under ostensibly similar selective pressure. At the present time about 30-40 per cent of *Esch. coli* strains are resistant to sulphonamides or ampicillin—a level of resistance which has increased only slowly over many years.

Since the increasing incidence of resistance is a consequence of selective pressure, it is not surprising that, as a corollary, when an antibiotic has been withdrawn from use in a circumstance where resistance to it has become widespread, there has commonly been a reduction in the number of resistant strains encountered.

DEFINITION OF RESISTANCE

Bacterial isolates have been labelled *sensitive* or *resistant* to antimicrobial agents ever since these agents were brought into use. Some of the criteria on which this categorization has been based have already been discussed in Chapter 7, where the concepts of the minimum inhibitory and minimum bactericidal concentrations (MIC and MBC) of an antibiotic have also been described. The decision whether a given bacterial isolate should be labelled sensitive or resistant ultimately depends on the likelihood that an infection with that organism can be expected to respond to treatment with a given drug. Making this judgement is less straightforward than might be supposed, since there is usually no simple relationship between the MIC (or MBC) of an antibiotic and clinical response. Therapeutic success depends not only on the intrinsic activity of the antimicrobial agent against the infecting organisms, but relies also on the drug reaching the site of infection in sufficient concentration (i.e. its pharmacokinetic behaviour) and the contribution that the host's own defences are able to make towards clearance of the offending microbes.

RESISTANT AND INSENSITIVE BACTERIA

If we look at whole bacterial species, rather than individual isolates, it is immediately apparent that bacterial species are not all intrinsically sensitive to all antibiotics (Table 11.1). Species vary widely in this respect and one would not, for example, attempt to treat a coliform infection with erythromycin or a streptococcal infection with an aminoglycoside, since the organisms are inherently resistant to these drugs. Similarly, *Pseudomonas aeruginosa* and the tubercle bacillus are natively resistant to most of the agents used to treat other, more tractable, infections. Some writers have used the term *insensitive* to describe this situation and have reserved the term *resistant* for variants of otherwise sensitive species that acquire the protection of resistance traits. The distinction is not trivial; the increasing importance of Gram-negative bacilli and the relative decline of the staphylococcus in surgical sepsis in part reflect the ways in which insensitive species may move into ecological niches made available by elimination of sensitive competitors by antibiotic use.

However, in considering the problems caused by resistance of bacteria to the action of antimicrobial drugs it is usually the emergence of resistance in previously sensitive bacterial species that is of concern. At least three different situations, each producing its own problems, can be distinguished:

Pre-existent resistance

Bacterial species in which most strains are sensitive to a newly introduced antimicrobial agent, but a few strains are already resistant at the time the drug is introduced. The classic example is *Staph. aureus* and penicillin as already described.

Table 11.1. Antimicrobial spectrum of some of the most commonly used antibacterial agents

Organism	Penicillins	Cephalosporins	Aminoglycosides	Tetracyclines	Macrolides	Chloramphenicol	Quinolones*	Sulphonamides	Trimethoprim	Metronidazole
Gram-positive bacteria										
Staph. aureus	V	S	(S)	(S)	(S)	S	V	(S)	S	R
Str. pyogenes	S	S	R	(S)	S	S	V	(S)	S	R
Str. faecalis	S	R	R	(S)	S	S	V	(S)	(S)	R
Other streptococci	S	S	R	(S)	S	S	V	(S)	S	R
Clostridium spp.	S	S	R	S	S	S	R	(S)	R	S
Gram-negative bacteria										
Esch. coli	V	V	(S)	(S)	R	(S)	S	(S)	(S)	R
Other enterobacteria	V	V	(S)	(S)	R	(S)	S	(S)	(S)	R
Ps. aeruginosa	V	V	V	R	R	R	S	R	R	R
H. influenzae	V	V	R	(S)	S	S	S	(S)	(S)	R
Neisseria spp.	V	S	R	(S)	S	S	S	(S)	R	R
Bacteroides spp.	R	V	R	(S)	S	S	R	(S)	R	S
Other organisms										
Mycobacteria	R	R	V	R	R	R	S	R	R	R
Chlamydia	R	R	R	S	S	S	S	S	R	R
Mycoplasmas	R	R	R	S	S	S	S	R	R	R
Fungi	R	R	R	R	R	R	R	R	R	R

S = Usually sensitive; R = usually resistant; (S) = considerable strain variation in sensitivity; V = variation among related drugs and/or strains.

* refers to newer fluoroquinolones such as ciprofloxacin, etc., not to nalidixic acid and earlier congeners.

Mutational resistance

Bacterial species which are fundamentally all sensitive to the agent under consideration, but which are able to mutate more or less readily to resistance. With these, in any large population of bacterial cells, a very few individual cells will be resistant at any one time. In the absence of the agent, these cells will have no particular survival advantage, but once the antibiotic is brought into use selective pressures again ensure replacement of sensitive by resistant lines. Many agents, including sulphonamides, fusidic acid, rifampicin, and many different bacterial species have shown this behaviour, in the laboratory and in the body, but it has been a particular problem in the treatment of tuberculosis with antituberculous drugs.

Transmissible resistance

The importance of those two situations has been overshadowed by the realization that genes conferring antibiotic resistance on bacterial cells can fairly readily pass from one bacterial cell to another both in the laboratory and in the wild. In fact, transfer and selection is a much more fruitful source of antibiotic resistance genes in bacterial populations than development of resistance *de novo*. Mechanisms by which resistance transfer takes place will be discussed in Chapter 13. Here it is sufficient to stress that however resistance appears in a hitherto sensitive bacterial cell or bacterial population, resistance will only become widespread under the selective pressures produced by the presence of appropriate antibiotics. Also, the development of resistant cells does not have to happen often or on a large scale. A single mutation or transfer event can, if the appropriate selective pressures are operating, lead to the replacement of a sensitive population by a resistant one. Without selective pressure, antibiotic resistance may be a handicap rather than an asset to a bacterium.

CROSS-RESISTANCE AND MULTIPLE RESISTANCE

These terms are often confused. *Cross-resistance* is resistance to a number of different members of a group of chemically related agents which are affected alike by the same resistance mechanism. For instance, there is almost complete cross-resistance between the different tetracyclines since tetracycline resistance is due to an exclusion mechanism which affects all members of the group. Among other antibiotic groups the situation is more complex. Resistance to aminoglycosides may be mediated by any one of a number of different drug-inactivating enzymes with different substrate specificities and the range of aminoglycosides to which the organism is resistant will depend on which enzyme it elaborates. Cross-resistance can occasionally arise between unrelated antibiotics. For example, a change in the outer membrane structure of Gram-negative bacilli may concomitantly deny access of unrelated compounds to their target sites.

Multiple drug resistance is shown when a bacterium has become successively resistant to several unrelated antibiotics. For example, if a staphylococcus is resistant to penicillin, streptomycin, and tetracycline, the resistances must have arisen independently, since the strain destroys the penicillin with a β-lactamase, has an altered target site for strepto-mycin and excludes the tetracycline from the cell.

It is not always easy to be sure when one is dealing with cross-resistance and when with multiple resistance. Genes conferring resistance to several unrelated agents can become linked together into one plasmid (accessory chromosome; see Chapter 13) and such linked resistances can be trans-ferred together *en bloc* from one bacterial cell to another. Shortly after the discovery of transferable drug resistance a large number of strains of coliform bacilli were isolated which were resistant to both streptomycin and sulphonamides. Strains resistant to either agent alone were uncom-mon, and in transfer experiments both resistances were always transferred together. It was logical to look for a common mechanism of resistance (cross-resistance) and it took some time for genetic analysis to yield formal proof that in these strains the resistance mechanisms were distinct (multiple resistance) although the genes conferring each were firmly linked into one plasmid.

THE CLINICAL PROBLEM OF DRUG RESISTANCE

Drug resistance is a clinical problem because it limits the number of therapeutically useful agents, puts constraints on those which can be used, and sometimes forces the use of more expensive, more toxic or more difficult agents than would otherwise be chosen. It is important not to overstate the resistance problem. Most specific infections, from anthrax to yaws, remain steadfastly susceptible to agents which have been available for many years, while our armoury is constantly being extended by the development of new and useful drugs. In contrast to non-bacterial infection, therapeutic failure today is seldom due to the primary resistance of infecting bacteria to all the drugs available for treatment. Indeed, it is unusual for therapeutic options to be restricted to only one or two anti-bacterial agents because of bacterial resistance, although other factors, e.g. drug allergy, may sometimes further constrain the physician's choice.

Nevertheless, the problem of resistance is a real one. In most situations in which antimicrobials need to be used treatment must be started, and is often completed, without the benefit of laboratory help. This is true both in domiciliary practice, where access to the laboratory may be limited and also in hospitals, where severe infections need treatment urgently and there is often no time to wait for the results of culture (and sensitivity) of the specimens already taken. In these circumstances, knowledge of local resistance trends may be as important as sensitivity testing of individual strains. There are well-defined areas, particularly with hospital-associated infections, in patients with chronic illness or impaired body defences, where the rational choice of antimicrobial agents is increasingly being hampered by the emergence of bacterial drug resistance. In these situations it is of paramount importance that the development and spread of resistance should be contained by sensible prescribing and by the implementation of agreed control of infection policies. Many hospitals now have control of infection teams of doctors (normally microbiologists) and nurses who have a roving commission to investigate outbreaks of infection. Such intervention is crucial in the containment of antibiotic resistance (see Chapter 14).

12

Mechanisms of resistance

In order to inhibit sensitive bacteria antibiotics must be able to enter the cells and attach to and inactivate target sites, which are often enzymes or other proteins. Polymyxins, almost alone among the clinically useful antibacterial agents, exert their effects at the cell surface, disrupting the cell membranes from without in a way which resembles the action of some detergents. Most other antimicrobial agents have to pass through the cell wall and outer membranes, and many are carried into the cell by active transport mechanisms more usually occupied in transporting sugars and other beneficial substances.

Some of the differences in susceptibility of different bacterial species for many antimicrobial compounds can be related to differences in cell wall structures. For example, the cell envelope of Gram-negative bacteria is a more complex structure than the Gram-positive cell wall and offers a relatively greater barrier to many antibiotics including penicillins and macrolides, while polymyxins attack the Gram-negative outer membrane not present in Gram-positive organisms.

It was formerly usual to classify resistant bacteria into two groups: those able to grow in the presence of levels of unchanged antibiotic lethal to sensitive cells and those able to destroy the drugs. In the light of recent discoveries it is more useful to consider four mechanisms by which resistance can arise. These are:

(1) alteration of the target site to reduce or eliminate binding of the drug to the target;

(2) blockage of transport of the agent into the cell;

(3) destruction or inactivation of the antibiotic;

(4) metabolic bypass—providing the cell with a replacement for the metabolic step inhibited by the drug.

ALTERATION OF THE TARGET SITE

This type of resistance has been described for many antibiotics, principally, but not exclusively, those concerned with ribosomal function. They include streptomycin, spectinomycin, erythromycin, fusidic acid, chloramphenicol, nalidixic acid, and rifampicin. Resistance usually arises from the selection of rare, but pre-existent mutants from within an otherwise sensitive bacterial population.

Streptomycin binds to a particular protein, designated S12, in the smaller (30S) ribosomal subunit in bacteria. A single mutational change in one amino acid in this protein can entirely prevent streptomycin binding and endow the bacteria with resistance to very high concentrations of the drug. Curiously, other aminoglycosides which are assumed to have an identical mode of action, such as kanamycin and gentamicin, are unaffected by this change.

A more bizarre mutational change can lead to the phenomenon of streptomycin dependence; the ribosomes misread the messenger RNA in the absence of the drug and the failing is corrected when the drug is supplied.

Changes in the proteins of the larger (50S) ribosomal subunit have occasionally been implicated in resistance to chloramphenicol and erythromycin. Erythromycin resistance in staphylococci and streptococci isolated from human infections is more usually due to methylation of the 23S ribosomal RNA by an inducible plasmid-mediated enzyme. Methylation of the ribosomal RNA also renders the bacteria resistant to other macrolides and to lincomycin and clindamycin. However, since erythromycin is a specific inducer of the enzyme, bacteria harbouring the plasmid are resistant to the other drugs only in the presence of erythromycin. This phenomenon is known as *dissociated resistance*.

Fusidic acid inhibits translocation of the growing polypeptide chain and mutational alteration of the protein involved renders the cell resistant to the action of this antibiotic.

The emergence of this type of resistance during therapy may be a cause of treatment failure with certain drugs, including rifampicin, nalidixic acid (and related compounds), fusidic acid, and the antituberculous drugs streptomycin, cycloserine, and isoniazid. Clinically, such resistance can be overcome by using antibiotic combinations, since the likelihood of double-resistance emerging is small; this strategy has been crucial in antituberculosis therapy.

Alterations in target proteins have also been implicated in the resistance of staphylococci to methicillin and other β-lactam antibiotics (MRSA; see Chapter 1, p. 21) and in penicillin-resistance in pneumococci. In contrast to the other examples cited, mutation to resistance to β-lactam antibiotics is uncommon; such resistance appears to have developed by rare mutational events and to have been subsequently disseminated under considerable antibiotic pressure.

INTERFERENCE WITH DRUG TRANSPORT

Variants exhibiting low levels of resistance to almost any antibiotic can be isolated readily from most bacteria. It is likely that these usually result from changes in permeability of the bacterial cell envelope. Such resistance can increase in a stepwise fashion and is usually accompanied by other phenotypic changes (e.g. slower growth rate, colonial variation on solid media, reduced virulence) which become more marked as the degree of resistance is increased. The clinical significance of this type of resistance has never been properly assessed, but it is likely that the slight shift in penicillin susceptibility of gonococci which has been observed over the years is due to such changes.

In two groups of antimicrobial agents, the aminoglycoside-aminocyclitol group and the tetracyclines, interference with the transport of drugs into the bacterial cell is of proven importance as a cause of resistance in clinical isolates.

Aminoglycosides

Aminoglycoside resistance is of particular interest because alteration in the transport mechanism is secondary to modification of the antibiotic by one or more of a series of enzymes produced by the resistant bacteria.

These aminoglycoside modifying enzymes are plasmid-coded and are classified according to the mechanism of the modification and to the site of modification on the aminoglycoside molecule. Three groups are recognized: aminoglycoside acetylating enzymes (AAC), adenylylating enzymes (AAD), and phosphorylating enzymes (APH) (Table 12.1).

It is apparent from Table 12.1 that a variety of patterns of cross-resistance can be shown by bacteria elaborating different enzymes, but the position is further complicated because there is no constraint which says a bacterium can only produce one such enzyme at any one time. Many clinical isolates are found to produce several enzymes with overlapping substrate ranges, and it becomes very difficult to predict which enzymes are present from consideration of the particular aminoglycosides against which resistance is shown. A more practical consideration is that when such complex patterns of cross-resistance can be shown by any isolate, sensitivity or resistance to one agent cannot be inferred reliably from sensitivity or resistance to another, and tests of sensitivity must be carried out against any of these agents which are considered for use in any clinical situation.

The acetylating enzymes, of which there are three main types, catalyse the transfer of acetate from acetyl coenzyme A to an amino group on the

Table 12.1. Aminoglycoside modifying enzymes

Enzyme	Typical substrates	Bacterial distribution	
		Gram-positive	Gram-negative
Acetyl transferases			
AAC (3)	Gentamicin, tobramycin	−	+
AAC (2′)	Gentamicin, tobramycin	−	+
AAC (6′)	Amikacin, tobramycin	+	+
Phosphotransferases			
APH (6)	Streptomycin	−	+
APH (3′)	Neomycin, kanamycin	+	+
APH (2″)	Gentamicin	+	−
APH (3″)	Streptomycin	+	+
Adenylyl transferases			
AAD (6)	Streptomycin	+	−
AAD (4′) (4″)	Amikacin, tobramycin	+	−
AAD (2″)	Gentamicin, tobramycin	−	+
AAD (3″) (9)	Streptomycin, spectinomycin	−	+
AAD (9)	Spectinomycin	+	−

The figure in brackets indicates the site of modification according to the internationally accepted numbering system for the various parts of the complex aminoglycoside molecule (see Fig. 12.1).

antibiotic molecule. These aminoglycoside acetyltransferases only attack deoxystreptamine-containing aminoglycosides and are, therefore, without effect on streptomycin or spectinomycin.

Aminoglycoside adenylyltransferases utilize ATP or other nucleotides as substrates and attach the nucleotide to exposed hydroxyl groups. Phosphotransferases also attack hydroxyl groups; these enzymes endow the cell with an altogether higher level of resistance than that conferred by acetylating or adenylylating enzymes.

Figure 12.1 shows the structure of kanamycin A, a typical amino-glycoside, and indicates the various sites at which modification can take place. Clearly, the presence or absence of available amino or hydroxyl groupings will affect the susceptibility to various enzymes and this is the basis of variability within the aminoglycoside group. The steric configuration of the groupings is also important: the semi-synthetic aminoglycoside, amikacin, for example, is structurally closely related to kanamycin A, but is much less susceptible to enzymic modification because of a hydroxy-

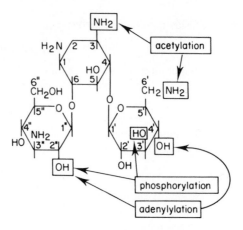

Fig. 12.1. Structure of kanamycin A, showing the sites at which enzymic modification can occur.

aminobutyric acid side-chain which fundamentally alters the steric configuration of the molecule.

When the aminoglycoside-modifying enzymes were first described they were considered to be examples of drug inactivation analogous to that found with chloramphenicol and many β-lactam antibiotics (see below). However, when resistance involves inactivation of the drug there is usually need for a critical concentration of bacteria elaborating the drug-destroying enzyme before resistance is apparent. A single cell is practically defenceless and MIC determinations show very marked inoculum effects. Furthermore, inactivated drug can be found in the culture medium. Bacteria resistant to aminoglycosides do not show much inoculum effect, the bacteria grow readily in high concentrations of the unmodified drug (indeed, it is difficult to show any altered antibiotic in the medium at all), modified and unmodified antibiotic appears to be absent from inside the cells and the ribosomes, when extracted, remain sensitive to the effect of the drug.

It appears likely that, in Gram-negative organisms at least, the amino-glycoside modifying enzymes are confined to the region of the cell envelope between the inner and outer membranes, the periplasmic space. They must be closely associated with the inner cytoplasmic membrane where they are accessible to acetyl coenzyme A and ATP. It seems that in this position the enzymes need to modify only small amounts of the antibiotics and that a few molecules of modified drug interfere with active transport mechanisms and block all further transport of drug into the cell.

Tetracyclines

The tetracyclines also inhibit protein synthesis. The uptake of tetracyclines into normal cells involves active transport which utilizes energy and which results in accumulation of drug inside the cell.

Plasmid-mediated resistance to tetracycline is common in both Gram-positive and Gram-negative bacteria. There is generally complete cross-resistance in that a strain resistant to one tetracycline is resistant to all the others, although exceptions may be found with minocycline. The precise mechanism of resistance is not completely understood, but is associated with decreased accumulation of the drug. There is no evidence of enzymic inactivation of tetracycline by clinical isolates of bacteria, or for alteration of the ribosomal target. However, some strains of bacteria produce a cytoplasmic protein which appears to have the function of protecting ribosomes from tetracycline attack.

Tetracycline resistance is generally inducible and full expression of resistance is obtained only after cells have been exposed to sub-inhibitory concentrations of the drug. In these circumstances, a new protein is synthesized which prevents accumulation of the drug within the resistant cell, apparently by the development of an active efflux system, so that drug entering the cell is simultaneously removed and never reaches an inhibitory level.

DRUG-DESTROYING MECHANISMS

These are probably the most important resistance mechanisms to be met in clinical practice, since they include the common modes of resistance to penicillins and cephalosporins, the most widely used of all therapeutic agents.

β-Lactam antibiotics

There are many different agents in this group (see Chapter 1) and a correspondingly large number of β-lactamases which catalyse hydrolysis of the β-lactam ring to form an inactive product (Fig. 12.2). In addition, varying levels of β-lactamase production as well as differences in cell envelope permeability play a considerable part in determining the differential susceptibilities of bacteria to this group of antibiotics.

The situation with β-lactamases is even more complicated than that found with aminoglycoside modifying enzymes. To begin with, all bacteria appear to contain enzymes capable of hydrolysing β-lactam antibiotics.

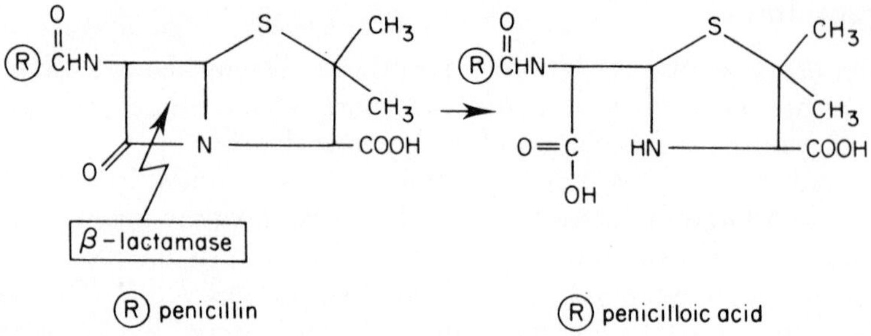

Fig. 12.2. β-Lactamase hydrolysis of penicillins to form the corresponding penicilloic acid which is antibacterially inactive. Cephalosporins may be attacked in a similar fashion, but the resultant cephalosporoic acid is usually unstable and disintegrates into smaller fragments.

Indeed, it has been suggested that the normal function and evolutionary origin of β-lactamases is to break a β-lactam structure that is a transitory intermediate in cell wall synthesis. These inherent enzymes are chromosomally mediated and are normally closely bound to the cell membrane. By and large, they attack cephalosporins more readily than penicillins and act relatively slowly. It is doubtful whether they have any clinical significance in most cases, but in certain organisms, notably *Enterobacter* spp. and *Pseudomonas aeruginosa*, derepression of chromosomal enzymes has been associated with treatment failures even with ostensibly 'β-lactamase-stable' cephalosporins.

From a clinical point of view most interest centres on a number of *plasmid-mediated enzymes* which are the major cause of bacterial resistance to penicillins and cephalosporins in clinical isolates. The picture is, however, complicated by the intrusion of *transposons* into the story. These genetic elements (described more fully in Chapter 13) allow translocation of genes between plasmid and chromosome so that the distinction between plasmid-mediated and chromosomally determined enzymes becomes blurred.

So far as plasmid-mediated β-lactamases are concerned, the simplest situation exists in Gram-positive cocci. The β-lactamases of *Staphylococcus aureus* are inducible exoenzymes conforming to a few biochemical types which are probably closely related. In streptococci, clinically significant β-lactamases are usually absent and these bacteria have consequently remained, with very few exceptions, steadfastly susceptible to benzylpenicillin. In contrast, the plasmid-mediated β-lactamases of Gram-negative bacilli embrace a wide variety of types which are physico-chemically quite distinct.

A number of different characters have been used to distinguish the different enzymes. Among these, substrate profile, isoelectric focusing and the action of enzyme inhibitors are probably the most useful.

Substrate profile refers to the hydrolytic activity of a β-lactamase preparation against a number of β-lactam substrates. Profiles are often expressed as ratios related to a value of 100 for a chosen reference substrate, often benzylpenicillin. *Analytical isoelectric focusing* is a method of separation in which proteins align themselves as sharp bands at their isoelectric points (pI) on a pH gradient produced electrophoretically in thin layers of polyacrylamide gel. The position of the β-lactamase in the gel can be detected using a special cephalosporin substrate, nitrocefin, which changes colour from orange to red when hydrolysed by the enzyme. The technique is sufficiently sensitive to detect β-lactamases in strains previously thought to lack any such enzyme and two or more β-lactamases produced by a single strain can be clearly separated. Inhibitors of enzyme activity include the isoxazolylpenicillins, the sulphydryl inhibitor, *p*-chloromercuribenzoate and β-lactam compounds such as clavulanic acid which, though exhibiting poor antibacterial activity themselves, are potent inhibitors of certain types of β-lactamases.

Using these and other techniques, it has been possible to distinguish about 30 different plasmid-mediated β-lactamases in Gram-negative bacteria and probably more remain to be characterized. The most widely distributed is that designated TEM-1 which is specified by a number of different plasmids and the genetic information for which resides on a transposon (see Chapter 13). This no doubt explains its wide distribution which includes many enterobacteria, *Ps. aeruginosa*, *Haemophilus influenzae*, and *Neisseria gonorrhoeae*. Other types of β-lactamase that are fairly widespread in Gram-negative bacilli include: TEM-2 (which has similar properties to TEM-1); SHV-1 (common in *Klebsiella* spp.); a group of enzymes which are capable of hydrolysing methicillin and isoxazolylpenicillins, OXA-1, -2, and -3; and several β-lactamases originally thought to be confined to species of *Pseudomonas* (PSE-1, -2, -3, and -4, which hydrolyse carbenicillin at least as fast as benzylpenicillin.

The clinical importance of staphylococcal β-lactamase has been much reduced by the availability of cloxacillin and other β-lactamase-stable penicillins. Some progress has also been made towards the control of resistance due to β-lactamases of Gram-negative organisms by the introduction of β-lactamase-stable cephalosporins and novel β-lactam compounds including the β-lactamase inhibitor, clavulanic acid. Plasmid-mediated β-lactamases have, however, been described that inactivate some, or all, available β-lactam agents. Fortunately, strains that elaborate such enzymes are presently uncommon.

Chloramphenicol

Resistance to chloramphenicol is another example of drug inactivation; in both Gram-positive and Gram-negative bacteria it is usually the result of acetylation of chloramphenicol by enzymes known as chloramphenicol acetyltransferases. The acetylated drug is unable to bind to the bacterial ribosome and is therefore without effect on protein synthesis. Many different chloramphenicol acetyltransferases have been described. Some appear to be genus- and species-specific; others, usually plasmid-associated, have achieved a wider distribution. This variety is a little surprising. Chloramphenicol has been less widely used than many other antibiotics of equivalent potency because of its rare but very serious toxic side-effects, and the selective pressures on the evolution of diverse inactivating enzymes must have been correspondingly less than with, for example, the penicillins.

METABOLIC BYPASS

Until recently, most of the common and relatively well-understood resistance mechanisms could be accommodated in one or other of the three groups already described. A fourth mechanism has now been shown to account for plasmid-mediated resistance, in some strains of bacteria, to sulphonamides and to trimethoprim.

Sulphonamides exert their bacteristatic effect by competitive inhibition of dihydropteroate synthetase, an enzyme which links para-aminobenzoate and pteridine to form dihydropteroate. Several strains of sulphonamide-resistant Gram-negative bacilli have been shown to contain a plasmid-determined dihydropteroate synthetase which is unaffected by sulphonamide, in addition to the normal chromosomally determined sulphonamide-sensitive enzyme. The plasmid-coded enzyme allows continued functioning of the threatened metabolic pathway, and growth in the presence of the drug.

Trimethoprim blocks a later step in the same metabolic pathway by inhibiting the dihydrofolate reductases of susceptible bacteria. Resistant strains have now been shown to synthesize a new, trimethoprim-insensitive and plasmid-coded dihydrofolate reductase, of which there are several types, as well as the normal drug-sensitive chromosomal enzyme. These are the only two known examples in which a plasmid provides the cell with an entirely new and drug-resistant enzyme that can substitute for the sensitive chromosomal enzyme which is also present unaltered in the cell.

The antimicrobial agents mentioned in this discussion of resistance mechanisms have been examples only, intended to illustrate the diversity of ways in which microbes can become resistant to the drugs we deploy against them. Study of mechanisms of drug resistance has led to the development of modified antimicrobial agents designed to circumvent the resistances. Attempts to limit the emergence and spread of drug resistance among bacterial species has demanded not only a knowledge of the mechanisms themselves, but also a description of the genetic bases by which these mechanisms are determined.

13

The genetics of resistance

The resistance of micro-organisms to antimicrobial agents nearly always has its basis in genetic changes in the microbial cell. In only a few instances have phenotypic changes been implicated in resistance. Consequently, a fundamental knowledge of microbial genetics is essential to the understanding of the development and spread of resistance to antimicrobial drugs. Since little is known about resistance determinants in non-bacterial micro-organisms, only bacterial genetics will be considered.

The heritable information which specifies a bacterial cell and which passes into daughter cells at cell division is carried in bacteria, as in all living cells, as an ordered sequence of nucleotide pairs along molecules of DNA. The processes of transcription of this information into messenger RNA and its translation into functioning proteins by ribosomes are also similar in bacteria and in other cells.

Each bacterial cell has one single chromosome, in the form of a single closed circular loop of DNA. In *Escherichia coli*, the organism most intensively studied, this single DNA molecule is about 1.4 mm in length and carries about four million nucleotide pairs.

The chromosome is coiled and looped into a compact bundle in the cytoplasm of the cell, but is not separated from the cytoplasm by any form of nuclear membrane. Transcription and translation of messenger RNA can therefore proceed simultaneously.

PLASMIDS

The bacterial chromosome carries all the genes necessary for the survival and replication of the bacterial cell under normal circumstances. Many, perhaps all, bacteria also carry additional molecules of DNA known as plasmids, which are separate from and replicate independently of the bacterial chromosome. Plasmids can contain genes which confer many properties on the cells which carry them. In general, these are properties which are not essential for the survival of the cell under normal circumstances, but which offer the cells a survival advantage in unusual or adverse conditions. Plasmids and chromosomes are all independent replicons, that is, they carry the genes necessary for their own replication inside the bacterial cell. The chromosome can be distinguished as the replicon which also carries the genetic information essential for cell division.

Several properties may be conferred on bacteria by plasmids.

1. Fertility—the ability to conjugate with and transfer genetic information into other bacteria. This property is only regularly exhibited by Gram-negative bacilli.

2. Resistance to many antibiotics.

3. Ability to produce bacteriocines—proteins inhibitory to other closely related bacteria which may be ecological competitors.

4. Toxin production.

5. Immunity to some bacteriophages.

6. Ability to use unusual sugars and other substrates as foods.

Plasmid compatibility

Many different kinds of plasmid have been described. They differ in size, DNA base composition, in the nucleotide sequences that can be recognized after treatment with endonucleases (endonuclease fingerprinting), and in compatibility behaviour. Compatible plasmids can coexist in the same host cell, while incompatible plasmids cannot, and so tend to displace one another. Plasmids are currently classified principally by incompatibility studies; there are at least 20 *incompatibility (Inc) groups* within the plasmids found in Enterobacteriaceae, and similar incompatibility schemes are used to subdivide staphylococcal plasmids and those found in strains of *Pseudomonas*. Most bacterial cells carrying plasmids will at any time only contain a single copy, or at most a very small number of copies, of any given plasmid. Plasmid replication is under stringent control by the host cell. The mechanism of incompatibility and the plasmid genes involved are not well understood, but appear to be related functionally to those involved in control of the replication and control of copy number. Although only a few genes are directly involved, plasmids belonging to the same Inc group often share greater DNA homology and show other similarities of structure and function than plasmids of different Inc groups.

The distinction between chromosomal genes and plasmid genes is not absolute. Where appropriate regions of DNA homology exist classical recombination can occur, both between different plasmids and between plasmid and chromosome. This process is relatively uncommon in bacteria because there are few regions of sequence homology between bacterial chromosome and bacterial plasmid which can be exploited. Another and more important mechanism by which genes pass from one bacterial replicon to another is the process known as transposition.

TRANSPOSONS

Transposition depends on the existence of a specific genetic element, the transposon, in which individual resistance genes or groups of genes are bounded by DNA sequences called *inverted repeats*—a sequence of bases at one end of the transposon which also appears, but in reverse order, at the other end. Often these inverted repeats are relatively short, of the order of 40 base pairs, but some much longer ones are known. One tetracycline resistance transposon, for example, is flanked by inverted repeats involving about a thousand nucleotide pairs each. It is likely that these DNA sequences provide highly specific recognition sites for certain restriction endonucleases which can catalyse the movement of transposons from one replicon to another without the need for regions of sequence homology.

Isolated DNA sequences analogous to the terminal sequences of transposons can also move from one replicon to another, or be inserted in any region of any molecule of DNA. These *insertion sequences* contain no known genes unrelated to insertion function, but in principle at least, two similar insertion sequences in appropriate orientation could bracket any assemblage of genes and convert it into a transposon. Thus, theoretically, all replicons are accessible to transposition and all genes transposable. This is of crucial evolutionary importance because it explains how genes of appropriate function accumulate on single replicons under the impact of selection pressure. Transposons play a vital part in plasmid evolution, as plasmids do in the evolution of bacteria themselves.

This process of evolution is still going on. We do not know the origin of any resistance gene carried by a plasmid, or even the origin of plasmids themselves, but we have been able to observe the steady increase in numbers of resistant bacterial strains which have followed the introduction of successive chemotherapeutic agents into clinical use. It has become increasingly apparent that transposition of resistance determinants has been involved in the spread of these determinants. For example, the transposon responsible for TEM-type β-lactamase production in enteric bacteria has been able to cross generic boundaries to cause penicillin-resistance in gonococci and ampicillin-resistance in *Haemophilus influenzae* by insertion into plasmids indigenous to these organisms.

BACTERIOPHAGES

Bacteriophages (phages) are viruses which infect bacteria. Most phages will attack only a relatively small number of strains of related bacteria; they have a narrow and specific host range.

Virulent phages inevitably destroy by lysis any bacteria they infect, with the release of numerous new phage particles from each lysed cell.

Temperate phages may lyse or may lysogenize sensitive bacterial cells. In lysogeny the infected phage chromosome becomes integrated into the chromosome of the host cell, where it is known as a *prophage*. The prophage coexists stably with the bacterium, replicating in step with and as part of the bacterial chromosome. Once in every few thousand cell divisions a prophage is released from the chromosome and enters the lytic cycle, with destruction of its host cell and release of a number of new phage particles into the medium.

TRANSFER OF GENETIC INFORMATION

There are three ways in which genetic information can be transferred from one bacterial cell into another: transformation, transduction, and conjugation.

Transformation. In this, lysis of a bacterial cell releases naked DNA into the surrounding medium, and some of this DNA can be taken up by neighbouring intact cells. This process has been much studied in the laboratory, but has not yet convincingly been shown to be responsible for gene transfer under natural conditions.

Transduction. This involves incorporation of bacterial DNA, either chromosomal or from a plasmid, into a bacteriophage particle which then acts as a vector carrying the incorporated genes into a susceptible bacterial cell.

Conjugation. In this, bacterial cells adhere to one another and DNA passes unidirectionally, from one cell termed the donor into the other, the recipient. Ability to conjugate depends on carriage of an appropriate plasmid by the donor cell.

The existence of these mechanisms means that bacteria do not necessarily have to evolve solely by a stepwise process of mutation and selection. They can also take in and express blocks of information which have been evolved and redefined elsewhere. They can, for example, acquire a plasmid-carrying gene conferring resistance to several different antibiotics and as a result, over a very short period of time following the receipt of such a plasmid by one cell, the organisms in a given niche may change from a state in which they are all sensitive to one in which it is difficult to find an antibiotic that is effective against them all. Of course, the ability to transfer genes in this way does not do away with the need to evolve them in the first place, but once they have evolved it does ensure their eventual widespread dissemination under appropriate selection pressures.

GENOTYPIC RESISTANCE

Genes conferring resistance to antibiotics may be part of the bacterial chromosome or may be carried on a plasmid, or very rarely as part of a phage genome. The distribution of these genes between the chromosome and plasmids reflects to some extent the biochemical mechanisms involved. For example, resistance which results from mutational alteration of a target protein will be chromosomal in location, and will map in the structural gene for the relevant protein. Streptomycin resistance arising from alteration in the ribosomal protein S12 is a chromosomal character behaving in this way. Rifampicin inhibits bacteria by binding to RNA polymerase. The gene for this enzyme is chromosomal and rifampicin resistance maps in the same locus as the polymerase gene. Mutational changes in permeability of the bacterial cell envelope also map on the bacterial chromosome.

When resistance genes code for entirely new enzymes, such as the aminoglycoside modifying enzymes, β-lactamases, or trimethoprim-resistant dihydrofolate reductases, the genes for these enzymes are commonly carried on plasmids. The evolutionary sequence leading to this kind of resistance must be complex. The evolution of any new enzyme is likely to be a very long process, and antibiotic-inactivating proteins are likely to have arisen only infrequently. Their location on plasmids only reflects the fact that transfer and selection must be a more fruitful source of antibiotic-resistance genes in bacterial populations than evolution of the genes afresh by each bacterial strain for itself.

Chromosomal and plasmid-mediated types of resistance may be equally important in the management of the individual patient. However, the plasmid-mediated variety has achieved greater notoriety because of the spectacular fashion in which bacteria may acquire resistance to a number of different agents through a single genetic event. Certainly, it has been plasmid-mediated resistance which has caused most problems in the highly selective environment of the hospital. Nevertheless, mutational resistance originating in the bacterial chromosome is a common cause of treatment failure with some compounds (see Chapter 12) and it is presumably a further example of Murphy's General Law of Cussedness which decrees that antibacterial agents for which resistance is not known to be transferred by plasmids (e.g. nalidixic acid and rifampicin) generally suffer from mutational resistance problems instead.

PHENOTYPIC RESISTANCE

So far as is known, phenotypic resistance to antibacterial agents is rare, although it is not always possible to be sure that phenotypic changes brought about in the microenvironment of a lesion do not contribute to insusceptibility of bacteria in the infected host. In the laboratory, phenotypic changes affecting antibiotic susceptibility can sometimes be induced; for example the outer envelope of *Pseudomonas aeruginosa* can be altered by varying the conditions of growth and this affects susceptibility to polymyxins.

The failure of penicillins and cephalosporins to kill *persisters* (those cells in a bacterial population that survive exposure to concentrations of β-lactam agents lethal to the rest of the culture) is not due to a genetic change, since the resistance is not heritable. In this case it is probable that the 'resistant' bacteria are caught in a particular metabolic state at the time of first encounter with the drug.

A peculiar form of phenotypic resistance is observed with mecillinam, a β-lactam antibiotic which, unusually among β-lactam agents, does not affect bacterial division. Mecillinam induces surface changes in susceptible Gram-negative bacilli which generally lead to death of the bacteria by osmotic rupture once sufficient damage has been incurred. However, those bacteria in the population which happen to have a low internal osmolality survive and, since mecillinam lacks the ability to prevent growth and division, such bacteria continue to grow in a morphologically altered form. On withdrawal of the drug the bacteria resume their normal bacillary shape and in due course revert to the same mixed susceptibility as the original parent culture.

SELECTION

Antibiotic resistance genes and the plasmids which carry them existed before the introduction of antibiotics into human medicine. The biochemical and genetic mechanisms involved are complex and intricate. One aspect of this problem, however, has become established beyond doubt: the emergence and survival of resistant bacterial populations is a result of the selective pressure resulting from the widespread use of antibiotics. Resistant cells survive in a given niche at the expense of sensitive companions of the same or other species. However, drug resistance, whether chromosomal or plasmid-mediated, does carry metabolic penalties for the cell. If the selective pressures of antibiotic use are withdrawn there is a gradual reversion to sensitivity. Individual cells lose their plasmids and a predominantly sensitive population replaces the resistant one. The implications of this situation for our efforts to control and limit the spread of bacterial drug resistance are discussed in the next chapter.

14

Control of the spread of resistance

Almost fifty years of antibiotic use have brought great benefits to man and animals. Foremost among these is the saving of life and relief of suffering by therapeutic use. Many of the killing bacterial diseases which were rife in the early years of this century have been successfully combated almost to the point of extinction. Pneumococcal pneumonia, tuberculosis, and streptococcal puerperal sepsis, for example, used to kill many hundreds of young people every year. Deaths from these and many other bacterial diseases are now rare in young adults, at least in developed countries.

Substantial amounts of antibiotics are also used outside normal therapy for prophylaxis and growth promotion in animal husbandry, and even in plant protection in agriculture. These wider uses have been very important in controlling losses due to infectious disease and in helping to meet growing demands for animal protein for food. The economic benefits of antibiotic use in food production are very large indeed.

Compared with most other drugs of similar potency, antibiotics are remarkably safe, and they are also remarkably effective. This has inevitably led to liberal, even lavish use, and concern has frequently been expressed that excessive and inappropriate use of these agents is the chief cause of the widespread emergence of resistant organisms. In August 1981, a statement was issued in the names of some 150 scientists from 25 countries, all of whom were actively engaged in plasmid research, drawing attention yet again to the worldwide public health problem of the spread and persistence of drug-resistant organisms. This, the latest in a long series of similar calls for regulation to 'curb the unnecessary use and flagrant misuse' of these drugs, clearly identifies the following practices as largely contributing to the present situation: dispensing antibiotics without prescription; using clinically useful antibiotics as growth promoters in animal feeds and on agricultural crops; prescribing antibiotics for ailments for which they are ineffective; misleading consumers by advertising antibiotics as 'wonder drugs', especially in areas where dispensing is not regulated; and using different labelling and advertising to sell the same product in different parts of the world. It goes on to point out that consumers, prescribers, dispensers, manufacturers, and government regulatory agencies are all involved in different ways, and all need to be convinced of the vital importance of prudent antibiotic use.

DISPENSING ANTIBIOTICS WITHOUT PRESCRIPTION

This is not a problem in the UK, where successively the Pharmacy and Medicines Act 1941, the Therapeutic Substances Act 1956, and the Medicines Act 1968, have provided a comprehensive system of control of the manufacture, importation, distribution, sale, supply, and description of medicinal products, including antibiotics, for human and veterinary use. The intention of this legislation is to give Health and Agriculture Ministers powers that will ensure eventually that all medicinal products offered for sale or supply in the UK are adequately tested for safety, quality, and efficacy, and enable the appropriate ministers to prohibit the retail sale or supply of any medicinal products except on the prescription of a doctor, dentist or veterinarian. The ministers are advised by several authoritative advisory committees and individuals, and exercise their powers by a comprehensive, but flexible system of product licences. There is, however, at present no body charged with advising specifically on antibiotics and antibiotic use, and there probably should be. There is no other example in therapeutics in which local misuse of an effective agent brings about a general diminution in its effectiveness.

Similar legislation covers much of Continental Europe and the USA. Indeed, the American Federal Authorities have been more often criticized for delaying the introduction or restricting the use of valuable agents than for permitting their indiscriminate use. In the rich, developed world the sale and distribution of antibiotics is fairly tightly controlled, while the poorer, but numerically much larger developing world provides a much bigger market in which the sale and distribution of these agents is largely unrestricted.

Paradoxically, the use of antibiotics in the Third World needs extending, not restricting, if standards of health are to be brought up to those of the developed world. However, this clearly needs to be done in a controlled manner, and over-the-counter availability of antimicrobial drugs is, in the end, going to create more problems than it solves. It was no great surprise that chloramphenicol-resistant typhoid bacilli first emerged in South America and penicillin-resistant gonococci in South East Asia.

The onus of providing the necessary legislation obviously rests with individual governments, with the advice and support of international agencies such as the World Health Organization. However, pharmaceutical houses also have a part to play in ensuring that their products are advertised and marketed to the same standards as those they apply in the countries of the developed world.

THE USE OF ANTIBIOTICS IN AGRICULTURE

Antibiotic-resistant bacterial populations arise in man and animals by the use of antibiotics, whether for therapy, prophylaxis, or growth promotion. The non-therapeutic uses have come under heavy criticism by those concerned in the treatment of infectious disease, despite their immense value in animal husbandry and food production. The extent to which resistant organisms in animals contribute to resistant organisms in man, as opposed to the re-cycling by cross-infection of resistant organisms within the human population, is still much in dispute. Accurate figures on antibiotic usage are hard to come by. In 1967 it was estimated that in the UK about 240 tons of antibiotics were used in human medicines, while 168 tons were sold for veterinary and agricultural purposes. No doubt those figures have increased considerably in the intervening years, but reliable up-to-date figures are not available. If the usage is re-calculated by taking into account the numbers of people and animals involved, current overall use of antibiotics in human medicine is at least four times that in animal husbandry and veterinary medicine per unit of body weight. It is likely therefore that human medical use contributes more to the human resistant bacterial population than non-human use does. Nevertheless, it has conclusively been shown that resistant bacteria, both commensal and pathogenic, arising in animal populations do pass to human hosts, and this source of human resistant bacteria cannot be ignored.

The Netherthorpe and Swann Reports

The use of certain antibiotics in restricted amounts to promote growth in livestock, mainly pigs and poultry, has been common practice in the USA since 1949 and in the UK since 1953. In the following few years, in the UK, concern about dangers resulting from the reported increase in resistant bacteria was voiced by both medical and veterinary professions, and led to the setting up by the Agricultural and Medical Research Councils in 1960 of a joint ARC/MRC Committee under the chairmanship of Lord Netherthorpe 'to examine the possible consequences of the feeding of antibiotics to farm animals and to consider whether this use constitutes any danger to human or animal health'. This Committee reported in 1962 that it saw no reason to discontinue the use of permitted feed additives (in the UK, penicillin, chlortetracycline, and oxytetracycline) and indeed recommended extending this use to young calves, although this was never implemented.

The growing incidence of resistance among salmonellas, especially in those associated with calf disorders, and the recognition of plasmid-borne transferable resistance led to a review of the evidence by the Netherthorpe Committee. In 1966 this Committee agreed that there was cause for concern and recommended the setting up of a new Committee with wider terms of reference to examine the whole problem of the use of antibiotics in veterinary medicine and animal husbandry. This recommendation led to the setting up, in 1968, of the Joint Committee on the use of Antibiotics in Animal Husbandry and Veterinary Medicine under the Chairmanship of Professor M. M. Swann, and the production, a year later, of what has come to be known as 'The Swann Report'. This report presented a masterly analysis of the whole problem of the use of antibiotics in animal husbandry, and made several recommendations, the most important of which were:

1. That permission to supply and use drugs without prescription in animal feeds should be restricted to antibiotics shown to be effective for this purpose, of little or no use for treatment of infections in man or animals and not likely to cause resistance against therapeutic agents in general use;

2. That therapeutic antibiotics should be available for use in animals only when prescribed by a member of the veterinary profession;

3. That a single committee should be set up with overall responsibility for the whole field of use of antibiotics and related substances whether in man, animals, food preservation, or for other purposes.

There were more than 20 further cogent recommendations, some of which have been implemented.

After 'Swann'

In the decade following the publication of the Swann report efforts were made to follow its recommendations and intentions, but with limited success. The direct commercial use of therapeutically useful antibiotics as growth promoters has been stopped, but the boundaries between feed additives for growth promotion, antibiotics prescribed prophylactically, and antibiotics used to treat sick animals have always been blurred. There has been widespread diversion of antibiotics properly prescribed for treatment of sick animals into feeds intended for well beasts. Antibiotics have been readily available without prescription on an illicit but extensive black market. Also, it has always been unclear how much the use of feed additives contributed to the resistance problem, compared with the equally extensive therapeutic use of antibiotics in veterinary medicine, which there was little attempt to control.

The Swann Report recommended the establishment of a single body charged with responsibility for overseeing the whole use of antibiotics in human and veterinary medicine and agriculture. A committee was set up; not the powerful committee with wide-ranging powers and extensive resources envisaged by the Swann Committee, but a joint advisory sub-committee of the Committee on the Safety of Medicines and the Veterinary Products Committee. This soon found its activities largely restricted to advising on the suitability of new products for use as feed additives; it was seldom consulted on problems of the use of antimicrobials in human medicine and when, at a politically inconvenient moment, it asked for increased powers and resources to fulfil its commitments under 'Swann', it was disbanded.

PRESCRIBING ANTIBIOTICS FOR INADEQUATE INDICATIONS

Whatever the contribution to the human load of resistant bacteria from the use of antibiotics in agriculture, the major selective pressure leading to human resistant organisms is the use of antibiotics in human medicine. A lot of antibiotic is used. It is often claimed that there is a lot of antibiotic misused, but this is difficult to substantiate. Practitioners most willing to open their prescribing habits to scrutiny are likely to be those whose prescribing is least likely to be at fault. Also, the ready exhibition of antibiotics for trivial bacterial or viral infections may prevent much of that infection developing beyond the trivial.

Nevertheless, the constant introduction of new agents makes it more and more difficult to be confident of choosing the right agent on every occasion, or even to be sure when an antibiotic is appropriate at all. Antibiotics which were once appropriate become less so as organisms become resistant to them, but may continue to be used because of their past effectiveness and despite increasing therapeutic failures.

ANTIBIOTIC POLICIES

The principles which should be followed in deciding which antibiotic, if any, to use in a given situation are discussed in Chapter 15. However, even in relatively straightforward clinical situations there are often several equally effective agents which might be used. Choice may then be determined by a locally agreed antibiotic policy. An antibiotic policy has been defined as a set of rules which superimposes on the definition of rational treatment several other considerations which lead to a decision as to which agent, among the several that are rational, should actually be used.

It is widely agreed that an antibiotic policy is desirable, at least in hospital practice. There is less unanimity about the form it should take and less again about how policy should be enforced. The basic principles of restriction—reserving some antibiotics for use only under very stringently defined circumstances; rotation of agents at intervals so that as resistance to one builds up another is brought into use to replace it; diversification, or the simultaneous use of a wide range of antibiotics, thus lessening the selective pressure of each; and use in combination, because the chance of emergence of resistance simultaneously to two agents is vastly lower than the chance of emergence of resistance to any one alone— have resulted in a bewildering array of suggestions for appropriate antibiotic use. This is not surprising, because local circumstances vary so much that any given policy is likely to be relevant only in a limited area and for a limited time. As local patterns of resistance alter, so antibiotic policies have to be adjusted to take account of changed circumstances.

Enforcement can occasionally be difficult. Individuals often resent the implication that another, the microbiologist or the Control of Infection Officer, or worse, a committee, should claim to know better than the involved clinician what should best be prescribed for a patient. Here, good communication within a hospital or a health area is of the utmost importance. Clinicians need to be aware of the local and changing patterns of infection and resistance in their locality. Information about new agents, together with some assessment of their likely place in the antimicrobial armoury; concerned discussion with colleagues to reach a consensus on appropriate usage; involvement of pharmacist and microbiologist as well as clinician; all these need to be brought into play. It may be that the most important function of an antibiotic policy is to provide a vehicle for ensuring that regular discussion between all concerned in antibiotic prescribing does take place.

CONTROL OF THE EMERGENCE OF RESISTANCE

All antibiotic use creates selective pressures which lead to the emergence of resistant bacterial strains. Antibiotics are vital to the practice of modern medicine; we cannot abandon them, or even unreasonably restrict their use. Resistant bacteria will continue to appear, and to cause problems in the treatment of the infections they cause. Surveillance of the use of antibiotics—locally, nationally, and internationally—coupled with the monitoring of emerging patterns of bacterial resistance will help influence prescribing practice and the development of meaningful antibiotic policies, as long as the people collecting the information ensure that it is passed on to the people who use the drugs. Few will recklessly continue to prescribe antibiotics to which local resistance is common, as long as they know that local resistance *is* common. The dissemination of accurate, up-to-date information is vital in establishing the appropriate use of antibiotics which, together with control of infection measures, is the best protection against the unrestricted spread of drug resistance.

Part IV

General principles of usage of antimicrobial agents

15

General principles of the treatment of infection

Antimicrobial agents are among the most commonly prescribed drugs. Their use has had a major impact on the control of most bacterial infections in man and to a lesser, although constantly increasing degree, is affecting the outcome of many fungal, viral, protozoal, and helminthic infections. The principles governing the use of antimicrobial agents to be discussed in this chapter apply specifically to the management of bacterial infections although the overall approach is similar when selecting treatment for other microbial diseases.

Antimicrobial therapy demands an initial *clinical evaluation* of the nature and extent of the infective process and knowledge of the likely causative pathogen(s). This assessment should be supported, whenever practical, by laboratory investigation aimed at establishing the microbial aetiology and, whenever possible, should provide evidence for its susceptibility to antimicrobial agents appropriate for the treatment of such an infection. The choice of drug, its dose route, and frequency of administration are also dependent upon an appreciation of the pharmacological and pharmacokinetic features of a particular agent. Furthermore, the range and predictability of adverse reactions of a particular compound should also be kept in mind.

CLINICAL ASSESSMENT

The clinical evaluation should define the anatomical location and severity of the infective process. The history and examination frequently determines such infective states as meningitis, arthritis, pneumonia, and cellulitis. Although such diseases may be caused by a wide variety of organisms, the range of pathogens is usually limited, and the pattern of susceptibility reasonably predictable. This, therefore, permits a rational selection of chemotherapy in the initial management of such infections.

The anatomical location is not only critical from the point of view of the most likely pathogen and the most suitable choice of drug, but also determines the *route of administration*. Superficial infections of the skin, such as impetigo which is caused by *Streptococcus pyogenes*, or infection of the mucous membranes such as oral or vaginal candidiasis, caused by *Candida albicans*, respond well to topical application. However, if infection is caused by the microbial invasion of tissues or the bloodstream, adequate tissue concentrations of a drug may only be achieved by either intramuscular or intravenous administration.

Other clues as to the nature of the infection are gleaned from epidemiological considerations such as the age, sex, and occupation of the patient. In tropical countries diseases such as malaria, amoebiasis, and typhoid fever are prime suspects in the investigation of fever and diarrhoea, and local knowledge about the prevalence of diseases like filariasis, schistosomiasis, and trypanosomiasis, which are circumscribed in distribution, may be used to advantage. In countries free from these diseases as indigenous problems, a history of overseas travel should alert the physician to consider exotic infections.

Pre-existing medical problems may predispose to infection; such conditions include valvular heart disease, underlying malignant disease, or the presence of prosthetic devices such as artificial hip joints, heart valves, or intravascular cannulae.

Under some circumstances the invading pathogen may be part of the host's normal flora. The normal host defences may be breached in a variety of ways. For example, the skin or mucous membranes, which are normally a most effective barrier against infection, may permit access of pathogenic organisms to the deeper tissues when traumatized by either a surgical incision or by accident. Similarly, burns can denude large areas of the body with subsequent infection by bacteria, notably *Pseudomonas aeruginosa*, *Staphylococcus aureus*, and *Str. pyogenes* which may be acquired from contact with patients or staff within the hospital.

The circulating and tissue phagocytes provide an important defence against infection. Therefore, an absolute or relative deficiency of circulating polymorphonuclear leucocytes is commonly associated with recurrent, frequently serious, infection. In patients with acute leukaemia, cytotoxic chemotherapy often depresses the circulating leucocytes to low levels for several days or weeks. Such patients are extremely vulnerable to serious episodes of infection, particularly Gram-negative bacillary bacteraemia, which carries a high mortality if untreated.

LABORATORY ASSESSMENT

Few infective conditions present such a typical picture that both a definitive clinical and microbiological diagnosis can be made without recourse to the laboratory. Therefore, whenever possible, a clinical diagnosis should be supported by laboratory confirmation. Such confirmation makes both the diagnosis and the management, in particular the selection of antimicrobial chemotherapy, more certain and allows for a more sound assessment of the likely prognosis. However, when infection is obvious or strongly suspected on clinical grounds therapy should be instituted as soon as appropriate specimens for laboratory investigation have been taken. In some cases (e.g. pneumococcal meningitis) the patient's chances of survival are directly related to the promptitude with which therapy is started. Furthermore, laboratory reports are not always contributory and several days may be lost trying to establish a microbiological diagnosis, during which time the patient's condition may deteriorate.

Serological tests which demonstrate antibody against specific microbial antigens are of no value in the initial selection of chemotherapy for the treatment of acute infective conditions. However, such testing is much more important in the diagnosis of more persistent infections such as syphilis, brucellosis, and Q fever.

SELECTION OF ANTIMICROBIAL CHEMOTHERAPY

In-vitro susceptibility

In-vitro testing of drugs provides indirect evidence of the likely clinical response of a particular pathogen to a specific drug or drugs. Confirmation of clinical efficacy can only be determined *in vivo* and, hence, the importance of clinical evaluation of all new antimicrobial agents. Controlled experimental evidence gained from the treatment of artificial infections in animals provides only indirect evidence of the likely clinical efficacy. Occasionally in-vitro evidence of activity is not borne out by in-vivo evidence of success. For example, *Salmonella typhi* is susceptible *in vitro* to many drugs active against Gram-negative bacilli, including gentamicin; however, typhoid fever only responds clinically to a limited range of drugs, including chloramphenicol, amoxycillin, or co-trimoxazole. This may in part be due to the intracellular location of *S. typhi* in this disease.

Bacteristatic or bactericidal agents

Antibacterial agents are often separated into either bactericidal or bacteristatic agents according to their ability to kill or inhibit bacterial growth. This separation is somewhat artificial since some bacteristatic drugs may be bactericidal either in higher concentrations or against different bacterial species. Bacteristatic agents must rely on host defences, in particular the phagocytic cells, to finally eliminate the infection, since if the drug is withdrawn bacteria have the opportunity to recover. Under most circumstances the choice between a cidal or a static agent is not critical. This is not the case in the treatment of infective endocarditis. Here bacteria are protected against phagocytic activity within the vegetations present on the deformed or prosthetic heart valve or adjacent endocardium. Under these circumstances it is important to use a bactericidal drug or combination of drugs which penetrate the vegetations and thus eradicate the infection. Similarly, patients with neutropenia from cytotoxic chemotherapy or other causes of bone marrow aplasia are extremely vulnerable to infection. Bacteristatic drugs are inappropriate in these cases and bactericidal agents should be selected.

Pharmacokinetic factors

The aim of chemotherapy is to eliminate an infection as rapidly as possible. To achieve this a sufficient concentration of the drug or drugs selected must reach the site of infection. The choice of agent is, therefore, as much dependent upon the pharmacological and pharmacokinetic features of the drug, which determine absorption, distribution, metabolism, and excretion, as upon its antimicrobial properties. These aspects are discussed in more detail in Chapter 16.

In general, drugs are administered either topically, by mouth, or by intravenous or intramuscular injection. Oral absorption is most erratic. Drugs must first negotiate the acid condition of the stomach before being absorbed, usually from the proximal small bowel. This occurs most readily when the stomach is empty and it is generally advised that they be swallowed approximately 30 minutes before a meal.

Absorption can be increased by protecting a drug from acid inactivation by a coating (so-called *enteric coating*) which subsequently breaks down once the tablet is beyond the stomach. Alternatively, the drug may be modified chemically to produce a more acid-stable formulation (see Chapter 16). For most minor infections, including skin, soft-tissue, respiratory tract, and lower urinary tract infection, oral therapy is appropriate.

In contrast to oral administration, intravenous administration avoids the vagaries of gastrointestinal absorption, and achieves rapid therapeutic blood and tissue concentrations. Intramuscular administration requires absorption through the tissue capillaries and is generally rapid except in conditions of cardiovascular collapse and shock when tissue perfusion is impaired. Relatively avascular sites such as the aqueous, and in particular the vitreous humour of the eye, are difficult sites in which to achieve adequate concentrations of drugs. In contrast, the presence of inflammation increases the permeability of many natural barriers such as the meninges and in this situation allows higher concentrations of certain drugs such as the penicillins, to be achieved within the CSF. Other drugs, most notably chloramphenicol, are little influenced by such inflammatory changes.

CHOICE OF ANTIMICROBIAL REGIMENS

Drug dosing

There are no universally applicable guidelines for drug dosing, which is frequently determined by factors such as tolerability and toxicity as well as the activity of a particular drug against a particular infecting organism. Some agents, most notably the penicillins, have such a wide margin of safety that enormous doses are frequently prescribed. Only in a few cases (e.g. treatment of *Ps. aeruginosa* infection with ticarcillin) does such antimicrobial overkill have a microbiologically rational basis. In an attempt to provide a rule of thumb in devising dosage schedules some authors suggest that blood levels four or eight times higher than the MIC of the organism are most likely to produce therapeutic tissue concentrations. However, for practical purposes dosages are based on experience gained from the treatment of a wide variety of infections. Guidance can sometimes be obtained by back titration of the patient's serum against his own infecting organism (see Chapter 8). A serum bactericidal titre of 8 or more obtained about 1 hour after a parenteral dose usually indicates adequate therapy in patients with infective endocarditis.

Length of therapy

Treatment should continue until all micro-organisms are eliminated from the tissues or the infection has been sufficiently controlled for the normal host defences to eradicate it. This end-point is in general determined by clinical observation and evidence of the resolution of the inflammatory process such as the return of body temperature and white cell count to normal.

Many infections come under control within a few days and 7 days' treatment is often sufficient. Uncomplicated urinary tract infections usually respond very rapidly to chemotherapy. Selection of the least dose compatible with complete resolution is desirable (see Chapter 21). In contrast, patients with pulmonary tuberculosis require 6-9 months' treatment with isoniazid and rifampicin if relapse is to be prevented (see Chapter 26). Furthermore, 10 days' penicillin treatment is necessary to eradicate *Str. pyogenes* from the throat in patients with streptococcal tonsillitis although symptomatic improvement occurs within a few days. There is no universally 'correct' duration of chemotherapy and each problem should be judged on its merits based on the clinical response to treatment.

ADVERSE REACTIONS

Antimicrobial agents, like all other therapeutic substances, have the potential to produce adverse reactions. These vary widely in their nature, frequency, and severity. Many such reactions are minor and short-lived such as gastrointestinal intolerance, but others may be serious, life-threatening, and occasionally fatal. Drug reactions are unfortunately a common cause of prolonged hospitalization or may precipitate hospitalization. Drug reactions may be predictable and dose-dependent, for example nephrotoxicity associated with the use of the antifungal agent, amphotericin B. However, many adverse reactions are unpredictable. The subject is discussed more fully in Chapter 18.

COMBINED THERAPY

In general, single drug therapy of established infections is preferred whenever possible. Such an approach is known to be effective and reduces the risks of adverse reactions and drug interactions that may accompany multiple-drug prescribing. Nonetheless, there are a few situations where combined chemotherapy has definite advantages over single drug therapy.

Initial therapy

In the management of acute and potentially life-threatening infections combined chemotherapy covering all likely pathogens is often used until the cause of the infection is established. It is common practice to combine flucloxacillin with an aminoglycoside, such as tobramycin or gentamicin, in the initial treatment of serious infections. However, should there be evidence that the infection has arisen in association with mucosal surfaces, such as the gut or female genital tract, then metronidazole or clindamycin is frequently added to meet the possibility of a mixed anaerobic and aerobic bacterial infection. Once a definitive diagnosis is established it is important to adjust the therapeutic regimen to one that is most appropriate.

Synergy

Under some circumstances combined chemotherapy is selected for its known synergic effect on a pathogenic organism. This increased ability to inhibit or kill the pathogen may speed resolution or reduce the risk of relapse when treating difficult infections. One of the commonest requirements for synergic therapy is the treatment of infective endocarditis caused by enterococci and occasionally by oral streptococci. The combination of two bactericidal drugs, penicillin and gentamicin (or streptomycin), is synergic both *in vitro* and *in vivo*, and is associated with a more favourable response to treatment than is single drug therapy.

Antagonism

On the other hand, some drugs may have an opposite effect and be antagonistic. For example, shortly after penicillin and tetracycline became available, it was shown that the two drugs together produced a worse clinical result in the treatment of pneumococcal meningitis than did either drug alone. In this situation a bacteristatic agent (tetracycline) prevents penicillin from achieving its bactericidal effect on the cell wall, which is dependent on bacterial growth.

Prevention of drug resistance

It is uncommon for the bacterium causative of an infection to become resistant during treatment, although some drugs including streptomycin, rifampicin, fusidic acid, and nalidixic acid are well known for encouraging the rapid emergence of resistant bacteria. These bacteria do not develop resistance in response to treatment, but small numbers of pre-existent resistant mutants proliferate when the sensitive population is suppressed.

In the treatment of tuberculosis combined chemotherapy is used specifically to prevent the emergence of resistant minority strains present in the tuberculous tissues.

COST

Antimicrobial drugs vary widely in their cost. In general, generic drugs cost less than proprietary preparations, whilst well established, widely used agents tend to be less expensive. Injectable preparations are usually more expensive than oral preparations, and syrups and drops are usually more expensive than tablets and capsules.

The use of very high dosage also escalates the cost. Sometimes this is unavoidable as in the treatment of *Ps. aeruginosa* infections with large doses of expensive antipseudomonal agents, but in general, high dosage should not be used without justification.

Among the most expensive antimicrobial agents are the parenteral cephalosporins, all antipseudomonal compounds, intravenous metronidazole, and most antiviral agents. It is, therefore, apparent that whenever drugs which are both equally effective and tolerated are available then it is reasonable to select the cheaper agent. This is a most important consideration in some developing countries where drug costs can account for 20 per cent of an already meagre health budget. *The British National Formulary* provides a useful approximate guide to the cost of drugs for doctors in the UK.

FAILURE OF ANTIMICROBIAL CHEMOTHERAPY

Patients with established infection may fail to respond to antimicrobial therapy for a variety of reasons.

Choice of therapy

Firstly, the choice of drug may be inappropriate for the infecting strain. This stresses the need to establish a microbiological diagnosis whenever possible so that the in-vitro susceptibility of the pathogen can be confirmed. On the other hand, some infections are caused by intracellular pathogens as in brucellosis, chlamydial disease, and typhoid fever. For treatment to be successful sufficient antibiotic must penetrate the cell and this limits the number of agents which are clinically effective. Failure may also result if the drug is inadequately concentrated at the site of the infection; this may occur if the dose is insufficient or the route inappropriate. By changing to the parenteral route or increasing the dose, therapeutic success may follow.

The route of excretion also requires consideration. For instance, in renal failure, drugs normally excreted by the kidneys may fail to reach therapeutic concentrations in the urine so that treatment of a urinary tract infection with drugs such as nalidixic acid and nitrofurantoin may be unsuccessful.

Presence of necrotic material

Treatment may also fail because of the presence of necrotic material, an eschar or abscess. Antibiotic penetration of such avascular material is poor so that surgical debridement of necrotic material or drainage of pus should be carried out early. Antibiotic treatment under these circumstances is an adjunct to such surgical management.

Presence of foreign material

Another related cause of failure of antimicrobial chemotherapy is infection that occurs in association with foreign material such as bladder catheters, intravascular devices, hip prostheses, or inanimate foreign material which gains access to the tissues following surgical or traumatic injuries. Under these circumstances total eradication of infection is rarely achieved until the foreign material is removed.

It can therefore be appreciated that if antimicrobial therapy is to be successful these drugs can only exhibit their full power as 'magic bullets' if used intelligently and if full recognition is paid to the need to individualize each course of treatment to both the patient and the pathogen.

16

Pharmacokinetics

Ehrlich's 'magic bullet' notion of chemotherapy foresaw substances which given as a single dose would localize in the sites of infection and destroy the organisms there. Despite the enormous advances made in the development of antimicrobial compounds none exhibits the remarkable properties Ehrlich visualized. The great majority of antimicrobial agents are widely distributed in the body in response to forces which have nothing to do with infection and may, in fact, result in the concentrations of the agent being least where they are most needed.

Amongst the many properties that must be exhibited by therapeutically useful chemotherapeutic agents, ability to achieve effective concentrations, and act in the complex environment of the infected lesion is essential. Most antibiotics are given systemically and the delivery and maintenance of effective concentrations at the site of infection is determined by the concentrations achieved in the blood which are in turn determined by the absorption, metabolism and excretion of the drug and by the way in which the blood-borne drug is distributed to the tissues. From serial measurements of the concentration of the agent in the serum, it is possible to calculate its rates of absorption and elimination and the volume in which the drug is distributed. The *volume of distribution* indicates whether it is largely confined within the vascular compartment or spreads out into the extracellular fluid—the site of most infections—or penetrates into cells where some organisms, for example, mycobacteria and brucella, multiply. The rates of transfer, volume of distribution and other key properties can be given numerical values which provide succinct and quantitative statements of the drug *pharmacokinetics*. For the present purpose, we will avoid such quantitative analyses and examine in turn each stage of movement of the drug from absorption to delivery to the infected site and the factors which influence each of the stages.

ABSORPTION

Many antibiotics do not produce adequate plasma levels when given by mouth and are available only as injectable preparations. However, the convenience of the oral route, particularly in domiciliary practice, means that whenever injectable agents with new and desirable properties are introduced demands quickly follow for oral preparations with similar properties. Where this can be achieved it sometimes requires the preparation of relatively complex derivatives of the original compound. This, combined with the need for properties such as stability in solution, means that pharmaceutical preparations (injections, capsules, and syrup) can contain different derivatives of the drug, sometimes with distinct properties.

Oral administration

The degree to which compounds are absorbed when given orally differs greatly. Chloramphenicol is so well absorbed that there is no place for an injectable form of the drug except in patients who cannot swallow. However, the taste of the drug is so bitter that it cannot be given as a syrup and a tasteless derivative is used for such preparations which is microbiologically inactive until it is hydrolysed in the gut with the liberation into the plasma of the active form. This device of producing derivatives which have some particularly desirable property but act in the body by the liberation of the parent drug is widely used and such preparations are collectively called *pro-drugs*.

Antibiotic esters

Erythromycin is irregularly absorbed and often produces low plasma concentrations. A number of derivatives have been produced in an attempt to overcome this difficulty, of which one is of general interest. This is erythromycin estolate which, like the tasteless chloramphenicol preparation, is microbiologically inactive, but it is much more lipid-soluble than the parent drug and much better absorbed in the small intestine where non-specific esterases liberate the active erythromycin into the portal vein. Esterification as the means of improving the oral absorption of drugs has been fairly widely used, other examples being the esters of ampicillin, such as pivampicillin, talampicillin, and bacampicillin.

Generally, esters show another important benefit in addition to the increased plasma levels obtained: their absorption, unlike that of the parent compound, is much less affected by the presence of food in the stomach. If patients are to take drugs at regular intervals it is very difficult to separate the administration of all doses from meal times and it is a great advantage in a drug to be unaffected by such influences. A further advantage of such pro-drugs is that they are not degraded by the bowel flora and, being microbiologically inactive, the fraction of the drug which is not absorbed does not disturb the gut flora as active antibiotics do—an effect believed to lessen the chances of post-antibiotic diarrhoea and of superinfection with resistant organisms.

Such esters, therefore, exhibit many advantages but they also show one potential disadvantage. If de-esterification in the gut wall is incomplete the intact ester can reach the liver and give rise to toxic effects. Fortunately, most of these compounds are rapidly degraded in the gut wall or the plasma.

Interference with absorption

The original tetracycline, chlortetracycline, is a good example of an oral agent which is not well absorbed. Moreover, its naturally low absorption is further depressed by the simultaneous administration of food, especially substances such as milk which contain high concentrations of calcium or magnesium with which tetracycline forms stable insoluble chelates. The unabsorbed compound is active and it powerfully disturbs the bowel flora, an effect that most probably underlies the bowel disturbances which commonly follow its use.

Attempts in the past to minimize these side-effects by the administration of the drug with milk or alkali secured any desirable effect they may have had in limiting the gastrointestinal symptoms at the expense of drug absorption.

Parenteral administration

Intravenous injection

The most direct way of ensuring adequate concentrations of antibiotic in the blood is by intravenous injection. The highest instantaneous concentrations are, of course, achieved by a single rapid intravenous injection, but any benefit of this may be offset by rapid excretion and many agents are given by infusion over 15 or 20 minutes. It was common practice at one time to add antibiotics to drip infusions, but this should be avoided since the slow rate of administration results in low plasma levels of the drug. Sometimes degradation of the drug in solution can occur over the prolonged period of administration, particularly if administration is combined with glucose. Certain combinations of penicillin and aminoglycosides mutually inactivate the other when mixed in intravenous solutions.

Rapid injection or infusion results in high concentration of the drug which then declines rapidly as the drug diffuses into the extracellular space and into the cells if they are accessible to it. There follows a period during which the concentration of drug falls more or less rapidly depending on the rate at which it is metabolized and excreted (fig. 16.1).

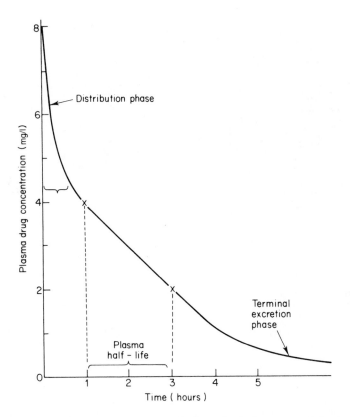

Fig. 16.1. Decline in plasma concentration of a drug after its intravenous injection. Three phases may be distinguished: an initial rapid fall as the drug is distributed from the plasma; a less rapid fall during the main period of excretion and metabolism; and a terminal slow decline representing, for example, the release of the drug from binding sites.

Plasma half-life

This phase principally determines the period for which active drug is available to the body and the time required for the concentration of drug in the plasma to fall by half is called the plasma half-life. Half-lives of different antibiotics vary considerably. That of benzylpenicillin, for example, is only 30 minutes while that of fusidic acid is 12 hours. Drug distributed into the tissues may be bound there and this drug as distinct from that in the plasma may be relatively slowly remobilized and excreted. When a drug behaves in this way the rate of elimination may be very slow and the *terminal half-life* very much greater than that during the main excretory phase.

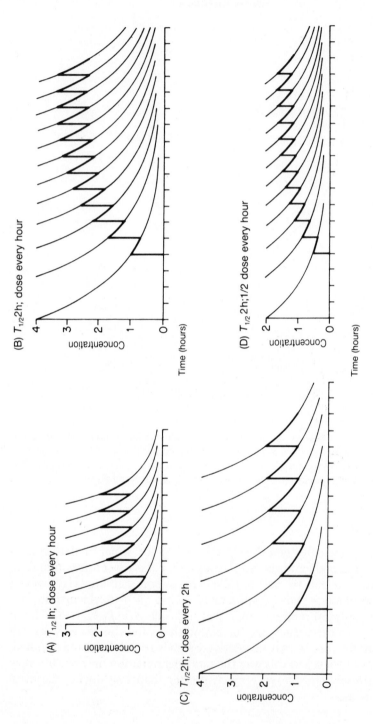

Fig. 16.2. Steady-state concentrations on various drug regimens. The thin lines are identical curves showing the fall in concentration of an agent with the half-life ($T_{1/2}$) shown. The thick lines indicate the concentrations achieved by doses given at intervals of (A, C) every half-life, and (B, D) twice every half-life. In each case a steady-state is eventually reached, but the time taken to achieve steady-state and the concentration achieved depends on the conditions. [From F. O'Grady (1971). *British Medical Bulletin* **27**, 142–7.]

(A) $T_{1/2}$1h; dose every hour

(B) $T_{1/2}$2h; dose every hour

(C) $T_{1/2}$2h; dose every 2h

(D) $T_{1/2}$ 2h;1/2 dose every hour

Time (hours)

Time (hours)

Concentration

Concentration

Concentration

Concentration

Drug accumulation

If large doses are given or the half-life of the drug is such that complete elimination has not occurred before the next dose is administered, the concentration of drug in the plasma will progressively rise. The excretion phase being logarithmic, the rate of elimination rises as the concentration of drug rises and eventually excretion proceeds as fast as the accumulation and the drug reaches a steady state (Fig. 16.2). This may be beneficial in achieving a constant exposure of the infecting organism to the agent, but it can also be hazardous if the agent is toxic. The possibility of accumulation and its consequences must be considered when an agent with a long half-life is administered or the patient's capacity to eliminate the agent is known or thought likely to be impaired.

Intramuscular injection

When all the drug is delivered directly into the plasma within a short time the plasma half-life is determined solely by the rate of elimination. When, however, uptake into the plasma is much slower then the persistence of the drug will depend not only on the rate at which it is eliminated but on the rate at which it is added. Absorption from intramuscular sites is usually rapid, but special *depot preparations* of drugs such as procaine penicillin have been developed which possess the special property that absorption from the injection site is slow and the plasma level correspondingly maintained for prolonged periods (Fig. 16.3).

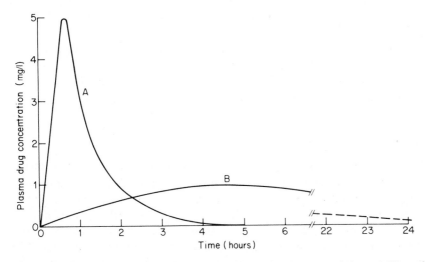

Fig. 16.3. Blood levels produced by the intramuscular administration of (A) penicillin and (B) procaine penicillin.

DISTRIBUTION

Protein binding

Compounds in the plasma generally reach the tissues by diffusion, but in some cases there is active secretion as in the saliva, the bile, and the urine. The most important factor affecting the diffusibility of compounds is the degree to which they are bound to plasma proteins, mostly albumin. With some drugs, such as cloxacillin, cephazolin, or fusidic acid more than 90 per cent of the drug is bound and is antibacterially inactive. Only the diffusible fraction of the drug reaches the tissues and only this fraction exerts any antimicrobial effect. As the unbound fraction diffuses away, more of the plasma-bound drug dissociates and the equilibrium between the bound and the free compound is maintained. Because of this effect in limiting the activity and diffusibility of the drug, high degrees of protein binding have been held to be highly disadvantageous.

Two things have to be considered. The first is that in order to be therapeutically effective adequate concentrations of free drug must be achieved at the site of infection. That this occurs with the compounds mentioned, despite high degrees of protein-binding, is clear from their clinical efficacy. The second is that bound drug will go wherever the protein goes and that includes the protein poured into the infected sites with inflammatory exudate. To this extent, protein-bound drug may be looked upon as a pro-drug with the valuable property of 'homing' on to sites of inflammation. Once in the site, as far as we know, the concentration of free and active drug is still defined by the equilibrium between free and bound drug.

Another important aspect of protein-binding is that protein-bound drugs compete with one another for binding sites and it is possible to displace one with another of higher affinity resulting in increased concentration and possibly toxic effects of the liberated drug (see Chapter 18).

Access to infected sites

The main interest in the distribution of antimicrobial agents is in the area which is least easy to study: the concentration achieved at the infected target. Some sites can be sampled directly, important examples being the CSF or the bronchial secretions. The difficulty is that there is good reason to believe that the distribution of drug in the subarachnoid space and the bronchi is far from homogeneous and a comprehensive view of the behaviour of the drug in these sites is hard to obtain. What is clear is that the specialized tissues which separate the drug circulating in the plasma from these important sites of infection are normally relatively impermeable to all but a few agents. Chloramphenicol and trimethoprim appear to be unusually well distributed agents, lipid solubility apparently playing a part in this, and it is claimed that the more lipid soluble tetracycline derivatives develop higher concentrations in the bronchi than the traditional compounds. Most drugs enter the infected site in high concentrations through increased permeability of the vascular endothelium produced by the inflammatory process, and an important result of this is that as the drug exerts its antibacterial effect and the inflammation subsides the drug is progressively excluded again. In some cases of meningitis treated with high doses of ampicillin, for example, exclusion of the drug as inflammation subsides leads to the recrudescence of infection and in such patients retreatment with chloramphenicol is generally undertaken.

Tissue concentrations

One of the most difficult areas to study is soft tissue infection. Some tissues, such as the tonsil, are accessible and by homogenizing samples of such tissue in suitable fluid the 'tissue' concentration of antibiotics can be measured. If this concentration is significantly higher than that of the blood the result is helpful although there is no way of knowing where precisely the drug is located in anatomical terms. If the concentration is less than that of the blood the measurements may represent simply the effect of diluting the drug present in the tissue blood vessels. This cannot be overcome by washing out the blood since this may artificially lower the tissue concentration by encouraging the diffusion of agent.

Attempts have been made to assess the antibiotic concentrations present in extracellular fluid by the creation of artificial collections of fluid which can be repeatedly sampled. In animals this has been achieved by implanting a sterile mesh into the subcutaneous tissue or muscle and allowing it to fill with fluid. In man, blisters can be raised on the skin by application of vesiculating agents such as cantharides. In general, the concentration of antibacterial agents rises and falls very much less rapidly in these spaces than it does in the plasma, and the concentrations achieved are considerably lower and more prolonged.

How closely these spaces mimic normal tissue spaces and particularly infected tissue spaces in their composition and fluid dynamics is much disputed. Interesting differences can be demonstrated in them in the behaviour of various antibacterial agents, but these do not appear to be decidedly reflected in differences of therapeutic performance. Perhaps the most extraordinary feature of antimicrobial pharmacokinetics is that after 50 years of intensive clinical and experimental study we still do not know what shape of drug concentration/time curve is needed at the site of infection to secure optimum antimicrobial effects. If we knew that we would be one step (of several required) towards more rationally based dosage schedules.

METABOLISM

As with other drugs, many antibiotics are modified in the body and the resulting metabolites are important for two reasons. Firstly, they are generally, though not always, significantly less active microbiologically than the parent compound. Some metabolites show not only different degrees, but different spectra of activity. The generation of such compounds can considerably complicate the microbiological assay of the drug and progress in our understanding of the more complicated situations of this kind has relied heavily on the development of such new methods of drug measurement as high pressure liquid chromatography. The second importance of the metabolites is that they may differ from the parent compounds in toxicity. If they are relatively inactive and more toxic, conventional microbiological assay of the drug will give very poor guidance as to the toxic hazard.

EXCRETION

The major route of excretion for most antibiotics is via the urine in which very high concentrations are often achieved. Many drugs excreted in this way are active against the organisms commonly responsible for urinary tract infections and the high concentrations of drug achieved in the urine play an important part in their elimination. Excretion is by glomerular filtration or tubular secretion and sometimes both. Metabolites and parent drugs may be differently handled by the kidney. In pyelonephritis the principal site of infection is in the peritubular areas of the medulla. Drug can reach this space by diffusion from the plasma, but high concentrations can also be achieved by non-ionic back diffusion. As the urine becomes more concentrated in its progress towards the collecting tubule, the concentration of drug rises markedly so that a large concentration gradient develops between the tubular contents and the interstitial space where organisms multiply. Only un-ionized species of drug are diffusible and the delivery of high tubular concentrations of the drug into the infected site therefore depends on the proportion of drug un-ionized at the pH of the tubular content. Nitrofurantoin, for example, is a weak acid and in renal tubular contents the greater part of the drug will be un-ionized and free to diffuse into the peritubular space.

Tubular secretion

The principal compounds excreted in the urine by active tubular secretion are the penicillins and cephalosporins. This process is so effective as to clear the blood of most of the drug during its passage through the kidney and plays a major part in determining the short half-life of compounds excreted in this way. The period for which inhibitory levels of rapidly excreted agents like benzylpenicillin are present in the blood can be increased by increasing the frequency of administration or by reducing the drug's tubular secretion. Many agents share the tubular route of excretion and will compete with one another for the active transport mechanism. The oral uricosuric agent, probenecid, is a potent competitor in this regard and its administration in conjunction with penicillins reduces the renal excretion and prolongs the plasma half-life.

The other important effect of active tubular transfer of β-lactam antibiotics is that it can alter the susceptibility of the cells to damage by aminoglycosides. Gentamicin has been the most extensively studied in this regard and the principal evidence of interaction is with cephaloridine. Simultaneous, or even shortly sequential administration of these two agents is likely to cause more impairment of renal function than is seen when either drug is given alone.

Some cells in other parts of the body behave in a way analogous to those of the proximal renal tubules. It is, for example, believed that active secretion of drug by cells of the choroid plexus is responsible for the rapid fall in CSF penicillin levels that is seen in patients treated for bacterial meningitis. It is likely that the same mechanism is responsible for the fall in CSF glucose levels at one time attributed to metabolism of the sugar by the infecting bacteria. Probenecid can be used to slow the active secretion of penicillin via the choroid plexus, but little use has been made of this method of conserving drug levels in the CSF.

Biliary excretion and enterohepatic recirculation

Some antibiotics, for example erythromycin, produce very low and sometimes undetectable levels in the urine. Many such compounds are excreted in the bile and metabolites produced in the liver may also, of course, follow this route. When the bile enters the small intestine a significant proportion of the drug may be reabsorbed and if so, enterohepatic recirculation can play a significant part in maintaining plasma levels of the drug. It is difficult in practice to obtain entirely satisfactory figures for the concentration of drugs excreted in the bile because of its relative inaccessibility. Most studies are done on bile obtained at operation or postoperatively when the bile is draining through a T-tube and conditions are plainly not physiological. Nevertheless, there is good evidence that some agents, including rifampicin and several cephalo-sporins, achieve unusually high biliary levels and are, therefore, valuable in the treatment of bacterial cholangitis. Naturally, this route of excretion ceases when the biliary tract is obstructed or hepatic function deranged and it is plainly prudent to avoid administering to such patients agents for which this is a major route of elimination.

17

Prescribing in the young and the elderly

Attitudes to prescribing in children and infants have changed considerably in recent years. Children are no longer considered to be small adults for the purposes of prescribing and the former practice of scaling down an adult dose on a weight basis is no longer readily accepted. Such scaling down may result in either subtherapeutic or toxic concentrations. This applies to the prescribing of all drugs in childhood, not only antimicrobial agents.

Similarly, the risks of adverse reactions increase significantly in elderly patients, especially if excretory organ (liver and kidney) function is impaired by age or disease. The evaluation of new drugs in paediatric and elderly patients presents particular problems and is extremely important, since the pharmacological handling of the drugs and their unwanted effects may differ considerably in infants, young children, the elderly, and normal adults.

PAEDIATRIC PRESCRIBING

In childhood, dosages may be adjusted according to surface area, which is more closely related to the ability to metabolize drugs. However, in infancy and early childhood the surface area is larger, relative to the older child and adult, hence there is a risk of overdosing when using such a system.

To arrive at a safe yet effective concentration of a drug is not without difficulties. In fact, for many drugs the dosages have not been accurately determined, even in adults. In the case of new antimicrobial agents pharmacological and toxicological investigations are more commonly carried out in an adult population so that information in children and particularly in infants and neonates may be extremely limited. Lack of such information may preclude the widespread use of a potentially useful agent in childhood.

To derive the necessary information in childhood requires painstaking and careful observations. Such observations are made in a population of sick children since volunteer pharmacokinetic information is not available from healthy children for ethical reasons.

Furthermore, owing to physiological differences, information in the preterm or low-birthweight infant cannot necessarily be applied to heavier or full-term infants. Very few centres have the expertise to carry out such exacting work.

Age-related epidemiology of infections

When selecting antimicrobial therapy knowledge of age-related infections is important in the initial management, before laboratory information is available. Many infections, although not entirely peculiar to infancy and childhood, are nonetheless much more frequently encountered in this age group. For example, the classical viral exanthems of rubella, measles, and varicella are primarily diseases of childhood. Such age-related infections reflect the ready transmission of these agents and the susceptibility of a relatively non-immune population. Similarly certain bacterial infections are much more common in this age group.

Neonatal meningitis is primarily caused by *Escherichia coli* and group B streptococci, whilst in the pre-school child *Haemophilus influenzae* is more frequent. Meningococcal infection is primarily a disease of childhood.

Upper respiratory tract infections are extremely common in childhood. Many are caused by viruses. For example, middle ear infection frequently follows such infection and is often complicated by secondary bacterial infections with *Streptococcus pneumoniae* or *H. influenzae*.

Cystic fibrosis is largely a disease of children although careful management is seeing an increasing number of sufferers survive into early adult life. A major complication of this disease is recurrent lower respiratory tract infection in which *Staphylococcus aureus* and *Pseudomonas aeruginosa* predominate. Such infections are difficult to control and it is often impossible to eliminate *Ps. aeruginosa* completely from the sputum.

Physiological considerations

Paediatric prescribing recognizes the fact that overall growth and development including organ function and metabolic pathways are frequently undergoing change in childhood. This is particularly so of the neonatal period in which both chronological age, gestational age and body weight are important considerations. Drug dosages, therefore, vary for many agents, including antimicrobials, on account of the state of flux of various physiological functions.

In particular, variation in renal maturity, differences in the extracellular fluid volume and the immaturity of various enzyme systems are important determinants of drug disposition, excretion, and metabolism. In the neonate, renal function is less efficient than in the older child since glomerular and tubular function continue to mature. The creatinine clearance rate in the neonate is approximately one third that of the older child. However, most infants achieve an adult glomerular filtration rate by the age of 12 months. Hence, drugs whose excretion is via the kidneys may require dose modification if toxicity is to be avoided.

Kidney function is not the only consideration. The volume of distribution of antibiotics is important in determining the dose that is necessary to achieve a therapeutic concentration at the site of infection. Agents which are essentially confined to the extracellular fluid, such as the aminoglycosides, will thus be affected by the proportionally larger extracellular fluid volume in the neonate compared with the older child and the adult. The extracellular fluid volume is approximately one-third of the body weight in the newborn.

To consider a specific example, the guidelines for prescribing aminoglycosides such as kanamycin and gentamicin vary according to body weight, and also the chronological age, against which the drugs' half-lives vary inversely. This takes into consideration both the immaturity of renal function, the different clearance rates and the differing volumes of distribution. For example, the mean half-life of kanamycin in neonates of 2000 g weight or less, and younger than 3 days of age, is approximately 8-9 hours; whereas for larger birthweight infants or those older than 9 days the half-life decreases to 3-4 hours. In like manner, a dose of gentamicin of 2.5 mg/kg every 12 hours is appropriate for infants up to 7 days old, whilst infants older than 7 days require the drug every 8 hours if therapeutic concentrations are to be achieved.

Metabolic considerations

Many drugs, including antimicrobial agents, undergo metabolic biotransformation prior to their elimination from the body. Such tranformation is effected by a variety of enzyme systems, many of which are present in the liver. In the neonate this organ and its enzymes are still maturing. For example, glucuronidation of chloramphenicol may be delayed in the neonate so that toxic blood and tissue concentrations develop. This can result in hypotension, cardiovascular collapse and death if unrecognized. The syndrome has been graphically described as the *grey baby syndrome*. Another example seen when novobiocin was more widely used was that of hyperbilirubinaemia. The drug interferes with glucuronyl-transferase which is important in the glucuronidation of bilirubin. Tetracyclines administered to children under 8 years of age may be deposited in the bones and teeth. In addition to producing dental staining, enamel hypoplasia may also result. Finally, deficiency of the red cell enzyme, glucose-6-phosphate-dehydrogenase, may result in acute haemolysis when either nitrofurantoin, sulphonamides, or the antimalarial primaquine is prescribed. This deficiency is genetically determined and remains a problem throughout life. Other problems of drug toxicity and drug interactions are not peculiar to childhood and are discussed in Chapter 18.

Placental passage of antimicrobial agents

Drugs including antibiotics are frequently prescribed to pregnant women although following the thalidomide disaster there is a more critical approach to prescribing in pregnancy. Antimicrobial agents are prescribed in pregnancy for a variety of reasons but most commonly for maternal urinary and respiratory tract infections. Such drugs may also be prescribed to the mother to treat intrauterine infections such as amnionitis, when further pharmacological considerations will determine the success or failure of therapy.

The placenta is not only an important defence against fetal infection, but also largely determines the concentration of a drug in fetal tissues. The transplacental passage of drugs may be by simple diffusion, or by an active transport system. As in other membrane situations, molecular weight, ionizability, lipid solubility and blood flow are all important considerations. Small molecular weight drugs below 1000 daltons tend to cross readily.

Antimicrobial agents which achieve good concentrations in fetal tissues include ampicillin, penicillin G, sulphonamides, chloramphenicol, and nitrofurantoin. The aminoglycosides cross moderately well and have occasionally been associated with fetal ototoxicity. The cephalosporins and clindamycin cross less readily whilst erythromycin is particularly poor in this respect.

The general caution restricting all unnecessary prescribing in pregnancy, in particular during the first 3 months, also applies to antimicrobial drugs. For example, the antifolate properties of trimethoprim and the sulphonamides carry a theoretical risk of inducing fetal abnormalities. However, of more importance is the complication of hyperbilirubinaemia that can result from the use of sulphonamides in the latter few weeks of pregnancy or during the neonatal period. Displacement of protein-bound bilirubin by sulphonamide may result in toxic concentrations of bilirubin and the risk of kernicterus.

Excretion of antimicrobial agents into breast milk

In common with other drugs, antimicrobial agents can enter human breast milk and therefore may potentially affect the suckling infant. The secretory process may either be active or passive and the final concentration is determined by factors such as molecular weight, lipid or water solubility, the degree of protein-binding and, of course, maternal serum concentrations. Breast milk has a neutral pH and drugs which ionize more readily tend to be weak bases.

There are few antimicrobial drugs which readily pass into breast milk and achieve concentrations similar to those in maternal blood. However, isoniazid and some sulphonamides such as sulphanilamide, which is now rarely used, do so. Tetracycline achieves moderate concentrations and could possibly cause discolouration of primary dentition and enamel hypoplasia. Chloramphenicol and erythromycin are found in concentrations approximately half those present in maternal blood. The penicillins and cephalosporins are generally poorly excreted into human breast milk.

In general, such concentrations are more of theoretical than of practical significance. However, there have been occasional reports of drug toxicity in children with glucose-6-phosphate dehydrogenase deficiency and disturbance of the bowel flora may also occur. Under most circumstances, the short-term administration of antimicrobial agents to lactating mothers need not interfere with breast feedings.

Patient compliance

Of particular importance in paediatric prescribing is the acceptability of the medication to the patient. Injections are understandably unpopular with children and their anxious parents and oral preparations are preferred whenever possible, provided their use does not compromise the likely success of therapy. In some cases antibiotics that are otherwise poorly absorbed when given by the oral route are available as esters or salts which exhibit greatly improved oral absorption, as for example with erythromycin. Similarly, chloramphenicol is extremely bitter; however, chloramphenicol palmitate is much more palatable. The need to make preparations palatable with syrup and flavourings is important if compliance is to be observed. Children generally find tablet and capsule preparations difficult to swallow and hence the popularity of syrup suspensions. One word of caution is necessary since many such preparations contain high concentrations of sucrose which may encourage caries formation. This applies essentially to children on long-term preparations which for the most part will be drugs other than antimicrobial agents.

In addition to palatability, compliance is increased by making the prescribing instructions clear and the least disruptive of the normal daily routine. Unnecessary disturbance of sleep patterns is a sure way to reduce compliance.

An important aspect of all prescribing and, in particular, paediatric prescribing, is the need to warn parents that any residual medication should be discarded in order to avoid the problem of accidental self-poisoning in childhood which may occasionally be life-threatening. This is particularly important with paediatric formulations which may be attractively coloured and sweet-tasting.

PRESCRIBING IN THE ELDERLY

As with most therapeutic agents, use of antibiotics is greatest in old age. This reflects the increased susceptibility to microbial disease in this age group, since the host response to infection is often impaired, either as a result of involution or the immunosuppressive effects of disease or drugs. Moreover, the inflammatory response is often dampened and this may lead to more serious infective states, which can have a profound effect on major organ function and thus modify response to antimicrobial therapy.

Age-related infection

Infection is an important cause of morbidity, and occasionally mortality, in the elderly. The classical infections of childhood (measles, mumps, chickenpox, etc.) have little impact in old age, whereas infections of the respiratory tract, urinary tract, and skin structures become substantially more common as one grows older. For example, the lower respiratory tract, often compromised by life-long exposure to cigarette smoke and atmospheric pollution, is an important target for infections that require medical consultation, hospital admission, and the administration of antibiotics.

Urinary tract infections increase substantially beyond the age of 50. In the male this is largely related to benign or malignant enlargement of the prostate; in the female it may have various causes, including sphincter disturbance, uterine prolapse, pelvic neoplasms, and poor hygiene compounded by periods of immobility.

Intra-abdominal infection may complicate gall bladder disease, diverticulosis, and malignancy of the bowel, while metabolic disorders, notably diabetes mellitus, predispose to infection of the urinary tract and septicaemia, as well as infected ischaemic or neuropathic ulcers of the feet.

Physiological changes in the elderly

In contrast to the situation in childhood, prescribing in the elderly must take account of the involution of many physiological systems. Host defences become progressively less efficient with age, and simultaneous degenerative, neoplastic, and metabolic disorders predispose to infection. Changes in excretory organ function can substantially alter drug disposition and elimination. This applies particularly to the functional integrity of the kidneys and liver, which are the major organs of drug excretion and metabolism; superimposed disease can further aggravate the natural decline in function. Loss of glomerular function is a normal concomitant of advancing years and may be clinically inapparent. For this reason all drugs should be used with caution in the elderly, especially those compounds for which the route of excretion is primarily renal. Use of aminoglycosides in older patient requires careful attention to dosage and monitoring of serum concentrations to ensure therapeutic, yet non-toxic levels.

Adverse reactions

Unwanted effects of antimicrobial drugs are more common in the elderly. This partly follows from the increased frequency of drug prescription in this group as well as the impaired efficiency of the excretory organs. However, certain drug reactions cannot be explained by such considerations as, for example, the increased frequency and severity of serious adverse reactions to co-trimoxazole seen in the elderly. Here, rashes, including the Stevens-Johnson syndrome with extensive skin and mucous membrane ulceration, and major blood dyscrasias are more common in the elderly. The effect is almost certainly related to the sulphonamide component of this drug.

Elderly patients are often prescribed multiple drugs and such polypharmacy raises important issues of drug interactions which may affect pharmacological activity as well as increasing the risks of side effects. Examples include the chelation of tetracyclines by antacids and the effect of H_2-antagonists on the activity of drugs such as the quinolones that are affected by alterations in pH. Likewise, the co-administration of theophyllines and quinolones, such as ciprofloxacin and enoxacin, can result in toxic concentrations of the former leading to agitation, confusion, and even seizures.

The principles of antimicrobial prescribing are common to all age groups, but greater attention to issues of drug distribution, excretion, and potential for adverse reactions is necessary in patients at the extremes of age. The burden of infection falls most heavily on the very young and the very old, and antibiotic prescribing is correspondingly more common in these age groups. In the treatment of infection in the young and the elderly it is essential, therefore, to choose the safest and most effective agent, and to use it in appropriate dosage for the shortest time necessary.

18

Adverse reactions to antibiotics

No antimicrobial agent is totally free from unwanted side-effects, and approximately 5 per cent of hospitalized patients prescribed antimicrobial therapy will develop an adverse reaction of some sort. Most are trivial, some merely inconvenient, but a few are life-threatening or fatal. Therefore, due caution should always be exercised before a patient is placed on antimicrobial therapy, to see whether there is an identifiable contra-indication to the use of such an agent. Unnecessary or inappropriate prescribing is to be deplored for several reasons, but in particular for unjustifiably running the risk of avoidable adverse reactions.

This chapter describes the various factors responsible for drug toxicity and the individual reactions seen with a variety of antimicrobial agents. However, it is important to keep a proper perspective on the relative frequency and this is indicated in Table 18.1.

DETERMINANTS OF TOXICITY

Genetic

A few adverse reactions are genetically determined. For example, patients deficient in the enzyme glucose-6-phosphate dehydrogenase are at risk of developing acute haemolysis when prescribed drugs such as the sulphon-amides, nitrofurantoin, and the antimalarial primaquine. Occasionally, the use of chloramphenicol, nalidixic acid, or PAS may be similarly complicated. This reaction may be avoided by screening for this X-linked erythrocyte enzyme defect, which is more commonly found among persons of Mediterranean, Far Eastern, or African stock. Similarly, the ability to acetylate the antituberculous drug, isoniazid, is genetically determined. In slow acetylators, isoniazid toxicity may occur.

Chemical

Many intravenously administered drugs, including antimicrobial agents, produce local irritation and frank phlebitis. To overcome this it may be

Table 18.1. Relative frequency of selected adverse reactions to antimicrobial agents

Antimicrobial agent	Frequent	Infrequent
Aminoglycosides	Ototoxicity Nephrotoxicity	Rashes
Cephalosporins	Hypersensitivity rashes *Candida* overgrowth	Nephrotoxicity (cephaloridine) Anaphylaxis Haematological toxicity
Chloramphenicol	Dose-related marrow toxicity	Aplastic anaemia Grey baby syndrome Optic neuritis
Clindamyin	Rash Diarrhoea	Hepatitis Pseudomembranous colitis
Co-trimoxazole and sulphonamides	Rashes (sulphonamide)	Megaloblastic anaemia
Erythromycin	Gastrointestinal intolerance	Cholestatic jaundice Deafness
Fusidic acid	Gastrointestinal intolerance (oral)	Hepatotoxicity (intravenous)
Nalidixic acid and other quinolones	Gastrointestinal intolerance Rashes	Confusion/convulsions Photosensitivity
Nitrofurantoin	Gastrointestinal intolerance	Hypersensitivity pneumonitis Haemolysis Peripheral neuropathy Rashes
Penicillins	Hypersensitivity reactions—mainly rashes	Haematological toxicity Encephalopathy Interstitial nephritis
Rifampicin	Hepatotoxicity Liver enzyme induction	Hypersensitivity 'Influenza syndrome' (intermittent treatment) Haematological toxicity
Tetracyclines	Gastrointestinal intolerance Candidiasis Dental staining and hypoplasia in childhood	Photosensitivity Nephrotoxicity Staphylococcal enterocolitis
Vancomycin	'Red man' syndrome	Nephrotoxicity

necessary to adjust the pH of an intravenous infusion by suitable buffering. In like manner, pain may accompany the intramuscular injection of a drug. For example, cephalothin is rarely administered by the intramuscular route because of local pain, whilst cefoxitin is given with a local anaesthetic, lignocaine, to counter the pain at the injection site.

Many drugs may produce gastrointestinal discomfort due to a local chemical irritation of the gastric and intestinal mucosa. Here, again, suitable buffering, enteric coating, or slow-release formulations may diminish these symptoms and increase the acceptability of a drug.

Metabolic

Drug accumulation

Drugs may be excreted unchanged, but this is unusual. More usually, they undergo degradation or modification to a greater or lesser degree prior to excretion. The liver is the major site of this metabolization although other organs such as the kidneys are also involved. When disease impairs either renal or hepatic function there is the risk of accumulation of the drug, or a metabolite, which may reach toxic concentrations in the tissues.

Similarly, in the premature or full-term neonate, both renal and hepatic function are physiologically immature so that some adjustments of dosaging may have to be made (see Chapter 17).

Enzyme induction

Certain drugs may cause hepatic enzyme induction. This is well known for barbiturates where it may have therapeutic effects. However, occasionally such enzyme induction may be undesirable. Patients simultaneously prescribed rifampicin and the contraceptive pill may conceive owing to inadequate circulating hormone concentrations that result from the induction of hepatic enzymes by rifampicin. Likewise, simultaneous administration of certain quinolones (e.g. enoxacin or ciprofloxacin) and theophyllines may result in the accumulation of toxic concentrations of the latter.

Electrolyte overload

Toxicity may also result from electrolyte overload. Certain antibiotics such as carbenicillin, being relatively inactive, are prescribed in large doses. Each 1 g of carbenicillin contains 5.4 mmol sodium. This can result in sodium overloading and congestive cardiac failure, particularly in patients who also have impaired renal function.

Dental staining

Tetracyclines are taken up by developing bones and teeth. In the former there are no significant long-term complications. However, staining of the dentition is unsightly and ranges from patchy cream to extensive brown deposits. In addition, enamel hypoplasia may also result. This ability to produce dental staining varies among the tetracyclines, being least with oxytetracycline. However, avoidance of all tetracyclines in children under 8 years of age will avoid such staining of the permanent dentition.

Histamine release

Too rapid infusion of vancomycin can result in the release of histamine, which, in turn, can produce acute flushing, tachycardia, and hypotension —a reaction known as 'red man' syndrome.

Drug interaction

Drugs may interact with other agents *in vitro* when mixed before administration, or *in vivo* once the drugs are ingested or injected. The study of drug interactions has become increasingly important and complex as new therapeutic agents become available. In general, many incompatibilities can be avoided by mixing the agents separately and administering them either by a different route or at different times.

In-vitro incompatibilities

Table 18.2 indicates the variety of in-vitro incompatibilities associated with antimicrobial agents. This list is far from complete and pharmaceutical advice should be sought whenever there is doubt concerning drug compatibility.

Table 18.2. In-vitro incompatibilities of selected antimicrobial agents

Antimicrobial agent	Agents with which incompatibility exists
Penicillin G	Ascorbic acid, tetracyclines, vancomycin, amphotericin B
Methicillin	Tetracyclines
Cephalothin	Erythromycin, tetracyclines, calcium gluconate, or chloride
Chloramphenicol	Tetracyclines, vancomycin, hydrocortisone, vitamin B complex preparations
Vancomycin	Chloramphenicol, hydrocortisone, heparin
Gentamicin	Carbenicillin

In-vivo interactions

In-vivo drug interactions occur for a variety of reasons. These include competition for plasma protein binding sites, inhibition or induction of liver enzymes, thus interfering with or potentiating other therapeutic effects. Table 18.3 indicates the variety of in-vivo effects that have been described. Among the more important drug interactions is interference with anticoagulant drugs, a problem that is commonly, but not exclusively caused by antimicrobial agents. For example, rifampicin and griseofulvin impair anticoagulation by enzyme induction whilst sulphonamides and chloramphenicol increase anticoagulation by enzyme inhibition, so that bleeding may occur.

Table 18.3. In-vivo incompatibilities of selected antimicrobial agents

Antibiotic(s)	Interacting agent(s)	Adverse reaction
Aminoglycosides	Curare-like agents	Neuromuscular blockade
Cephaloridine	Frusemide, ethacrynic acid	Nephrotoxicity
Chloramphenicol Sulphonamides Isoniazid	Phenytoin	Phenytoin toxicity
Enoxacin Ciprofloxacin	Theophylline	Agitation, convulsions
Gentamicin	Cephaloridine, frusemide, ethacrynic acid	Nephrotoxicity
Griseofulvin	Warfarin	Decreased anticoagulation
Metronidazole	Alcohol	Nausea and vomiting (disulfiram effect)
Rifampicin	Oral contraceptives	Decreased efficacy
Sulphonamides Nalidixic acid	Anticoagulants	Increased anticoagulation
Tetracyclines	Oral antacid preparations and oral iron	Decreased tetracycline absorption

Hypersensitivity

Among the antibiotics the β-lactam compounds have the greatest potential to produce hypersensitivity reactions. Because of the similar structure of the penicillins, hypersensitivity to one agent is usually accompanied by hypersensitivity to the whole group. Moreover, the structural similarities between the cephalosporin antibiotics and the penicillins are accompanied by a degree of cross-hypersensitivity between the two groups. Approximately 10 per cent of patients who are hypersensitive to the penicillins will show cross-hypersensitivity to the cephalosporins. However, the monobactam compounds, of which aztreonam is the only one presently available, appear to be less allergenic and may be administered to patients with a history of hypersensitivity to other β-lactam antibiotics. This suggests that the sensitizing moiety of these drugs is not the β-lactam ring.

Immediate reactions

Immediate hypersensitivity reactions to the penicillins and cephalosporins can occur within minutes and produce nausea and vomiting, pruritus urticaria, wheezing, laryngeal oedema, and cardiovascular collapse. In extreme cases the patient may die unless the attack is controlled with adrenaline and attention to the integrity of the airway. The estimated frequency for anaphylaxis is 1–5 for every 10 000 courses of penicillin prescribed.

Delayed reactions

Other hypersensitivity reactions tend to be delayed, and include drug fever, erythema nodosum, and a serum sickness-like syndrome. Hypersensitivity rashes are particularly common with the semi-synthetic penicillins such as ampicillin and its analogues and the cephalosporins. The rashes take a variety of forms, but, in general, are maculopapular and pruritic. They may also be vesicular, bullous, urticarial, or scarlatiniform. In addition, the use of ampicillin is associated with a generalized maculopapular eruption in more than 90 per cent of patients suffering from infectious mononucleosis (glandular fever) and, less frequently, in association with cytomegalovirus infection. The reason for these hypersensitivity rashes in association with such viral infections is uncertain. However, the response is short-lived and does not reflect long-lasting penicillin hypersensitivity, so that future use of penicillins is not contraindicated in these patients.

Other antimicrobial agents that commonly produce hypersensitivity drug rashes are the sulphonamides and clindamycin. The sulphonamides and co-trimoxazole are responsible for a wide variety of eruptions which range from urticarial to maculopapular to erythema multiforme and its more severe variant, the Stevens–Johnson syndrome, in which there is both cutaneous and mucous membrane involvement and a significant mortality rate.

Hypersensitivity reactions may also involve individual organs. For example, the penicillins occasionally produce an interstitial nephritis. Nitrofurantoin may affect the lungs and erythromycin estolate is associated with hypersensitivity cholestasis. Other rare hypersensitivity reactions including haemolytic anaemia, neutropenia, and thrombocytopenia may occasionally occur with the penicillins, cephalosporins, and sulphonamides.

Predicting hypersensitivity

This is difficult. Some individuals have a strong family history of drug allergy or of allergic disease such as asthma or eczema. Skin testing is occasionally carried out, but is unfortunately unreliable. It is therefore imperative to inquire about any previous episodes of hypersensitivity. When reactions occur they should be carefully documented and explained to the patient, so that serious hypersensitivity reactions can be avoided in the future.

Altered microbial flora

Antimicrobial drugs cannot distinguish between pathogenic organisms and those that make up the normal flora of the host. Even so-called 'narrow-spectrum' antibiotics like penicillin have a profound effect on the normal flora of the mouth and gut to eliminate or suppress penicillin-sensitive strains of streptococci and anaerobic bacteria. As a rule this alteration of the normal flora is without consequence and is rapidly reversed on stopping treatment.

Some agents have a greater potential to suppress the normal flora which may be complicated by the overgrowth of drug-resistant organisms which in turn may give rise to superinfection. In general, the worst culprits are broad-spectrum antibiotics such as the tetracyclines, ampicillin, and cephalosporins. Their use is occasionally associated with the overgrowth of yeasts, particularly within the oral cavity where they may result in oral candidiasis, also known as monilia or thrush. Occasionally, this overgrowth may extend throughout the gut and produce a serious enterocolitis.

In the past, hospitalized patients receiving tetracycline and other broad-spectrum drugs such as chloramphenicol, also experienced overgrowth with antibiotic-resistant strains of *Staphylococcus aureus* with a resultant enterocolitis. This was much feared, particularly in the postoperative patient, where mortality rates were high. For reasons that are not entirely clear this complication is nowadays seldom seen.

More recently, the syndrome of antibiotic-associated colitis caused by toxin-producing strains of *Clostridium difficile* has been recognized. This may follow the use of one or a large number of agents although clinda-mycin, ampicillin, and the cephalosporins are most commonly incrimin-ated. It is thought, but not proven, that antibiotic use selectively favours proliferation of the causative organism. The colitis caused by the toxin may be severe, even life-threatening. Oral vancomycin has been success-fully used to control the condition when it arises.

Finally, patients treated with antimicrobial agents are at risk of acquiring organisms from the environment. Because of the intensive selection pressure operating in many hospital units, organisms acquired in hospital are often more virulent and frequently exhibit resistance to a variety of antibiotics, putting the patient at increased risk.

TISSUE- AND ORGAN-SPECIFIC TOXICITY

Gastrointestinal tract

Antimicrobial agents are commonly administered orally provided that absorption from the bowel is satisfactory. It is scarcely surprising therefore that a variety of gastrointestinal side-effects are associated with their use. Nausea, vomiting, and increased bowel movement, sometimes amounting to diarrhoea, are common, but are generally of minor inconvenience and do not interrupt treatment. Diarrhoea occurs in approximately 5–10 per cent of patients taking oral ampicillin or clindamycin. However, the most serious gastrointestinal complications are overgrowth of *Candida*, *Staph. aureus*, or toxin-producing strains of *Cl. difficile* (see above).

Skin

Skin rashes are among the more frequent adverse reactions caused by antimicrobial drugs. The majority of such reactions are caused by hyper-sensitivity, as already described, but a wide variety of other eruptions may occur and these include maculopapular, vesicular, and bullous eruptions, exfoliation, and erythema multiforme. Delayed hypersensitivity reactions with sulphonamides may result in erythema nodosum, which may be part of a serum sickness-like syndrome with drug fever and arthralgia.

Photosensitivity eruptions occur with long-acting sulphonamides, the tetracyclines, particularly demeclocycline, and also nalidixic acid. The skin becomes red, oedematous, and vesicular. This side-effect is more common in hot climates.

Finally, a lupus syndrome is occasionally seen with the penicillins and sulphonamides. The eruption primarily affects the skin and although the blood is positive for anti-nuclear factor, the phenomenon is rarely associated with severe systemic disease. Cessation of therapy is associated with resolution of the condition although this may take some time.

Respiratory tract

Antibiotics have a variety of effects on the normal respiratory tract. Hypersensitivity reactions manifested by bronchial asthma and pulmonary eosinophilia may occur, usually in sensitized individuals. Asthmatic reactions are most likely in those who have an underlying bronchospastic tendency. Nitrofurantoin, para-aminosalicylic acid, the sulphonamides, and β-lactam antibiotics may produce such reactions. Nitrofurantoin has also been associated with a chronic intestinal pneumonitis progressing to fibrosis. This has occurred with long-term use and the changes may only be partially reversible on stopping the drugs.

An indirect side-effect of antibiotic therapy is opportunistic lung infection. This usually occurs in those patients with underlying malignant disease and those receiving cytotoxic or immunosuppressive therapy. Patients who are artificially ventilated are particularly vulnerable. The normal flora becomes modified and opportunistic pulmonary infection occurs.

Liver

The liver is a major organ of drug metabolism and excretion, and is consequently vulnerable to a variety of adverse effects. Antibiotics may affect the liver to produce an acute hepatitis or cholestasis. Such reactions are often unpredictable although pre-existing liver disease suggests caution in prescribing potentially hepatotoxic drugs.

Several antimicrobial drugs including carbenicillin, clindamycin, and para-aminosalicylic acid may produce minor elevations of liver enzymes which uncommonly progress to a frank hepatitis with nausea, vomiting, and a tender enlarged liver. Cholestasis may be seen in association with nitrofurantoin and erythromycin derivatives.

Isoniazid is a frequent cause of hepatitis which is uncommon below the age of 20 but increases significantly in persons of middle-age and beyond. Symptoms usually develop within the first 2 months of treatment and subside on stopping treatment. Transient asymptomatic elevation of liver enzymes is common but of little significance. Routine testing of liver function is not justified unless symptoms develop.

Rifampicin may also produce elevation of liver enzymes although when used in combination with isoniazid, as it may be in the treatment of tuberculosis, clinical hepatotoxicity appears to be no more frequent than when isoniazid is used alone.

Another more serious variety of liver toxicity may follow the use of intravenous tetracycline either in patients with pre-existing liver disease or if administered during pregnancy. Under these circumstances liver necrosis is recognized which may prove fatal.

Neurological system

Central nervous system

Ototoxicity is an important side-effect of the aminoglycoside antibiotics. However, their individual potential for either vestibulotoxicity or cochleotoxicity varies and is least for tobramycin. Vestibulotoxicity is recognized by unsteadiness of gait and nystagmus whilst cochleotoxicity is recognized by a hearing loss which initially affects high frequencies that may only be detected by audiography.

Although penicillins are (setting aside penicillin allergy) the least toxic of antibiotics, encephalitic reactions may occur with massive parenteral doses of penicillin G of 20 million units or more per day. There is no conceivable therapeutic benefit in such heroic doses, which should be avoided. If intrathecal therapy with penicillin is contemplated the adult dose should not exceed 20 000 units because of the risk of convulsions. Other β-lactam antibiotics such as the cephalosporins may also be associated with convulsions and encephalopathy when given in high doses. High doses of nalidixic acid may also produce convulsions. The phenomenon of benign intracranial hypertension may follow the use of nalidixic acid, tetracycline, and occasionally, penicillin. This effect is reversible on stopping treatment. Optic neuritis is a rare complication of the use of chloramphenicol, whilst ethambutol is also associated with dose-related optic nerve damage and retinopathy.

Peripheral nervous system

Several agents may be associated with a peripheral neuropathy, although the mechanisms are not well understood. Isoniazid is known to interfere with pyridoxine metabolism. Nitrofurantoin competes with thiamine-pyrophosphate and thus interferes with pyruvate oxidation. Metronidazole may produce a peripheral neuropathy with prolonged use which is reversible on stopping the drug.

Neuromuscular blockade, although rare, is a potentially serious adverse reaction and occurs in association with the use of the aminoglycosides, polymyxins, tetracyclines, and lincomycin. The aminoglycosides produce neuromuscular blockade by a curare-like anticholinesterase effect and by competing with calcium; this is more likely to be seen following the use of muscle relaxants during anaesthesia.

Kidneys

Owing to the fact that the kidneys are the major route of drug excretion it is not surprising that nephrotoxicity is relatively frequent. It is often dose-related and is more common in those with either pre-existing renal failure or in those who are receiving other nephrotoxic agents.

Sulphonamides

These were among the first antimicrobial drugs shown to be nephrotoxic. Some of the early sulphonamides which were rapidly secreted and poorly soluble, were prone to deposit crystals within the urinary tract, sometimes causing tubular damage and ureteric obstruction. This complication is uncommon with modern sulphonamides, which are generally more soluble and more slowly excreted.

Penicillins

Benzylpenicillin and, occasionally, other penicillins may produce a hyper-sensitivity interstitial nephritis. This is recognized by haematuria, pro-teineuria, and such features as pyrexia and eosinophilia.

Cephalosporins

These vary in their nephrotoxic potential. Cephaloridine (no longer available in the UK) is nephrotoxic when more than 6 g per day is pre-scribed, particularly if prescribed in combination with a diuretic, such as frusemide or ethacrynic acid. The evidence in favour of other cephalo-sporins being nephrotoxic is equivocal although cephalosporins may potentiate aminoglycoside toxicity.

Tetracyclines

These may occasionally be nephrotoxic. This applies particularly to patients with pre-existing renal insufficiency and the elderly with physio-logical impairment of renal function. The degree of renal failure produced varies, but is usually reversible. An explanation of the phenomenon may lie in the anti-anabolic effect of tetracyclines. Outdated (time-expired) preparations of tetracyclines may cause tubulotoxicity with consequent electrolyte and amino acid loss.

A specific effect of demeclocycline is the production of nephrogenic diabetes insipidus, a phenomenon that has been put to therapeutic advantage in the management of the syndrome of inappropriate anti-diuretic hormone secretion.

Among tetracyclines, doxycycline is unique in being devoid of nephro-toxicity, reflecting its primary hepatobiliary route of excretion.

Aminoglycosides

These are the antibiotics most frequently associated with nephrotoxicity. Their nephrotoxic potential varies and nephrotoxicity occurs in decreasing order of frequency with kanamycin, gentamicin, tobramycin, amikacin, and netilmicin. Nephrotoxicity is potentiated by pre-existing renal disease, prolonged or repeated courses of treatment or the simultaneous administration of other nephrotoxic agents. In many instances, the renal insufficiency produced is reversible although permanent impairment including renal failure does occur.

Haematological toxicity

Antimicrobial agents may result in a variety of haematological adverse reactions. Bone marrow toxicity may be either selective and affect one cell line, or be unselective and produce pancytopenia and marrow aplasia. Furthermore, immune-mediated haemolysis may occur in which Coombs' antibodies are detected. Bleeding may occur from platelet dysfunction or from thrombocytopenia. Eosinophilia may represent a hypersensitivity reaction.

β-Lactam antibiotics

The penicillins may rarely produce both a primary haemolytic anaemia and also Coombs' antibody positive disease. In addition, a selective white cell depression has been described with ampicillin, methicillin, and carbenicillin whilst the latter may also produce bleeding due to drug-induced platelet dysfunction or interference with fibrin formation. This may be important in the seriously ill patient with bone marrow suppression. Similarly, the cephalosporins may be associated with a positive Coombs' test although frank haemolysis is uncommon. Eosinophilia occurs with variable frequency as does the selective depression of white cells, and occasionally platelets, following the development of platelet antibodies. A vitamin K-dependent bleeding disorder has been associated with certain cephalosporins which possess a methyltetrazole-thiomethyl side chain. These include cephamandole, cefotetan, cefoperazone, and latamoxef. Although uncommon, bleeding has been identified largely in elderly or malnourished patients undergoing major surgery. It is both treated and prevented by the administration of vitamin K.

Sulphonamides

Among the more important groups of agents to produce haematological side-effects are the sulphonamides and sulphonamide-containing mixtures such as co-trimoxazole. Marrow toxicity may result in aplastic anaemia, or a selective neutropenia, or thrombocytopenia. In addition, haemolysis may either be primary or related to glucose-6-phosphate dehydrogenase deficiency. Co-trimoxazole may produce megaloblastic bone marrow changes or, less commonly, a peripheral megaloblastic anaemia. This tends to occur with prolonged therapy and is related to the joint antifolate action of the two components of co-trimoxazole.

Chloramphenicol

This has achieved notoriety for inducing marrow depression which is manifested in two ways. Firstly, the more common dose-related bone marrow depression is seen when the daily dose exceeds 4 g. There is a progressive anaemia, neutropenia, and sometimes thrombocytopenia which is reversible on either discontinuing treatment or reducing the dosage. The other far more serious reaction is that of total bone marrow depression and aplastic anaemia. This is unpredictable but is estimated to occur with a frequency of 1 in 24 000–1 in 40 000 treatment courses. Mortality from aplastic anaemia is still in excess of 50 per cent. Thiamphenicol, a derivative of chloramphenicol, available in some parts of the world, appears to be devoid of the irreversible toxic effects on the bone marrow.

PREVENTION OF ADVERSE REACTIONS

There are major difficulties in preventing adverse drug reactions. Patients frequently respond idiosyncratically to antimicrobial agents as to other drugs and the chief problem, especially with the rarer side-effects, is their unpredictability. Awareness of the possibility of adverse effects is obviously important and a close working relationship with either a clinical pharmacologist or specialist in the use of antimicrobial agents will help to overcome problems as they arise.

When toxic effects develop or are suspected the decision has to be made as to whether to stop or change the patient's treatment. The drug may frequently be continued provided the dose is adjusted, either by reducing each individual dose or prolonging the interval between doses.

Antibiotic assays (Chapter 8) are an important method for determining whether dosage adjustment is necessary, particularly in the case of aminoglycosides with which the leeway between effective and toxic levels is small. Chloramphenicol should be assayed when used in the newborn child, to prevent excessive accumulation.

Finally, the reporting of adverse drug reactions, whether caused by antimicrobial agents or other drugs, remains the responsibility of all practising doctors. In the UK the Committee on Safety of Medicines operates a voluntary adverse reactions reporting system (see Postscript).

19

Chemoprophylaxis

Chemoprophylaxis is the prevention of infection by the administration of antimicrobial agents as distinct from prevention by immunization. Individuals who require prophylaxis differ from the normal population in that they are known to be exposed to a particular infectious hazard and/or their ability to respond to infection is impaired.

Prophylaxis should be confined to those periods for which the risk is maximum, so that the problems of disturbance of the normal flora, super-infection with resistant organisms, untoward reactions, and cost will be minimized. If chemoprophylaxis is to have a place in the management of infection it is likely to be most effective when we can identify:

(1) individuals in whom the risk of infection is high;

(2) the organisms likely to be responsible;

(3) the agent likely to be active against those organisms.

Failure to establish and adhere to such guidelines has made unnecessary chemoprophylaxis the commonest form of antibiotic misuse in hospitals.

PATIENTS WITH NORMAL RESISTANCE

A clear example is provided by the need to protect travellers to areas where malaria is common. The chances of acquiring the disease are high, the results can be grave, and the period at risk is well defined: from arrival in the area until 6 weeks after departure—the time taken for any parasites that may have been acquired to be finally eliminated. There are agents which are specifically active against the malaria parasite and suitable for prophylaxis, and there is only one complication: the parasite may be resistant to the chosen prophylactic drug and it is plainly important to ensure that the agent used is active against the local parasite (see Chapter 30).

Not all situations are as clear cut as this, however, and a good example of the sort of uncertainties that arise is provided by the situation in which a child develops meningococcal meningitis. Any of the family, the school and social contacts, and the medical attendants might acquire meningococci from the child and become nasopharyngeal carriers. Some of those carriers could themselves develop meningitis. Should all receive chemoprophylaxis? Epidemiological evidence indicates that children are much more likely to develop the disease than adults and that acquisition requires close contact. The general advice, therefore, is to offer chemoprophylaxis only to close contacts and to medical attendants only if they have been exposed to unusual opportunities for transmission of the organism as, for example, during mouth-to-mouth resuscitation.

Again, the choice of agent is complicated by microbial resistance. Sulphonamides are extremely effective in prophylaxis, but sulphonamide-resistant meningococci are now common. This is particularly unfortunate because other agents such as penicillin which are equally effective in the treatment of the disease are much less effective (for reasons which are imperfectly understood) in prophylaxis. In the absence of information as to whether the organism is sulphonamide-sensitive, rifampicin should be used. Evidence is accumulating that ciprofloxacin may be equally effective.

Surgical sepsis

The commonest circumstance in which patients with otherwise normal resistance to infection become susceptible is in the course of surgical operations. Here two situations must be distinguished: those in which the tissues involved are infected and those in which they are not.

Uninfected tissues

Here, the patient becomes liable to infection through the breach in the normal protective integument by organisms, almost invariably staphylococci, derived from the patient's own carrier sites or from the surgical team. On the face of it, this might appear to fulfil the criteria for necessary prophylaxis: a known organism (*Staphylococcus aureus*) of known susceptibility (to cloxacillin) with a risk of infection over a clearly defined period. In fact, there is no justification whatsoever for the use of chemoprophylaxis in this way. The incidence of wound sepsis following operations on uninfected tissues, such as thyroidectomy, should be extremely small and the effect in the otherwise normal patient should in any case be easily controlled. If wound sepsis following such operations is common, something is seriously wrong with the hygienic management of the patients and the source and mode of spread of infection must be identified and eliminated. The use of antimicrobial agents in this situation diverts attention from the real problem and, by failing to control spread, facilitates infection with resistant strains.

Infected tissues

Under this heading we can conveniently dismiss operations conducted in the presence of infection: for example, incision of an abscess, the removal of infected bone, or prostatectomy in the presence of urinary infection. Antibiotics are commonly given in conjunction with such operations, often with the specific intention of controlling any spread of organisms locally or into the bloodstream as a result of the procedure. In this sense, such therapy can be regarded as prophylaxis, but it is more appropriately regarded as part of the treatment which will often already have begun prior to surgery when the causative organism and the appropriate agent will ordinarily be known from prior laboratory tests.

Contamination by normal flora

True chemoprophylaxis may be required where operations involve organs which are not infected, but which harbour a normal flora, notably the oropharnyx, the gut, and the vagina. As in the case of the skin, the orpharyngeal flora seldom gives rise to local infection following simple procedures such as tonsillectomy, and systemic chemoprophylaxis is not required. However, if there is much tissue damage or local impairment of the blood supply such as may be seen in destructive wounds, chemically-induced abortion, or elaborate vaginal repairs, implanted organisms may give rise to infection. In such cases infection often involves anaerobic organisms and several different species may act in concert to produce a so-called synergic infection. Such conditions require chemoprophylaxis and, where there is necrotic tissue, surgical debridement.

Upper gut surgery

The normal flora of the gut is uniform neither in its distribution nor its composition. The mouth contains copious organisms, but the oesophagus, stomach, and small gut normally contain only a few passengers derived from the mouth or the food, many of which are destroyed in the acid of the stomach and the rest hurried by peristalsis to the terminal ileum where the mixed flora typical of the large bowel contents begins to develop. This is notable for its content of Gram-negative rods, both aerobic and anaerobic, and for the extraordinarily high concentrations of bacteria which develop as the gut contents are progressively dehydrated.

It is to be expected from the scanty flora harboured that operations on the upper gut are seldom complicated by infection and do not call for chemoprophylaxis. Indeed, prophylactic antibiotics given to patients undergoing operations on the upper gut are likely to pave the way for the acquisition of hospital strains of bacteria that are highly resistant to antibiotics. A particular hazard is colonization of the anterior nares by antibiotic-resistant staphylococci and facilitation of their access to the stomach by the passage of pernasal gastric tubes. Protection of such patients by tetracycline or other broad-spectrum agents has, in the past, led to severe and sometimes fatal staphylococcal enterocolitis. Similar arguments might apply to operations on the biliary tract, which is normally sterile; antibiotic administration should only be required in patients with bacterial cholangitis and this is treatment, not prophylaxis. Unfortunately, the presence of bacterial infection can only be determined with certainty at the time of operation and antibiotics are, therefore, usually given routinely to patients undergoing cholecystectomy. Because the majority of infecting organisms are aerobic Gram-negative rods, cephalosporins are commonly used.

Large bowel surgery

The situation in the large bowel is quite different. No other organ is so laden with bacteria able to infect normal tissues and post-operative infection rates of 30 or 40 per cent are not uncommon. The problem of controlling microbial spillage from the large bowel in the course of surgery has been approached in the following ways.

Bowel sterilization   The first and original procedure was to remove as far as possible the large bowel contents by purging and enema. Poorly absorbed agents, such as neomycin and some sulphonamides, were (and in some places still are) widely used in conjunction with mechanical cleansing of the gut to 'sterilize' the bowel before operation. In fact, this failed to render the residual bowel contents sterile because of inactivity against the most numerous bowel inhabitants, the non-sporing Gram-negative anaerobic bacteria. Nevertheless, vigorous pursuit of these procedures sometimes managed to leave the large bowel sufficiently microbially denuded for the patients to become superinfected with antibiotic-resistant hospital strains of staphylococci and to suffer severe and even fatal staphylococcal enterocolitis.

Tissue sterilization   An alternative approach is to attempt to sterilize all the tissues exposed to faecal organisms by irrigation at the end of operation with a potent antiseptic or antibiotic. Considerable reduction in the incidence of post-operative sepsis has been obtained following the use of antibiotics, commonly tetracycline, or non-specific agents such as povidone-iodine or noxytiolin. Unfortunately, absorption of drugs from large raw areas or the peritoneum is at least as rapid as from intramuscular injections and, as a result, the local concentration of agent rapidly falls and the patient is exposed to remote toxic effects of the drug just as if it had been parenterally administered.

Systemic chemoprophylaxis   Recognition of this problem has led to prophylaxis based on two separate procedures: elimination, as far as possible, of faecal organisms by mechanical means (possibly supplemented by oral antibacterial agents) and systemic administration of drug active against the principal potential pathogens over the period during which implantation and invasion by the organism is likely to occur. In some places, systemic antibiotics have been given for a week or two before operation—a procedure which offends against many of the rules of effective prophylaxis; it contributes nothing beyond the most recent dose to the concentration of drug in the tissues at the time of operation, it exposes patients to the risk of superinfection with resistant organisms and to increased risk of untoward reactions, and it increases the cost.

What is required is concentrations of agent adequate to dispose of any organism likely to establish infection implanted in the tissues in the course of the operative procedure. Plainly, this does not include any period before the operation begins, but in order to secure adequate concentrations at the time of operation, the first dose of agent should be given up to an hour before. If intravenous drugs are used, these are often administered by the anaesthetist at the time of induction of anaesthesia. The question of how long tissue concentrations must be maintained cannot be answered with any certainty, but obviously must cover the time of the operation. No trial has convincingly established the period of risk, but the physiology of wound healing suggests that it is relatively short. Many regimens continue post-operative prophylaxis for 48 hours. For short operations, for example, uncomplicated appendicectomy, single dose prophylaxis is usually adequate.

Choice of agent Convincing scientific evidence is also lacking on the optimum agent to be used for this purpose. Success was obtained many years ago with chloramphenicol, though the prophylactic use in large numbers of patients of an agent with so potentially dangerous a side-effect as aplastic anaemia must be deplored. The attraction was that it was active against almost all the organisms likely to be involved in bowel infection including the predominant anaerobes. Later, cephaloridine was shown significantly to reduce the sepsis rate after large bowel surgery, although it has no activity against anaerobes. It was generally believed that by eliminating aerobes which consume oxygen and thereby provide the conditions necessary for anaerobic growth, anaerobic activity was abolished. It later become clear that this cannot be the whole explanation when metronidazole, which is active only against anaerobic bacteria, proved to be a most effective chemoprophylactic agent in both large bowel and gynaecological surgery.

Despite this success, there was concern that metronidazole has no effect against aerobic bacteria and it was consequently combined with agents such as gentamicin, widely active against Gram-negative rods, and cloxacillin active against staphylococci. Many believe this clumsy therapy to be unnecessarily comprehensive and the cloxacillin is often omitted, the antistaphylococcal activity of gentamicin being deemed to be sufficient. All would prefer a single agent if one could be agreed upon, but impeccable comparative trials are hard to do and valid comparisons between series hard to make. Some rely on metronidazole alone, believing that the anaerobic element in synergic post-operative sepsis is so dominant that elimination of that alone will abort the process. Others prefer agents with significant intrinsic activity against both aerobes and anaerobes, and cefoxitin, or the combination of amoxycillin and clavulanic acid, have been effectively used for this purpose.

PATIENTS WITH IMPAIRED RESISTANCE

What has been said so far applies to patients in whom there is no reason to suspect any impairment of the natural bacterial clearance mechanisms. There are important differences in patients with impaired resistance. Bacterial infection may be caused by a much greater variety of organisms including commensal bacteria; the occasions of exposure may be everyday occurrences and, therefore, much less easy to identify and the role of chemoprophylaxis in eliminating implanted bacteria is more decisive than supportive.

Impaired resistance is of two forms: local and general. Local impairment occurs where, for example, the blood supply to the area is defective or foreign bodies are present or for some other reason the local defences are not mobilized. Important examples are amputations through the mid-thigh for obliterative arterial disease, implantation of surgical prostheses, and rheumatic endocarditis.

Amputation

Surgery in obliterative arterial disease is associated with a specific serious risk. Even in the most fastidious, the perineum, upper thighs and lower abdomen can be soiled with gut organisms amongst which clostridia are common. Clostridial spores are highly resistant to antiseptics and skin preparation before operation cannot be relied upon to destroy them. Implantation of such organisms into the oxygen-deprived tissues of the ischaemic limb at amputation provides precisely the conditions most favourable to their proliferation with the production of tissue necrosis and gas gangrene. Only clostridia are responsible for this condition and all are susceptible to penicillin which, given prior to operation and for 48 hours after, can be relied upon to prevent this disastrous complication and must be administered whenever such amputations are contemplated. Post-amputation sepsis occurring despite penicillin prophylaxis is commonly caused by *Bacteroides fragilis*, *Staph. aureus* or aerobic Gram-negative rods.

Implantation of surgical prostheses

The deliberate introduction of foreign bodies such as cardiac valves or hip joint prostheses carries a risk of infection the results of which can be disastrous. Chemoprophylaxis is consequently universally used, but its efficacy is almost impossible to calculate, since the incidence of infection even without chemoprophylaxis is extremely low. A very large study mounted by the Medical Research Council and the Public Health Laboratory Service in the UK has shown a significant reduction in sepsis rates in hip replacement operations when peri-operative antibiotics were used. The study also examined the benefits of 'clean air' theatres and meticulous antisepsis. The combination of such special operative techniques and anti-microbial prophylaxis reduced the infection rate to about 0.1 per cent.

There is no unanimity of opinion as to which antibiotic is most appropriate and little likelihood of settling the question by clinical trial since huge numbers of comparable patients would have to be enrolled to detect differences in the efficacy of different agents. Since *Staph. aureus* is often incriminated in orthopaedic sepsis, the agent chosen should clearly be active against this organism. Many orthopaedic surgeons use cephradine, which combines adequate antistaphylococcal activity with useful cover for many Gram-negative organisms.

In cardiac surgery, broad-spectrum cover with an anti-staphylococcal penicillin and an aminoglycoside has been advocated, but the common occurrence in some units of strains of staphylococci resistant to these agents has led to the adoption of vancomycin as a prophylactic agent, despite its cost.

Infective endocarditis

Patients with certain congenital cardiovascular abnormalities, prosthetic heart valves, rheumatic carditis, or arteriosclerosis are subject to deposition of vegetations on the endocardium which are liable to become infected with bacteria transiently liberated into the bloodstream. For example, salivary organisms enter the blood when a tooth is extracted and gut organisms can enter the blood during large bowel operations. In normal subjects these organisms are quickly cleared by the reticulo-endothelial system, but in patients with pre-existing endocardial vegetations they may become trapped and grow in the vegetation to give rise to bacterial endocarditis. A great variety of bacterial species can occasionally infect the valves in this way, but much the most important organisms are viridans streptococci from the mouth and enterococci from the gut or bladder (Chapter 23).

Identification of patients at risk

Despite the availability of many agents active against the infecting organisms, treatment of bacterial endocarditis is still far from satisfactory in terms of prolonged survival. Protection against the risks of such infection is therefore essential. The difficulty is that almost none of the requirements of soundly based chemoprophylaxis can be met in full, and because of the infrequency of infection it is impossible to measure the efficacy of chemoprophylaxis and the relative merits of competing regimens.

The best that can be done is to identify all patients with relevant heart disease undergoing all procedures likely to give rise to relevant bacteraemia, recognizing that this will fail to protect those patients who give no history of heart disease—and increasing numbers of older patients in whom the original nidus is presumably arteriosclerotic fall into this category—and those who give no history of dental or other relevant manipulations. This is an unsatisfactory situation, but the alternative is frequent prophylaxis for a much wider section of the population with all the attendant problems of emergent resistance, side-effects, and cost.

Prophylactic regimens

Thus, the choice of subjects and necessary occasions of chemoprophylaxis are hard to establish. The choice of agents and duration of treatment are scarcely less so. Since bactericidal agents are essential to eliminate the causal bacteria of endocarditis, it follows that they are essential for prophylaxis. Penicillin has long been the drug of choice in chemoprophylaxis for dental procedures where the risk is from oral streptococci which are usually penicillin-sensitive.

Dentists object to regimens which require injections and are, thus, unsuited to the dental surgery and likely to add substantially to the difficulties of persuading children (and not a few adults) to undergo necessary dental treatment (itself an important part of prophylaxis against infective endocarditis). This has led to the advocacy of large single doses (3 g) of amoxycillin, which has the advantage of being well absorbed when given by mouth when it produces concentrations of drug in the blood bactericidal for the majority population of sensitive streptococci for 24 hours. Where enterococci are likely to be liberated into the blood, supplementation of this treatment with streptomycin or gentamicin is essential. In patients allergic to penicillins oral erythromycin (or clindamycin) or intravenous vancomycin can be substituted for amoxycillin. Parenteral therapy is recommended only for dental procedures carried out under general anaesthesia.

As in the case of surgical sepsis, it is not established (probably cannot be established) how long bactericidal concentrations of agents must be maintained, but the episodes of bacteraemia are very short and chemoprophylaxis for more than a few hours cannot be necessary. Again, it is important that the agent should be given an hour or so before operation so that the peak concentration is present in the blood at the time of maximum risk.

LONG-TERM CHEMOPROPHYLAXIS

Rheumatic carditis

This is an unusual form of special susceptibility to infection in that the patients are susceptible not to the infection itself—streptococcal pharyngitis—but to remote immunological sequelae involving the heart. The chemoprophylaxis of the condition rests on unusually secure grounds: only one organism is responsible—the haemolytic streptococcus—and that has remained, to date, steadfastly sensitive to penicillin which will eradicate the organism from the throat. Penicillin is therefore uniquely indicated. Moreover, the patients at risk are clearly identified by having already suffered an attack of rheumatic endocarditis, it being well established that subsequent attacks of streptococcal pharyngitis lead to further cardiac damage. As a fresh attack of pharyngitis may occur at any time and the risk of further cardiac damage persists at least through adolescence, penicillin prophylaxis must be continuous until puberty. This requires the oral administration of phenoxymethylpenicillin several times every day or, more conveniently, intramuscular injections of benzathine penicillin which produce adequate concentrations of penicillin in the blood for a month.

Immunocompromised patients

Prolonged penicillin prophylaxis of rheumatic subjects is successful because only one organism can cause the disease, no resistant strains have emerged, and prolonged penicillin treatment is seldom complicated by side-effects. Had the disease been caused by one of the organisms which has become successively resistant to a great variety of agents, for example, the staphylococcus or *Escherichia coli*, frequent changes of therapy would have been required ending almost certainly with the need to choose between abandoning prophylaxis and contemplating long-term therapy with relatively toxic agents. This kind of dilemma has often to be faced in other situations where the patient's resistance to bacterial infection is reduced for prolonged periods. Examples are in patients suffering from immunodeficiency or diseases associated with impaired defences or treated with immunosuppressive agents. Such patients are subject to invasion from their own microflora and from organisms acquired in the hospital environment, including opportunist organisms such as *Pseudomonas* which can give rise to generalized disease. The management of such patients is an intensified variant of that used for surgical patients. Great care is taken to deny access of hospital organisms to them; they may, for example, be physically isolated from the ward in elaborate mechanical isolators, fed sterile food and given mixtures of poorly absorbed antibiotics such as neomycin, vancomycin, bacitracin, polymyxin, and nystatin, collectively active against all the organisms including both anaerobes and *Candida*, likely to enter the blood from the gut. A refinement of this blunderbuss approach is to attempt *selective decontamination* with two or three agents that remove most of the organisms from the oropharnyx and bowel, but preserve the anaerobic flora. This tactic is intended to discourage overgrowth of resistant organisms in the alimentary tract by a process known as *colonization resistance.* Selective decontamination regimens often combine oral and parenteral drugs, although systemic chemoprophylaxis has been objected to in the past on the grounds that the appropriate agents may be required for therapy if infection occurs despite the elaborate precautions.

The unconscious patient

Normally, the respiratory tract below the larynx is sterile in the sense that there is no resident flora, but organisms stray into the bronchi from the oropharynx and are removed by the mucociliary mechanism. Excess mucus excited by attempts at microbial establishment is removed together with the entrapped microbes by coughing. In the unconscious patient this process is suspended and if artificial means to maintain bronchial toilet are inadequate, multiplication of oropharyngeal organisms in the depths of the bronchi will give rise to bronchopneumonia. It is tempting to guard against this by chemoprophylaxis directed against the common pathogenic organisms: *Streptococcus pneumoniae* and *Haemophilus influenzae*, for example, with ampicillin. In practice, the effect of such therapy is to facilitate the establishment of resistant Gram-negative rods in the oropharynx which then promptly follow the same route into the depths of the lung where they establish an infection which is more difficult to treat and may well extend to fatal septicaemia. Several studies have confirmed the expectation that chemoprophylaxis in such circumstances increases rather than decreases the mortality from respiratory infection.

Chronic urinary tract infection

In contrast, the long-term chemoprophylaxis of intractable urinary infection in patients who cannot be controlled by short-term therapy is highly successful. Why should this form of long-term chemoprophylaxis succeed when the evidently analogous situation in the respiratory tract is at best a failure and at worst a disaster? The reasons appear to be twofold. Firstly, the agents most widely used for the purpose, nitrofurantoin and trimethoprim, do not encourage the emergence of resistant strains in the gut—from which the urinary infecting organisms are derived—in the way that resistant organisms are encouraged in the oropharynx. Secondly, the drugs are excreted into the urine in very high concentrations, while agents used in the treatment of respiratory infection achieve concentrations in the bronchial secretions which are often considerably lower than those in the blood. The essential ingredients of success, therefore, are unusually favourable pharmacokinetic properties and unusual failure to facilitate the emergence of resistant strains. Continuing freedom from resistance can never be relied upon and there is already some suggestion that the favourable position of trimethoprim in this regard is threatened.

Urinary tract surgery

Having said that the urinary tract is unusually suited for successful long-term chemoprophylaxis, important exceptions must be noted. Unfortunately, patients are still infected in hospital in the course of instrumentation or surgery. Some of these patients have gross abnormalities of the urinary tract and may have greatly impaired defence mechanisms. Catheterization carries a significant risk of urinary infection and short-term chemoprophylaxis (for example, with nitrofurantoin) to cover the period of risk is highly successful. This success is not, however, maintained if the period of catheterization is prolonged. The defences are then set aside in a way that resembles that of the respiratory tract in the unconscious patient. Prolonged chemoprophylaxis results in superinfection with resistant organisms. This is also true of attempts to reduce infection by instillation of antiseptics into the bladder or by impregnation of catheters with antibacterial compounds. The lesson is always the same: patients in hospital, whose defences are impaired, are continuously at risk and must be continuously protected against the access of hospital organisms by appropriate hygienic measures. Attempts to prevent infection by prolonged chemoprophylaxis while hygiene is neglected can be relied upon to ensure infection with resistant organisms that may be inaccessible to treatment.

Apart from special examples in which unusual features of the organism or the agent can be readily identified, chemoprophylaxis is likely to be successful only over short periods of identifiable exposure to identifiable organisms susceptible to identifiable agents. It is likely to be worthwhile only if the risk to the patient of developing the infection it is desired to prevent clearly outweighs the possible untoward effects and cost of chemoprophylaxis.

Part V

The therapeutic use of
antimicrobial agents

20

Respiratory tract infection

It has been traditional to subdivide the respiratory tract into upper and lower regions, above and below the epiglottis, and to talk of upper respiratory tract infection and lower respiratory tract infection separately. To a large extent this is reasonable; the upper respiratory tract has a rich and varied microbial population at all times, which contributes to its reaction to pathogenic invaders, while in most healthy people most of the time the lower respiratory tract, protected by ciliated epithelium, mucus, and macrophages, is virtually free from microbes.

Similarly, fairly well recognized collections of symptoms and signs have been held to define different illnesses which can be diagnosed with more or less confidence. These include the common cold, pharyngitis, tonsillitis, otitis media, croup, bronchitis, bronchiolitis, and pneumonia as well as specific infections, such as influenza, diphtheria, and whooping cough.

Some bacteria and viruses can, however, play a part in several of these conditions, and there is considerable overlap between lower and upper tract disease. Fever, excess serous and mucous secretion in the nose and paranasal sinuses, inflammation of the throat and respiratory passages, stimulation of the cough reflex, loss of ciliary activity, shedding of superficial mucosa, spasm of bronchial smooth muscle, and collapse of alveoli can all be found in many respiratory infections. Between them they give rise to the runny noses, headache, earache, cough, sputum production, malaise, and chest pain which, in different combinations, make up the varying clinical pictures of acute respiratory disease.

Respiratory infections are caused by viruses, or bacteria, or both. If the illness is entirely viral in origin, an antibiotic will not help. If there is a bacterial component, antibiotic treatment will probably help, and may be vital. It is often difficult to recognize when bacteria may be involved. Secondary bacterial infection is often, but not always, present in otitis media, sinusitis, and pneumonia, and few would withhold antibiotics for these conditions. Other conditions such as pharyngitis (sore throat) and croup are more controversial.

UPPER RESPIRATORY TRACT INFECTION

Sore throat

This is one of the commonest problems seen in general medical practice, and also one of the most controversial. The most important causal organism is *Streptococcus pyogenes*, which has been said, in different surveys, to account for from less than 20 per cent to more than 50 per cent of all sore throats. All authorities agree that viruses, and particularly the adenoviruses, account for most of the others.

Streptococcal sore throat is important because it may lead to serious complications. It is not possible on clinical findings alone to distinguish between streptococcal and non-streptococcal sore throat. The question is therefore whether to take a throat swab for culture before starting specific treatment or to treat all sore throats as though they were streptococcal, without culture.

The aims of treatment are:

1. to prevent non-suppurative sequelae (rheumatic fever and acute glomerulonephritis);
2. to prevent suppurative complications such as sinusitis, peritonsillar abscess, otitis media, cervical adenitis, and pneumonia;
3. to decrease the spread of infection;
4. to shorten the course of the disease.

Antibiotic treatment of streptococcal sore throat will prevent subsequent rheumatic fever, which may follow from 0.4 to 2.8 per cent of untreated cases, even if treatment is delayed for up to 9 days after onset. Patients who have had an attack of rheumatic fever should be treated with continuous oral penicillin for at least 5 years, to prevent a recurrence. There is no convincing evidence that acute nephritis can be prevented by treating a streptococcal sore throat. Suppurative complications are also markedly decreased by prompt treatment, as is spread of infection to contacts. Treatment probably shortens the duration of the sore throat, but not by much. Controlled studies are unconvincing. On balance, since little is lost by delaying the start of treatment by 24 hours, where adequate bacteriological facilities are available it is worthwhile treating with antibiotics only those sore throats shown to be streptococcal by culture. In the absence of bacteriological guidance it is reasonable to err on the side of caution and to treat as though all were streptococcal. There is, however, room for discretion and many general practitioners are guided more by the severity of the disease and the social circumstances of their patients than by any consideration of the presumed aetiology.

The antibiotic of choice is either penicillin or, for penicillin-hypersensitive patients, erythromycin, and there is evidence that these should be given for at least 10 days to eradicate the organism. Ampicillin should not be used, as it will cause a rash if the sore throat is the herald of glandular fever. Tetracyclines are also inappropriate because of the high incidence of resistance among streptococci.

Diphtheria

At present uncommon in Britain, and indeed everywhere that an effective vaccination policy is practised, diphtheria is nevertheless important in the differential diagnosis of sore throat. Diagnosis must be made on clinical grounds—the severity of the illness, the presence of a diphtheritic membranous exudate—as treatment of the acute illness with antitoxin is life-saving and must be started before bacteriological confirmation can be completed. Penicillin and erythromycin are both effective in eradicating the organism, but cultures should be repeated 2 or 3 weeks after treatment to detect patients who continue to harbour the organism. Most of these will be cleared by a repeat course of antibiotic.

Croup

Noisy difficult breathing, hoarseness, and stridor are common signs of acute laryngo-tracheo-bronchitis in children in winter. This distressing condition is usually viral in origin; para-influenza viruses, the respiratory syncytial virus, and adenoviruses being particularly common causes. Treatment is supportive; the condition is usually self-limiting and resolves in 2-4 days if uncomplicated. Endotracheal intubation or tracheostomy may be needed to relieve respiratory obstruction.

Acute epiglottitis

This is a much less common, but much more dangerous cause of croup caused by infection with *Haemophilus influenzae* of serotype b. There is systemic illness as well as local respiratory difficulty, and the swollen oedematous epiglottis can cause complete airway obstruction with dramatic suddenness. It is this complication which makes acute epiglottitis such a life-threatening condition. Treatment is as much concerned with maintaining the airway as with controlling the infection, but as soon as the condition is suspected treatment should be started with parenteral chloramphenicol or, if that is not readily available, intramuscular ampicillin. Some strains of *H. influenzae* are resistant to chloramphenicol or ampicillin (occasionally both). In areas where resistant strains are known to be prevalent, cefotaxime should offer a logical alternative, but firm evidence for its efficacy is presently lacking.

Pertussis (whooping cough)

Antibiotics are notoriously ineffective in controlling the distressing cough of pertussis; nevertheless, erythromycin has been shown to eradicate the organism from the respiratory tract and can also be used for the protection of susceptible close contacts.

Acute otitis media and sinusitis

Mild catarrhal inflammation spreading up the Eustachian tubes and into the paranasal sinuses is a common accompaniment of most viral upper respiratory infections, and often resolves without chemotherapy as the cold subsides. More severe illness, with toothache, facial pain and tenderness, and a purulent nasal discharge, or earache, pain on moving the pinna, and a red bulging eardrum, indicates bacterial infection and demands antibiotic treatment.

Acute sinusitis and acute otitis media are both caused predominantly by *H. influenzae* and *Streptococcus pneumoniae*. Staphylococci, *Str. pyogenes*, *Branhamella catarrhalis*, and alpha-haemolytic streptococci are less often involved. The antibiotic of choice is amoxycillin; erythromycin and co-trimoxazole are logical alternatives and may be necessary if β-lactamase-producing *H.influenzae* is involved. The optimal duration of therapy is unknown, but 10 days is conventional. Supportive measures such as elevation of the head of the bed, humidification, analgesics, and decongestants may be helpful. Patients with acute fulminating infection which fails to resolve rapidly should be referred to an ENT surgeon for possible surgical drainage.

Acute bacterial parotitis

As a rule bacteria reach the parotid gland by retrograde passage from the mouth. The infection is usually unilateral and used to be a common complication of abdominal surgery. Today, good control of post-operative fluid balance, prompt blood replacement, and attention to oral hygiene have made post-operative parotitis a rarity, and the condition is now more often seen in debilitating medical disease, as a result of a dry infected mouth. Occasional cases may follow obstruction of the parotid duct by calculus or a foreign body, or even occur as an embolic complication of septicaemia.

Treatment consists of correction of dehydration, oral toilet and antibiotics. As the infection is usually due to *Staphylococcus aureus* the antibiotic of choice is flucloxacillin. Surgical drainage may be necessary if these measures fail to bring prompt relief.

Infection in the mouth

Almost all acute suppurative mouth infections originate in the teeth, and are usually the result of dental caries and periodontal disease. Both of these are caused by the metabolism of sugars by oral bacteria, mainly streptococci. The sugars are converted into dextrans and mucopolysaccharides which accumulate as dental plaque, localizing the bacteria to the tooth surface and gingival margins, and allowing acid production to attack the tooth substance.

Chronic gingivitis

When plaque develops under the gingival margin and the periodontal membrane is broken, particles of food accumulate and become infected. The gums retract and become inflamed, and chronic gingivitis results. Acute infection may punctuate the course of chronic periodontal disease, but is usually well localized as an acute dental abscess.

The bacteria usually involved are streptococci, mainly of the alpha-haemolytic and non-haemolytic varieties, and when antibiotic treatment is indicated, penicillin and erythromycin are both effective. The mainstay of treatment and prevention is, however, proper mouth hygiene, dental care, and attention to diet. Soft sugary foods cause dental disease; crisp abrasive fibrous foods prevent it.

Vincent's gingivitis

This is an acute ulcerative gingivitis accompanied by, and probably caused by, proliferation of two normal mouth microbes, a spirochaete, *Treponema vincenti*, and a fusiform bacillus. The main symptoms are bleeding gums, soreness of the mouth, a bad taste, and offensive breath. The disease always occurs in a mouth already ravaged by pre-existing gingivitis and poor oral hygiene. There is extensive gingival ulceration, and contact ulcers may form on the sides of the tongue and the cheek. Occasionally, the infection may spread to cause an acute ulcerative tonsillitis and pharyngitis, a condition known as Vincent's angina.

Vincent's infection responds rapidly to penicillin or metronidazole. When the condition has subsided proper attention should be given to dental care and the correction of underlying mouth disease. Acute ulcerative gingivitis may be an early sign of serious haematological diseases, such as acute leukaemia or agranulocytosis, and these should be excluded.

Thrush

In contrast to the other mouth infections already mentioned, thrush is not associated with poor oral hygiene or dental problems. It is caused by infection of the mucous membrane with the yeast *Candida albicans* and is predominantly a neonatal infection. Candida is a common vaginal commensal, especially in pregnancy, and infection is acquired by the infant during passage through the birth canal. It presents in the first few days of life as white curdy patches on cheeks, lips, palate, and tongue. Treatment is with local nystatin.

In adults, oral thrush is more sinister and is almost always indicative of serious underlying disease, among which endocrine disturbances such as diabetes mellitus, severe blood dyscrasias, and disseminated malignancy are prominent. The condition may complicate treatment with broad-spectrum antibiotics or steroids. A less sinister, but more common manifestation of oral candida infection is the chronic atrophic candidosis which may plague people wearing ill-fitting dentures. In all these conditions oral nystatin or oral amphotericin B may be used to control the candida, but treatment is essentially that appropriate to the underlying condition.

Actinomycosis

This is another condition closely associated with poor oral hygiene, gingivitis, dental decay and especially tooth extraction, in which a normal mouth organism, *Actinomyces israelii*, gains access to already unhealthy tissues and causes a subacute or chronic suppurative infection.

Actinomyces israelii is an anaerobic gram-positive bacillus which shows true branching. On the rare occasions on which it invades tissues it causes an intense polymorphonuclear neutrophil reaction. The most usual mode of infection is through a tooth socket after extraction. Within 1–6 weeks after extraction, the patient notices a small swelling over the mandible. This enlarges and, if untreated, the infection spreads to form an extensive abscess cavity, with extension to involve overlying skin and the formation of one or more sinuses. The pus characteristically contains 'sulphur granules' which are colonies of the actinomycete and the diagnosis is confirmed by culture. Usually, medical advice is sought before the abscess points. Incision, drainage, and treatment with penicillin will control the infection, but the antibiotic needs to be given for 2 or 3 months if relapse is to be avoided. Fusidic acid, clindamycin, erythromycin, and tetracycline are all also active against actinomyces, but again prolonged treatment is necessary to effect cure.

LOWER RESPIRATORY TRACT INFECTION

Acute bronchitis

Most cases of acute bronchitis in a previously healthy adult are caused by viruses, although some may be caused by *Mycoplasma pneumoniae*. The illness is characterized by chest tightness, wheeze, breathlessness and cough. Usually mild, it can be severe in the very young, the very old, the debilitated and in acute exacerbations of chronic bronchitis. If mild, treatment is symptomatic and antibiotics are rarely indicated, especially when the sputum remains mucoid. Purulent sputum or severe illness makes secondary bacterial infection likely, and the most probable offending organisms are *Str. pneumoniae* and *H. influenzae*. The possibility of *M. pneumoniae* infection makes erythromycin or a tetracycline a logical choice of antibiotic, but ampicillin or co-trimoxazole are also effective in most cases.

Chronic bronchitis

This term covers a very wide range of disease, from the irritating, trivial, but persistent cough with some sputum most days in winter and little else, to advanced chronic obstructive airways disease with severe disability and constant respiratory distress. This makes the role of antibiotics in the management of chronic bronchitis particularly difficult to assess. The aim of treatment has been to control acute exacerbations when they occur; long-term prophylaxis has been used for patients with advanced illness and constantly purulent sputum. It now seems clear that those patients who regularly suffer frequent acute exacerbations throughout winter do benefit from long-term antibiotic treatment throughout the winter months, but that for the majority of patients prompt early treatment of acute exacerbations as they occur is just as good. Tetracyclines, ampicillin, amoxycillin, and co-trimoxazole can all be used, and there is little to choose between them. Patient preference and experience of side-effects often decide which is used. A supply of the chosen drug is given at the beginning of winter and the patient instructed to start taking it as soon as the need is felt.

Pneumonia

Any interference with the defences of the respiratory tract or the normal drainage of the lung may predispose to pneumonia. Such interference may be caused by an antecedent upper respiratory infection such as a common cold, and a high proportion of patients with pneumonia give a history of such an infection. At any time, but usually within a week of the onset of the cold, the patient rapidly becomes more ill, with a rise in temperature, cough, at first dry and painful, but later productive of viscid purulent or blood-stained sputum, pleuritic pain, and rapid respiration. The diagnosis is made by finding clinical or radiological evidence of consolidation.

Most pneumonias are caused by infective agents, although chemical or allergic pneumonias do occur. The consolidation may be confined to part or the whole of one or more lobes of the lungs—lobar pneumonia—or may be patchily distributed in a lobular pattern throughout the lung fields —bronchopneumonia.

Pneumococcal pneumonia

The pneumococcus is by far the commonest cause of lobar pneumonia in previously healthy children and adults, and is also prominent in pneumonias following acute exacerbations of chronic bronchitis, together with *H. influenzae*, and occasionally staphylococci, klebsiellae, and a variety of upper respiratory organisms. Nevertheless, lobar pneumonia is not always pneumococcal; any anatomical type of pneumonia can on occasion be caused by almost any respiratory pathogen. Patients with pneumonia require treatment before the results of bacterial investigation are known, and it is seldom possible to be sure of the cause before starting therapy. In the previously healthy child or relatively young adult it is reasonable to assume that the infection is pneumococcal and to start treatment with penicillin by injection. Ampillicin or amoxycillin by mouth are just as effective and have the advantage of being effective against *H. influenzae* as well. Alternatively, a combination of ampicillin and erythromycin can be used. This covers not only for pneumococci and *H. influenzae*, but also for *L. pneumophila* (*vide infra*) and *M. pneumoniae*, a fairly common cause of atypical pneumonia which occurs in epidemic waves and often affects young adults in schools, colleges, or army camps.

Legionnaire's disease

Recently, *Legionella pneumophila* has proved to be a surprisingly frequent cause of lobar pneumonia, accounting for 10 per cent or more of cases in some series. It can occur in explosive outbreaks, but is more commonly sporadic, and contrary to popular belief far more often relatively mild and self-limiting than fulminating and lethal. More than half the cases diagnosed in the UK are found retrospectively by antibody studies on follow-up after recovery from the acute illness. Erythromycin is the antibiotic of choice, and is usually given together with rifampicin in proven cases of *Legionella* pneumonia.

Staphylococcal pneumonia

This serious infection is uncommon except during epidemics of influenza. It is an occasional complication of viral pneumonia at any age, but is especially dangerous in infancy. Any patient who becomes rapidly and gravely ill with pneumonia should be assumed to have a staphylococcal infection, and should be treated with large doses of flucloxacillin.

Opportunistic infections

Patients developing pneumonia while in hospital or as a complication of some other serious underlying disease are at special risk of infection with unusual organisms. Hospital staphylococci and a variety of Gram-negative organisms including *Klebsiella* and *Pseudomonas* are important. Speculative treatment with a combination of an aminoglycoside (e.g. gentamicin) and flucloxacillin or an expanded spectrum cephalosporin (e.g. cefotaxime) is indicated while an attempt is made to isolate a significant organism from sputum, blood, pleural fluid, lung puncture, or trans-tracheal aspirate.

Pneumonia developing in association with neutropenia following treatment with cytotoxic drugs, or in patients with immunosuppression, including those suffering from AIDS, may be due to *Pneumocystis carinii*, fungi, or viruses. Tissue obtained by needle biopsy or open biopsy may be necessary for diagnosis. *Pneumocystis* pneumonia is treated with high dose co-trimoxazole and fungal pneumonias with amphotericin B, with or without flucytosine. In patients with AIDS treatment of *Pneumocystis* pneumonia with co-trimoxazole is accompanied by an unusually high rate of adverse reactions. In these cases, pentamidine isethionate is recommended; this is also highly toxic, but unwanted effects can be considerably reduced by instilling the drug directly into the lungs in aerosolized form by use of a nebulizer.

It must be stressed that in the treatment of all severe pneumonias general medical and nursing care is as important as antibiotic administration. Close monitoring of blood gases, prompt relief of hypoxia, a readiness to resort to mechanical ventilation early, the correction of dehydration, and the relief of pain are all of great importance in the management of this condition.

Empyema

The commonest cause of empyema (purulent pleural effusion) is extension of infection from the lung, but infection can also result from penetrating chest wounds, as a complication of thoracic surgery or by extension upwards from a sub-phrenic abscess. The commonest infecting organisms are *Staph. aureus, Str. pneumoniae, Str. pyogenes*, anaerobic streptococci,

Bacteroides, and other anaerobic bacteria. Mixed infections are frequent, and even when bulk pus from the empyema is cultured the causal organism may not be isolated in up to a quarter of cases, usually because of prior antibiotic treatment. Treatment is by drainage of pus and administration of antibiotics. Initial treatment with penicillin and metronidazole can be modified when the results of examination of the aspirated pus become known, but chemotherapy must in any case be continued for several weeks or until the empyema cavity is satisfactorily obliterated. A similar regimen of high dose penicillin or flucloxacillin and metronidazole should also be used in the treatment of aspiration pneumonia and lung abscess, in which a similar range of organisms may be involved.

Tuberculosis

The other major cause of respiratory disease, *Mycobacterium tuberculosis*, is considered in Chapter 26.

21

Urinary infections

TYPES OF INFECTION

Symptoms of urinary tract infection are usually frequency. of micturition and dysuria. Lower abdominal pain, loin pain, and fever are less often seen with acute uncomplicated cystitis—in which infection is confined to the bladder—but are invariably found in acute pyelonephritis, or other upper tract disease involving the kidney.

Bacteriuria

This, the presence of bacteria in a freshly passed mid-stream specimen of urine, is a laboratory finding. When more than 10^5 organisms/ml are cultured from a specimen of urine the term 'significant' bacteriuria is used. This figure correlates well with urinary infection, but should not be taken to imply that lower numbers are necessarily 'insignificant'. The figure of 10^5 has been established as the cut-off point for significance in order to exclude perineal contaminants which may be present in urine in considerable numbers.

Asymptomatic bacteriuria

This is found frequently in surveys of normal populations and the prevalence increases with age. Except at both extremes of life it is found more frequently in females—an indication of the ease of ascent of organisms from the introitus to the bladder. Asymptomatic infection does not need to be treated except where it has been shown to lead to upper tract infection as, for example, in pregnancy.

Acute cystitis

Infection confined to the lower urinary tract is usually self-limiting. The hydrodynamic effect of continual urine production and micturition tends to wash organisms out of the bladder. The natural defences of the urinary epithelium, both phagocytic and humoral, also limit the natural history of urinary infection. Unless there are anatomical abnormalities—partial obstruction or an inability to empty the bladder completely—or a focus of infection such as a renal calculus (stone) or abscess, infection of the urinary tract often lasts only a few days although the duration of symptoms may be shortened by appropriate chemotherapy. Indeed, old remedies such as high fluid intake may be as efficacious as the newest antibiotic!

Recurrent bacteriuria

In some patients recurrent bacteriuria may be shown to be associated with pyelonephritis. This is an indication for treatment and further investigation.

Symptomatic abacteriuria

In general practice about half the patients presenting with frequency and dysuria have sterile urine cultures. This abacteriuric condition is sometimes referred to as the *urethral syndrome*—a common, but largely unexplained condition.

Post-operative infection

Bacterial infection following surgery or instrumentation of the urinary tract is often seen in hospitalized patients and presents special problems in therapy because of the relatively antibiotic-resistant organisms found in many of these cases. The presence of foreign material such as a urinary catheter which may act as a focus of infection, also makes treatment more difficult.

Urinary infection in children

This is especially important in the very young whose kidneys are growing, because of the possible sequela of pyelonephritis, an important cause of terminal renal failure. Making an accurate laboratory diagnosis is difficult; collecting an uncontaminated urine from an infant requires patience and skill in catching it. In some cases it is necessary to collect supra-pubic aspirates by direct needle puncture through the abdominal wall. This method is of particular value in babies where it is relatively easy to perform.

LABORATORY METHODS

The confirmation of urinary tract infection is made in the laboratory by quantitative culture of an uncontaminated specimen. Skin and perineal flora shed into urine in sufficient numbers will multiply in a few hours at room temperature and give false positive results. These can be reduced by refrigeration and rapid processing in the laboratory. Alternatively, the possibility of contaminants growing in the urine during transit can be circumvented by culturing the urine as soon as it is passed. This is achieved by using dip-inoculum methods which consist of agar attached to slides or spoons which are dipped in the urine, drained, and transported in a stoppered bottle to the laboratory where any bacterial cultures are counted after overnight incubation at 37 °C. A rough quantification is possible by this method or by other simple methods of direct plating of a fixed volume of urine on appropriate culture media. Simple identification of the resulting significant isolates is made and antimicrobial susceptibility tests performed as described in Chapter 7. The common bacterial causes of urinary infection and their usual antibiotic sensitivity patterns are listed in Table 21.1. Many of the bacteria listed may be present as truly infecting organisms or as contaminants. This is a particular problem in urine collected from women which is commonly contaminated with

Table 21.1. Frequency of isolation and usual antibiotic susceptibility of organisms causing urinary tract infection

Organism	Percentage isolates		Sulphonamides	Trimethoprim	Ampicillin	Nitrofurantoin	Nalidixic acid	Gentamicin	Ciprofloxacin
	Hospital	General practice							
Escherichia coli	50	75	(S)	S	(S)	S	S	S	S
Proteus mirabilis	14	8	S	(S)	S	R	S	S	S
Klebsiella aerogenes	12	5	(S)	(S)	R	S	S	S	S
Other coliforms	4	1	R	(S)	(S)	S	S	S	S
Staphylococci	6	7	S	S	R	R	R	S	S
Enterococcus faecalis	10	3	R	(S)	S	R	R	R	S
Pseudomonas aeruginosa	3	<1	R	R	R	R	R	S	S
Candida albicans	<1	0	—Use antifungal agents—						
Mycobacterium tuberculosis	< <1	< <1	—See Chapter 26—						

S = usually sensitive; R = usually resistant; (S) = resistance common.

perineal or vaginal organisms. Mixtures of bacteria usually indicate contamination although mixed infections do occur in catheterized patients.

THERAPY

Choice of agent

In a condition with such a high spontaneous cure-rate it may not be always possible to judge comparative efficacy of different regimens. Urinary infections have been the subject of numerous trials and for most antibiotics a cure-rate of over 80 per cent is expected. In acute, uncomplicated cystitis seen in general practice over 90 per cent of patients would be expected to be asymptomatic after a few days' antibiotic and remain free from bacteriuria for some weeks following. In an early study of the use of sulphonamides in urinary infection a better response was shown in patients infected with bacteria shown in the laboratory to be sensitive than in those infected with sulphonamide-resistant bacteria—a slight justification for the microbiology laboratory! It is an advantage to know the susceptibility of the infecting strain before starting treatment, but delay is justified only in asymptomatic and chronic recurrent cases. The vast majority of acute urinary infections present with painful symptoms and treatment should start before sensitivity results are available. A 'best guess' antibiotic should be selected based on past history, knowledge of likely pathogens and local resistance patterns. In domiciliary practice *Escherichia coli* predominates and the majority will be fully sensitive to all the commonly used antimicrobials listed in Table 21.1. However, in some communities, sulphonamide- and ampicillin-resistant coliforms are sufficiently common for these drugs to be abandoned in favour of trimethoprim or one of the other urinary antimicrobials. The use of co-trimoxazole is not recommended in the treatment of a urinary infection, since the sulphonamide component plays an insignificant role and one might as well use the less toxic trimethoprim alone unless the infecting organism is known to be resistant.

Two agents, nitrofurantoin and nalidixic acid, achieve adequate concentrations only in urine and are exclusively of use in urinary tract infection. Nitrofurantoin is cheap, but it often causes nausea. It is only effective in an acidic urine and thus in *Proteus* infections where the ammonia-producing bacteria raise the pH to over 8 it is ineffective. Nalidixic acid and its early congeners (including cinoxacin, oxolinic acid, flumequine, and pipemidic acid) are inactive against staphylococci and streptococci, and may also exhibit some unpleasant side-effects. However, the more recently developed fluoroquinolones, such as ciprofloxacin, norfloxacin, and ofloxacin combine much improved intrinsic activity with an expanded spectrum which covers not only Gram-positive cocci, but also problem bacteria such as *Pseudomonas aeruginosa*.

Alternative agents to the drugs so far mentioned are often less effective. Oral cephalosporins and mecillinam often fail to produce better results than the traditional drugs. Tetracyclines are effective against many urinary pathogens, but resistance is common and they have sufficient side-effects not to be widely used in practice. The combination of amoxycillin and the β-lactamase inhibiting compound, clavulanic acid, is useful in the therapy of resistant strains.

In countries in which it is available, fosfomycin has proved useful in the treatment of cystitis. The spectrum of activity of this antibiotic embraces most urinary tract pathogens, but the calcium salt commonly used for oral administration is erratically absorbed and resistance may supervene if insufficient concentrations are achieved in urine. The trometamol salt of fosfomycin, developed in Italy, has much better bioavailability and is potentially advantageous for the oral treatment of bacterial cystitis.

Therapeutic regimens

Conventional treatment of urinary infection has been extrapolated from general principles of therapy of tissue infections, often without due regard to the special circumstances obtaining in the infected urinary tract. Thus, it has been advocated for many drugs that they be taken several times a day for 7-10 days. In fact, many antibacterial drugs are preferentially excreted into the urine and attain very high concentrations there, sometimes for long periods. Moreover, in the treatment of bacterial cystitis (in contrast to pyelonephritis or infections complicating urinary tract abnormalities) antibacterial drugs are generally needed only to tip the balance in favour of normal clearance mechanisms. Several studies have shown that much curtailed regimens, lasting for 1-3 days, are as successful as prolonged therapy in curing bacterial cystitis. Indeed, longer courses are wasteful of resources especially since many patients, wiser than their doctors, abandon treatment once the symptoms abate.

Short course treatment has an additional potential benefit in serving to identify those few patients (the ones who fail short-course therapy) who are likely to require more extensive urological investigation. Many of the commonly used antibacterial agents are suitable for this type of approach, although those, like trimethoprim, the newer fluroquinolones or trometamol fosfomycin, which are slowly excreted into urine over a long period, have an advantage over rapidly excreted compounds (β-lactam agents and nitrofurantoin) which achieve high, but transient, concentrations in bladder urine. The practice of giving one or two massive doses of amoxycillin, which is sometimes advocated, would seem to have little to recommend it, since the enormous urinary levels produced are no more bactericidal than those achieved by conventional doses.

Symptomatic abacteriuria (urethral syndrome)

The 'urethral syndrome' is usually seen in young women and although the patients are generally given antibiotics, the symptoms are probably self-limiting. Some patients get intractable symptoms and seek relief from non-medical practitioners; as there may be a psychological element to the urethral syndrome this is reasonable practice. It is, however, important to exclude any known microbial cause. A proportion of women suffering from the urethral syndrome do display intermittent bacteriuria, and sexually transmitted diseases may mimic the frequency and dysuria syndrome. Anticholinergic preparations are commonly used in the management of cystitis and may be beneficial—an example is emepronium (Cetiprin).

Sexual and emotional difficulties may aggravate symptoms and counselling is important. Frequency and dysuria are sometimes related to vaginal hygiene and deodorants or to sexual technique.

The chronic sufferer from frequency and dysuria is a persistent visitor to the surgery and may consume more antibiotics than most patients, hoping for relief from this distressing condition.

Difficult infections

In a small minority of patients symptoms persist or rapidly recur after short course therapy. Inappropriate choice of agent accounts for a few of these, but many of them will be shown to have abnormalities on intravenous urogram. Radiological assessment of patients failing therapy or presenting with recurrent urinary infection is important and must be considered mandatory in children and young adult males. Urograms and micturating cystograms often show an anatomical abnormality such as vesico-ureteric reflux or a contracted kidney indicative of pyelonephritis. Bacteriuria in such patients is an indication for antibiotics even in the absence of symptoms. If repeated conventional courses of treatment fail to prevent relapse and bacteriuria relatively soon after stopping the drug there is a case for long-term antibiotics to suppress the infection. There is some debate about how long this prophylaxis should continue and which patients should receive it. In adults the decision should not be taken lightly and it should be reviewed every 6 months. It is common practice to maintain children with vesico-ureteric reflux and evidence of kidney damage on suppressive antibiotics until they reach puberty. Co-trimoxazole and, more recently, trimethoprim alone are the most widely used agents for this purpose. There is very little evidence for the emergence of tri-methoprim-resistant strains on this regimen. Drugs which rapidly select resistant mutants during a course of treatment such as nalidixic acid are not suitable, but nitrofurantoin may be useful, if tolerated, in patients who develop infection with trimethoprim-resistant organisms. Adverse reactions and superinfection limit the choice of antimicrobial when used long-term and it may be necessary to ring the changes after a few years.

Calculi

Stones in the collecting system are a common cause of urinary tract obstruction and this may predispose to urinary infection. Some calculi, especially those containing hydroxyapatite, may harbour the infecting organism within the substance of the stone. Urease-positive bacteria such as *Proteus* species are commonly incriminated because the alkaline conditions produced by the production of ammonia by the bacterial enzyme favour stone formation. Large infected calculi cannot be treated by chemotherapy and surgery or lithotripsy is necessary. Infection often relapses after lithotomy and there may be small stones left in the kidneys which can act as a further source of bacteriuria. Long-term drug suppression is indicated for these patients. Trimethoprim is the most favoured drug for this indication as nitrofurantoin is ineffective against *Proteus* infections.

Catheters

Urinary catheterization is an essential and commonly performed pro-cedure, but it is not without complications to the patient, the commonest of which is infection. Organisms may be introduced into the bladder on insertion of the catheter or may ascend between the catheter and urethra or up the lumen of the tube. Ascending infection results first in bladder colonization with no symptoms except a 'cloudy' urine followed by cyst-itis which may lead to bladder calculi. In some cases with long-term indwelling catheters, infection may reach the kidneys to result in pyelone-phritis. Instrumentation or catheter removal from an infected urine may give rise to bacteraemia which may present as a mild 'catheter fever' or a life-threatening Gram-negative septicaemia.

Prevention of bacterial colonization is obviously a desirable goal, but even with careful aseptic technique and the use of closed drainage sys-tems bacteriuria is a frequent finding in patients after the catheter has been in position for a few days. The decision to use an indwelling urinary catheter should be tempered by awareness of this complication. In the management of the young chronically sick with neurogenic bladders, many authorities advocate intermittent self-catheterization to overcome the inherent problems of a foreign body in the bladder. Attempts at chemo-prophylaxis with antibiotics inevitably lead to colonization with resistant organisms including, eventually, *Candida*. Hexamine (methenamine), the oldest antibacterial drug used in urinary infection, may have some benefit when used prophylactically since the active component, formaldehyde, which is released in the acid conditions of the urine, is active against all bacteria and yeasts. In the face of established infection, however, hexamine is ineffective. Prophylactic bladder irrigation with antiseptics, such as chlorhexidine and noxytiolin, is sometimes advocated, but this has the disadvantage of breaking the closed drainage system which offers the best means of keeping infection at bay and infection rates are not improved. Again, in the face of long-term bacteriuria the procedure is of limited value and may provoke bacteraemia.

Treatment of catheter-associated urinary infection with antibiotics is only of short-term value. However, in the symptomatic febrile patient Gram-negative septicaemia may supervene and it is important to abort this complication. The chances of treatment being successful are consider-ably improved if the catheter can be removed. Symptomless infection present at the time of removal of a catheter can be treated as an ordinary urinary infection. In patients with indwelling urinary catheters and minimal symptoms there is little to be gained by chemotherapy as candiduria will inevitably follow.

Choice of antimicrobial to treat infection in a catheterized patient may be severely limited as the organisms responsible are often antibiotic-resistant nosocomial strains and infections are frequently due to mixed organisms.

22

Gastrointestinal infections

Gastrointestinal infections are among the commonest infections suffered by mankind. Worldwide it has been estimated that on any one day 200 million people are suffering from acute infective gastroenteritis. The morbidity produced is also profound and even in Britain the economic impact is significant. For example, approximately 4.3 million working days per annum are lost as a result of acute diarrhoea, much of which is infective in origin. Death may occur from electrolyte and fluid loss, particularly in the very young, elderly, or malnourished who can ill-withstand such severe metabolic disturbances that sometimes accompany acute infectious diarrhoea.

Gastrointestinal pathogens are transmitted directly from person to person or indirectly through faecal contamination of the environment, food, or water supply. Hence, the high frequency of such infections in underdeveloped countries where the absence of a clean water supply and safe sewage disposal compound the problems of poverty. Some pathogens, most notably salmonellae, are common to both man and farm animals.

Food may be contaminated by various gut pathogens or their toxins. When illness occurs as a sudden outbreak which can be traced to a common meal, the term *food poisoning* is applied. Non-microbial food poisoning occasionally results from the ingestion of chemicals, fungi, and other toxins such as scombrotoxin and ciguatoxin.

CLINICAL MANIFESTATIONS

The incubation period of gastrointestinal infections varies according to the ingested dose, the site of infection in the gut and the pathogenic mechanism of diarrhoea. The shortest incubation periods are seen with *Staphylococcus aureus* food poisoning where a pre-formed toxin produces symptoms within ½–8 hours of ingestion. Longer incubation periods are associated with salmonellosis and shigellosis in which microbial replication within the bowel may take a day or so before disease is produced.

Symptoms of nausea and vomiting are more frequently associated with small bowel infection. Large bowel involvement is often associated with tenderness over the colon. In dysentery, diarrhoea is accompanied by a profuse, bloody exudate. Regardless of the major site of action, colicky pain is the commonest symptom associated with gastrointestinal infection. The severity of illness is essentially dictated by the degree of fluid loss. Losses of less than 3 per cent body weight are usually undetectable. Once fluid loss exceeds 10 per cent body weight oliguria, cyanosis, and cardiovascular collapse develop and may be fatal unless rapidly corrected.

Systemic symptoms of fever, headache, and rigors are seen in shigellosis and salmonellosis where the intestinal mucosa is involved. Bacteraemia may complicate a severe attack of gastrointestinal salmonellosis and occasionally result in metastatic infection.

GENERAL MANAGEMENT

The management of acute gastroenteritis is largely dictated by the severity of the illness. Most attacks are self-limiting and adequate oral fluid replacement is usually possible. Admission to hospital may be required when vomiting persists or clinically detectable dehydration has developed. In most instances oral fluid replacements are successful. In infants oral treatment with glucose-electrolyte solution is usually given and milk feeding temporarily stopped since lactose deficiency frequently complicates gastroenteritis in early childhood. Therefore, unhydrolysed lactose remaining in the bowel is broken down by gut organisms to lactic and acetic acid which produce diarrhoea through the effects of an osmotic load. Older children and adults can usually replace fluid losses by drinking water, fruit juices, or soft drinks. Few patients require intravenous fluid replacement. However, under such circumstances normal saline and bicarbonate are usually rapidly effective in the severely dehydrated.

Use of antibiotics in gastrointestinal infections

The use of antibiotics carries the risk of directly irritating an inflamed bowel mucosa, or of producing diarrhoea from superinfection. In addition, their use may encourage transferable drug resistance among such pathogens as *Salmonella*.

None the less, there are specific circumstances where antibiotics are appropriate for gastrointestinal infections and associated with clear benefits. Table 22.1 summarizes the chief indications for antimicrobial therapy.

Bowel sedatives and adsorbents

Various agents are available for the symptomatic control of gastrointestinal symptoms. They are frequently prescribed yet little definite evidence exists for their efficacy. They act either by slowing gastrointestinal motility or by fluid adsorption. Diphenoxylate with atropine, loperamide, and codeine slow gastrointestinal motility, and may have an additional mild analgesic effect. Adsorbants include kaolin, chalk, aluminium hydroxide, and cellulose, which tend to increase the stool bulk. Their use should not minimize the importance of adequate fluid and electrolyte replacement. This is especially important in infancy and early childhood where bowel sedatives may induce an ileus and mask fluid loss. Moreover, excessive dosing with diphenoxylate may induce respiratory depression in the young child.

VIRUS INFECTIONS

Viral infections of the bowel are common and produce both sporadic and epidemic disease. Many viruses may cause infection; however, numerically the most important is *rotavirus* which causes both community- and hospital-acquired gastroenteritis. The virus can be demonstrated by electron microscopy. Several other viruses may be associated with acute gastroenteritis; these include adenoviruses, Norwalk agent, caliciviruses, and astroviruses. The infections are usually self-limiting and antimicrobial chemotherapy is not indicated.

CHOLERA

Cholera is an important worldwide cause of serious gastrointestinal infection. It is prevalent throughout the Indian subcontinent and South East Asia where every few years waves of infection radiate from the Ganges basin. The infection is spread by faecal contamination of water supplies.

The cholera vibrio is present in large numbers in the stools of infected patients. The present pandemic is caused by the El Tor biotype.

The onset of cholera is sudden with the development of profuse, pale, watery diarrhoea which may reach several litres a day; the so-called rice-water stools which are isotonic with plasma. The patient rapidly becomes dehydrated, and unless fluid and electrolytes are replaced, becomes apathetic with subsequent hypotension and death. Mortality is highest in the elderly, the very young, and the malnourished.

Recognition of the pathophysiological role of cholera toxin in the production of the disease by stimulation of cyclic AMP has justified the

Table 22.1. Major gastrointestinal infections and their antimicrobial therapy

Organism	Major site of infection	Disease produced	Antimicrobial therapy	Comments
Bacillus cereus	SB	Food poisoning (nausea and vomiting)	None	Reheated rice often incriminated
Campylobacter jejuni	SB	Enteritis	(None)	Erythromycin in severe cases
Clostridium botulinum	CNS	Botulism (neural paralysis)	Penicillin	Neurotoxin: antitoxin more important than antibiotics
Clostridium difficile	LB	Pseudomembranous colitis	Vancomycin or metronidazole	Antibiotic-associated
Clostridium perfringens (welchii)	SB	Food poisoning (diarrhoea)	None	Due to toxin production
Entamoeba histolytica	LB*	Amoebic dysentery	Metronidazole	See Chapter 30
Escherichia coli	SB	(i) Infantile diarrhoea		Rare above age of two. Fluid replacement more important than antibiotics
		(ii) Traveller's diarrhoea	(Prophylactic co-trimoxazole or trimethoprim)	Due to cholera-like toxins; usefulness of antibiotics unproven; self-limiting
Giardia lamblia	SB	Giardiasis	Metronidazole	See Chapter 30
Rotavirus	SB*	Diarrhoea	None	Hospital and community outbreaks occur

Salmonella typhi (and *S. paratyphi*)	Extraintestinal	Enteric fever	Co-trimoxazole or chloramphenicol	Antibiotic treatment mandatory: resistant strains occur
Other salmonellae	SB*	Diarrhoea	None, unless complicated by systemic infection	Antibiotics prolong excretion
Shigella sonnei	LB*	Sonnei dysentery	None	Usually self-limiting
Sh. dysenteriae *Sh. flexneri* *Sh. boydii*	LB*	Bacillary dysentery	Co-trimoxazole, ampicillin	Antibiotics only in severe cases
Staphylococcus aureus	SB	(i) Food poisoning (nausea and vomiting)	None	Due to toxin; usually self-limiting
		(ii) Enterocolitis	Flucloxacillin + fusidic acid	Antibiotic-associated
Vibrio cholerae	SB	Cholera	Tetracycline	Fluid replacement essential, but antibiotics reduce disease severity
Yersinia enterocolitica	SB	Mesenteric adenitis/ diarrhoea/ileitis	(Co-trimoxazole tetracycline)	Antibiotics only in severe cases

LB = large bowel; SB = small bowel; * = mucosal invasion; CNS = central nervous system.

empirical benefit of a glucose-electrolyte oral replacement regimen. The addition of glucose considerably reduces the total volume of replacement fluid required by enhancing the absorption of sodium and water from the small bowel.

Cholera is one of the few gastrointestinal diseases which merit antibiotic treatment as an adjunct to fluid replacement therapy. It has been shown that the duration of cholera is abbreviated by 60 per cent by the use of an oral tetracycline such as doxycycline, prescribed for 4 days. The vibrio is eliminated from the bowel and toxin production ceases rapidly. The carrier state does not occur. Resistance to tetracycline is, unfortunately, increasing and may limit the usefulness of antibiotic therapy in the future.

CAMPYLOBACTER INFECTION

Campylobacter jejuni is now recognized as one of the commonest world-wide causes of acute gastrointestinal infection which may be sporadic or epidemic. The organism produces infection in all age groups, but most frequently in young adults and pre-school children. Epidemics have occurred involving several thousand people following the ingestion of contaminated milk or water supplies. The organism itself is widespread in nature, producing infection in both domestic and farm animals, including poultry, and hence there are many opportunities for spread to man.

Campylobacter gastroenteritis generally lasts for a few days, but may occasionally be more protracted with marked abdominal symptoms of colicky pain and tenderness as well as profuse diarrhoea. Acute appendicitis may be mimicked. Attacks are self-limiting and managed by increasing the oral fluid intake. More severe attacks sometimes require hospital-ization and under these circumstances oral antibiotic treatment with erythromycin is indicated.

There is little information to suggest that any of the different salts or esters of erythromycin has any advantage over erythromycin base although the former are more readily absorbed from the bowel. The drugs are well tolerated, but occasional gastrointestinal intolerance may aggravate the patient's condition. Campylobacter infection is common, but fatalities are rare. Excretion ceases soon after clinical recovery.

Campylobacter pylori is a newly described spiral organism that appears to be involved in certain types of chronic gastritis and, possibly, peptic ulceration. Treatment with amoxycillin in combination with bismuth salts clears the infection, but relapse may occur. Macrolides and quin-olones seem to be ineffective.

SALMONELLOSIS

Gastrointestinal salmonellosis is increasing in importance and is only second to campylobacter as a cause of gastrointestinal infection in the UK where several thousand cases are reported annually. There are more than 1700 different serotypes of salmonella but relatively few produce human disease with any regularity. Some common strains are *Salmonella typhimurium*, *Salmonella enteritidis*, *Salmonella hadar* and *Salmonella virchow*. Frozen poultry is a particularly common source of human infection.

Illness is commonly associated with systemic features of fever and malaise, in addition to the gastrointestinal symptoms. Bloodstream invasion may also occur following mucosal penetration. This occurs more frequently in the very young, the elderly, and those with underlying diseases such as alcoholism and cirrhosis. Achlorhydria from pernicious anaemia, atrophic gastritis, gastrectomy or H_2-receptor antagonists enhances the risk of salmonellosis by eliminating the protection afforded by the normal gastric acid.

Treatment of acute gastrointestinal salmonellosis is essentially directed at the replacement of any lost fluid or electrolytes, either by mouth or intravenously. Antibiotics are contraindicated in the management of gastrointestinal salmonellosis, unless there is secondary bloodstream invasion, since they do not reduce either the duration of illness or the period of excretion. The latter may in fact be prolonged.

Enteric fever

This is caused by *Salmonella typhi* or *Salmonella paratyphi* A, B, or C. The illness is usually designated typhoid or paratyphoid fever when the aetiological agent is known. Enteric fever is primarily a septicaemic illness acquired by ingestion. The gastrointestinal mucosa is readily penetrated, and the pathogen gains access to the lymphatics and blood from where it infects the liver and other parts of the reticuloendothelial system. The bowel is also involved since the lymphoid tissue in Peyer's patches is inflamed and often ulcerates. Constipation is more common than diarrhoea. Perforation and peritonitis are not uncommon in the untreated disease.

Enteric fever is potentially fatal and, unlike gastrointestinal salmonellosis, should always be treated with antibiotics. The bacteria are frequently located intracellularly and not all drugs shown to be active *in vitro* evoke satisfactory clinical response. The drug of choice is chloramphenicol, which produces the most rapid resolution of fever and best cure rates. Treatment must be continued for 2 weeks and, even so, relapse may occur. Alternative agents include co-trimoxazole and high-dose amoxycillin. Both regimens are effective although the time taken for resolution of the fever may not be as rapid as with chloramphenicol and relapses also occur. Relapses should be treated with a further 2 weeks' treatment.

Following clinical recovery salmonella may be excreted in the stool for several weeks. Should this continue for a period in excess of 3 months it is likely that the patient will become a persistent carrier.

In general the chronic carrier state is harmless to the individual. However, there is a potential threat to his household and the community should lapses in personal hygiene produce contamination of food or water supplies. For this reason chronic excretion precludes employment requiring the handling of food. Prolonged high-dose ampicillin therapy is occasionally curative; ciprofloxacin may also prove useful.

SHIGELLOSIS

In its severe form shigellosis produces classic bacillary dysentery characterized by profuse diarrhoea with blood and pus. Infection is worldwide but is more common in underdeveloped countries where sanitation and levels of hygiene are low. In Britain outbreaks occur, particularly among young children in low socioeconomic circumstances and also in long-stay institutions such as prisons and hospitals for the mentally ill. The spectrum of illness ranges from mild diarrhoea to a fulminating attack of dysentery. The more severe forms of disease are in general associated with *Shigella dysenteriae* whilst more mild attacks are associated with *Shigella sonnei*. *Shigella flexneri* and *Shigella boydii* tend to produce disease of intermediate severity although there is considerable individual variation. *Shigella sonnei* is the most frequent isolate in Britain. *Shigella flexneri* is frequently associated with disease in immigrants. The other species are uncommon in Britain.

Shigella spp. are amongst the most virulent gastrointestinal pathogens, requiring only a few bacteria to produce disease. The organism multiplies in the small bowel with subsequent invasion of the mucosa of the terminal ileum and colon. The intense inflammatory response produces a hyperaemic bowel which readily bleeds. Despite the severity of the infection, bloodstream invasion is uncommon in shigellosis. Some strains, notably *Sh. dysenteriae* also produce an enterotoxin which stimulates fluid secretion within the small bowel so that watery diarrhoea may precede frank dysenteric symptoms.

Treatment of shigellosis is dependent upon the severity of the diarrhoea and blood loss. Mild attacks may be managed with fluid and electrolyte replacement by mouth whereas more severe cases may require hospitalization and intravenous fluids. In shigellosis there is a definite place for antibiotic therapy for the severe attack, and to curtail the milder attacks associated with epidemic disease. Unfortunately, resistance among *Shigella* is increasing and laboratory testing of antibiotic susceptibility is important.

Ampicillin, co-trimoxazole, or tetracycline are appropriate choices and may be administered orally provided they are shown to be active *in vitro*. Antibiotic therapy shortens the illness, controls symptoms and speeds elimination of the organism from the bowel. For most mild attacks of *Sh. sonnei* antibiotics are unnecessary.

YERSINIOSIS

Infection with *Yersinia enterocolitica* may produce mesenteric adenitis, terminal ileitis and also acute diarrhoea. For obscure reasons it is more common in Scandinavia, but its occurrence is worldwide. Erythema nodosum and a reactive arthritis may complicate such infections. The illness is usually self-limiting and unless complicated by extragastrointestinal symptoms, is infrequently suspected. Tetracycline or co-trimoxazole are effective if an antibiotic appears justified.

FOOD POISONING

Food may be contaminated at source, in the abattoir, subsequent to marketing or during preparation. Storing at ambient temperatures encourages microbial growth, hence the importance of adequate refrigeration. Foods frequently associated with outbreaks of disease include poultry, meats, shellfish, and those containing dairy products, notably cream. Foodhandlers may excrete salmonellae and contaminate food by lapses in personal hygiene, whilst staphylococcal food poisoning is often the result of contamination of food from infected skin lesions.

Clostridium perfringens (welchii) produces powerful exotoxins which may contaminate meats, gravies and sauces that are either inadequately refrigerated or partially reheated. True mucosal invasion is uncommon with *Cl. perfringens* food poisoning although a severe invasive infection, enteritis necroticans, may rarely occur. This has been described from New Guinea where pork feasts produce disease known locally as 'pig bel'.

Occasional outbreaks of gastroenteritis are caused by *Bacillus cereus*, most frequently in association with the reheating of rice in restaurants. The organism is ubiquitous and produces disease by elaborating an enterotoxin. The disease is self-limiting.

Botulism is fortunately a rare disease which develops after ingesting inadequately sterilized canned products. Spores of *Clostridium botulinum* produce a powerful neurotoxin that is readily absorbed from the gut and produces neural paralysis which in particular affects the respiratory musculature. Treatment is aimed at supporting the patient whilst the fixed neurotoxin undergoes degradation. Prompt treatment with antitoxin is essential to prevent more severe disease.

In all these various forms of food poisoning specific antimicrobial chemotherapy is contraindicated, with the single exception of symptomatic bloodstream invasion complicating gastrointestinal salmonellosis. Treatment is essentially supportive with the notable exception of the use of specific antitoxin for botulism.

Escherichia coli

Acute gastroenteritis is common among travellers to tropical and subtropical regions where it has been known to generations of travellers as 'Delhi belly', 'Gyppy tummy', or 'Montezuma's revenge'. In many instances disease is caused by toxin-producing strains of *Esch. coli*. The toxins have many similarities to the cholera toxin and the pathophysiology of the illness is similar. *Enterotoxigenic* strains differ from the *enteropathogenic Esch. coli* responsible for infantile gastroenteritis which is associated with a few clearly defined serotypes. The latter illness, once a scourge of obstetric units, is now uncommon, at least in the UK, although it may still produce severe dehydration, requiring intravenous fluids. Two other kinds of pathogenic *Esch. coli* are recognized: *enteroinvasive* strains that can produce severe invasive infection of the bowel, but are fortunately uncommon; and *enterohaemorrhagic* strains that produce a toxin detectable by a cytotoxic effect on Vero tissue culture cells (Vero toxin), and have been associated with haemorrhagic colitis and haemolytic uraemic syndrome.

Antimicrobial therapy is unhelpful in the management of traveller's diarrhoea or infantile gastroenteritis caused by *Esch. coli*. Attempts at chemoprophylaxis against traveller's diarrhoea with oral doxycycline or co-trimoxazole have been reasonably successful, but their widespread use for this indication is not recommended. Drug resistance among *Esch. coli* strains is an increasing problem in developing and tropical countries where enterotoxigenic strains are endemic; resistance would inevitably increase further with widespread prophylactic use.

ANTIBIOTIC-ASSOCIATED DIARRHOEA

Paradoxically, the use of antimicrobial agents is occasionally complicated by diarrhoea. This is usually due to a direct irritating effect on the bowel mucosa. However, alteration of the bowel flora may be followed by frank infection with *Candida* or *Staph. aureus*.

A more serious consequence of antibiotics is disease caused by toxin-producing strains of *Clostridium difficile*. In severe cases bloody diarrhoea and a frank colitis develop. The bowel appearances are characteristic and aptly described by the term pseudomembranous colitis. Use of clindamycin or β-lactam antibiotics are most frequently complicated by this disease which occurs in sporadic or epidemic form in hospital practice. The condition is potentially fatal and should be treated with oral vancomycin or metronidazole.

INTESTINAL PARASITES

Symptoms ranging from mild diarrhoea to severe dysentery may be caused by some protozoa and helminths. These are considered in Chapters 5 and 30.

23

Bacteraemia and endocarditis

BACTERAEMIA

Bacteraemia refers to the presence of bacteria in the blood, detected in the laboratory by blood culture. The clinical manifestations range from transient, asymptomatic bacteraemia to fulminating septicaemia, with shock and death occurring within a matter of hours. When bacteraemia is associated with clinical manifestations it is known as *septicaemia*. Thus, bacteraemia is a laboratory finding, whereas septicaemia is a clinical diagnosis.

Any traumatic procedure that facilitates entry of organisms from an infected cutaneous lesion or bacteria-laden mucosal surface may cause bacteraemia (Table 23.1). In addition, invasive infections such as pneumococcal pneumonia, meningitis, or osteomyelitis may be associated with bacteraemia.

In the last 45 years changes have taken place in the type of organism most frequently encountered. In the pre-antibiotic era *Streptococcus pyogenes* and *Streptococcus pneumoniae* accounted for the majority of positive blood cultures and fatalities, but by 1960 *Staphylococcus aureus* had become dominant. Today, staphylococci and pneumococci are still important, but are outnumbered by Gram-negative bacilli as causes of septicaemia and death. Anaerobes such as *Bacteroides fragilis* are also encountered more frequently, perhaps because of improved anaerobic techniques.

The increase in bacteraemic infections due to Gram-negative bacilli follows the success of antibiotics in controlling many Gram-positive infections, but advances in medical and surgical expertise have also played an important part: Gram-negative septicaemia is common in patients undergoing extensive surgery, aggressive immunosuppressive therapy and invasive procedures at the extremes of age, in the very ill or in patients whose normal defence mechanisms are already compromised by the underlying disease. These infections are mostly hospital-acquired, the widespread use of antibiotics having promoted the selection of Gram-negative organisms (which may be resistant to many antibiotics) in the hospital environment.

Table 23.1. Procedures that may produce transient bacteraemia

Predominant organism	Procedure
Viridans streptococci	Dental extraction
	Periodontal surgery
	Surgery or instrumentation of upper respiratory tract
Enterococci	Surgery or instrumentation of the urinary tract
	Surgery or instrumentation of the digestive or biliary tract
	Obstetric/gynaecological surgery
Staphylococcus aureus	Drainage of an abscess

The use of vascular catheters has become an indispensable feature of medical management and this has resulted in an increase in bacteraemia caused by Gram-positive cocci, notably *Staphylococcus aureus* and *Staph. epidermidis*. Polymicrobial bacteraemia and recurrent bacteraemia have also become more common in recent years.

Bacteraemia may be *transient, intermittent*, or *continuous*. The danger of transient bacteraemia depends on the host and the organism. Thus, transient bacteraemia due to viridans streptococci after dental extraction is of no consequence in an otherwise healthy individual, but in those patients with abnormal heart valves it may produce endocarditis (see below). *Staphylococcus aureus* may localize in the metaphyses of long bones and lead to osteomyelitis in children. Transient bacteraemia with Gram-negative bacilli following instrumentation of an infected urinary tract may produce rigor and fever.

Continuous bacteraemia is the hallmark of intravascular infection and also occurs in infections in patients with neutropenia, overwhelming septicaemia, acute haematogenous osteomyelitis, and infections with intracellular organisms such as *Salmonella typhi* and *Brucella* sp., during the early stage of the illness.

Intermittent bacteraemia is characteristic of abscesses and also occurs in certain types of chronic infection such as meningococcal or gonococcal septicaemia or brucellosis.

Antibiotic therapy

If death is to be prevented and shock avoided, the clinician must react promptly and aggressively to the early signs of septicaemia with appropriate parenteral therapy. At least two separate sets of blood cultures and other appropriate specimens from likely sites of infection should be sent to the laboratory. Antimicrobial therapy must start before the culture results are available and rational therapy must take into account the clinical setting and thereby the probable type of bacteraemia.

Secondary bacteraemia

When bacteraemia is secondary to a focus of infection which is readily apparent or clinically suspected it is usually possible to predict the most likely organisms from the clinical presentation (Table 23.2). The most appropriate antibiotic or combination can then be chosen in the light of local knowledge of resistance patterns and changed later, if necessary, on the basis of bacteriological findings. Often, a Gram-stained smear of a specimen from the presumed primary site of infection gives the vital clue on which the choice of 'best-guess' therapy can be based.

Primary bacteraemia

Certain groups of patients give no clue as to the primary focus of infection or its likely source. Such 'primary' bacteraemia of unknown source may occur in neonates, compromised patients, and, rarely, normal individuals.

The neonate   The newborn baby is comparatively susceptible to bacterial invasion of the bloodstream, but the recognition and localization of infection may be difficult because the manifestations are frequently non-specific. However, it is imperative that the diagnosis is made early and antibiotic treatment started at once to avoid complications like meningitis or death. The initial 'blind' choice is a combination of benzylpenicillin and an aminoglycoside, which covers the two most common organisms, *Escherichia coli* and group B haemolytic streptococci as well as most other bacterial infections in this age group. If there is obvious staphylococcal skin infection, flucloxacillin should be substituted for benzylpenicillin.

Compromised patients   Bacteraemia frequently develops without previous surgery or instrumentation in compromised patients, especially those with haematological disease, whose underlying condition and/or therapy increases susceptibility to infection. Among the major predisposing factors are profound neutropenia, mucosal ulcerations, and administration of corticosteroid, cytotoxic, and immunosuppressive drugs. Neutropenic patients are unable to localize an infection at the point of entry due to their inability to mount an inflammatory response; bloodstream invasion occurs frequently without any clinical evidence of the source of bacteraemia. Most of these patients will die within 48 hours if left untreated, so it is essential to begin empirical treatment as soon as blood and other cultures are taken. Since the infecting organisms are unknown, and may include bacteria like *Pseudomonas aeruginosa*, broad-spectrum cover should be used. Therapy with an aminoglycoside (e.g. gentamicin) together with either an antipseudomonal penicillin (e.g. azlocillin or ticarcillin) or an expanded spectrum cephalosporin (e.g. cefotaxime or ceftazidime) has been widely used. Precise choice will depend on local experience and knowledge of resistance patterns. Newer agents, such as the imipenem/cilastatin combination or ciprofloxacin may prove useful in these patients, but clinical experience at the time of writing is limited. In patients with vascular catheters infections with *Staph. epidermidis* should be borne in mind. These organisms are commonly resistant to the standard agents and vancomycin may be added to the regimen in selected cases.

Normal individuals   Primary bacteraemia in normal individuals is rare. *Neisseria meningitidis*, which may produce a fulminating septicaemia, is the most common type in children or adults. There is great urgency in starting treatment, preferably with benzylpenicillin. A delay of a few hours may lead to death of the patient.

Streptococcus pneumoniae and *Haemophilus influenzae* occasionally cause bacteraemia in an otherwise healthy, but febrile child. Those aged 6 months to 2 years are most at risk. Although such bacteraemias may resolve spontaneously, a small minority of patients remain ill and a few develop severe disease, including meningitis. Antibiotic therapy with amoxycillin is warranted.

Other important causes of primary bacteraemia include *Salmonella typhi* and *S. paratyphi* (see Chapter 22), *Brucella abortus*, and *Brucella melitensis*. In the UK brucellosis in man is usually caused by *Br. abortus*, acquired by direct contact with animals, or from consumption of unpasteurized milk and its products. It is difficult to culture *Br. abortus* from blood, even in the acute stages. The diagnosis may rest on clinical presentation with a history of occupational exposure or of drinking raw milk. Serological tests are also helpful. Doxycycline, given in combination with rifampicin for at least 6 weeks, is emerging as the treatment of choice. Co-trimoxazole has also been used, but seems to be associated with a high relapse rate.

INFECTIVE ENDOCARDITIS

Endocarditis is an inflammation of the endocardial surface of the heart. An infection of the endocardium with micro-organisms is known as 'infective' endocarditis, which is preferable to the old term 'bacterial' endocarditis, since fungi, rickettsiae, or chlamydiae may be involved. Although the infection may be located anywhere in the heart chamber,

Table 23.2. Guide to 'best-guess' therapy in secondary bacteraemia

Primary focus of infection	Most likely organism in blood culture	Initial choice of antibiotic
Respiratory tract		
Lobar pneumonia	*Str. pneumoniae*	Benzylpenicillin
Gastrointestinal tract		
Peritonitis	Coliforms; *Bacteroides*	Gentamicin + metronidazole
Ascending cholangitis	Coliforms; *Enterococcus faecalis*	Gentamicin + ampicillin
Liver abscess	Coliforms; anaerobes; streptococci	Gentamicin + ampicillin + metronidazole
Diarrhoea	*Salmonella*	Chloramphenicol *or* co-trimoxazole
Genitourinary tract		
Cystitis/pyelonephritis/instrumentation	Coliforms; *E. faecalis*	Gentamicin + ampicillin
Perinephric abscess	Coliforms; *Staph. aureus*	Gentamicin + flucloxacillin
Pelvic abscess	Coliforms; anaerobes; *N. gonorrhoeae*	Gentamicin + ampicillin + metronidazole
Central nervous system		
Meningitis	*Str. pneumoniae*; *N. meningitidis*; *H. influenzae*	See Chapter 27

Cardiovascular system		
Bacterial endocarditis	Viridans streptococci, etc.	See Table 23.4
Septic thrombophlebitis	*Staph. aureus*	Flucloxacillin
Intravascular devices	*Staph. aureus; Staph. epidermidis*	Flucloxacillin
Skeletal system		
Osteomyelitis/septic arthritis	*Staph. aureus*, etc.	Flucloxacillin (see Chapter 25)
Soft tissue		
Surgical wound (non-abdominal)	*Staph. aureus*	Flucloxacillin
Burns	*Ps. aeruginosa; Staph. aureus*	Gentamicin + flucloxacillin
Carbuncle	*Staph. aureus*	Flucloxacillin
Spreading cellulitis	*Str. pyogenes*	Benzylpenicillin
Periorbital cellulitis	*Str. pyogenes; H. influenzae; Staph. aureus*	Ampicillin + flucloxacillin

the lesion is usually on the heart valves. The words *acute* and *subacute* are still used to describe endocarditis, though the terms originated in the pre-antibiotic era when all patients with endocarditis died and those who died following a fulminant course were said to have 'acute' endocarditis, whereas those who suffered a more indolent course and died after more than 6 weeks (and sometimes up to a year) of illness were said to have 'subacute' endocarditis.

Nowadays, most patients are cured by appropriate antibiotics and it is more useful to classify endocarditis according to the infecting organism, which, besides giving an idea of the probable course of the disease, has therapeutic implications suggesting the antibiotic regimen to be used.

Infective endocarditis, although not common (about 1000 cases per year in England and Wales), is still a very dangerous condition. The initial reduction in mortality to about 30 per cent achieved by antibiotics has still not been much improved, although the pattern of disease has changed, in the antibiotic era. Whereas in the past the mean age of patients was less than 40, today more than half the patients are over 50. One reason for this is the decline in rheumatic fever, but advances in medical and surgical technique have also played a part by increasing survival in patients at risk of acquiring endocarditis, such as those with rheumatic or congenital heart disease. Moreover, demographic trends in age distribution are associated with an increase in degenerative heart disease and this may also be a predisposing factor. Infective endocarditis in drug addicts occurs predominantly in young adults. In about one-third of patients the disease appears to be naturally occurring in that there is no evidence of underlying heart disease.

Pathogenesis

Infective endocarditis is most likely to result from the interaction of several events.

1. Structural alteration of the endothelial surface of the valve.
2. Deposition of platelets and fibrin on the edges of the valve, resulting in the formation of a non-bacterial thrombotic vegetation (NBTV).
3. Colonization of NBTV by micro-organisms transiently circulating in the blood.

Transient bacteraemia is a common event (Table 23.1). Certain streptococci capable of producing extracellular dextran tend to stick to fibrin-platelet vegetations and are known to produce infective endocarditis more frequently than non-dextran-producing strains. Once colonization occurs there is rapid deposition of additional fibrin and platelets over the bacterial colonies and within 24–48 hours marked proliferation of bacteria occurs.

Aetiological agents

Any organism can cause infective endocarditis, but streptococci and staphylococci account for more than 90 per cent of culture-positive cases. Streptococci are still the commonest causes of the naturally occurring type of endocarditis, accounting for about 70 per cent of all cases. Most common of all are the 'viridans' streptococci, a heterogeneous group including *Streptococcus mutans*, *Streptococcus sanguis*, and *Streptococcus mitior*, normally present as commensals in the mouth. Enterococci and *Streptococcus bovis*, which are predominantly gut commensals, are found with increasing frequency. Other streptococci are occasionally incriminated. Endocarditis caused by *Staph. aureus* often presents as a fulminating infection; in about half of these patients there is no evidence of underlying heart disease.

Endocarditis associated with prosthetic heart valves is frequently due to staphylococci, Gram-negative bacilli, diphtheroids, and *Candida*. The organisms may gain access at the time of surgery, or later as a consequence of bacteraemia following infection at a distant site. The infection may manifest itself within 2 months of operation (early onset) or appear long after this period (late onset), when viridans streptococci again become the commonest organisms. Occasionally, organisms acquired at operation may take more than 2 months to manifest themselves.

Staphylococcus aureus is the commonest organism causing endocarditis in drug addicts, although a wide variety of other organisms may be involved. The infection originates in the use of unsterile material used for injection, or is endogenous.

The relative frequency with which the various aetiological agents are encountered is shown in Table 23.3.

Laboratory diagnosis

Blood culture remains the single most important laboratory investigation in patients with suspected endocarditis. Bacteraemia is usually low grade, but continuous, so it does not really matter when blood cultures are taken. Because of the possibility of bacteraemia being missed and the common problem of contamination of blood cultures with skin flora, it is recommended that at least three sets of blood cultures are taken, irrespective of temperature, over a 24-hour period, provided there is no clinical urgency. Cultures should be taken before the start of antibiotic therapy. It is not always possible to distinguish potential contaminants such as *Staph. epidermidis* and diphtheroids from infecting bacteria, and isolation of the same organism from each of several cultures may be important presumptive evidence that such an isolate is genuine. If the patient is seriously ill

Table 23.3. Aetiological agents in infective endocarditis

Predisposing factor	Streptococci		Staphylococci		Gram-negative bacilli	Candida sp.	Others
	viridans	enterococci	aureus	epidermidis			
'Naturally' occurring endocarditis	+++	+	++	+	−	−	+
Cardiac surgery/prosthetic heart valves							
(a) early onset: up to 2 months	+	+	+++	+++	+++	++	+
(b) late onset: more than 2 months	+++	+	++	++	++	+	+
Drug addicts	+	+	+++	+	++	+	−

+++ =Very common; ++ =common; + =rare; − =very rare.

and urgent therapy is required, three sets of cultures should be taken over a period of 1-2 hours from separate venepunctures. It may be difficult to isolate bacteria from patients who have received antibiotics in the preceding 2 weeks and if the clinical situation permits, repeated blood cultures spread over several days may be necessary.

To avoid contamination with skin flora it is immensely important to pay strict attention to skin preparation and to aseptic technique while performing the venepuncture and inoculating the culture bottles. Casual rubbing of the skin with a swab followed by use of an ungloved finger to palpate the vein is a sure way to cause contamination of the cultures. Similarly, blood should not be drawn through an indwelling catheter, since peri-catheter contaminants may be picked up. All blood culture bottles must be taken to the laboratory promptly and put inside an incubator.

In a certain number of patients suspected of having infective endocarditis, blood cultures are persistently negative. Likely explanations are:

(1) prior administration of antibiotics;

(2) infection with fastidious organisms including rickettsiae or chlamydiae;

(3) infection with *Candida*, in which only 50 per cent of blood cultures may be positive;

(4) infection on the right side of the heart, which is occasionally accompanied by negative blood culture;

(5) disease other than infective endocarditis (e.g. left atrial myxoma).

When blood cultures are negative, paired samples of sera (one taken on admission and another 10-14 days later) should be examined for antibodies against other infective agents of endocarditis.

General principles of therapy

For most other infections bacteristatic agents are capable of eradicating the offending microbe in support of host defence mechanisms. However, in endocarditis a population of about 10^9 organisms/g of tissue is situated within the depths of layers of fibrin protected from phagocytosis and humoral defences. Hence, bactericidal antibiotics are necessary which must sterilize the lesion on their own without any help. Bacteristatic agents such as tetracyclines or chloramphenicol may produce a symptomatic response, but once discontinued, relapse is common and they should not be used.

The most commonly used bactericidal agents are the penicillins, in particular benzylpenicillin. In penicillin-hypersensitive patients vancomycin or a cephalosporin offer suitable alternatives. Aminoglycosides, though generally bactericidal, have little activity against streptococci and cannot be used alone (see below for use of aminoglycosides in combination therapy).

From experimental work it is known that organisms buried deep in infected vegetations exist in a state of reduced metabolic activity and bactericidal antibiotics that have a cell wall site of action (e.g. penicillins) are relatively inactive in this situation so that the antibiotic must be administered for a prolonged period. Short-term therapy is associated with relapse and no patient with infective endocarditis should be treated for less than 4 weeks.

The administration of antimicrobial agents by the parenteral route is the only reliable way of ensuring that sufficient antibiotic is present in the serum to guarantee its penetration into the vegetation. With the added risk of patient non-compliance oral treatment cannot be recommended unless facilities exist for frequent monitoring of serum bactericidal activity when it may be used in selected cases of naturally acquired endocarditis.

Laboratory control of antibiotic therapy

Ordinary laboratory sensitivity tests are not recommended in the laboratory management of infective endocarditis. Instead, the MIC and MBC of the antibiotic for the organism involved should be precisely determined (see Chapter 7). In difficult cases tests for antibiotic synergy may also be required to determine optimal combination therapy.

As an additional control of adequate therapy, testing of the bactericidal activity of the patient's serum just before and 1 hour after administering a dose is widely practised, although controversy surrounds its value. The patient's own infecting organism is used for the test and a peak bactericidal titre of, at least, 1 in 8 is considered satisfactory. If aminoglycosides are included in the treatment regimen periodic assays may need to be done as well.

Treatment of specific infections

Highly sensitive viridans streptococci

Approximately 80 per cent of viridans streptococci are highly sensitive to penicillin (MIC 0.1 mg/l or less) and in the past such cases have been treated with penicillin alone. It has been suggested that an aminoglycoside such as gentamicin might be added on the grounds that the duration of treatment may be shortened from 6 to 4 weeks and the few relapses that occur may be prevented completely. The rationale for this comes from studies *in vitro*, supported by animal experiments using the rabbit endocarditis model. Such investigations indicate that the combination of penicillins and aminoglycosides achieve a more rapid and complete kill than that obtained with penicillin alone. In elderly patients with impaired renal function aminoglycosides are best avoided and 4 weeks parenteral penicillin should be used.

Patients who have the naturally acquired type of infection and have responded well during the first 2 weeks of combination therapy may be continued on oral amoxycillin for the remainder of the treatment. Serum bactericidal activity should be determined periodically during oral therapy.

Enterococcal endocarditis

This is the third most common type of endocarditis and is among the most difficult to treat. Mortality is around 20 per cent and relapses are not uncommon. Penicillin alone is not completely bactericidal for most strains of enterococci, but the additional presence of an aminoglycoside produces a marked enhancement of killing and a combination of penicillin and an aminoglycoside is established as the treatment of choice. In the past, streptomycin was the aminoglycoside used, but it is now known that about 40 per cent of enterococcal strains contain ribosomes that are completely insusceptible to the action of streptomycin and in such strains synergy cannot be demonstrated. Ribosomal resistance to gentamicin is still rare, and synergy between gentamicin and penicillin can be demonstrated with virtually all strains of enterococci. For this reason gentamicin is now the preferred aminoglycoside.

The combination of gentamicin and vancomycin is also synergic against enterococci and is the alternative combination therapy in patients who are allergic to penicillin. Cephalosporins, including the new generation compounds, have no useful activity against enterococci.

Viridans streptococci that are relatively resistant to penicillin (MIC >0.1 mg/l) or 'tolerant' (MBC : MIC ratio ≥ 32) are increasingly encountered. Endocarditis caused by such strains is best treated in the same way as enterococcal endocarditis, although 2 weeks of combination therapy followed by penicillin alone should be adequate for 'tolerant' strains.

Staphylococcal endocarditis

Endocarditis caused by *Staph. aureus* results in rapid and severe valvular destruction and the mortality, even with appropriate treatment, is high (50 per cent). Patients with prosthetic heart valves often need further surgery to replace the infected valve and antibiotic treatment may have to be continued for longer than 4 weeks in these patients. Since the vast majority of staphylococci are able to destroy penicillin, the initial choice is a penicillinase-stable penicillin such as flucloxacillin. Gentamicin may be included for the first 2 weeks of therapy to ensure complete killing. In selected cases of naturally occurring staphylococcal endocarditis, oral flucloxacillin may be used for the last 2 weeks of therapy.

If the staphylococci are multi-resistant (as is commonly the case with *Staph. epidermidis*) a triple regimen of rifampicin, vancomycin, and gentamicin has been found to be useful.

If laboratory tests reveal that the staphylococci are sensitive to penicillin, this may be used. Treatment is then the same as that used for endocarditis due to highly sensitive viridans streptococci. So-called tolerant strains of staphylococci, which are inhibited, but not killed by penicillins, should be treated with combination therapy.

Endocarditis due to other bacteria

Haemophilus influenzae, Haemophilus parainfluenzae, Haemophilus aphrophilus, Cardiobacterium hominis, Actinobacillus actinomycetem-comitans, Erysipelothrix rhusiopathiae, Listeria monocytogenes, and *Rothia dentocariosa* are just some of the species which are occasionally isolated from blood cultures in endocarditis. Infection due to these more exotic organisms, though rare, is on the increase. Some of these organisms are slow-growing and sensitivity tests may be difficult to perform or interpret. They are probably best managed empirically with combination therapy using penicillin (or ampicillin) and gentamicin. Serum bactericidal activity is monitored if possible.

Endocarditis due to Gram-negative enteric bacteria

Although these organisms commonly produce bacteraemia, they are extremely uncommon in endocarditis, except in patients with prosthetic heart valves or who are drug addicts. Combination therapy with a β-lactam antibiotic plus an aminoglycoside is usually required, the choice depending on the results of antibiotic sensitivity tests. Medical treatment alone is rarely successful and surgery is needed in most cases. Mortality is high.

Fungal endocarditis

This is usually due to *Candida* spp. and occurs in patients who have had cardiac surgery or who are drug addicts. Occasionally, it occurs as a complication of an infected central venous line. Peripheral embolus occluding a major vessel to a limb is not uncommon. When this occurs, culture of material obtained at embolectomy may yield the offending organism when blood cultures are negative. Surgery is essential to replace infected valves since antifungal drugs alone are unlikely to be effective. Combined therapy using amphotericin B and 5-fluorocytosine is the recommended antifungal treatment.

Table 23.4. Summary of the treatment of some of the commoner types of infective endocarditis

Organism	Treatment of choice				Alternative to penicillin if patient is allergic	Comments
	1st week	2nd week	3rd week	4th week		
Viridans streptococci Other streptococci	Gentamicin Benzylpenicillin				Cephalosporin	Consider changing to oral amoxycillin after 2 weeks
Enterococci	Gentamicin Benzylpenicillin				Vancomycin	Combination therapy may be prolonged if duration of symptoms more than 3 months
Staph. aureus Staph. epidermidis	Gentamicin Flucloxacillin				Vancomycin	1. Consider changing to oral flucloxacillin after 2 weeks 2. Use benzylpenicillin if the strain is sensitive 3. Use vancomycin for methicillin-resistant strains
Str. pneumoniae N. gonorrhoeae	Benzylpenicillin				Cephalosporin	
Culture-negative endocarditis	Gentamicin Benzylpenicillin				Vancomycin	1. Use flucloxacillin if the patient has a prosthetic heart valve or is a drug addict 2. Change to tetracycline if *Coxiella burneti* or chlamydial antibodies detected

Note: patients with infected prosthetic heart valves may need prolonged parenteral therapy or surgery, or both.

Culture-negative endocarditis

Rarely, *Coxiella burneti* or chlamydiae may be involved and should be excluded by serology in all cases since the management is different: tetracycline is used for prolonged periods, but surgery is required for cure. Mortality with antibiotic treatment alone is high.

The remaining cases are managed according to the clinical setting, based on assumptions of the most likely microbial cause.

Table 23.4 summarizes the antibiotic regimens for the common types of infective endocarditis. Acutely ill patients in whom endocarditis is strongly suspected should receive benzylpenicillin, flucloxacillin, and gentamicin until culture results have revealed the offending organism.

Surgical therapy

Persistent infection and intractable congestive heart failure are indications for surgical intervention. In addition, valve replacement at any stage of the disease may be life-saving in selected patients.

24

Skin and soft-tissue infections

GENERAL CONSIDERATIONS

At birth the skin of the infant becomes rapidly colonized with a variety of organisms from the mother, the attendants, and the environment. Only a limited number of species finally become resident flora of the normal skin, for example *Staphylococcus epidermidis*, micrococci, *Propionibacterium acnes*, and coryneform bacteria—all essentially non-pathogenic. In an intact skin these organisms usually prevent potentially pathogenic organisms such as *Staphylococcus aureus* and group A haemolytic streptococci from gaining a permanent foothold. However, if the integrity of the skin is breached by trauma (accidental or surgical), burns, foreign body, or primary skin diseases (psoriasis, atopic dermatitis), then these potentially pathogenic organisms are not only capable of establishing themselves as 'residents', but may also produce infection of the skin and subcutaneous tissue. Other factors which may predispose to skin infection include underlying immune deficiency diseases, diabetes mellitus, and systemic or topical use of steroids. However, in one of the most common of skin infections, namely a boil or a furuncle, there is usually no evidence of any breach in the skin nor any other predisposing factor.

Many different organisms may be involved in skin and soft-tissue infections, but the commonest causes are *Staph. aureus*, *Streptococcus pyogenes* (Group A haemolytic streptococci), *Clostridium perfringens* (*welchii*) and the bacteroides group of organisms. Each of these organisms will be considered in turn and reference made to other organisms where appropriate.

STAPHYLOCOCCAL INFECTIONS

Staphylococcus aureus is the commonest cause of infection of traumatic wounds (accidental or surgical), burns and skin diseases. The normal intact skin does not readily accept *Staph. aureus* except as 'transient' flora, but about 25 per cent of people carry the organism in the nose. In addition, some individuals, especially adult men, may carry *Staph. aureus* in the perineal or axillary regions. In contrast, newborn infants are extremely susceptible to colonization of the skin with *Staph. aureus*.

Skin infection with *Staph. aureus* may involve the hair follicles or the surface and the lesions produced may be pustular or exfoliative.

Pustular lesions

Such lesions of the skin are by far the commonest bacterial infection in man. Fortunately, the majority are mild and self-limiting and do not need medical attention. Pustular lesions commonly encountered include:

1. *Folliculitis* (pimple)—where the infection is confined to the hair follicle without involvement of the surrounding skin or the subcutaneous layers of the skin;
2. *Furuncle* (boil)—when the folliculitis has spread deeper with an area of surrounding cellulitis;
3. *Carbuncle*—when several furuncles have coalesced together to form a large indurated painful lesion containing loculated pus with multiple drainage points.

Exfoliative lesions

These involve the superficial layers of the skin and are characterized by stripping of the epidermis due to the action of an exfoliative toxin produced by certain phage types of *Staph. aureus*. When such lesions are localized and limited the condition is known as *impetigo*, but this form may be due to group A haemolytic streptococci rather than staphylococci (see below). Not infrequently, both organisms can be isolated from the lesions. In newborns the more pronounced lesions may result in large flaccid bullae, the so-called *bullous impetigo*, which occasionally may spread in an epidemic form in the neonatal unit. Rarely, in the very young or the immunocompromised adult, extensive, continuous lesions affect large areas of the body. The patient is systemically unwell with fever and skin tenderness, and the epidermis may separate in sheets in response to gentle stroking (Nikolsky's sign). Various names have been given to this generalized form of the disease, such as staphylococcal scalded skin syndrome, toxic epidermal necrolysis, Ritter's disease, and pemphigus neonatorum. *Staphylococcus aureus* may not be found in the skin lesions and the infection may be at a remote site (e.g. the conjunctiva) from where the toxin causing the generalized skin lesions is absorbed.

Toxic shock syndrome

Certain phage types of *Staph. aureus* produce toxins which cause a multi-system disease characterized by sudden onset of fever, myalgia, vomiting, diarrhoea, hypotension, and an erythematous rash: the 'toxic shock syndrome'. Originally thought to be limited to menstruating women using a particular type of tampon, it is now known to be a rare sequel of any type of staphylococcal infection.

MANAGEMENT OF STAPHYLOCOCCAL INFECTIONS

Large pustular lesions

Minor, well-localized staphylococcal skin lesions are self-limiting and, usually, do not need medical attention. However, larger boils, carbuncles, and infected wounds need not only surgical drainage, but also systemic antimicrobial therapy, which may have little or no effect on the local lesion, but prevents local extension or metastatic infection. This is most important in patients who have lesions on the face where the consequences of retrograde spread via the emissary veins to the cavernous sinus are grave, and as such, even small lesions around the nose and lips are usually treated with a suitable antistaphylococcal agent. It is safe to assume nowadays that the *Staph. aureus* is a penicillinase producer and, therefore, resistant to penicillin. It is, therefore, necessary to use a penicillinase-stable penicillin such as flucloxacillin. Erythromycin or clindamycin are suitable alternatives for patients who are allergic to penicillin. Treatment should be commenced prior to surgery to prevent haematogenous dissemination, and in high-risk situations it should be given parenterally in the initial stages. Treatment is continued until all evidence of acute inflammation has subsided. Where facilities exist, pus obtained at drainage should be submitted for culture in order to definitively establish the causal organism (which may turn out to be an organism other than *Staph. aureus*) and its antibiotic sensitivity.

Acne

These minor pustular lesions are probably not bacterial in origin, but commensal bacteria may be involved and tetracyclines or topical clinda-mycin may help in keeping the lesions under control.

Exfoliative lesions

Minor lesions, for example impetigo, can be managed by the use of topical agents only (see Chapter 31), but if group A haemolytic streptococci are involved, systemic penicillin must be used for at least 10 days to eradicate the organisms from skin lesions and thereby avoid the possible risk of post-streptococcal glomerulonephritis. Erythromycin is suitable for patients who are allergic to penicillin. Extensive impetigenous or bullous lesions, as well as staphylococcal scalded skin syndrome and toxic shock syndrome, require urgent medical attention. A suitable antistaphylococcal agent such as flucloxacillin or erythromycin must be used parenterally.

Recurrent boils

Management of patients with recurrent boils poses a special problem. The management of any one episode is the same as in any other patient, but to prevent further episodes the site of staphylococcal carriage (which may involve another member of the family) should be ascertained, and steps taken to eradicate the source of infection (see Chapter 31).

STREPTOCOCCAL SKIN INFECTIONS

Group A haemolytic streptococci do not form part of the normal skin flora and in the UK primary streptococcal skin infections are far less common than those due to *Staph. aureus*. Streptococci probably enter the skin through areas of minor trauma (e.g. cuts, scratches, or puncture wounds) or become superimposed on some pre-existing skin disease. Lapses in personal hygiene favour initiation of the infective process.

Impetigo

Streptococcal impetigo is very similar to the non-bullous form of staphylococcal impetigo, except that regional lymphadenopathy is commoner with the streptococcal variety. Characteristically, a preschool child presents with lesions round the mouth and nostrils, or on the extremities. Streptococcal impetigo was not routinely treated with systemic antibiotics until an outbreak of impetigo in Trinidad in 1971 revealed that some of these streptococcal strains were nephritogenic. Indeed, in certain parts of the world, impetigo is currently the commonest form of streptococcal infection preceding acute glomerulonephritis. Since the risk may be as high as 1-2 per cent it is advisable to treat all cases with systemic antibiotics, preferably penicillin, limiting topical antimicrobials to patients with small numbers of lesions or as supplemental therapy. Antibiotic treatment is also justified as a public health measure to decrease the streptococcal reservoir and hopefully to limit the spread of potentially nephritogenic strains.

Cellulitis

Cellulitis in its broadest interpretation is an acute infection of the sub-cutaneous tissues, usually streptococcal or staphylococcal in origin. A more superficial form, *erysipelas*, which usually affects the face or lower limbs, is almost always caused by group A streptococci. In the neonate erysipelas may develop from an infection of the umbilical stump.

Previous trauma (accidental or surgical) or an existing skin lesion are the usual predisposing factors in cellulitis, but rarely blood-borne organisms localize in subcutaneous tissue, or an underlying osteomyelitis may present as a cellulitis. If material for bacteriological examination is difficult to obtain—as may be the case if there is no exudate or superficial skin lesion—clinical appearances may be helpful in differentiating staphylococcal from streptococcal cellulitis. In a typical streptococcal case the involved lymphatic ducts show up a red streak extending towards the regional lymph nodes which are enlarged and tender. Bacteraemia is common. Various kinds of haemolytic streptococci other than *Str. pyogenes* may be involved, but penicillin remains the drug of choice for treatment. Staphylococcal cellulitis requires flucloxacillin or erythromycin. If the bacterial aetiology is in doubt flucloxacillin (or erythromycin) alone will provide cover for both organisms. *Haemophilus influenzae* (type b) is an important causative agent of cellulitis in infants under 3 years of age. Facial swelling, often of the cheek or periorbital region, is a common presenting feature and blood cultures are usually positive. In such cases cefotaxime or chloramphenicol should replace benzylpenicillin in therapy.

Anthrax, an animal disease that occasionally spreads to workers handling animal hides, wool or animal products contaminated with *Bacillus anthracis* spores, may present as an oedematous cellulitis. Characteristically, a large, painless necrotic lesion ('malignant pustule') develops on the face, neck, or arms over 2-3 days, sometimes leading to a potentially fatal septicaemic disease. The characteristic lesion and the patient's occupation should alert the doctor to this rare condition. Parenteral penicillin is the treatment of choice. For those allergic to penicillin, tetracyclines are suitable.

Necrotizing infections

The classification and nomenclature of necrotizing, subcutaneous infections is confusing and controversial. *Necrotizing fasciitis* (streptococcal gangrene) is a life and limb threatening type of cellulitis involving skin, subcutaneous tissue, and fascia. Most cases are caused by group A streptococci either alone, or in combination with other organisms, including *Staph. aureus*, coliforms, and anaerobes. The initial cellulitis advances aggressively and the patient becomes toxic. Blood cultures are often positive and streptococci can also be isolated from the bullous lesions. *Progressive bacterial synergistic gangrene* usually complicates surgical abdominal wounds. It starts as an ulcer near the wound and can spread to affect much of the anterior abdominal wall. Classically, microaerophilic streptococci, together with *Staph. aureus* (occasionally coliforms) have been isolated from such lesions.

Management of these rare conditions include radical debridement of all necrotic tissue together with appropriate antibiotics to deal with the various organisms present, as indicated by bacteriological investigations.

CLOSTRIDIAL INFECTION

Gas gangrene (clostridial myonecrosis) is a life-threatening invasive infection caused by several species of *Clostridium*, principally *Cl. perfringens*. These organisms form part of the normal bowel flora of man and animals and clostridial spores are common in soil. Gas gangrene only develops when impaired blood supply, tissue necrosis, or the presence of foreign bodies, produces low oxygen tension in the tissues suitable for the germination of the spores. It is most likely to develop when there is gross soft tissue injury contaminated with soil or dirt, for example, compound fracture in a road traffic accident. Most important are immediate surgical debridement of devitalized tissue and removal of any foreign body, but prophylactic penicillin should also be given. Patients undergoing above-knee amputation for peripheral vascular disease are at risk of developing gas gangrene from faecal clostridia contaminating the buttocks and should be given penicillin prophylaxis (see Chapter 19). Gas gangrene may rarely complicate other surgical wounds, particularly after bowel or biliary surgery, or be a complication of septic abortion.

Clostridial anaerobic cellulitis occurs under similar circumstances, but exploration of the wound usually reveals that the muscle is spared.

Management of gas gangrene

Once gas gangrene is diagnosed on clinical grounds, immediate and aggressive surgical excision of all involved tissues is essential. In the case of gas gangrene of the abdominal wall this means excision of subcutaneous tissue and muscle; if a limb is affected it may need amputation and a patient with septic abortion may need hysterectomy. High-dose parenteral benzylpenicillin should also be commenced promptly. For patients allergic to penicillin, metronidazole may be used. Some authorities also recommend local irrigation with penicillin and hydrogen peroxide, or the use of hyperbaric oxygen.

Despite these heroic and mutilating measures, mortality in gas gangrene remains high. Antitoxin therapy has no place in the management of gas gangrene, whereas in tetanus, the other important clostridial disease, caused by *Clostridium tetani*, antitoxin is much more important than antibiotic therapy.

ANAEROBES OTHER THAN CLOSTRIDIA

Bacteroides fragilis and other non-sporing Gram-negative anaerobes form a major part of the normal bacterial flora of the upper respiratory, gastrointestinal, and female genital tracts. These organisms and anaerobic streptococci are often found in mixed infections with coliforms in intra-abdominal sepsis following appendicectomy, abdominal, ano-rectal, and gynaecological surgery.

In the elderly, diabetic, or obese patient, post-operative infection or infected pressure sores may give rise to a rapidly spreading infection involving deeper tissues, including muscle, to produce *synergistic necrotizing cellulitis*—a variant of necrotizing fasciitis. *Fournier's gangrene*, another form of necrotizing fasciitis involving the perineum, scrotum, or penis is also associated with mixed organisms including anaerobes. Infection may spread to the anterior abdominal wall. The incidence of post-operative infection following certain types of abdominal surgery is very high (up to 40 per cent) and this is one area in which antimicrobial prophylaxis is certainly indicated (see Chapter 19). For established infection surgical intervention is most important and antimicrobial therapy plays a supportive role. Antibiotics used must cover coliforms and anaerobes and a combination of gentamicin and metronidazole is reasonable. Wound infection following 'clean' surgery (e.g. thyroidectomy or mastectomy) is uncommon and when it does occur, *Staph. aureus* remains the commonest aetiological agent.

MISCELLANEOUS INFECTIONS

A wide variety of organisms, alone or in combination, may occasionally produce infection of, for example, human or animal bites, or diabetic gangrenous lesions. Wounds close to bones or joints may involve these structures. A definitive bacteriological diagnosis should be sought and appropriate treatment instituted on the basis of laboratory findings.

25

Bone and joint infections

SEPTIC ARTHRITIS

Septic or pyogenic arthritis can be defined as invasion of the synovial membrane by micro-organisms, usually with extension into the joint space to produce a closed-space infection. In most cases, organisms reach the joint via the blood stream from a distant focus of infection, e.g. septic skin lesions, otitis media, pneumonia, meningitis, gonorrhoea, or urinary tract infection. At times, spread of infection to the joint may occur without an identifiable primary focus. Rarely, micro-organisms may be introduced directly into the synovial space following a penetrating wound, articular surgery, or during intra-articular injection. Alternatively, the joint may become infected by direct spread from adjacent osteomyelitis or cellulitis. Once infection in the joint is established it may lead to secondary bacteraemia.

Aetiology

In the UK, *Staphylococcus aureus* is by far the commonest cause of septic arthritis in all age groups, accounting for 60-90 per cent of all proven infections. Other organisms may be important in selected age-groups, for example *Escherichia coli* and group B streptococci in neonates; pneumococci, group A streptococci and coliforms in the elderly; and *Haemophilus influenzae* (type b) in children less than 6 years of age. *Neisseria gonorrhoeae* occasionally causes septic arthritis in healthy young adults. Rarely, patients with meningococcal meningitis may develop septic arthritis during the course of their illness. Other rare causes of septic arthritis include *Mycobacterium tuberculosis*, atypical mycobacteria, *Brucella* spp., fungi, and *Borrelia burgdorferi*, the spirochaete that causes Lyme disease.

Clinical and diagnostic considerations

In approximately 90 per cent of cases a single joint is involved. In both children and adults the knee is most commonly affected and the hip the next most common site. Classically, the patient is a young child with a high temperature and a red, hot, swollen joint with restricted movement. However, septic arthritis is not uncommon in the elderly and the debilitated, who may present with non-specific symptoms. Patients with rheumatoid arthritis have an increased incidence of septic arthritis, but the clinical diagnosis may be delayed or overlooked, a fact which may partly explain the poor prognosis.

A presumptive diagnosis of septic arthritis rests on the immediate examination of the joint fluid, for clinically it is difficult to rule out other conditions which may mimic septic arthritis (e.g. exacerbation of rheumatoid arthritis, gout, acute rheumatic fever, or trauma to the joint). Typically, the fluid is cloudy or purulent with a marked excess of neutrophils. The Gram-film is of immediate help not only in the diagnosis of septic arthritis but also in the choice of the most appropriate antimicrobial therapy. In patients who have not had antibiotics prior to arthrocentesis and are infected with Gram-positive organisms, the offending bacteria may be seen microscopically in between 75 and 95 per cent of cases. Blood cultures must always be taken and sometimes the organism is isolated only by this means. In suspected gonococcal arthritis, cervical, urethral, rectal, and throat swabs must also be taken for culture prior to antimicrobial therapy.

Guidelines to antibiotic therapy and management

It is imperative that a diagnosis is made rapidly and appropriate therapy instituted immediately since permanent damage to the joint may occur leading to long-term residual abnormalities. The majority of patients who are treated promptly, recover completely. Infection of the hip-joint is more difficult to treat, for in addition to antibiotics, urgent open surgical drainage is needed because of the technical difficulty of needle aspiration. The key to success in managing a patient with septic arthritis is a combination of antibiotics and drainage. In most cases this is achieved by needle aspiration which should be repeated daily, if indicated, in an attempt to 'drain the joint dry'.

The choice of initial antibiotic therapy depends upon the age of the patient and the Gram-film findings. If the Gram-film is positive the offending organism can be identified with a high degree of probability before culture (see Table 25.1) and the appropriate antibiotic for that particular organism is the automatic choice irrespective of the age. If, however, the Gram-film is negative then the initial choice is influenced by the age of the patient and/or the underlying disease; antibiotic therapy is chosen to cover the most likely organism (Table 25.2) and can be modified

Table 25.1. Initial antimicrobial therapy in septic arthritis, when organisms are seen in the Gram-film of the joint aspirate

Description of the Gram-film	Probable organism	Initial choice of antibiotic	Comments
Gram-positive cocci in clusters	Staphylococci	Flucloxacillin	Fusidic acid may be added
Gram-positive cocci in long chains or diplococci	Streptococci	Benzylpenicillin	
Gram-negative coccobacilli	*H. influenzae*	Cefotaxime or chloramphenicol	May change to ampicillin if sensitive
Gram-negative large rods	Coliforms or *Pseudomonas*	Cefotaxime + gentamicin	Change cefotaxime to ceftazidime if *Ps. aeruginosa*
Gram-negative diplococci	*Neisseria*	Benzylpenicillin	

subsequently if a causative organism is identified on culture. Most antimicrobial agents given parenterally achieve therapeutic levels in the infected joint and, therefore, intra-articular injection of antibiotics is not recommended, particularly as it may induce chemical synovitis. There is no consensus of opinion about the type of surgical intervention that is appropriate in septic arthritis and haematogenous osteomyelitis; nor about the choice of antibiotics, route of administration and duration of treatment. A sequential intravenous-oral regimen, carefully monitored at the time of oral therapy, is widely used in children. In all cases, initial treatment must be with parenteral antibiotics until the condition of the patient has stabilized (usually 7-10 days) and the joint is reasonably dry. In selected patients high-dose oral therapy may be used in the last 2-3 weeks of treatment provided patient compliance can be guaranteed and serum bactericidal levels are satisfactory (see Chapter 8). The duration of treatment depends on the organism and the age of the patient. Neonates and young infants in whom there may be concurrent osteomyelitis should receive intravenous therapy for at least 3-4 weeks. Ten to fourteen days' therapy may be adequate for septic arthritis caused by group A haemolytic streptococci, pneumococci or *Neisseria* spp., whereas *Pseudomonas aeruginosa* may require as long as 6-8 weeks. Most cases of septic arthritis caused by *Staph. aureus* or *H. influenzae* are treated for at least 3-4 weeks.

Table 25.2. Initial antimicrobial therapy in septic arthritis when no organisms are seen in the Gram-film of the joint aspirate

	Most likely organism							Initial choice of antibiotic
Age	Staph. aureus	Streptococci Group A	B	Str. pneumoniae	H. influenzae	Gram-negative bacilli	N. gonorrhoeae	
Newborn–2 months	+ +		+ +			+ +		Flucloxacillin + gentamicin
2 months–6 years	+ + +	+		+	+ +			Flucloxacillin + cefotaxime
7–14 years	+ + +							Flucloxacillin
15–adults	+ + +						+	Flucloxacillin
Elderly*	+ + +	+		+		+		Flucloxacillin + gentamicin

* Or patients with underlying disease. + + + =very common; + + =common; + =rare.

OSTEOMYELITIS

Osteomyelitis is infection of bone usually caused by bacteria. In the pre-antibiotic days osteomyelitis was a dreaded disease not only because it was frequently fatal, but also because those who survived were often left seriously crippled with chronic discharging sinuses from the affected bones. This complication may still happen when a patient has not sought medical advice early enough or when acute osteomyelitis has not been treated promptly and adequately. Unlike infection of soft tissues, bone is a rigid structure and cannot swell so that as infection proceeds and pus forms there is marked rise of pressure in the affected part of the bone, which, if unchecked or unrelieved, may impair blood supply over a wide area resulting in areas of infected dead bone. Once this chronic phase of osteomyelitis is established surgical intervention to remove dead and necrotic bone (sequestrum) becomes mandatory to eradicate infection in addition to the use of antibiotics.

Pathogenesis and aetiology

Haematogenous osteomyelitis

Most commonly bone is infected by staphylococci reaching the site from a boil or other focus of infection via the bloodstream. In many patients the primary focus of infection is not apparent. Acute haematogenous osteo-myelitis is primarily a disease of children under 16 in whom over 85 per cent of cases occur. The usual sites are the long bones (femur, tibia, humerus), near the metaphysis, where the blood supply to the bone is most dense. However, when the disease occurs in adults the vertebrae are commonly affected. *Staphylococcus aureus* accounts for about half of all cases and for over 90 per cent of cases in otherwise normal children. In the elderly with underlying malignancies and other diseases, and in drug addicts, Gram-negative bacilli (coliforms and *Ps. aeruginosa*) are being reported with increasing frequency; coliforms are also commonly involved in vertebral osteomyelitis. In neonates, the diagnosis of osteomyelitis is often difficult, multiple bone involvement is common and the adjacent joint may be involved. In addition to *Staph. aureus*, *Esch. coli*, and group B haemolytic streptococci are the main offenders. For some reason group B streptococci have a predilection for the humerus in neonates. As in septic arthritis, *H. influenzae*, group A haemolytic streptococci and *Strepto-coccus pneumoniae* may occur (Table 25.2), but they are even less common in osteomyelitis.

Rare causes of haematogenous osteomyelitis include *M. tuberculosis*, *Brucella abortus*, and particularly in parts of the world where sickle-cell anaemia is prevalent, salmonellae.

Non-haematogenous osteomyelitis

Bones may also be infected by the introduction of organisms through post-traumatic or post-operative wounds. *Staphylococcus aureus* is still the commonest cause, but Gram-negative organisms are also occasionally found. *Pseudomonas aeruginosa* may occasionally produce osteomyelitis of the metatarsals or calcaneum following a puncture wound of the sole of the foot and *Pasteurella multocida* infection may follow animal bites. Finally, patients with infected pressure sores overlying a bone or those with peripheral vascular disease and/or diabetes mellitus may develop osteomyelitis with mixed aerobic and anaerobic organisms (coliforms and *Bacteroides* species) though *Staph. aureus* is still an important organism.

Clinical and diagnostic considerations

The classical manifestations of acute haematogenous osteomyelitis include abrupt onset of high fever, toxicity, with marked redness, pain and swelling over the involved bone. In adults, the manifestations may not be so dramatic. The most important and valuable physical sign is bony tenderness in the metaphysis; this is especially helpful in older children and adults in whom the local and systemic manifestations of infection are not so pronounced. In vertebral osteomyelitis there may be general malaise, with or without low-grade fever and low back pain. If the infection is not controlled it may spread to produce spinal epidural abscess with consequent neurological symptoms.

The conclusive diagnosis of osteomyelitis rests on the isolation of the causative organism from the lesion. Thus, bone aspiration is essential. This will also reveal any abscess which will require surgical drainage. Bone scanning techniques may be helpful if the exact localization of infection is in doubt. At least two sets of blood cultures must be taken; this will clinch the diagnosis in about 50 per cent of cases and obviate the need for bone biopsy. In patients with chronic osteomyelitis it is misleading to base antibiotic treatment on the results of culture of pus obtained from a draining sinus which may bear no relation to the organism obtained at surgery; for precise bacteriological diagnosis material must be obtained during surgical removal of dead bone and tissue or by deep needle aspiration of exudate.

Guidelines to antibiotic therapy and management

It is generally agreed that acute haematogenous osteomyelitis can be cured with antibiotics alone provided they are given early enough (usually within the first 72 hours of the development of symptoms) while the bone retains its blood supply and before extensive necrosis has occurred. Therefore, therapy must start immediately after bone aspirate and blood cultures have been obtained. Gram-film results of aspirated material may help in the initial choice of antibiotic. If no organisms are seen, *Staph. aureus* is the prime suspect in any age group, and an antistaphylococcal agent that penetrates well into bone and pus should be used. Penicillins and fusidic acid fulfil this criterion; however, since *Staph. aureus* is usually resistant to benzylpenicillin and resistance to fusidic acid arises easily when it is used alone, a combination of flucloxacillin and fusidic acid is recommended. If the patient is a young child less than 6 years of age, flucloxacillin and cefotaxime should be used to cover the rare possibility of *H. influenzae*; in the neonate, where group B streptococci are a distinct possibility, benzylpenicillin may be used instead of cefotaxime. Alternative antistaphylococcal agents include clindamycin, vancomycin, and rifampicin.

To ensure adequate concentration at the site of infection high doses of antibiotics should be given parenterally. If an abscess has already formed when the patient is first seen, or if there is no significant clinical improvement within 24 hours of instituting parenteral therapy, then surgical drainage of the abscess becomes essential.

The duration of antimicrobial therapy of acute staphylococcal osteomyelitis should be not less than 4 weeks and may need to be much longer. However, this is a long period for any patient to be on intravenous therapy, particularly when that patient is a young child. It has, therefore, been recommended that after a week or so parenteral therapy should be changed to high-dose oral therapy for the remaining 3-4 weeks. This should only be done if the initial clinical response is good, if patient compliance can be guaranteed, and if facilities exist for monitoring antibiotic activity in serum. Flucloxacillin and fusidic acid are suitable for oral therapy. The recommended duration of treatment of osteomyelitis due to *Str. pneumoniae* or group A haemolytic streptococci is 10-14 days, but this may need to be prolonged in individual cases.

Management of osteomyelitis caused by enteric Gram-negative bacilli is difficult. Appropriate surgical intervention should be accompanied by prolonged intravenous therapy with an aminoglycoside in combination with an expanded-spectrum cephalosporin, such as cefotaxime (enterobacteria) or ceftazidime (*Ps. aeruginosa*). Until recently, there was a lack of a suitable oral agent that was both active and achieved good penetration into bone. Preliminary results with the newer fluoroquinolones, such as ciprofloxacin, are encouraging, but the development of resistance may be a problem. At the time of writing it is too early to predict whether combination therapy with fluoroquinolones will improve prognosis in these difficult infections.

In chronic osteomyelitis where surgery is essential, high-dose oral antibiotics have to be continued post-operatively for several months if infection is to be eradicated.

26

Mycobacterial disease

TUBERCULOSIS

Tuberculosis is an infectious disease of worldwide distribution and great antiquity. The pulmonary form was described by Hippocrates and characteristic lesions of tuberculosis of the spine have been demonstrated in the mummies of ancient Egypt. It attacks both man and animals, affects all ages and every organ in the body, and ranges in severity from latent to hyperacute (the 'galloping consumption' of Victorian times), killing young and old alike. Once known as the 'Captain of the Kings of Death', it has probably been responsible for more deaths in the world than any other bacterial disease. However, the last 30 years have seen enormous progress in the understanding of the epidemiology, prevention, and especially the treatment of tuberculosis and, although far from being eradicated, this age-old killer of man has at last become a preventable and curable disease. This chapter will deal principally with the treatment of pulmonary tuberculosis, because that is the most common form of the disease and practically the only form responsible for transmission from man to man.

Landmarks in the treatment of tuberculosis

Before the advent of chemotherapy, the treatment of tuberculosis was largely restricted to attempts to increase the patient's resistance to the disease. Prolonged rest in hospital and sanatoria, special diets, and avoidance of physical activity were all thought to be important. Attempts were made to immobilize affected lung tissue by artificial pneumothorax, removal of ribs, or, more radically, removal of affected lung tissue itself. Amputation of affected limbs was common, as was surgical resection of other diseased tissues. Today, most of these methods have become almost forgotten history, as the action of drugs on the tubercle bacillus itself has assumed overwhelming importance.

The main landmarks in this story are summarized in Table 26.1. The first was the discovery, in 1940, of the bacteriostatic effect of sulphonamides in guinea pigs infected with tubercle bacilli. The most effective

Table 26.1. Landmarks in the treatment of tuberculosis

Year	Treatment
1944	Streptomycin
1949	Combination chemotherapy—streptomycin and PAS
1952	Isoniazid
1956	Ambulatory outpatient treatment
1964	Intermittent regimens, fully supervised
1972	Short-course chemotherapy

were diamino-sulphones such as dapsone, and the discovery was less than earth-shattering because these agents were found to have little if any activity against tuberculosis in man. They were, however, effective in the treatment of leprosy and remain so today.

The next major advance was the introduction in 1944 of streptomycin, the first drug shown to be effective in the treatment of human tuberculosis. It remains a most important antituberculous drug today. Its use was, however, limited by the ready emergence of streptomycin resistance in tubercle bacilli during treatment, and also by adverse reactions to the drug. In 1949, it was discovered that combined therapy with para-amino-salicylic acid (PAS) and streptomycin prevented the emergence of strains resistant to either, and since then the administration of two or more drugs in combination has been considered essential for adequate treatment of tuberculosis.

The third of the classical antituberculous drugs, isoniazid (INH) was introduced in 1952 and, for the first time, uniformly successful primary chemotherapy of tuberculosis became possible. Initial treatment with streptomycin alone, in courses lasting from 6 weeks to 3 months, had a very high relapse rate after cessation of treatment, while prolonged treatment led to a high incidence of toxicity from the drug and emergence of drug resistance was common. The addition of PAS almost eliminated the emergence of resistant strains, and allowed treatment to be prolonged to 12 months or longer. Relapses after treatment were still common, but longer periods of treatment with streptomycin, which could only be given by injection, were increasingly unacceptable to patients and it needed the introduction of INH, another oral agent, for really long course treatment to be possible. Eventually, a classical regimen evolved in which streptomycin, PAS, and INH were given for 2-3 months, followed by PAS and INH for a further 18 months to 2 years. Until the late 1950s patients were usually confined to hospital for most of this time. This was a very successful regimen (more than 90 per cent of patients completing the course were cured), but it was also a very exacting ordeal in itself, and patients commonly absconded from treatment. Among absconders, relapse was common.

Between 1955 and 1960 a controlled clinical trial was carried out in Madras to compare the effect of 12 months of chemotherapy in two groups of patients: one group treated under good conditions in a sanatorium, the other under poor conditions at home. The results were startling. Despite good accommodation, nursing, rich diet, and prolonged bed rest the sanatorium patients did no better than similar patients treated in overcrowded homes, who had a poor diet, much less rest, and who often worked long hours under poor conditions. The risk to close family contacts was studied for over 5 years, and showed that there was no difference in the incidence of disease between the contacts of patients treated at home and those of sanatorium patients. The major risk to contacts lay in exposure to the index case before diagnosis was made and treatment initiated. Once effective treatment had been started there was little further risk to contacts. Also, the study showed that treatment in a sanatorium is no safeguard against irregularity of drug taking unless the patient is actually seen to swallow every dose. It was this study which caused the dramatic change from institutional to ambulatory outpatient treatment as a general policy.

During the 1960s several new antituberculous drugs were brought into use, of which three—rifampicin, pyrazinamide, and ethambutol—have emerged as of particular importance. Exploitation of these drugs has allowed investigation of intermittent chemotherapy regimens, in which individual drug doses are given at intervals of more than a day (in some cases only one or twice a week)—of particular importance in developing countries where fully supervised daily medication is difficult to deliver—and also, more recently, the development of much shorter regimens, several being curative in less than 12 months.

Factors involved in the response to chemotherapy

Tubercle bacilli: number, site, and activity

In man, in pulmonary tuberculosis, most of the tubercle bacilli are found in the walls of cavities in the lungs open to the bronchi. Here the pH is relatively high, at least on the alkaline side of neutrality. The oxygen tension is also high and the bacilli are actively multiplying. However, there is another smaller population of bacilli, dormant in closed cavities, or in caseating tissue, or inside macrophages, where the pH and oxygen tension are both low, and bacterial multiplication slow.

Antituberculous drugs and their mode of action

The drugs available for the treatment of tuberculosis differ in their activity against tubercle bacilli under different conditions. For example, streptomycin and INH are bactericidal against actively multiplying bacteria under alkaline conditions, while pyrazinamide acts largely on intracellular organisms in an acid medium. Rifampicin is active against both extracellular and intracellular organisms, and also on those dormant in caseous nodules. Bactericidal activity against actively multiplying bacteria largely determines the acute response of the sick patient to chemotherapy, but sterilizing activity against the dormant 'persisters' in the bacterial population is most important when considering the incidence of relapse after cessation of treatment.

Effects of the body's defences and immune response

Host factors and defence mechanisms have, in recent years, been shown to be of much less importance in determining the outcome of tuberculous infection than the effective use of antituberculous drugs. However, species differences in the response to tuberculosis are of considerable interest and have been the source of some confusion. In the mouse, unlike man, tubercle bacilli multiply readily inside macrophages, while there is much less multiplication in cavities and tissue spaces. In the guinea-pig, multiplication of bacilli more nearly resembles that in man, but the human immune response, based on the bacteristatic effect of low pH and low oxygen tension in caseous tissue, is nearer that of the mouse than the guinea-pig. The effect of these differences on the experimental investigation of the drug treatment of tuberculosis has been to complicate an already difficult picture. For example, streptomycin has high bactericidal activity in man and moderate activity against actively multiplying bacilli in the guinea-pig, but is virtually inactive in the mouse. Pyrazinamide, bactericidal in the mouse, is without effect on tuberculosis in the guinea-pig. The practical implication is that the development of effective antituberculous regimens in man has depended almost entirely on the use of large-scale controlled trials of different regimens in appropriate human populations. There is still no suitable in-vitro or animal model from which information can be transferred to man without reservation.

The antituberculous drugs

Streptomycin

This was the first effective drug against tuberculosis in man. Like all aminoglycosides it is not absorbed when given orally, and must be administered as an intramuscular injection. In patients over 40 years of age the dose is reduced because of an increased incidence of vestibular damage, leading to dizziness and ataxia. Hypersensitivity reactions also occur.

Para-aminosalicylic acid (PAS)

This was particularly effective in preventing the emergence of isoniazid-resistant organisms when the two drugs were used together. Very large doses were given, up to 10-12 g a day, orally, in two or three doses. The drug tastes most unpleasant, and gastrointestinal intolerance was common. PAS has now been replaced by more effective and better tolerated drugs, such as ethambutol.

Isoniazid (isonicotinylhydrazine; INH)

This is active only against the tubercle bacillus, not against other microbes, but against this organism it is potent and bactericidal. It penetrates rapidly into all tissues and lesions, its activity is not affected by the pH of the environment, it is well tolerated and is cheap. It is not surprising, therefore, that it is the drug most widely used in the treatment of tuberculosis. The drug is given in a single daily dose as it is more important to achieve a high peak concentration than to maintain a continuously inhibitory level. In intermittent regimens large doses can be used and very high peak levels attained. Isoniazid is metabolized mainly by acetylation, at a rate which varies from one individual to another. Patients can be divided into two groups—*rapid* and *slow inactivators*. This is of little clinical importance in patients treated daily, or even twice weekly, but with intermittent regimens in which the drug is only given once a week, rapid inactivators fare less well than slow inactivators, and there is some practical value in determining, by relatively simple tests, to which group a patient belongs, when an intermittent regimen is contemplated.

Adverse reactions include peripheral neuropathy (which can largely be prevented by giving pyridoxine), drug-induced hepatitis, and toxic psychosis. All are uncommon.

Pyrazinamide

This has a special sterilizing effect on intracellular tubercle bacilli, and has therefore found an important place in short-course chemotherapy, in which the important factor is the incidence of relapse after cessation of treatment. It is given orally. Adverse reactions are rare, but hepatic toxicity has been a problem, and hypersensitivity reactions and photosensitivity of the skin also occur.

Rifampicin

One of the most exciting and potentially valuable of the antituberculous drugs has been rifampicin. Active also against a wide range of other bacteria, it has proved a most potent drug against human tuberculosis, both for primary treatment and in treatment of relapses given daily or intermittently. The daily dose is usually 450-600 mg orally. In intermittent regimens, 900 mg twice a week or 1200 mg once a week can be given. However, rifampicin has not yet become a universally used standard drug, because it is expensive, and it has troublesome side-effects requiring special supervision and care. Curiously, several of these are far more common on intermittent regimens than when the drug is taken daily, and typically begin 2-3 hours after the single morning dose. Once-weekly regimens give more toxicity than twice-weekly, and with daily regimens side-effects are uncommon and trivial. The side-effects are usually mild, and can usually be controlled by reducing either the dose size or the interval between doses. The exception is that the occurrence of purpura is an indication to stop the drug and not give it again.

Thiacetazone and ethambutol

These are alternatives to PAS in many antituberculous regimens. Thiacetazone is one of the oldest antituberculous drugs, being known since before 1950. It has about the same rate of toxicity as PAS, with rashes, jaundice, bone marrow depression, and gastrointestinal upsets prominent. It is more convenient to the patient than PAS (one tablet instead of several cachets a day), is much cheaper, and is stable in tropical climates, where PAS tends to deteriorate. Ethambutol is also an effective drug. Its only serious side-effect is retrobulbar neuritis, which is dose-dependent, rare, and reversible when the drug is stopped. Ethambutol would largely have replaced PAS and thiacetazone by now had it not been far more expensive.

Ethionamide

Because of its gastrointestinal side-effects—anorexia, salivation, nausea, abdominal pain, and diarrhoea—ethionamide is one of the most unpleasant of all antituberculous drugs to take. It needs great determination in a patient and his medical attendants to persist in a course of treatment. Its role is almost entirely in the treatment of patients whose bacilli are resistant to INH and streptomycin.

Cycloserine, viomycin, kanamycin, and capreomycin

These are four rather weak antituberculous drugs used only in three-drug regimens as reserves for the treatment of tuberculosis resistant to the major antituberculous drugs.

Short-course and intermittent therapy

The discovery that both pyrazinamide and rifampicin are active against dormant as well as actively dividing tubercle bacilli prompted the investigation, mainly in East Africa and Hong Kong, of shorter periods of treatment with a variety of combinations of antituberculous drugs. In the first East African trial streptomycin and isoniazid were used alone and with either pyrazinamide, thiacetazone, or rifampicin. This trial clearly showed that all four regimens were effective in controlling the acute stage of the disease, but that, in addition, the regimens containing rifampicin or pyrazinamide would cure more than 90 per cent of patients in 6 months.

Further trials explored different combinations and also the effect of intermittent treatment (Table 26.2). It soon became apparent that all regimens containing two of the three drugs, isoniazid, pyrazinamide, and rifampicin would cure more than 90 per cent of patients in 6 months and virtually all in 9 months. The limitations of treatment became those of cost and of patient compliance in the face of unpleasant side-effects of the drugs. In the developing world the aim was to find acceptable fully supervised mass treatment at a cost the communities could afford.

Affluent countries have different aims. These countries need very effective unsupervised regimens for use where patient motivation is high and good compliance can be assumed. Studies in these countries have shown that rifampicin plus isoniazid daily for 9 months, with streptomycin

Table 26.2. Antituberculous regimens

Study	Regimen*	Percentage cure rate after:		
		9 months	8 months	6 months
Britain	2 ERH/RH	100		95
France	2 SRH/RH	100		95
Singapore	2 SRHZ/RH			99
E. Africa	RH	100		95
E. Africa	2 SRHZ/TH		100	90
E. Africa Madras	} 2 SRHZ/S$_2$H$_2$Z$_2$		100	95
E. Africa	1 SRHZ/S$_2$H$_2$Z$_2$		98	90
E. Africa	1 SRHZ/TH		90	80
Hong Kong	4 S$_3$R$_3$H$_3$Z$_3$/S$_2$H$_2$Z$_2$		99	95
Hong Kong	S$_3$H$_3$Z$_3$	95		75

* E = Ethambutol; H = isoniazid; R = rifampicin; S = streptomycin; T = thiacetazone; Z = pyrazinamide. Initial figure is length in months of intensive phase. Subscript figure is number of doses a week.

or ethambutol for the first 2 months will cure virtually all patients with pulmonary tuberculosis, and these regimens have become standard treatment in Europe. More recently, it has been shown that the total length of treatment can be reduced from 9 to 6 months if pyrazinamide is added for the first 2 months. The British Thoracic Society now recommends a 6-month course of treatment in which rifampicin, isoniazid, and pyrazinamide are given together with either ethambutol or streptomycin for 2 months, then treatment continued for a further 4 months with the two drugs rifampicin and isoniazid. There is increasing evidence that the fourth drug (ethambutol or streptomycin) can be omitted from this regimen without detriment. Almost all regimens contain an initial intensive phase with three or four drugs as it is important to bring the acute illness under control as rapidly as possible.

Drug-resistant tuberculosis

There is wide variation between different parts of the world in the number of patients found to be infected with tubercle bacilli resistant to one or more antituberculous drugs at the time the disease is diagnosed. High rates, particularly to isoniazid, have been reported from Egypt (34 per cent), India (27 per cent), Korea (24 per cent), and low rates from Scotland (5 per cent), England (3 per cent), and Algeria and Finland (2 per cent each). Short-course chemotherapy may be successful even in the presence of initial drug resistance to both isoniazid and streptomycin providing the regimen includes rifampicin and pyrazinamide in the first 2 months, and rifampicin in the continuation phase. This is because initial resistance to rifampicin and pyrazinamide is low everywhere at present, and is another important justification for the use of the complex four-drug regimens already noted. Where adequate facilities exist for determining drug sensitivities, regimens can be devised for individual patients taking account of both initial resistances and resistances emerging during treatment. Modern drug regimens are designed to prevent the emergence of drug resistance, and failure is usually due to the patient not adhering to the regimen prescribed. This is the main impetus behind the development of intermittent fully supervisable regimens.

Extrapulmonary tuberculosis

Tuberculous meningitis

This is the most serious form of tuberculous infection, and is invariably fatal when untreated. It is a frequent complication of untreated miliary tuberculosis, and may vary from an abrupt and severe illness resembling other acute bacterial meningitis to a subtle and chronic disease extending over several months. As in other forms of tuberculosis, appropriate chemotherapy is vital. Treatment should always include isoniazid and rifampicin. The isoniazid should initially be given in larger than usual dose, with a pyridoxine supplement. During the first intensive phase, these drugs should be accompanied by either pyrazinamide or ethambutol and streptomycin. After about 2 months, these can be discontinued, but the isoniazid and rifampicin should be continued for at least a further 8 months. Intrathecal antibiotics are unnecessary but additional treatment with corticosteroids should be considered in severe cases.

Other forms of tuberculosis

Tuberculosis can affect any system in the body, including bones, joints, and kidneys. Generally, the principles described for the treatment of pulmonary tuberculosis are also appropriate for the treatment of other forms, although few regimens have been given controlled clinical trials. Surgical intervention is sometimes necessary to establish the diagnosis, or to drain large abscesses, relieve pressure from tuberculous masses or repair damage from tuberculous scar tissue, but is no longer the mainstay of antituberculous treatment.

ATYPICAL MYCOBACTERIA

Species of mycobacteria other than *Mycobacterium tuberculosis* or *Mycobacterium leprae* can cause disease in man. The so-called atypical species include *Mycobacterium kansasii*, *Mycobacterium marinum*, *Mycobacterium intracellulare*, *Mycobacterium fortuitum* and several others. The isolation of pathogenic atypical mycobacteria does not prove that disease is present; colonization with these organisms is not uncommon. Nevertheless, disease caused by these organisms may be indistinguishable from true tuberculosis.

Atypical mycobacteria are usually more resistant to the standard antituberculous agents than *M. tuberculosis*. However, standard antituberculous chemotherapy is usually effective, although it may have to be prolonged and more often needs to be accompanied by surgical resection of affected tissue.

Atypical mycobacteria of the *avium-intracellulare* group have come into prominence since the appearance of AIDS. Patients with AIDS seem particularly prone to develop infection with these mycobacteria and the disease may be associated with a severe 'wasting syndrome'. Mycobacteria of the avium-intracellulare group are usually highly resistant to the common antituberculous drugs and infected patients respond poorly to antimicrobial therapy. Compounds related to rifampicin, including rifabutin (ansamycin) and rifapentine, as well as the fluoroquinolone, ciprofloxacin, are often active against these organisms *in vitro*, but their clinical efficacy remains unproven at the time of writing.

LEPROSY

This is a chronic communicable tropical disease caused by infection with *M. leprae*, and characterized by skin lesions and involvement of peripheral nerves causing anaesthesia, muscle weakness, paralysis and consequent injury and deformity. Two major types are described, *lepromatous* and *tuberculoid*. In lepromatous leprosy there is diffuse involvement of skin and mucous membranes, with ulceration, iritis, and keratitis; scrapings of skin or mucous membranes contain numerous acid-fast bacilli. The tuberculoid form is more localized, but nerve involvement occurs early; only scanty bacilli are present. In both forms, progress of the disease is slow. The tuberculoid form may heal spontaneously in a few years. Death is usually due to other causes.

The mainstay of treatment of leprosy has been oral dapsone (diaminodiphenylsulphone; DDS) given for 1 or 2 years in tuberculoid disease, but for up to 10 years in lepromatous leprosy. However, resistance to dapsone has become common and leprologists now recommend triple therapy, whenever possible, with rifampicin, clofazimine, and dapsone. Rifampicin is more rapidly bactericidal than dapsone, but resistance may arise if it is used alone. It is also expensive, which is a considerable constraint to its use in countries where it is most needed. Clofazimine is effective, but the compound is pigmented and some patients find the discoloration of the skin that it produces unacceptable. Ethionamide or prothionamide are useful, but more toxic alternatives.

In multibacillary, lepromatous leprosy, triple therapy with monthly rifampicin and daily clofazimine (or alternatives), and dapsone should be given for at least 2 years, or until bacilli can no longer be seen microscopically; in paucibacillary disease, 6 months' therapy with rifampicin and dapsone may be adequate. With such long and complicated regimens, patient compliance is naturally a problem, particularly in areas of the world where leprosy is most prevalent.

It should be remembered that patients with leprosy may also have tuberculosis; the triple therapy regimen used for the treatment of leprosy is inadequate for the treatment of tuberculosis.

27

Meningitis and brain abscess

MENINGITIS

Meningitis is an inflammation of the membranes covering the brain and spinal cord. Infection may be due to bacteria or viruses. Despite the advent of modern antimicrobial therapy, it remains a very serious cause of morbidity and mortality. Fortunately, viral meningitis is usually self-limiting, but before the introduction of chemotherapy the outcome in bacterial meningitis was almost uniformly fatal. Today, the outlook is no longer so grim; the mortality has been reduced to about 15-20 per cent. However, this varies with age, the bacterium and the state of consciousness of the patient; in neonatal meningitis due to Gram-negative bacilli and in pneumococcal meningitis in patients over the age of 50, the death rate may be as high as 50 per cent. If death is to be averted and neurological complications minimized, the clinician must suspect meningitis early, diagnose it accurately, and initiate correct therapy aggressively.

In the UK about 2500 cases of bacterial meningitis occur annually and some 75 per cent of these are due to infection by one of three organisms: *Neisseria meningitidis*, *Haemophilus influenzae* (type b) and *Streptococcus pneumoniae*. The remaining 25 per cent of cases have a varied aetiology with *Escherichia coli* and group B haemolytic streptococci dominant in the neonatal period.

In the UK, *N. meningitidis* is the commonest cause of acute bacterial meningitis, although the incidence of *H. influenzae* meningitis has increased in recent years and *Listeria monocytogenes* has also become more common. The frequency with which the common bacterial causes of meningitis are found in different age-groups is shown in Table 27.1.

Pathogenesis

Bacterial meningitis most commonly follows haematogenous spread of the micro-organism from a distant site of infection or colonization and blood cultures frequently yield the offending organism. The choroid plexus of the lateral ventricles is probably the initial site of entry of blood-borne bacteria into the CSF. Primary foci of infection may exist in the naso-

Table 27.1. Bacterial aetiology and classification of meningitis

Classification and age	Organism						
	Neisseria meningitidis	Haemophilus influenzae	Streptococcus pneumoniae	Escherichia coli	Streptococcus group B	Listeria monocytogenes	Others*
Primary meningitis							
Neonates	–	–	–	+++	+++	+	+
Infants / Young children under 6 yrs	+++	+++	++	–	–	–	–
Children 6 yrs and over	+++	–	++	–	–	–	+
Adults under 40 yrs	–	–	+++	+	–	–	+
Adults 40 yrs and over	–	–	+++	–	–	+	+
Recurrent meningitis							
Any age	–	+	+++	–	–	–	–

+ + + = Very common; + + = common; + = rare; – = very rare. * 'Others' = Enterobacteria, *Pseudomonas* sp. or *Staph. aureus* (neonates; meningitis complicating trauma or neurosurgery); *M. tuberculosis* (children and adults); *Cryptococcus neoformans* (immunocompromised patients).

pharynx, middle ear, lung, heart valves, skin, gastrointestinal, or genito-urinary tracts. Less commonly bacteria may reach the CSF by direct extension from neighbouring infected tissues or a ruptured intracranial abscess. Rarely, micro-organisms may be directly implanted into the subarachnoid space through dural defects of congenital or traumatic origin.

Once a pathogen is introduced into the subarachnoid space in sufficient numbers, an intense inflammatory process is set up in the meninges with marked congestion, oedema, and outpouring of exudate. Usually, the classical symptoms and signs of infection, fever, malaise, and leucocytosis are accompanied by characteristic signs of increased intracranial pressure and meningeal irritation. In neonates, infants, and the aged the signs and symptoms may be non-specific and subtle.

Laboratory diagnosis

Diagnosis of purulent meningitis is a medical emergency. Delay in examining CSF jeopardizes the institution of appropriate therapy and specimens should be sent to the laboratory as soon as lumbar puncture is performed, day or night. As well as being examined bacteriologically, cell count and estimation of protein and glucose concentration should be carried out. Typical laboratory findings in bacterial and viral meningitis are given in Table 27.2. Gram-staining of a centrifuged deposit of CSF is essential and may reveal the causative organism in 85 per cent of cases, allowing appropriate therapy to be started while cultural results are awaited. Occasionally, the Gram-stain is positive when cultures prove negative, especially if treatment has been given before lumbar puncture. Similarly, blood culture may reveal the organism in treated patients, and for this reason blood cultures should also be taken.

Meningococcal meningitis

Neisseria meningitidis primarily affects infants, children, and young adults (Table 27.1). Less than 10 per cent of cases occur in patients over 40 years of age. The organism is carried asymptomatically in the naso-pharynx of a small proportion of the population and this represents the reservoir of infection. The onset of illness may be remarkably sudden and the patient may die of overwhelming septicaemia before there is time to develop a full-blown picture of meningitis. Luckily, this is relatively rare; far more commonly signs and symptoms of meningitis appear over 1–3 days. A macular, petechial, or purpuric rash is present in about 60 per cent of patients suffering from meningococcal meningitis.

Sulphonamides used to be useful for the treatment of meningococcal

Table 27.2. Typical CSF changes in bacterial and viral meningitis

	Normal CSF	Bacterial meningitis*	Viral meningitis
Appearance	Clear; colourless	Purulent or cloudy	Clear or slightly opalescent
Cell count (per μl)	0–5	100s or 1000s	10s or 100s
Main cell type	(Lymphocytes)	Polymorphs †	Lymphocytes ‡
Protein concentration	0.1–0.4 g/l	High (may be several g/l)	Normal or slightly raised
Glucose concentration	C. 60% of blood glucose	<40% of blood glucose	Unchanged
Gram film	Negative	Positive	Negative

* Excluding tuberculous meningitis.
† Exceptions: partially treated pyogenic meningitis; tuberculous, listeria, or leptospiral meningitis, in which a lymphocytic response is common.
‡ In early cases an increased polymorph count may be seen.

meningitis, but sulphonamide-resistant strains account for about 40 per cent of isolates in the UK and as many as 70 per cent in parts of the USA. Sulphonamides are thus no longer reliable in treatment, although they still have a role in prophylaxis, since they are more effective than any other agent in eradicating meningococci from the throat, providing the strain is susceptible. Penicillin or chloramphenicol are the drugs of choice for treatment, although they are unsuitable for prophylaxis. However, reports are beginning to emerge of strains of *N. meningitidis* that are resistant or of reduced sensitivity to penicillin, and all isolates should be tested for susceptibility.

Haemophilus meningitis

Almost all cases of meningitis due to *H. influenzae* are caused by capsulated type b strains. The disease is largely confined to a narrow age group between 3 months and 6 years of age (Table 27.1) probably reflecting the absence of anticapsular antibody in this age group. It is occasionally encountered in older children and adults. The onset is often insidious, progressing over a period of 3–5 days. In some infants the illness may be limited to fever, vomiting, and diarrhoea in the early stages, making the diagnosis of meningitis difficult.

In the past, virtually all strains of *H. influenzae* type b were sensitive to ampicillin, but this is no longer the case. In the UK about 18 per cent of isolates are now resistant to ampicillin, although chloramphenicol resistance is still extremely rare. In certain parts of the world resistance to ampicillin or chloramphenicol is more common and isolates resistant to both are not unusual.

Pneumococcal meningitis

Pneumococcal meningitis may occur in young infants, but is relatively rare in children older than 1 year. It reappears in young adults and after the age of 40 it is the most common organism causing bacterial meningitis (Table 27.1). Pneumococcal meningitis is often a complication of infection in the chest, middle ear, and sinuses. The onset may be sudden and the course rapid with death within 12 hours of admission to hospital. More than 50 per cent of patients are either semiconscious or unconscious on admission. The outlook is grim in those over 50 years of age: out of 18 cases reviewed in a study in Nottingham, only two survived. Some patients die despite apparently optimal chemotherapy and sterilization of the CSF. Survivors often suffer residual neurological effects.

Pneumococci are the commonest cause of recurrent or post-traumatic meningitis, for example, following closed head trauma when organisms may reach the meninges via abnormal communications between the nasopharynx and the subarachnoid space. Immunodeficiency also predisposes to recurrent meningitis. Patients who have had splenectomy are particularly prone to fulminating pneumococcal meningitis.

Nearly all isolates of pneumococci encountered in the UK are exquisitely sensitive to penicillin, but in certain parts of the world penicillin resistance is quite common and susceptibility can no longer be assumed anywhere. For this reason all isolates from CSF or blood should be tested. Penicillin resistant strains can be readily detected in the laboratory by a markedly reduced zone of inhibition round a disc containing 1 μg of oxacillin, which is more reliable for this purpose than benzylpenicillin.

Neonatal meningitis

The neonate, within the first 2 months of life, is at the highest risk of developing meningitis, the incidence being about 0.3 per 1000 live births. Predisposing factors include prematurity, low birthweight, and delivery after prolonged rupture of the membranes.

Any organism present in the vagina or in the neonatal environment can cause meningitis, but *Esch. coli* and group B streptococci are much the most common in the UK. Less common organisms include *Listeria monocytogenes* (which may also be acquired transplacentally), various enterobacteria and *Pseudomonas aeruginosa*.

The early signs and symptoms of neonatal meningitis are frequently vague: lethargy, refusal of feeds, and fever. A bulging fontanelle is a relatively late sign. The mortality rate is considerable (about 20-50 per cent depending on the organism and predisposing factors), and a high degree of suspicion and prompt investigation with lumbar puncture is essential. Of those who survive, about half will have some evidence of neurological damage.

Neonatal meningitis is usually managed with a combination of antibiotics (see below); since the susceptibility of the organisms involved is far from predictable, the chosen therapy should be backed up by appropriate laboratory tests.

Culture-negative pyogenic meningitis

About 40 per cent of patients presenting with meningitis will already have received antimicrobial therapy prior to lumbar puncture. Antibiotics which penetrate CSF poorly should produce minimal changes, but those drugs which enter the CSF in significant amounts may cause failure of attempts to isolate the organism. Prior therapy does not seriously alter cell counts or protein and glucose concentrations and it is usually still possible to differentiate between bacterial and viral meningitis.

Although prior therapy may confuse the clinical picture it is not detrimental to the individual patient who has as good a prognosis as those who are untreated. 'Best guess' therapy should be aimed at all three common bacterial pathogens.

Rarer forms of meningitis

Listeria meningitis

As well as causing meningitis in neonates, *L. monocytogenes* also produces meningitis in adults, particularly those who are immuno-suppressed or have some underlying disease. The source of infection in most sporadic cases is unclear, but at least 1 per cent of humans carry the organism in the gut and food has been implicated in some cases.

The organism is sensitive to a variety of agents, but large doses of ampicillin, with or without gentamicin is the treatment of choice. Cephalosporins have no useful activity against these organisms.

Streptococcal meningitis

In addition to group B streptococci, other streptococci may cause meningitis following head injury, neurosurgical procedures or rupture of cerebral abscess. Benzylpenicillin is the drug of choice.

Staphylococcal meningitis

Staphylococcus aureus may produce meningitis in fulminating pneumonia, endocarditis, or as a complication of head injury, neurosurgery, or ruptured cerebral and epidural abscess. *Staphylococcus epidermidis* is important in shunt-associated meningitis, where removal of the infected shunt may be necessary in addition to antibiotic therapy. Almost all strains of *Staph. aureus* are sensitive to flucloxacillin or cloxacillin and high-dose therapy with one of these drugs is the mainstay of treatment. *Staphylococcus epidermidis* may be resistant to flucloxacillin and systematic and intraventricular therapy with vancomycin may be necessary.

Cryptococcal meningitis

This is a rare form of meningitis, caused by *Cryptococcus neoformans*, a yeast found in the environment. The disease occurs mainly in those who are immunocompromised due to disease or drugs. Amphotericin B was the only useful drug until the less toxic 5-fluorocytosine became available; however, there are reports of resistance emerging during therapy with the latter drug. Synergy has been demonstrated between amphotericin B and

5-fluorocytosine *in vitro* and a combination of low-dose amphotericin B and 5-fluorocytosine is now recommended in cryptococcal meningitis. The new azole derivative, fluconazole, penetrates well into CSF and is undergoing trial in cryptococcal meningitis in patients with AIDS.

Tuberculous meningitis

This can affect any age after the neonatal period. It is uncommon, but cases can be missed unless the physician is aware of the possibility and the laboratory is keen to exclude tuberculous meningitis in all cases where abnormal clinical or CSF findings (increased lymphocytes, raised protein, low CSF glucose) have not been satisfactorily explained. The presentation is less dramatic and the illness is usually spread over a period of 2 weeks or more. The numbers of tubercle bacilli in CSF is small and success in finding them in direct smears depends on the intensity of the search. Failure to demonstrate the bacilli in smears does not exclude the diagnosis and therapy should be started presumptively in strongly suspected cases.

The principal treatment, with combination therapy, remains the same as for pulmonary tuberculosis (see Chapter 26). Fortunately, most currently used antituberculous agents, with the exception of streptomycin, penetrate reasonably well into CSF in tuberculous meningitis.

Therapeutic considerations

Bacterial meningitis was difficult or impossible to treat before the advent of sulphonamides. Today, with a battery of potent antimicrobial agents, success rests on prompt initiation of treatment, started on the basis of Gram-film findings and on the appreciation of certain principles and guidelines.

Penetration of antibiotics into CSF

In bacterial meningitis infection is located in a closed space within the CSF which represents an area of impaired host defence. Hence, it is imperative to ensure that the antimicrobial agent used is both lethal to the invading organism and able to penetrate into the CSF in therapeutic concentration. All organic compounds entering CSF must traverse the blood-brain barrier: a lipid membrane in the brain capillary, the epithelial layer of the choroid plexus, or both. The choroid epithelium is highly impermeable to lipid insoluble molecules. The penetration of antibiotics into the CSF is dictated mainly by:

(1) lipid solubility;
(2) degree of ionization;

(3) molecular size and structure;

(4) serum concentration of the drug;

(5) protein binding;

(6) degree of meningeal inflammation.

The commonly used antimicrobial agents can be subdivided into three broad groups according to their ability to penetrate into CSF.

1. Those that penetrate inflamed and non-inflamed meninges, even when used in standard doses. These include chloramphenicol, sulphonamides, trimethoprim, metronidazole, and the antituberculous agents isoniazid and pyrazinamide.

2. Those that penetrate when the meninges are inflamed, or when used in high doses. These include benzylpenicillin, ampicillin, flucloxacillin, extended-spectrum cephalosporins of the cefotaxime type, vancomycin, and rifampicin.

3. Those that penetrate poorly even when the meninges are inflamed. These include aminoglycosides, the earlier cephalosporins, erythromycin, tetracycline, and fusidic acid.

Choice of antimicrobial agent

Sensitivity to benzylpenicillin and ampicillin can be predicted with a high degree of confidence for *N. meningitidis* and *Str. pneumoniae*, although resistant strains do occur.

In *H. influenzae* meningitis, a combination of ampicillin with chloramphenicol is often used initially to cover the possibility of resistance, with one or other agent discontinued once sensitivity results are known. Although this combination has been considered potentially antagonistic, this does not appear to be the case with *H. influenzae* (or the other common meningeal pathogens) against which chloramphenicol is bactericidal. Ampicillin resistance is usually due to β-lactamase production and this can be detected rapidly by any one of several laboratory tests. Chloramphenicol-resistant strains are presently rare in the UK, but in some countries strains that are resistant to both ampicillin and chloramphenicol are quite common.

Cefotaxime, ceftizoxime, and ceftriaxone exhibit excellent activity *in vitro* against all strains of *H. influenzae*, as well as *Str. pneumoniae*, *N. meningitidis*, *Esch. coli* and group B streptococci. Intravenous therapy with high doses of these agents usually results in CSF concentrations many times those necessary to kill the organisms. Clinical trials suggest that these antibiotics offer reasonable alternatives to chloramphenicol in the initial empirical therapy of meningitis in areas where β-lactamase-producing *H. influenzae* are common, as well as in patients known to be hypersensitive to penicillins.

Neonatal meningitis Treatment of neonates is particularly difficult, since a wide variety of organisms may be involved. Chloramphenicol has been widely used, but this drug, despite its excellent penetration into CSF, is not bactericidal to *Esch. coli* and relapse has been recorded. Moreover, chloramphenicol may, on rare occasions, cause irreversible bone marrow aplasia and produce 'grey syndrome' in the neonate.

High doses of cefotaxime (or other extended-spectrum cephalosporin) in combination with gentamicin provide synergic bactericidal activity against *Esch. coli* and other enterobacteria. Combination therapy should be continued for at least 3 weeks. In meningitis caused by group B strepto-cocci, at least 2 weeks of high dose therapy with benzylpenicillin, together with gentamicin for the first 7–10 days, is recommended. For *L. mono-cytogenes*, high dose ampicillin should be used in combination with gentamicin for at least 2 weeks.

If the CSF Gram-film does not reveal any organisms, the initial choice of agents in neonatal meningitis must cover *Esch. coli*, group B strepto-cocci, and *L. monocytogenes*.

A summary of current recommendations for the initial therapy of pyogenic meningitis is outlined in Table 27.3.

Route of administration

Intravenous administration of antibiotics is preferred in all cases of bacterial meningitis, for the essence of specific treatment is not merely to kill the organisms, but to kill them quickly. Since β-lactam antibiotics enter the CSF reluctantly, it is essential to give these antibiotics parenter-ally in high and frequent doses to ensure that, even at the lower levels of diffusion, therapeutic concentrations can be achieved. When chlor-amphenicol is used for treating meningitis, the oral route can be used after the initial acute stages of illness, but oral penicillin V, oral ampicillin preparations, or amoxycillin, have no place in the treatment of meningitis.

Duration of therapy

The duration of treatment in most cases of uncomplicated meningitis is short. Antibiotic treatment of meningococcal meningitis need last only 5 days, whereas *H. influenzae* and pneumococcal meningitis are best treated for a minimum of 7–10 days to ensure complete eradication of the organism and to prevent relapse. In neonatal meningitis and adult meningitis due to unusual organisms, more prolonged therapy may be indicated and each case should be reviewed in consultation with a microbiologist.

Table 27.3. Antibiotic treatment of pyogenic meningitis

Age of patient	Gram-film findings	Presumptive organism	Start therapy with	Comments
<2 months	Gram-negative bacilli	'Coliforms'	Cefotaxime + gentamicin	Change if necessary when culture and sensitivity known
	Streptococci	Group B streptococci	Benzylpenicillin + gentamicin	
	Gram-positive bacilli	L. monocytogenes	Ampicillin + gentamicin	
	No bacteria seen	Esch. coli, group B streptococci, or L. monocytogenes	Ampicillin + gentamicin	Change according to culture and sensitivity results
2 months to 6 years	Gram-negative diplococci	N. meningitidis	Benzylpenicillin	Chloramphenicol if allergic to penicillin
	Gram-positive diplococci	Str. pneumoniae	Benzylpenicillin	May be changed to ampicillin if sensitive
	Small Gram-neg. bacilli	H. influenzae	Chloramphenicol or cefotaxime	
	No bacteria seen	Any of above 3	Chloramphenicol or cefotaxime	May be changed to ampicillin or benzylpenicillin when culture result known
>6 to <40 years	Gram-negative diplococci	N. meningitidis	Benzylpenicillin	
	Gram-positive diplococci	Str. pneumoniae	Benzylpenicillin	
	No bacteria seen	Either of above 2	Benzylpenicillin	
>40 years	Gram-positive diplococci	Str. pneumoniae	Benzylpenicillin	May be changed to benzyl-penicillin if pneumococci isolated
	Gram-positive bacilli	L. monocytogenes	Ampicillin + gentamicin	
	No bacteria seen	Either of above 2	Ampicillin + gentamicin	

BRAIN ABSCESS

Brain abscess is a localized collection of pus within the brain parenchyma. It is a life-threatening condition which used to carry a mortality of 40 per cent. This has now been reduced to about 10 per cent by the introduction of computerized tomography, leading to earlier diagnosis and more precise localization, by improvements in surgical and bacteriological techniques, and by the use of appropriate antibiotics. About 4–10 cases a year are seen in neurosurgical units.

Brain abscesses may follow penetrating head injuries or neurosurgery, but are more commonly secondary to a focus of infection in an adjacent area (e.g. an ear or sinus) or a distant site (e.g. lung abscess, bronchiectasis, or endocarditis). Blood-borne spread often causes multiple abscess formation. In about 20 per cent of cases the primary focus is unrecognized.

Brain abscess secondary to middle ear or mastoid infection is usually located in the temporal lobe or cerebellum, whereas the frontal lobe is the usual site when infection spreads from the sinuses. The organisms involved reflect those found in the primary focus of infection. With proper attention to technique, the role of anaerobes and polymicrobial infection has become apparent. Anaerobes such as *Fusobacterium* spp., *Bacteroides* spp., anaerobic streptococci and *Actinomyces* spp. are commonly isolated alone or together with other major pathogens including *Streptococcus milleri*, enterobacteria, *Staph. aureus*, and *Haemophilus* spp.

Lumbar puncture is unhelpful in diagnosis and may be hazardous, but blood cultures may be positive and should be taken.

Surgical drainage of the abscess, either by burr-hole aspiration or craniotomy, is essential and the pus obtained should be sent to the laboratory for urgent microscopy and culture. Because mixtures of aerobic and anaerobic organisms are likely, chemotherapy should cover both possibilities. Chloramphenicol penetrates well and its broad-spectrum covers most anaerobes. However, chloramphenicol alone is not bactericidal to enterobacteria, which are common in otogenic brain abscess, and its use, either alone or in combination with β-lactam antibiotics has been associated with high mortality. The combination of chloramphenicol and gentamicin has been found to be antagonistic in experimental meningitis. Moreover, the potential toxicity of chloramphenicol puts it at a disadvantage, since therapy may need to be maintained for 4–6 weeks.

Metronidazole is bactericidal for almost all anaerobes and is of proven efficacy in brain abscess. Furthermore, therapeutic concentrations are achieved in the brain even after oral administration; however, metronidazole has no activity against aerobes.

The precise choice of antimicrobial chemotherapy in brain abscess depends on the site of the abscess, any predisposing factors, and the results of laboratory tests on the pus. Frontal lobe abscess of sinus origin should be treated with high doses of benzylpenicillin in combination with metronidazole, since *Str. milleri*, with or without anaerobes, is the chief culprit. Temporal lobe or cerebellar abscess of otogenic origin is treated with a combination of high dose cefotaxime and metronidazole. Gentamicin should be added to this regimen if coliform organisms are seen on the Gram-film or are grown in culture.

The duration of antimicrobial therapy remains unsettled. It is our practice to administer antibiotics parenterally for at least 3 weeks to all surgically treated patients, often followed by oral treatment for 6-8 weeks.

28

Viral infections

Viral infections are ubiquitous. In many cases the illness is of known aetiology, but in others a virus is often involved even though laboratory evidence is lacking. In communities, viruses appear as uninvited guests able to circulate freely under the conditions covering many human activities and disease is largely determined by the absence of specific immunity. To initiate infection virulent particles are required in sufficient numbers to gain a foothold in a susceptible host. Spread is dependent on the proportion, density, mobility, and immunity of the populations at risk, plus the amount of interchange taking place among them. As the herd immunity increases, spread declines and finally ceases although under natural conditions this seldom becomes complete. For example, in urban communities some 85 per cent of the adult female population is immune to rubella, yet the seasonal spread among non-immune children leaves the remaining adult females at risk.

Severity may be accentuated at the extremes of age or when the virus infection complicates pre-existing disease such as bronchitis, leukaemia, or immune deficiencies generally. Sometimes the effect is secondary, e.g. pneumonia in influenza or chickenpox, paralysis or meningitis in polio-myelitis, or damage to liver or kidneys as immune complex phenomena in serum hepatitis or tropical haemorrhagic fevers.

Not unusually, viruses pave the way for bacterial infections and the rationale of the often-criticized use of antibiotics in certain viral infections is to prevent such secondary bacterial invasion.

In terms of spread, viruses are fragile outside the cellular environment and, since they consist largely of protein complexes, they are readily inactivated at a temperature of 60-65°C which will coagulate protein. Even at 37°C viruses usually survive only a matter of hours. At lower temperatures there is more variation between the different virus groups with most able to survive for days at 4°C. For indefinite preservation in the laboratory temperatures of $-70°C$ or lower are preferable.

The control of virus disease has predominantly focused on stimulating host immunity through active immunization. Short-lived passive immunity can be produced by the use of pooled human serum or more concentrated preparations of hyperimmune globulin for the prevention of specific infections. Thus, immune serum globulin can be used to prevent hepatitis A, and hyperimmune serum is used for post-exposure prophylaxis against hepatitis B or rabies infection.

The chemotherapeutic management of virus disease remains limited, although considerable progress has been made in recent years. The intimate relationship of virus and host cell creates difficulties in developing drugs which are selectively toxic to the virus whilst being harmless to the host. Early compounds such as cytosine arabinoside, although inhibitory to herpes viruses, were too toxic in clinical use. The specificity of acyclovir, which is activated only in cells infected with virus, is a major breakthrough. Acyclovir is a safe and effective drug in the treatment and prevention of herpes simplex and varicella-zoster infections. Other types of antiviral chemotherapy will be discussed within the general review of virus infection.

TYPES OF INFECTION

Acute generalized illness

A marked feature of many virus diseases is the effective and durable immunity which follows one attack. This is exemplified by common exanthemata such as measles, mumps, and rubella, all due to viruses having a single serotype. From the time of infection there is a build up of virus within the body. During this incubation period the patient remains well and is non-infectious until the virus attains its sites of election and illness develops. Excretion then occurs over a brief period just before and during the acute stage. The illness is followed by the development of immunity which peaks during convalescence and then declines slowly. Reinfection may not always be prevented, but clinical manifestations are unusual, although late sequelae arising from deficiencies in host immunity may rarely occur; for example, measles may be followed by giant-cell pneumonia or subacute sclerosing panencephalitis. Treatment in general is symptomatic. Antiviral drugs, even if available and given early in the illness, are likely to be too late to influence the course of events in the acute exanthems except perhaps in the immunocompromised host.

Acute superficial illness

In this type of illness repeated attacks are common and mainly affect the respiratory tract. Common colds and influenza come under this heading. There is usually a short incubation period during which virus multiplication occurs in the nasopharynx. The site of infection is accessible to local treatment and antiviral drugs could theoretically abort or reduce the severity of an attack. In practice, protection of contacts who are most at risk from complications is likely to be a more fruitful line of approach. For example, amantadine has proved an effective prophylactic, but only for infection caused by influenza A. Recurrent infections stem from the range of virus groups and from the number of serotypes within each group which can give rise to similar clinical syndromes. Immunity is short lived and limited to the homologous virus. Furthermore, influenza A viruses can alter their antigenic determinants by changes in the surface configuration. These alterations are known as *antigenic shift* for major changes and *antigenic drift* for minor ones and lead to the occurrence of major and minor epidemics of influenza. Another common viral pathogen of the respiratory tract is respiratory syncytial virus. This causes trivial infections in adults, but may lead to fatal bronchiolitis and pneumonia in young children. Topical (aerosolized) ribavirin may be of value in severe cases.

Persistent low grade infections

Such illnesses are characterized by a primary attack, often during early childhood, when the illness is often mild in character, followed by periodic recurrences. The herpes group of viruses is particularly involved. So-called fever blisters and cold sores are common manifestations of infection by *Herpesvirus hominis* type 1; recurrent infections may result from a variety of factors including stress, fevers, and pneumonia or a waning immunity. Genital vesiculation, sometimes recurrent, is due to *Herpesvirus hominis* type 2. Varicella-zoster is another herpes virus which causes chickenpox as the primary disease and shingles or zoster in later life, when infection occurs as a painful, localized eruption.

Antiviral chemotherapy has made no impact on eliminating persistent viruses and treatment is restricted to relieving the acute manifestations of infection. For herpetic infections of the eye and skin, idoxuridine, as a 0.1 per cent aqueous solution, or 0.5 per cent ointment is available for local application. The drug is too toxic for parenteral use although a 5 per cent solution in 40 per cent dimethylsulphoxide is available for cutaneous application to herpes simplex and severe herpes zoster skin lesions. Vidarabine, as a 3 per cent ointment applied locally to the eye, or by parenteral injection, has been used in chickenpox or disseminated herpes zoster in immunosuppressed patients. However, these agents have been superseded by acyclovir for systemic use in the treatment of severe acute herpes simplex and varicella-zoster infection in the immunocompromised and non-compromised patient.

AIDS

Human immunodeficiency virus (HIV) is the cause of AIDS (acquired immune deficiency syndrome) and is acquired by sexual contact, blood transfusion, or intravenous drug abuse; infants of infected mothers are also at risk. HIV persists in its target cell, the CD4 lymphocyte. The incubation period varies from a few weeks to several years, although approximately half those infected will develop symptomatic disease from opportunistic infections or malignancies. Antibody activity does not appear to be protective and, hence, much research is directed at chemotherapeutic control. Zidovudine (azidothymidine) acts on the enzyme reverse transcriptase and is of value in controlling the rate of disease progression in those with AIDS. However, toxicity to the bone marrow may result in the necessity for blood transfusions to correct drug-induced anaemia.

Slow virus infections

These diseases of the central nervous system are characterized by an indefinite, but prolonged incubation period of up to 2 or 3 years, an insidious onset and an ultimately fatal progressive encephalopathy with spongiform degeneration. They include Creutzfeldt–Jakob disease in man, scrapie in sheep and goats, and mink encephalopathy. The causative agents, though ill-defined, are transmissible. In some other progressive diseases, such as multiple sclerosis, the search for a definitive viral aetiology has proved inconclusive at the time of writing. No chemotherapeutic agent has yet emerged that is capable of arresting the inexorable course of these diseases.

Congenital infections

Any virus circulating in maternal blood during pregnancy can cross the placental barrier and cause infection which may induce fetal damage. Rubella and cytomegalovirus are most commonly pathogenic to the fetus. The effects will vary according to the nature of the virus and the stage of pregnancy. They can range from fetal destruction and death leading to abortion to less serious complications such as deafness which may not be noticeable for several years. In addition, there may be selective damage with abnormalities of the heart, eyes, internal organs, skeleton, or brain. In these infections excretion of virus in urine of the child may persist for several months and be a source of infection to non-immune contacts.

Prevention is the key to the reduction of congenital virus infections. An effective rubella vaccine is available (*vide infra*). A vaccine for cytomegalovirus is at an experimental stage, but as with other herpes virus vaccines there are problems relating to viral persistence in the host and carcinogenic potential.

Inapparent infections

There is wide variation in virulence among naturally occurring viruses and antibody surveys have frequently shown persons to be immune without having suffered a clinical attack. For example, in poliomyelitis, even before vaccine became available, the ratio of those immune to those with manifestations of the disease exceeded 100:1. Obviously, inapparent infections do not present a therapeutic problem, but are important when assessing benefits of vaccination.

Carrier states

Persistent viral excretion is rare in human infections, although rabies virus may be excreted in the saliva of the dog or the bat for long periods. One important, though more artificial, human problem brought about by the transfusion of blood and its products, is the carriage of the virus and surface antigen particles of serum hepatitis (hepatitis B) in the blood of persons who manifest no symptoms of the disease. Virus excretion is minimal and such persons need not normally be regarded as infectious, except to close contacts such as sexual partners. However, the blood is highly infectious and the virus may be transmitted by transfusion or by the use of shared syringes by drug addicts. Medical and paramedical personnel handling blood are also at risk, as are babies of maternal carriers. In the UK the carrier rate is of the order of 0.1 per cent; it is much higher in tropical regions. Because of the transfusion risk, blood donors are routinely screened for evidence of hepatitis B antigens. Hepatitis due to viruses antigenically distinct from both hepatitis A and B (so-called non-A, non-B hepatitis) is also transmissible by blood. It is being recognized more frequently though identification of the viruses and their carriers presents problems.

Antiviral prophylaxis has nothing to offer those at risk and protective immunization of selected groups is the only suitable approach to prevention. Currently, two varieties of hepatitis B vaccine are available: one is derived from the serum of human carriers; the other is manufactured by techniques of genetic engineering. They are currently recommended for health care staff at risk of infection and sexual partners of infected persons. Passive protection for persons exposed to hepatitis B infection is available in the form of specific hyperimmune globulin.

The special form of viral carriage exhibited by latent viruses may also cause problems. Herpesviruses are an increasing problem in immuno-suppressed patients due to their heightened susceptibility and lack of resistance. Recurrent varicella may affect acute leukaemic patients under treatment. Cytomegalovirus and Epstein–Barr (EB) virus may be transferred in blood or in organs, while latent infections may undergo reactivation especially in transplant recipients. Ganciclovir, an antiviral agent that is related to acyclovir, but is much more toxic, may be of value in serious cytomegalovirus infection.

PREVENTION OF VIRUS INFECTIONS

Specific antiviral therapy for the prevention of viral disease is in its infancy, although available for selected infections. The emphasis has largely depended upon control through immunization and the use of isolation to circumvent virus spread.

Immunization

This method of pre-empting natural infection aims not only to give protection to the individual, but is also used to cover a high proportion of the population, and thus provide herd immunity. Live attenuated virus vaccines give a longer immunity requiring fewer booster doses. They also provide the opportunity for transfer to non-vaccinated individuals; on rare occasions such transfer may involve revertants that exhibit increased virulence. Inactivated virus vaccines are safe but require multiple primary doses and immunity may be short-lived.

Poliovirus vaccine

This is a mixture of the three poliovirus serotypes, given by mouth to provide circulating and local intestinal immunity. The primary course in babies is of three doses at 3-4 months of age, 6 months, and 10-12 months with the aim of ensuring infection of the gut by all serotypes and of overcoming any interference from other enteroviruses. Booster doses are advocated at the beginning and end of schooling, and before travel to any part of the world where the disease is endemic. Parents may with advantage, be revaccinated when their baby is given the first dose.

Measles vaccine

This is advocated for children early in the second year. The disease is highly infectious and although overall mortality is low the incidence of complications, ranging from middle ear disease and bronchopneumonia to encephalitis, may be considerable. Because mild fever may develop in some children after vaccination the simultaneous injection of small amounts of immune globulin is sometimes advocated.

Rubella vaccine

This is available in the UK for 11–13-year-old girls to ensure protection against rubella in the child-bearing years. It can also be given to adult women who lack immunity if pregnancy is avoided for 3 months after vaccination. This proviso avoids possible contact between the vaccine virus and the fetus in early pregnancy. In such women it is useful to confirm the development of antibody after vaccination.

Mumps vaccine

Although this is available it has seldom been advocated in the UK because of the generally mild natural disease. However, administration of a combined measles, mumps, and rubella vaccine to pre-school children has been spectacularly successful in preventing these diseases in the United States and a number of countries, including the UK, now have similar programmes.

Yellow fever vaccine

This is available at special centres for persons visiting areas where the disease is endemic.

Rabies vaccine

Various forms of this vaccine have been used since the pioneering work of Pasteur in the late nineteenth century, for the post-exposure treatment of rabies. The vaccine stimulates antibody formation, which takes a little time to develop and is not active intracellularly. Yet the virus, after local multiplication tracks to the brain along nerve fibres and out of reach of the antibody. Vaccine is best given *as soon as possible* after the exposure in a small series of injections under preliminary cover from specific anti-rabies globulin. The current inactivated vaccine prepared in human diploid cells is potent and has few side effects, unlike the earlier brain tissue vaccines which carried a considerable risk of inducing allergic encephalomyelitis.

Influenza vaccine

This is an inactivated combination of current influenza A and B virus strains, whose content is revised annually to keep pace with the surface antigen changes. The vaccine is not advocated for general use, but is valuable as a protective measure for workers in vital industries or professions, as well as for groups at special risk such as the elderly and those suffering from chronic bronchitis. Because of the frequent antigenic changes vaccination needs to be repeated annually.

Standard immune globulin

Because of its antibody content, this may provide short-term protection against some virus diseases if given prophylactically or shortly after exposure. It is expensive to prepare, requires deep subcutaneous injection which may cause some local pain, and can only be considered marginally effective. It is of most use in children with hypogammaglobulinaemia or those undergoing immune suppressive therapy who have been exposed to common exanthemata such as measles or chickenpox. In rubella, where it is often difficult to get an accurate history of exposure, it has seldom proved effective in practice. Although it has been widely given to travellers for protection against hepatitis A, its efficacy is in doubt because of uncertainty over the antibody status of the recipients.

For rabies, specific immune globulin can provide some immediate protection until there is response to vaccine. However, because it may interfere with the response to antigen, booster doses of vaccine are needed. In serum hepatitis (hepatitis B) specific immune globulin, if given soon after exposure, may prevent the onset of the disease or suppress a clinical attack. This treatment has also been advocated for babies born of maternal carriers particularly if there is evidence of virus particles and 'e' antigen in the mother's serum, as well as surface antigen. Such a combination is indicative of a high degree of infectiousness.

29

Venereal diseases

Venus has a lot to answer for if she was responsible for the conditions that bear her name! These afflictions of love are a motley collection of microbial diseases (Table 29.1); some, like syphilis, are potentially very serious; others, like trichomonal vaginal discharge, are merely a nuisance. When two human beings are in close contact, their mucous membranes in apposition, transfer of microbes is facilitated. Not all cases of VD, however, have genital infections; varieties in sexual technique allow for many different parts, not necessarily private, to be in sufficient contact to lead to a clinical lesion.

The explosive increase in sexually transmitted disease (STD) worldwide makes it important for all doctors to have a knowledge of their treatment. In some parts of the world STD are so common that their treatment constitutes a disproportionate part of the total health care budget. Moreover, the recognition that acquired immune deficiency syndrome (AIDS) is usually spread sexually has greatly increased public awareness of these conditions.

LABORATORY DIAGNOSIS

Microscopy will give accurate rapid confirmation of a clinical diagnosis in many cases. The examination of exudate from a syphilitic chancre must be done by dark ground microscopy within a few minutes of collecting the specimen; the presence of motile spirochaetes makes the diagnosis as it is not possible to cultivate these organisms in artificial media. Typical Gram-negative intracellular diplococci in a Gram-stained film of a urethral discharge in the male is strongly supportive of the diagnosis of acute gonorrhoea. Culture of cervical swabs from women and from extragenital sites in both sexes is necessary because examination of Gram-stained smears is unreliable. The unstained 'wet' film of vaginal secretions is the most widely used method for the diagnosis of trichomoniasis and may also reveal *Candida* and cells suggestive of non-specific bacterial vaginosis.

Table 29.1. Venereal diseases and their treatment

Condition	Pathogen	Antimicrobial
Urethral discharges		
Gonorrhoea	*Neisseria gonorrhoeae*	Penicillin (amoxycillin)
Non-specific (NSU)	*Chlamydia* or *Ureaplasma*	Tetracycline (erythromycin)
Vaginal discharges		
Thrush	*Candida albicans*	Nystatin (clotrimazole)
Trichomoniasis	*Trichomonas vaginalis*	Metronidazole
Non-specific	*Gardnerella vaginalis* and *Mobiluncus* spp.	Metronidazole
Genital sores		
Syphilis	*Treponema pallidum*	Penicillin (erythromycin)
Chancroid	*Haemophilus ducreyi*	Sulphonamides (tetracycline)
Lymphogranuloma venereum	LGV (chlamydia)	Tetracycline (erythromycin)
Herpes	Herpes simplex type 2	Acyclovir
Warts	Wart viruses (human papillomaviruses)	Local podophyllin (cryotherapy)

Direct microscopic examination is of utmost importance in venereology clinics as it confirms many clinical diagnoses and for this reason many STD clinics have laboratory facilities on site. In the majority of cases a sufficiently accurate microbiological cause can be ascribed to the patient's complaints to enable specific chemotherapy to be given.

Few genital pathogens can be cultivated easily. The most commonly sought, *Neisseria gonorrhoeae*, is a fastidious organism requiring special media and growth conditions. Selective media containing antibiotics to inhibit commensal bacteria are used. Isolation of *Chlamydia trachomatis* requires cell culture. These obligate intracellular bacteria may also be seen by direct fluorescence microscopy; alternatively, the antigenic particles may be detected by enzyme immunoassay techniques.

Serological investigation may also be valuable in STD, particularly in syphilis where it may be the only way of confirming the diagnosis. The Wassermann reaction, employing a non-spirochaetal antigen, was used for many years, but this test yields some false-positive results. More specific treponemal antigens are available nowadays. One disadvantage of the newer tests [the *Treponema pallidum* haemagglutination antibody (TPHA) and the fluorescent treponemal antibody (FTA) tests] is that they often remain positive for life, even after effective treatment.

TREATMENT OF VENEREAL DISEASE

Many patients with STD default treatment. It is therefore important to render as many patients as possible non-infectious after a single visit to the clinic. Concomitant treatment of the sexual partner(s) is essential to prevent reinfection and contact tracing can help to keep the spread of the disease within bounds, particularly in the control of spread of antibiotic-resistant strains of *N. gonorrhoeae*.

Syphilis

Curing 'the pox' holds an important place in the history of chemotherapy. Heavy metals, in particular mercury, were used for many centuries and the development in the first decade of the twentieth century of arsenicals such as Salvarsan heralded the start of modern chemotherapy. It is difficult to imagine nowadays the horror which was felt about the disease and the importance of finding a cure. It held something of the mystery and fear in the minds of laymen later occupied by cancer and now by AIDS. In its medieval heyday syphilis was apparently a more virulent infection than it is today and earned the adjective 'great', diminishing the importance of 'smallpox', a disease feared later in history. Syphilis is a chronic disease capable of involving nearly every organ of the body. The old student adage 'know syphilis and you will know medicine' indicates how widespread the disease may be and how it can mimic other conditions. The progression of the infection varies greatly; even in untreated cases, latent periods of many years frequently occur.

Penicillin has been the mainstay of therapy since 1943 when the drug was first used to treat syphilis. The primary sore (chancre) will respond to relatively low doses of many antimicrobials, but such treatment may only suppress the disease, which reappears in its later manifestations. This danger exists in treating a patient with non-syphilitic STD who may also be incubating syphilis. For this reason serological tests for syphilis should be done on all high-risk patients attending venereology clinics and repeated after 6 weeks.

Animal work suggests that *T. pallidum* is exquisitely sensitive to penicillin: as little as 0.002 mg/l is bactericidal. There is no evidence of variation in sensitivity and resistance is not known to occur. Other antibiotics with treponemicidal activity include erythromycin, tetracyclines, chloramphenicol, and cephalosporins, but none is thought to be as active as penicillin, which is the drug of choice in all cases except those where there is definite evidence of allergy.

Even in the early stages of the disease, spirochaetes divide relatively slowly and in latent and tertiary syphilis division presumably occurs infrequently. Since β-lactam antibiotics require active growth to achieve a killing effect a low concentration of penicillin is required over a prolonged period. This is achieved by using forms of the drug which are released slowly from an intramuscular depot. Aqueous procaine penicillin (600 000 units) will give an adequate concentration for 24 hours; if combined with oil and aluminium monostearate (PAM) the effect will be maintained for 72 hours. PAM is no longer used in the UK, where benzathine penicillin, which gives greatly prolonged release, is usually preferred. In tertiary syphilis treatment for several weeks is necessary, but since benzathine penicillin does not achieve adequate CSF concentrations it is not recommended. Frequent high doses of benzylpenicillin are recommended in the treatment of neurosyphilis.

A common hazard of syphilis therapy is the Jarisch-Herxheimer reaction observed with a few hours of treatment with penicillin (or arsenicals). This is a hypersensitivity reaction due to spirochaetal endotoxin and is not related to penicillin allergy. The Herxheimer response is of little significance in primary cases, but may occasionally be fatal in some tertiary or late cases.

GONORRHOEA

In 1829 *The Lancet* published a series of lectures to students at St. Bartholomew's Hospital, London, by Mr Lawrence. In his paragraph on how to cure a clap he proclaims 'If anyone could find a speedy and effectual mode of accomplishing this he would undoubtedly immortalise himself. The ladies of Fleet Street and the Strand would be inclined to erect a statue to his memory!'

Modern antibiotics have revolutionized the practice of venereology and no more so than in 'curing the clap'. Acute gonococcal urethritis occurs 2-10 days after contact and in the male is nearly always obvious, presenting as a visible thick yellow discharge accompanied by dysuria and itching. Asymptomatic cases represent less than 5 per cent of male infections, but 50 per cent of female infections. Prompt treatment with appropriate antibiotics will cure the majority of patients with no residual effects: it is hard to imagine that only 60 years ago gonorrhoea was treated by weeks of local irrigation and many sufferers were left with urethral strictures. Nowadays, the major problems of the disease are seen in women, especially with disseminated gonococcaemia. It is one of the main causes of infertility in the world.

Neisseria gonorrhoeae is sensitive to many antimicrobial agents, but penicillin has remained the drug of choice since it replaced sulphonamides in the later stages of the Second World War. Its value has been maintained by increasing the dose to keep ahead of bacterial resistance. This strategy worked successfully until the emergence of strains completely resistant to penicillin in 1976. In the late 1950s in-vitro testing showed that some strains of *N. gonorrhoeae* were becoming less sensitive to penicillin. In one of the clearest demonstrations of the relevance of laboratory tests to clinical practice, Curtis and Wilkinson demonstrated that failure of penicillin was directly related to the MIC of penicillin for the infecting strain. In this study 300 000 units penicillin was unable to cure any patient infected with gonococci for which the penicillin MIC was 0.5 units/ml (0.3 mg/l) whereas all those infected with strains displaying an MIC ≤0.015 units/ml were cured. Proportionately reduced cure rates were observed with organisms of intermediate susceptibility.

In the 1960s the widespread and increasing resistance of gonococci to penicillin became well recognized and standard therapy for acute gonorrhoea increased to 4.8 or 5 megaunits in some parts of the world. In countries where antibiotics can be purchased in the market place the prevalence of resistant gonococci is very high. For many of these strains the MIC of penicillin is greater than 1 mg/l which makes treatment with that drug almost impossible and resistance to sulphonamides, tetracyclines and newer drugs is common. Since the discovery of *N. gonorrhoeae* capable of producing β-lactamase, the position has worsened. These gonococci contain a transmissible plasmid (R-factor) from Enterobacteriaceae which renders them completely resistant to penicillin, ampicillin and amoxycillin. In parts of the Far East and Africa over one-third of all strains are β-lactamase producers. Recommendations for the therapy of gonorrhoea must be tempered with a knowledge of the antimicrobial susceptibilities of local strains.

In the acute disease a single dose of penicillin giving high tissue concentrations for 12 hours is sufficient. Procaine penicillin has been widely employed for this purpose together with oral probenecid to delay renal excretion. Where most strains are relatively sensitive, as in the UK, 2.4 megaunits is sufficient, but double or even larger intramuscular doses have been advised in other parts of the world. The size of the buttock becomes a critical factor and often these enormous doses have to be divided into two injections. A single oral dose of 2 or 3 g amoxycillin with probenecid has replaced injections in many clinics, but oral drugs are mistrusted by some patients who think they are not as good as the injection, and by doctors who worry that patients will not comply, especially if multiple doses have to be given without supervision. Patients with acute gonorrhoea are amongst the highest defaulters in VD clinics. There is therefore great importance in a single curative dose and more studies have been performed comparing different regimens of treating gonorrhoea than almost any other condition. Most give a greater than 90 per cent cure rate and many 'failures' may in fact be re-infections as patients attending VD clinics do not always give accurate information.

For patients infected with β-lactamase-producing strains of *N. gonorrhoeae*, spectinomycin has been widely used. However, the newer cephalosporins, especially cefotaxime and, where available, ceftriaxone, are also commonly used. Amoxycillin-clavulanate and the newer quinolones, such as ciprofloxacin, are also effective. If there is known hypersensitivity to penicillin, cephalosporins may be used, but if the reaction was previously severe the danger of cross-allergy is too great and a non-β-lactam alternative (e.g. co-trimoxazole or ciprofloxacin) should be employed.

Antibiotics give a speedy and complete cure in most cases of acute gonorrhoea. Occasional complications such as epididymitis, arthritis, and pelvic infection in the female require admission to hospital and prolonged antibiotics. Non-genital gonococcal infection also requires more than a single dose of penicillin to effect a cure.

Ophthalmia neonatorum

This occurs within a few days of birth in babies born to infected mothers. Gonococci in the female genital tract are implanted in the conjunctivae during delivery and the neonate develops a purulent discharge from one or both eyes. There may be considerable cellulitis and if untreated the infection may lead to destruction of the cornea. Treatment should be prompt with parenteral penicillin and frequent local instillations of chloramphenicol. The condition may be prevented by silver nitrate drops placed in the eyes immediately after birth. This therapy (Credé's method) is still used in areas where the risk of infection is high but does have a risk of inducing a chemical conjunctivitis especially if the concentration of $AgNO_3$ is too high.

NON-GONOCOCCAL URETHRITIS

In many men presenting with urethral discharge, gonococci cannot be demonstrated and a diagnosis of non-specific (NSU) or non-gonococcal urethritis (NGU) is made. Such cases are seen more frequently than gonorrhoea in the UK and are common everywhere. Although the primary disease is less severe and the complications fewer than with gonorrhoea, satisfactory treatment is more difficult. Thorough microbiological investigation has determined the aetiological role of *Chlamydia trachomatis* in nearly half these cases. Some are probably due to ureaplasma, a form of mycoplasma and a few to *Trichomonas vaginalis*, herpes virus, urinary tract infection, and local causes such as trauma or tumours.

The most useful therapeutic agents are tetracyclines, but short courses are ineffective. The duration of therapy should be at least 7–10 days. In spite of this, failures are common; some are due to failure of compliance or re-infection, but many genuine relapses occur, confirming the view that chlamydial infections may have a latent phase. Since laboratory facilities for the diagnosis of chlamydial infection are not universally available (and even where they are, results take some time to obtain) 'blind' therapy is necessary. Chlamydial disease commonly remains undiagnosed and untreated. In the UK it has been estimated that there are about 20 000 untreated infections in women each year. Throughout the world it causes significant morbidity in terms of pelvic infections, infertility, and eye disease (trachoma).

Complications of NGU are most often seen in women and the newborn. Although the majority of women who are culture-positive for chlamydia are asymptomatic and are only investigated because of urethritis in a partner, they are able to pass infection to the newborn during delivery. Neonatal conjunctivitis due to chlamydia is a less severe form of ophthalmia neonatorum than that caused by gonococci. It may be so mild as to be unsuspected clinically and, like all the conditions due to chlamydia, it is underdiagnosed. In spite of its mild, self-limiting course it can cause permanent eye damage and, whenever suspected, chlamydial conjunctivitis should be treated. Without appropriate laboratory facilities an accurate diagnosis cannot be made, but an index of suspicion is an indication for using tetracycline eye ointment. Local treatment is often difficult to apply adequately and many clinicians advise giving erythromycin orally, in addition, to prevent the development of chlamydial pneumonia. Erythromycin is preferred in the infant because systemic tetracycline stains teeth and bones. Therapy needs to be for at least 3 weeks as with all complicated chlamydial infections. It is self-evident that the parents should be examined and treated as for non-specific urethritis.

VAGINAL DISCHARGE

The normal bacteria flora of the adult vagina before the menopause consists of numerous lactobacilli, diphtheroids, and anaerobes. This maintains locally a pH between 4 and 5 which is inhibitory to coliforms. However, yeasts flourish in acid conditions as wine-makers will know.

Candidiasis

Candida albicans, the commonest pathogenic yeast, may be found in up to a quarter of healthy women of child-bearing age and frequently the delicate balance between the resident flora and intruding *Candida* is disturbed to produce clinical 'thrush'. Oral antibiotics, in particular tetracyclines, are prone to produce this side-effect which is also more common in pregnancy. The male, especially if uncircumcized, may occasionally have clinical balanitis due to *Candida* and the organism is not infrequently carried by healthy individuals. Venereal transfer is probable in these circumstances, but as thrush can occur without intimate contact it is not a recognized STD. Local applications of antifungal agents, such as nystatin or one of the imidazoles (clotrimazole, or miconazole) are sufficient, but prolonged and repeated courses are required in a few intransigent cases and oral ketoconazole or fluconazole is sometimes used. The partner must be concurrently treated as with all venereally spread conditions.

Trichomonal infection

Trichomonas vaginalis is a flagellated protozoon commonly found throughout the world. It favours a more alkaline pH than *Candida* and causes a foul-smelling yellow vaginal discharge often noticed because of staining of clothes and itching. It has been found in a high proportion of asymptomatic women in antenatal clinics, but may cause symptoms sub-sequently, especially after menstruation. In some patients the organism invades the anterior urethra and symptoms of dysuria and frequency may lead the clinician to make a tentative diagnosis of urinary tract infection. Some patients labelled as 'urethral syndrome' may be suffering from trichomoniasis. The organism is sometimes carried transiently and asymptomatically by the male, but a low-grade non-specific urethritis may occur.

The treatment of trichomonal infection has been revolutionized by the advent of metronidazole. Treatment is given orally; the local applications previously employed were often ineffective and messy. Metronidazole should not be used during pregnancy because of possible teratogenic effects; patients on metronidazole should also avoid taking alcohol because of a reaction similar to that caused by disulfiram (Antabuse). However, most patients under treatment for venereal diseases are asked to abstain from alcohol and sex; the former to reduce the willingness for the latter and so reduce spread.

Non-specific vaginitis

This is a term employed for a symptomatic discharge for which no obvious cause can be found. As with NSU there are likely to be many possible aetiological agents—not all microbial. There is evidence that a proportion of these cases are associated with a pleomorphic, Gram-variable rod previously named *Haemophilus vaginalis* or *Corynebacterium vaginale*, but now called *Gardnerella vaginalis*. Like many a potential pathogen it can be found in normal healthy individuals. Metronidazole appears to improve symptoms associated with this organism, but its role may be to inhibit associated microaerophilic, curved bacteria, called *Mobiluncus*. This condition has been called anaerobic or bacterial vaginosis.

OTHER GENITAL LESIONS

Every genital sore thought to be venereal in origin must be considered potentially syphilitic. The long-term complications of treponemal infection are so serious that it is essential not to miss an early infection. Although with clinical experience it is possible to distinguish between the causes of such lesions, mixed infections are not rare in STD.

Herpes simplex type 2

This virus causes vesicles, usually on the penis or labia, similar to 'cold sores' found around the mouth. Proctitis is common in passive homosexuals. The painful vesicles burst to form superficial erosions which can be secondarily infected. Women may carry the virus in the cervix where there is a possible complication of infection of the newborn which may occasionally be fatal. The arrival of acyclovir has altered the therapy of herpes infections; local treatment of established lesions is not completely satisfactory, but the duration of a primary attack is reduced.

Warts

The other common viral disease seen in VD clinics is warts. Genital warts (*condylomata acuminata*) are similar to the common skin complaint and local therapy is palliative in many cases. A long course of chemical applications such as podophyllin or burning the lesions with diathermy or liquid nitrogen is often required; in some patients the warts disappear spontaneously, giving rise to the myths of 'charmers'. There is a strong association between these warts, which are caused by some types of human papillomaviruses, and cancers of the cervix and penis. The treatment of genital warts occupies a good part of the work of VD clinics and is often unrewarding. Workers in venereology await a safe and effective remedy.

Chancroid (soft sore)

This is caused by *Haemophilus ducreyi*. The genital lesions are painful and often multiple with large associated inguinal glands which may suppurate to form a 'bubo'. Sulphonamides and streptomycin alone or in combination for at least 10 days were the standard drugs. Tetracyclines work in the majority of cases except in the Far East where resistance occurs. Short courses of amoxycillin-clavulanate or fluoroquinolones have also been successfully used. Chancroid is rarely seen in the UK but in warmer countries there have been several epidemics.

Lymphogranuloma venereum (LGV)

This is also a predominantly tropical condition, but caused by a chlamydial agent. It starts as a small ulcer which may be unnoticed until inguinal glands enlarge and become matted together. Associated inflammation may give the appearance of elephantiasis as a late complication and breakdown of abscesses may give recto-vaginal fistulae. Tetracyclines, sulphonamides or erythromycin may be used but as with other chlamydial infection 2-3 weeks of therapy is required.

AIDS

The treatment of STD has been complicated by the AIDS pandemic. HIV infection, itself, may require (or demand) drug treatment (see Chapter 28); the opportunist infections associated with the syndrome also require specific therapy. Sexually transmitted diseases are an important link in the spread of the infection. Every occasion on which a patient presents with an STD should be used as an opportunity to reach the high-risk community with a health education message. In those already at risk of contracting HIV infection, counselling and advice should be available at the clinic. Those with 'full-blown' AIDS may also have intractable STDs such as herpes. This may, indeed, be the signal for the diagnosis, so that clinicians expert in the field may be alerted to deal with the patient.

30

Parasitic diseases

Examples of the more important parasites have been examined in Chapter 4 and this chapter will restrict itself to specific problems of the therapy of parasitic disease. The organisms considered as 'parasites'—that is the pathogenic protozoa and helminths—tend to cause chronic disease and many individuals, once infected, may become long-term carriers. This ensures that in the warmer countries of the world where poorer standards of hygiene often prevail, there is a high prevalence of infection and a high incidence of new cases all the time. The areas with the highest parasitic burden tend to have the poorest medical care because of poverty, a legacy of inadequate facilities, and the logistics of reaching the majority of people living in scattered rural communities. In many countries the total annual health care budget would not be sufficient to treat a fraction of their population even if it were all spent on antiparasitic drugs.

HOST-PARASITE RELATIONSHIP

One of the peculiarities of treating parasitic infections is the varied relationship between man and microbe. The life cycles often ensure that at some stage the organism is not susceptible to a particular drug either because it is in a resting phase or in an inaccessible site. In many cases the host and parasite reach a steady state of coexistence with no symptoms at all. Parasites restricted to the gut lumen such as the protozoon, *Giardia lamblia* (also known as *Giardia intestinalis*), or many helminths often reach this stage and the intruder is only discovered when stools are examined. In other cases, for example filariasis, the disease becomes 'burnt-out' after years. All these late asymptomatic cases may be diagnosed by chance during routine investigations or as part of mass screening campaigns. The contribution of the parasite burden to overall health is usually impossible to estimate and if the only available drug is potentially toxic the decision to treat an apparently healthy individual is difficult to make. Another factor in making such a decision is the likelihood of re-infection from the community or environmental reservoirs. Intestinal parasites are found in over 70 per cent of the population in some tropical countries and a child living in a rural environment will inevitably be quickly in contact with the parasite again. Treatment of an individual case without taking care to prevent re-infection is wasting resources and is not good practice. If the drug is non-toxic and inexpensive there is some justification in treating asymptomatic individuals, especially if the infection may at some stage cause further problems.

Some intestinal protozoa such as *Entamoeba coli* may be classed as true commensals for there is no evidence to incriminate them in human disease. Their only significance may be in mis-identification in stool microscopy. Similarly, some helminths like the whipworm, *Trichuris trichiura*, rarely cause problems. However, many other parasites do clearly have a pathogenic role and in those cases an accurate laboratory diagnosis is essential if antiparasitic therapy is to be useful.

THERAPEUTIC DIFFICULTIES

In addition to the factors peculiar to treating parasitic infections, many of the general principles mentioned in Chapter 15 apply. Any therapy of extended duration in relatively healthy individuals in the community will be difficult to monitor and compliance may be a problem, especially if the drug is unpleasant to take and has conspicuous side-effects. This can occur even with well-educated travellers taking antimalarials.

Many of the remedies for the major parasitic infections are potentially toxic and it is always necessary to weigh the consequences of iatrogenic disease against the benefit of therapy which might not always be able to effect a complete cure. These considerations must still be borne in mind nowadays, even though less toxic compounds are gradually becoming available for some parasitic diseases.

MALARIA

Figure 30.1 shows the worldwide distribution of malaria, which is the most important of all parasitic diseases in terms of mortality. Although indigenous malaria is now virtually restricted to the tropics and sub-tropics it is commonly imported into many temperate countries because of the rapid increase in world travel. The volume of international business travel continues to expand each year, and 'package' holidays to East and West Africa or other tropical destinations are becoming increasingly popular. It is therefore not surprising that the importance of imported malaria in non-malarious countries continues to grow. Over 30 000 cases of imported malaria were recorded in Europe in the decade 1973-1982; the figure is likely to be grossly underestimated because of considerable under-reporting

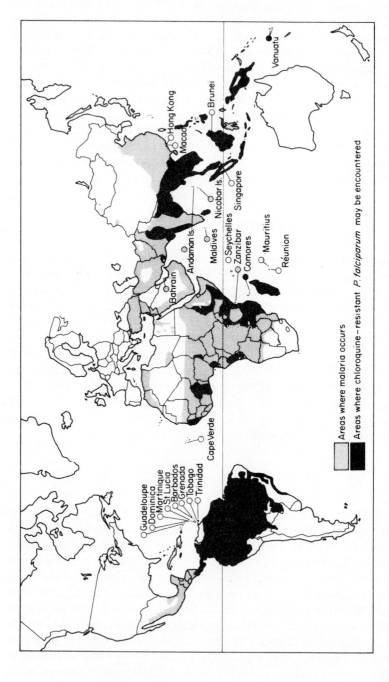

Fig. 30.1. Map showing world distribution of malaria (situation as at December 1985) and areas where chloroquine-resistant *P. falciparum* may be found. [Redrawn from: *World Health Organization Weekly Epidemiological Record* (1987). **22**, 160–1.]

in some countries. A total of 245 fatalities from malaria were reported among European travellers during this same period and the tragedy is that these were all preventable. However, this is insignificant compared with the damage malaria inflicts on the populations of the tropical world; in parts of West Africa it is estimated that at least 10 per cent of children die of falciparum malaria before they reach the age of 5.

Acute malaria

The drug of choice in the treatment of acute malaria is chloroquine, a 4-aminoquinoline derived from the traditional remedy, quinine. These agents are active against the blood forms of the parasite which is important in the symptomatic stage of the disease when rapidly dividing schizonts cause red cell lysis; it is particularly important in falciparum malaria when infected erythrocytes block small cerebral blood vessels to give rise to the rapidly fatal form of cerebral malaria. In such a medical emergency parenteral therapy is necessary. Intravenous chloroquine is not without hazard as a rapid infusion may cause cardiac irregularities. Even subcutaneous administration in infants may cause a fatal reaction. In its time chloroquine revolutionized the treatment and prophylaxis of malaria, but we are now beginning to pay the penalty for its extensive use by the appearance of resistant strains of *Plasmodium falciparum*. Although other species of *Plasmodium* retain susceptibility to the drug, chloroquine resistance in *P. falciparum* has become a major clinical problem in South East Asia, Central and South America, and East Africa. The spread seems inexorable and it has lately become clear that resistance now has a firm foothold in tropical West Africa where falciparum malaria is hyperendemic and responsible for many thousands of deaths each year. Many chloroquine-resistant strains are also resistant to alternative drugs such as the combinations of pyrimethamine with sulphonamides (Fansidar) or dapsone (Maloprim). Indeed, quinine has returned to favour as the drug of first choice in severe falciparum malaria if chloroquine resistance is thought to be possible. Resistance to quinine is presently quite rare, but resistance to other antimalarials throughout the world has become such a problem that the need for new antimalarial compounds has become acute. Mefloquine, a quinolinemethanol derivative developed by the Walter Reed Army Institute of Research in Washington is active against drug-resistant strains and has been successfully used for treatment. However, resistance to mefloquine is known to emerge readily and there are fears that widespread use will quickly negate its value. Derivatives of a Chinese herbal remedy, qinghaosu (artemisinine) are also undergoing trials; first indications are that intravenous sodium artesunate or intramuscular artemether might be useful in treatment.

Recurrent malaria

To effect a radical cure in recurrent malarias with an exoerythrocytic cycle, such as 'benign tertian' malaria due to *Plasmodium vivax*, it is necessary to employ an 8-aminoquinoline. Primaquine is the most commonly used drug for this purpose. It is necessary first to make an accurate diagnosis by examining thin and thick blood films. Secondly, it is important to treat the acute erythrocytic attack with chloroquine before administering primaquine. Thirdly, patients must be screened for glucose-6-phosphate dehydrogenase (G-6-P D) deficiency. Low levels of this red blood cell enzyme occur in many populations in endemic areas and administration of primaquine to such individuals may lead to an acute haemolytic crisis worse than the original malaria. Iatrogenic reactions of this sort have given 8-aminoquinolines a bad name in India. Laboratory screening tests for G-6-P D deficiency are not difficult to perform and should be available widely in endemic areas. Primaquine should not be used during pregnancy.

Antimalarial prophylaxis

Advice on prophylaxis against malaria presents a great problem because of the difficulty in predicting drug resistance. Chloroquine has been widely used, but its usefulness has been seriously undermined by the spread of resistance in *P. falciparum*. Moreover, it has a bitter taste and more serious side-effects, such as skin photosensitization and retinal damage may become apparent after prolonged use. For these reasons and because of the danger of further encouraging the emergence of chloroquine resistance, it is probably unwise to use the drug as a long-term prophylactic, even in areas known to be free of resistance. In general, it is preferable to use an antifolate agent (pyrimethamine or proguanil) whenever possible, but the unpredictability of resistance has led some authorities to recommend combinations of antifolates with chloroquine in an attempt to reduce the chances of breakthrough of protection. The 4-aminoquinoline drug amodiaquine should not be used for prophylaxis because of the risk of agranulocytosis and other blood dyscrasias.

The most important aspect of chemoprophylaxis is regular medication and continuance of therapy for at least 4 weeks after the last possible exposure. Some patients can remember to take daily drugs better than others and prefer proguanil. Otherwise, the traditional 'Sunday–Sunday' tablet of pyrimethamine is used. Although it is not essential to pre-medicate patients before travelling it is advisable to start a routine a week prior in order to ensure acceptability and enable adequate drug concentrations to be achieved before exposure. In highly endemic areas where the risk of malaria is high a double dose may be given. With weekly drugs such as pyrimethamine or chloroquine a dose can be given in the middle of the week. This should not be continued long-term with chloroquine due to chronic toxicity.

Sulphonamide and sulphone-containing mixtures should be avoided in persons known to be hypersensitive to these compounds. If antifolate agents are used during pregnancy folic or folinic acid supplements should also be given. Of great importance, but often neglected, are practical hints to minimize exposure: wearing long clothes, using insect repellants and sleeping under mosquito nets. It is also important to stress to all travellers that prophylaxis may not be effective; so that any fever should be treated with suspicion until malaria has been excluded by examination of adequate blood slides.

AMOEBIASIS

Entamoeba histolytica may live harmlessly in the lumen of the gut, usually in the cyst form, or may invade the gut mucosa to cause amoebic dysentery. The factors that govern the transformation from harmless commensal to invasive pathogen are poorly understood. Secondary spread from the primary intestinal focus sometimes occurs to give rise to abscess formation in various parts of the body, usually the liver.

The treatment of symptomless cyst-passers, especially those living in endemic areas, is not worthwhile unless there is evidence of recurrent attacks of dysentery. Acute intestinal amoebiasis is characterized by bloody diarrhoeic stools. Motile amoebae with phagocytosed red cells are seen on direct microscopy of a freshly passed specimen. This is an indication for therapy to relieve symptoms and prevent possible complications: either local haemorrhage or invasion. Metronidazole is the agent of choice in a high initial dose which should be continued for 3-5 days. This drug gives a high cure rate; if there is a relapse and cysts are seen in the stool an agent more active against them such as diloxanide furoate should be given.

Invasion of trophozoites into tissues, especially into the liver, may occur without dysentery and the first indication of amoebiasis may be a hepatic abscess. Metronidazole has replaced emetine and older remedies in the treatment of invasive amoebiasis. Therapy needs to be of longer duration than with uncomplicated disease. There is no evidence of drug resistance in amoebae. Metronidazole is easy to administer and gives rise to few adverse reactions. The only drawback in the poorer countries of the world where amoebiasis is hyperendemic is cost and availability. In such situations emetine hydrochloride may be given parenterally. There is a severe risk of cardiac toxicity and treatment must be given in hospital with complete bed-rest which nullifies any cost benefit. Exercise should be forbidden for 1 month after therapy. Oral di-iodohydroxyquinoline is a safer, but less effective alternative for amoebic colitis. Chloroquine may be used as an alternative for the treatment of amoebic liver abscesses.

GIARDIASIS

The flagellate protozoon *G. lamblia* is found only in the intestinal lumen. There is no invasion of the surface, the trophozoite being attached to the mucosa of the small intestine, especially the jejunum. Cysts are passed in the stools and infection is transmitted by contamination of food and water. *Giardia* is a frequent cause of chronic diarrhoea and is often underestimated as a pathogen. However, many infections are asymptomatic and, even with a heavy infestation in adults, the symptoms may be mild: nausea, flatulence, and steatorrhoea. In young children the condition may give rise to malabsorption. Although worldwide in distribution this intestinal infection, like most, is more common in less hygienic communities. Giardiasis is common in the UK as well as being the most frequently imported parasitic disease.

Metronidazole is the treatment of choice administered in a similar regimen to that used to treat amoebic dysentery although lower doses may suffice. Cases which do not respond to metronidazole require mepacrine after re-infection has been excluded.

AFRICAN TRYPANOSOMIASIS

Although extensively found in livestock and game in the tsetse fly belt, human trypanosomiasis due to *Trypanosoma rhodesiense* is a sporadic disease in East and Central Africa although occasional outbreaks occur. The clinical course of the disease found in this area is more acute than that caused by *T. gambiense* which is a major health hazard in rural West Africa. Both parasites eventually infect the brain to give the clinical manifestations of 'sleeping sickness'. Before this stage a clinical diagnosis is difficult because of the non-specific nature of the symptoms. However, an early diagnosis is important as treatment is more effective and less toxic at this stage. Laboratory confirmation may be difficult to obtain except in specialized centres because the trypanosomes are often scanty in peripheral blood. Before CNS involvement suramin or pentamidine may be used in therapy but when a lumbar puncture indicates meningo-encephalitis it is necessary to use an organic arsenical. Melarsoprol has replaced the more toxic tryparsamide for this purpose. All the anti-trypanosomal drugs are toxic; treatment should be given in hospital and expert advice sought.

CHAGAS' DISEASE

This form of trypanosomiasis is widespread in South America. The causative organism, *T. cruzi*, invades heart muscle causing myocardial damage which may be fatal. The condition had no known therapy until the recently introduced nitrofuran, nifurtimox, appeared. This drug may succeed in eradicating parasites in the acute stage of the disease at the expense of some toxicity. Its value in established infection is more dubious. Similar considerations appear to apply to the nitroimidazole derivative, benznidazole.

LEISHMANIASIS

Kala-azar

This is an important disease which has returned to prominence in recent years because of large epidemics in India and Africa. The vectors, the small blood-sucking sandflies, *Phlebotomus* spp. increased greatly when insecticide spraying against malaria-carrying mosquitoes was stopped. Visceral leishmaniasis is a chronic, often fatal, condition characterized by fever, anaemia and gross splenomegaly. Microscopy and culture of bone marrow or splenic aspirate confirms the diagnosis. Pentavalent antimonials remain the agents of choice although relapse possibly due to drug-resistance or inadequate dosage and duration of treament is not uncommon. Sodium stibogluconate (Pentostam) is given by the parenteral route in high dosage for at least 30 days and preferably longer. The possibility is being investigated of reducing the toxicity of antimonials by packaging them in artificially made liposomes—minute fat globules that are phago-cytosed into infected cells of the reticulo-endothelial system where they release the drug at the target site. Unfortunately, preparation of the carrier is not easy and it has a short life due to disruption of the particles. At present this limits the widespread use of this method in endemic areas, where the disease is usually found in scattered rural communities. Drug resistance is not uncommon; some of these may be suppressed by high-dose antimonials for extended periods, but toxic effects such as cardiac irregularities are inevitable. Pentamidine has been used as an alternative for many years but patients fare little better on this toxic compound.

Cutaneous and muco-cutaneous leishmaniasis

These forms of the disease are less serious and can be treated with lower total doses of pentavalent antimonial. Most respond to local excision.

PNEUMOCYSTIS INFECTION

Pneumonia is a common terminal event in patients with malignant disease. In those with immunodeficiencies a wide range of potential pathogens may give rise to respiratory disease (see Chapter 20). One particular opportunist parasite, *Pneumocystis carinii*, gives rise to an interstitial pneumonia in immunocompromised patients especially those with AIDS. Prevention of this disease is possible using co-trimoxazole and this is advocated in the USA where the condition is diagnosed more frequently than in the UK. Treatment of an established infection is more difficult but co-trimoxazole is a safe alternative to pentamidine, which is also effective. Unfortunately, AIDS sufferers experience a high rate of hypersensitivity reactions to sulphonamides. This has led to greater use of pentamidine, which appears to be safe and effective for both prophylaxis and treatment when administered by inhalation via a nebulizer. It was increased demand for pentamidine which first alerted the Communicable Diseases Centers in Atlanta, Georgia, to the appearance of the AIDS problem in the USA.

FILARIASIS

In some areas of the tropics nearly the whole population is infected with filarial worms. Diagnosis is made by microscopical demonstration of the larval forms (microfilariae) in blood or, in the special case of *Onchocerca volvulus*, in superficial shavings of skin. Some of the blood microfilariae exhibit a curious periodicity in that they are found in peripheral blood during only the day (*Loa loa*) or the night (*Wuchereria bancrofti*). *Brugia malayi* usually exhibits a less complete nocturnal periodicity. *Wuchereria bancrofti* and *B. malayi* cause a clinically identical condition resulting in severe cases of elephantiasis due to blockage of the lymphatics of the lower trunk. This condition is seen in many parts of the tropics and probably over 250 million people are affected. The clinical syndrome is due to a variety of factors depending on degree of exposure and host reaction to the worms, and in any area a small proportion will have gross elephantiasis. Often by this stage the disease may be 'burnt out' and an anthelminthic may do little to improve the patient's condition, for which surgical and supportive measures are all that is left.

It is important to recognize *B. malayi* (which is restricted to South East Asia) because therapy with diethylcarbamazine (DEC) produces severer reactions than with Bancroftian filariasis. One of the factors limiting individual and mass therapy of filariasis is the frequent occurrence of hypersensitivity reactions to dead worms. This problem is seen particularly in the treatment of filariasis due to *O. volvulus*, the causative parasite of 'river blindness', which affects large numbers of people in West Africa and Central America. As with the other filariasis, many infected persons exhibit only minor symptoms such as skin swelling and itching. The decision to treat is tempered by a knowledge of the natural history of the disease, the patient's complaints and the likelihood of reinfection in a hyperendemic community. The chances and severity of possible reactions must be balanced against any possible benefit. This was particularly true when DEC was the only effective microfilaricide. The introduction of ivermectin has changed the therapy of filariasis. This relatively non-toxic oral drug has shown great promise in field trials in West Africa, especially in the treatment of onchocerciasis. One of the benefits of the use of ivermectin is that reactions to treatment are a good deal milder than with DEC and it is likely to become the drug of choice now that it is more widely available through an agreement between the manufacturers, Merck, Sharp and Dohme, and the World Health Organization.

TOXOCARIASIS

Infection with the dog roundworm, *Toxocara canis*, may cause a condition known as 'visceral larva migrans' which may result in serious eye infection usually presenting as a visual loss in childhood. Although not a common disease it is found worldwide and is probably under-recognized. The larvae of the worm migrate to the retina, setting up an inflammatory response. Treatment with DEC has been recommended but hypersensitivity reactions may require steroids to be given as well. There is some anecdotal evidence that thiabendazole may offer an effective and less toxic alternative.

INTESTINAL HELMINTH INFECTIONS

Single doses of the common agents such as tetrachloroethylene, piperazine and bephenium give acceptable cure rates. Table 30.1 shows the differential activity of these and the newer oral agents which have a broader

Table 30.1. Spectrum of activity of drugs used in the treatment of intestinal helminthiasis

Drug	Ancylostoma duodenale	Necator americanus	Ascaris lumbricoides	Strongyloides stercoralis	Trichuris trichiura	Enterobius vermicularis
Tetrachloroethylene	+	+ + +	-	-	-	-
Piperazine	-	-	+ + +	-	-	+ + +
Bephenium	+ + +	+	+	-	-	-
Levamisole	+ +	+ +	+ + +	-	-	-
Pyrantel pamoate	+ +	+ +	+ + +	+	+ +	+ + +
Thiabendazole	+ +	+ +	+ + +	+ +	-	+ +
Mebendazole	+ +	+ +	+ + +	+	+ +	+ + +

+ + + = Highly effective; + = poorly effective; - = no useful activity.

spectrum but are more expensive. In the warmer countries with poor water supplies and inadequate methods of sewage disposal, re-infection is almost inevitable, yet a few words of health education such as advice on wearing shoes to prevent hookworm, may be extremely valuable.

SCHISTOSOMIASIS

Schistosomes (also known as bilharzia, or blood flukes) give rise to a chronic debilitating condition with hepatosplenomegaly and diarrhoea or haematuria. The adult worms adopt a more-or-less benign relationship with the host and it is fibrosis and tissue damage arising from the deposition of eggs which is responsible for most of the unpleasant manifestations of schistosomiasis.

In the days when trivalent antimonials were the only available agents for therapy of bilharzia, the decision to treat a specific case would depend on similar factors to those mentioned for filariasis: balancing the toxic effects of treatment with the severity of the patient's illness and the likelihood of rapid re-infection.

However, no area of antiparasitic chemotherapy has undergone such a transformation in recent years as has the treatment of schistosomiasis. As well as antimonials, a whole battery of drugs is now available including one, praziquantel, which appears to offer the possibility of effective single-dose therapy for mass treatment campaigns. Available drugs are not equally effective against all three types of schistosome infecting man; their differential activity is summarized in Table 30.2.

With the advent of these relatively safe and cheap antischistosomal drugs, it has become possible to use chemotherapy as a means of control

Table 30.2. Spectrum of activity of drugs used in the treatment of schistosomiasis

Drug	*Schistosoma mansoni*	*Schistosoma haematobium*	*Schistosoma japonicum*
Trivalent antimonials	+ + +	+ +	+ +
Niridazole	+	+ + +	+
Lucanthone	+	+ +	−
Hycanthone	+ +	+ + +	−
Metriphonate	−	+ + +	−
Oxamniquine	+ + +	−	−
Praziquantel	+ + +	+ + +	+ + +

+ + + = Highly effective; + = poorly effective; − = no useful activity.

of the disease in conjunction with the use of molluscicides to control the snail host and the provision of safe means of disposal of excreta. Unless there is development of drug resistance on a wide scale, such methods offer a good hope for the control of one of the major parasitic scourges of mankind. The outlook is not so bright for the other major diseases mentioned in this chapter, although control of onchocerciasis may be possible with ivermectin.

31

Topical use of antimicrobial agents

The concept of applying drugs directly to clinical lesions is appealing: problems of absorption and pharmacokinetics do not apply and agents too toxic for systemic use may be safely applied to skin or mucous membranes. The major drawback is that, even in the most superficial skin lesion, there may be areas inaccessible to a topical approach. Furthermore, collections of pus may prevent the agent reaching the infecting organisms and for this reason the management of any abscess includes drainage of pus.

Although skin, the largest and most accessible organ of the body, is the most obvious target for topical antimicrobials other sites are available for this approach to therapy: the mucous membranes of the mouth and vagina, and the external surfaces of eyes and ears. Direct application of antibiotics into normally sterile sites, such as joints, spinal fluid or the urinary bladder, or instillation into surgical wounds prior to suture may also be considered as a form of topical therapy, but will not be specifically dealt with in this chapter. Application of topical agents to mucous membranes or damaged skin may lead to considerable systemic absorption and the possibility of systemic toxicity should be borne in mind.

The chief reasons for using topical antimicrobial agents are:

(1) to achieve high drug concentrations at the site of infection;
(2) to treat trivial infections where use of a systemic drug is unjustified;
(3) to prevent infection in a susceptible site (e.g. burns);
(4) agents may be used that are too toxic for systemic use;
(5) cost: topical agents are generally cheaper than systemic drugs.

ANTISEPTICS

Disinfectant is a general term for chemicals which can destroy vegetative micro-organisms; those disinfectants that are sufficiently non-injurious to skin and exposed tissues to be used topically are called *antiseptics*. In order to achieve adequate antimicrobial activity, high concentrations of antiseptics are required and this serves to distinguish them from *antibiotics* in Waksman's original sense of 'substances produced by micro-organisms antagonistic to the growth or life of others in high dilution'. In many cases, true antibiotics are used topically in high concentration and might thus be classed as antiseptics. In fact, antiseptics and antibiotics are often used in exactly the same situations in dermatological practice and there has been some difference of opinion as to which class of agent to use in, for example, the treatment of infected ulcers or wounds. Antiseptics are usually cheaper and have the advantage that bacterial resistance rarely, if ever, develops. Preparations commonly employed include chlorhexidine, cetrimide, iodophors (non-irritant iodine complexes), and solutions liberating hypochlorite, such as Eusol or Dakin's solution.

METHODS OF APPLICATION

Drugs which are dissolved in aqueous solutions (*lotions*) have the disadvantage of running off the skin and cooling it by evaporation. This method of delivering antimicrobial agents to the site of infection is inefficient and not often used, except as ear or eye drops. For use in eye infections, frequent application onto the cornea and conjunctiva is necessary, because the drug is only in contact for a short time and much of the active component runs down the cheek as an expensive tear! The value of aqueous preparations resides mainly in their irrigant and cleansing action and much of the therapeutic success may be due to these properties.

It is usual to apply drugs to the skin in a fat base, either as an oil and water *cream*, or a largely lipid *ointment*. Drug solubility affects the achievable concentration in each component, while availability at the lesion depends on diffusion from the applicant and absorption from the skin. Antibiotics which are lipid soluble and freely diffusible, for example fusidic acid, are at an obvious advantage in this respect.

Sticky ointments may remain in contact with the infected site for a considerable time and application may be needed only once daily, but this obviously depends on the frequency of washing.

Some of the commonly used topical preparations are listed in Table 31.1. Many of the formulations designed for topical use contain combinations of antimicrobials. Mixtures are intended to cover a wide antibacterial spectrum and to be compatible.

Table 31.1. Some of the most commonly used topical antimicrobial agents. The numerous topical antiseptics available are omitted

Agent	Application	Indication*	Comments
Antibiotics			
Chloramphenicol †	Drops/ointment	Eye/ear	Very broad spectrum
Fusidic acid †	Ointment/drops	Skin only	Best against *Staph. aureus*
Gentamicin †	Cream/ointment/drops	Ear/nose/eye	Should not be used in hospitals
Mupirocin	Ointment	Nose	Macrogol-based ointment unsuitable for nasal application
Neomycin (framycetin)	Cream/ointment/drops/powder	Ear/nose/eye	Often combined with gramicidin or bacitracin and/or polymyxin B
Nystatin (and other polyenes)	Cream/pessary/suspension/lozenges	Mouth/vagina	For thrush (candidiasis)
Tetracycline †	Ointment/cream/drops	Ear/eye	Broad-spectrum; resistance common
Sulphonamides and other antimicrobial agents			
Mafenide	Cream/drops	Burns/eye	} May cause sensitization
Silver sulphadiazine	Cream	Burns only	
Nitrofurazone	Ointment/drops	Ear	
Acyclovir †	Ointment/cream	Eye/genitalia/mouth	} Antiviral agents: for use on herpes lesions
Idoxuridine	Ointment/drops	Eye/genitalia/mouth	
Vidarabine †	Ointment	Eyes	
Imidazoles (clotrimazole, etc.)	Cream/pessaries/gel/powder	Vagina	Antifungal: for use in skin infections and vaginal thrush

* = Indications other than skin, for which most are used. † = Compounds that are also used systemically.

CHOICE

The results of laboratory tests may be helpful if adequate specimens are sent to the laboratory, but frequently colonizing microbes are isolated from the surface of deep lesions while the true underlying pathogen remains undetected. The clinician must be careful not to use a battery of antimicrobials to treat harmless commensals colonizing an unoccupied niche.

Conventional antimicrobial sensitivity testing is often irrelevant because susceptibility of organisms to antiseptics can usually be assumed. Moreover, laboratory criteria of susceptibility to antibiotics usually apply to systemic use, not the high concentrations achievable by topical application. Nevertheless, complete resistance in laboratory tests is a contraindication to use of a particular agent. Regular monitoring of hospitalized patients with large skin lesions, such as ulcers and burns, is useful to determine the nature and prevalence of resistant organisms, as well as the extent of cross-infection.

Choice, if not based on microbiological evidence, must include agents active against all likely pathogens. Topical antiseptics and hydroxyquinolines are to be preferred to antibiotics on microbiological grounds of avoidance of resistance, but many users prefer antibiotics because it is claimed that a quicker response is generally obtained. Tetracyclines are often recommended by clinicians, but not by microbiologists, who point to the prevalence of tetracycline-resistance and the readiness with which such prevalence increases under selective pressure. Combinations of antibiotics, such as bacitracin and neomycin, or bacitracin, neomycin, and polymyxin are often used, and a corticosteroid is sometimes added for good measure. These antibiotics are not usually used for systemic therapy, so possible problems of compromising the activity of systemically useful agents by encouraging the emergence of resistance are minimized (see below). Nevertheless, it should be remembered that the topical use of neomycin might generate strains of bacteria cross-resistant to other aminoglycosides such as gentamicin.

One antibiotic, mupirocin (pseudomonic acid) has been marketed solely for topical use. The spectrum of activity of this agent is virtually restricted to Gram-positive cocci. Mupirocin is unsuitable for systemic use since it is quickly metabolized in the body. It has a unique mode of action (on protein synthesis) and cross-resistance is not a problem.

In practice, one of the most important limitations to choice is the availability of a particular drug as a topical product. Manufacturers are well aware that it makes little commercial sense to market a relatively cheap topical formulation if it is going to encourage resistance which diminishes the usefulness of more expensive parenteral forms of the drug. Here, at least, the interests of industry and the consumer coincide.

BACTERIAL SKIN INFECTIONS

Trivial skin sepsis, often due to staphylococci, is common, but usually self-limiting in healthy individuals. Impetigo is frequently a more severe and widespread condition which may involve both *Streptococcus pyogenes* and *Staphylococcus aureus*. In general, mild infections of the skin respond to local measures involving cleansing of the crusted areas and application of topical agents, such as fusidic acid or mupirocin, to the raw surfaces. More severe staphylococcal and streptococcal skin lesions may require systemic therapy and this is discussed in Chapter 24.

Nasal carriage

In recurrent sepsis with *Staph. aureus* it may be necessary to attempt to eradicate the organism from the body. This is also desirable in patients and staff colonized with antibiotic resistant strains, particularly methicillin-resistant *Staph. aureus* (MRSA) which can cause serious cross-infection problems. The external surface of the skin can be washed in antiseptics, but nasal carriage of staphylococci is often resistant to this treatment. For this purpose, nasal creams should be applied at least twice a day for 5 days. Chlorhexidine/neomycin cream (Naseptin) has been widely used, but does not appear to be as effective as mupirocin in the eradication of nasal carriage of MRSA. The normal dermatological preparation of mupirocin, which is in a macrogol (polyethylene glycol) excipient is unsuitable for nasal application and a paraffin-based ointment should be used for this purpose.

ACNE

The role of bacteria in the pathogenesis of acne vulgaris is still under debate, although commensal diphtheroids, such as *Propionibacterium acnes* are thought to play some part. Systemic antibiotics, including tetracycline and erythromycin, do improve severe intractable cases and success has also been claimed for topical antimicrobials, in particular for clindamycin. Treatment with any of these agents needs to be prolonged and is an adjunct to other measures aimed at improving the condition.

BURNS

The treatment of burns is an enormous specialized topic that cannot be covered adequately in this chapter. However, topical agents do have definite value in the prevention of infection in patients with burns so it is appropriate that their use should be mentioned.

Initially, a thermal burn renders the skin sterile, but bacterial colonization is inevitable, even with scrupulous aseptic technique. Indeed, infection, usually with *Str. pyogenes*, *Staph. aureus*, or *Pseudomonas aeruginosa*, is an important determinant in the outcome of extensive burns, since it is a major cause of delay in skin healing and of death.

Prophylaxis with topical antibiotics and antiseptics has been shown significantly to reduce colonization and sepsis. Mafenide, a sulphonamide derivative, was widely used, but has been largely replaced by silver sulphadiazine or chlorhexidine in the UK. None of these agents will reliably prevent infection by multiply resistant Gram-negative rods, especially *Ps. aeruginosa* (an organism that has replaced *Str. pyogenes* as the major scourge of burns units), or fungi. Aggressive surgical approaches of early wound closure by skin grafting after debridement has reduced the requirement for topical applications to burned surfaces.

In cases where infection becomes established, systemic drugs will often have to be employed, the choice being dictated by laboratory tests. However, since the penetration of antibiotics to surface lesions with a poor blood supply may be inadequate, topical dressings are additionally required.

Urinary and respiratory infections are commonly encountered in the burned patient, as is septicaemia, which has a poor prognosis. These infections require, of course, systemic therapy, but choice may be limited by bacterial resistance since many burns units are notorious for the prevalence of highly resistant strains, especially of *Ps. aeruginosa*.

SKIN ULCERS

Ulceration of the skin of the leg or the area overlying the sacrum may arise from a variety of pathological states and infection is usually a sequela, not an initiating event. Disorders of the circulation, including obliterative arterial disease, small vessel damage consequent on diabetes mellitus and varicose veins are the most common underlying conditions and correction of the underlying cause is essential to the healing of any ulcer. Continuous pressure is another common factor in the formation of a break in the skin, particularly in the bed-ridden. Such bed sores are difficult to prevent without scrupulous nursing care. This problem has led to the development of special air beds and cushions to minimize local vascular occlusion to the skin overlying bony areas such as the sacrum.

The presence of infection in a skin ulcer may be detected by odour, local cellulitis and appearance of pus, which in the case of pseudomonas infection may be characteristically green. Gas in the tissues, detected as crepitus on palpation, may indicate anaerobic infection. Swab reports showing the presence of potential pathogens do not prove infection since colonization of a large raw skin area is inevitable. *Staph. aureus*, environmental and gut bacteria are the organisms most commonly found in these sites. *Pseudomonas aeruginosa* is frequently found in long-standing ulcers because of its intrinsic resistance to many antibiotics and chemical agents used as antiseptics. In some cases infection is sufficiently invasive to warrant systemic treatment and metronidazole should be given to patients in whom *Bacteroides fragilis* infection is suspected.

Local therapy with antiseptics, combined with measures to improve the nutrition of the site are the mainstays of management of skin ulcers. Chlorine- or iodine-containing compounds (especially *iodophors*, which are iodine complexes that do not stain the skin and are less irritant) are often used, but older remedies such as honey, sugar, and vinegar may also have a place. In addition, topical antibiotics such as tetracycline are often used in severe infected ulcers which do not respond to conservative management. Many weeks of regular dressing combined with bed rest may be required to heal large ulcers; admission to hospital often speeds up the process. Skin grafting is frequently used for the most recalcitrant cases.

SUPERFICIAL FUNGAL INFECTIONS

Confirmation of the diagnosis of superficial fungal infections such as ringworm and tinea pedis of the skin, or thrush of the mouth or vagina, depends on laboratory investigation of appropriate specimens from the affected area (nail, hair, skin scrapings, swabs of lesions of mucous membranes). Microscopy alone will be sufficient to establish a fungal cause in most cases, but culture is necessary to identify the aetiological agent. Susceptibility testing presents technical difficulties, but dermatophytes may usually be assumed to be susceptible to appropriate agents (see Chapter 4, Table 4.1). *Candida albicans* may acquire resistance to some drugs, but this is only of great importance in invasive candidiasis.

The limiting factor in treating dermatophyte infections is penetration of the agent. For superficial skin infections old-fashioned remedies, such as benzoic acid-containing ointments (e.g. Whitfield's ointment) are perfectly effective, but for hair and nail infections, agents which penetrate into keratinized tissue are needed. Oral griseofulvin is uniquely suited to this purpose, since it is absorbed from the gastrointestinal tract and is preferentially concentrated in keratin. Because of the slow turnover of nail and hair, treatment for several months may be required; indeed, fungal infections of toenails may not completely clear, even after a year's treatment with griseofulvin, despite susceptibility of the infecting fungus.

Thrush responds in most cases to an appropriate antifungal agent, applied topically (e.g. nystatin or an imidazole), but precipitating factors, such as diabetes or antibiotic therapy, must also be corrected if they are present. If there is clinical evidence for invasive infection, as, for example, *Candida* oesophagitis, appropriate systemic drugs, such as amphotericin B, 5-fluorocytosine, fluconazole or ketoconazole must be added.

DISADVANTAGES OF TOPICAL THERAPY

Topical therapy is not without its hazards. Although the direct toxic effects of drugs given systemically are reduced, exposed tissues and mucous membranes offer a fairly efficient site for drug absorption. For example, aminoglycoside ototoxicity has been reported following local application of neomycin, especially in the newborn. A more frequently observed effect is sensitization to the agent so that subsequent use of the drug, either topically or parenterally, produces a hypersensitivity reaction. Penicillin, in particular, is prone to sensitize the host and because of possible anaphylactic reactions it is not advisable to use any β-lactam antibiotic on the skin. A further hazard of topical therapy is that local irritation may lead to a delay in wound healing, even though the actual infection is controlled.

Superinfection with resistant bacteria or with fungi is a common consequence of using any topical antibiotic for a prolonged period. Widespread use of one particular agent will lead to a larger reservoir of resistant organisms and the possibility of cross-infection. This is particularly likely to occur in burns units and dermatology wards, where there are many patients with large open skin lesions. Prevention of infection and cross-infection by aseptic methods is desirable, but often difficult in practice.

Of equal concern is the development of bacterial resistance during therapy. It has been shown that topical neomycin can select resistant *Staphylococcus epidermidis* strains, which can transfer resistance to *Staph. aureus* on the skin. The emergence of gentamicin-resistant *Ps. aeruginosa* and coliforms has been associated with topical use of that aminoglycoside, particularly on leg ulcers. In some instances the resistance is plasmid-mediated. In this manner, topical agents select multi-resistant organisms which may subsequently cause systemic infection in the patient or, by cross-infection, others. This is the most powerful argument against the indiscriminate use of topical antibiotics, and since antiseptics lack this disadvantage, they are to be preferred wherever possible.

32

Postscript: The development and marketing of antimicrobial drugs

The vast majority of new antimicrobial agents now emerge by a process of chemical modification of existing compounds. A few naturally occurring compounds continue to be described, but no entirely novel antimicrobial agent has emerged on to the therapeutic scene in recent years. The proliferation of agents continues, but the emphasis may be shifting. Of ten new antimicrobial agents released on to the UK market during 1987 and 1988 (Table 32.1) three were antiviral agents and one was antifungal; two of the six antibacterial agents were variants of older compounds.

The progress of a new antibiotic from discovery to marketing is outlined in Fig. 32.1. When a new antimicrobial drug is discovered or invented, the first indications of its activity and spectrum are usually gleaned from fairly crude in-vitro inhibition tests against a few common representative organisms. In-vitro screening tests will not detect potentially useful activity if in-vivo metabolism of the compound is a prerequisite for the antimicro-

Table 32.1. New antimicrobial agents 1987–88 (UK)

Compound	Therapeutic category
Aztreonam	Antibacterial
Cefuroxime axetil	Antibacterial
Ciprofloxacin	Antibacterial
Fluconazole	Antifungal
Ganciclovir	Antiviral
Imipenem	Antibacterial
Mupirocin	Antibacterial (topical)
Ticarcillin/clavulanate	Antibacterial
Tribavirin	Antiviral
Zidovudine	Antiviral

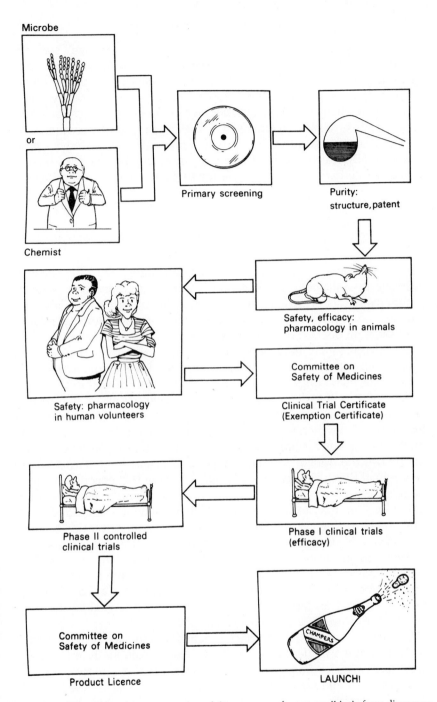

Microbe

or

Chemist

Primary screening

Purity:
structure, patent

Safety, efficacy:
pharmacology in animals

Safety: pharmacology
in human volunteers

Committee on
Safety of Medicines

Clinical Trial Certificate
(Exemption Certificate)

Phase II controlled
clinical trials

Phase I clinical trials
(efficacy)

Committee on
Safety of Medicines

Product Licence

LAUNCH!

Fig. 32.1. Diagrammatic representation of the progress of a new antibiotic from discovery to marketing.

bial effect (e.g. Prontosil; see Historical introduction), nor will such tests reveal agents which might modify microbial cells sufficiently to render them non-virulent or susceptible to host defences, without actually preventing their growth. Furthermore, conventional laboratory culture media occasionally contain substances which interfere with the activity of certain antimicrobial compounds, which may consequently go undetected.

Despite these difficulties, in-vitro screening offers an extremely simple and generally effective way of detecting antimicrobial activity which has yielded a rich harvest of therapeutically useful compounds over the years.

DEVELOPMENT OF NEW COMPOUNDS

Those compounds that pass the initial screening tests must be made available in sufficient quantities and in sufficiently pure form to enable preliminary tests of toxicity and efficacy to be carried out in laboratory animals, and more extensive and precise in-vitro tests to be performed. Pilot-stage production usually presents little problem, although considerable difficulties may be experienced in scaling up production at a later date, when relatively large quantities are needed for clinical trials and subsequent marketing.

Animal tests of toxicity, pharmacology, and efficacy are an indispensable part of the development of any new drug, but they also have considerable limitations. Idiosyncratic reactions may suggest toxicity in a compound that would be safe for human use or, more importantly, adverse reactions peculiar to the human subject may go undetected. The pharmacological handling of the drug may be vastly different from that encountered in the human subject. As regards efficacy testing, animals have important limitations in that experimental infections seldom correspond to the supposedly analogous condition in man, either anatomically or in the relationship of treatment to the natural history of the disease process.

If preliminary tests of toxicity and efficacy indicate that the compound is worth advancing further, full-scale acute and chronic toxicity tests are carried out in animals. These include long-term tests of mutagenic capacity, effects on fertility, and teratogenicity. Mutagenicity tests may also be performed in microbial systems (Ames test).

Providing the animal toxicity studies reveal no serious toxicity problems, the first tentative trials are undertaken in healthy human volunteers (usually employees of the company involved) to investigate the pharmacology and safety of the new drug in man. Once these tests have been successfully completed, application may be made to the drug licensing authority for permission to undertake clinical trials.

CLINICAL TRIALS

The proof of the pudding is in the eating, and no amount of in-vitro or animal testing can replace the ultimate test of safety and efficacy: therapeutic use in human infection.

Nevertheless, the clinical trial stage remains, in many ways, the least satisfactory aspect of the testing of any new antimicrobial drug. The reasons for this are not difficult to find: 'infection' is not a static condition in which therapeutic intervention produces an all-or-none effect. Many factors, such as mobilization of the patient's own immune response, drainage of pus, or treatment of an underlying surgical or medical condition, may crucially affect the response to therapy. The patient may improve subjectively, even though the antimicrobial therapy has demonstrably failed to eradicate the supposed pathogen; conversely, the patient's condition may deteriorate despite bacteriological 'success'.

Clinical trials should not be undertaken lightly. They are difficult to design, tedious to perform and are fraught with ethical difficulties. The conduct of the trial requires close supervision by a medical practitioner dedicated to the task, who needs to have the full support of reliable and motivated nursing and laboratory staff. Before undertaking a trial, a detailed protocol should be drawn up, defining the conditions for which the new treatment is intended, the dosage regimens to be used and the treatment with which it is to be compared. Participating laboratories should be consulted to ensure that full facilities are available for the monitoring of microbiological progress and the detection of adverse reactions.

Careful consideration should be given as to whether the trial should be open, single-blind (treatment known to the prescriber only) or double-blind (treatment randomly allocated in a fashion unknown to prescriber or recipient). In general, uncontrolled, open trials are unsatisfactory, except as preliminary indicators of safety and efficacy. Controlled, double-blind trials are the most desirable scientifically, but are subject to ethical difficulties in that the prescribing doctor does not have full control over the patient's treatment.

Ethical considerations need to be taken fully into account. The basic principles which should govern all research involving human subjects are embodied in the *Declaration of Helsinki*, which was adopted by the 18th World Medical Assembly in 1964 and revised by the Assembly in 1975. Most health authorities now have ethical committees which monitor clinical trial protocols. The committee will need assurance that the safety of a new compound has been satisfactorily established and will wish to know what form of patient consent is to be obtained. It will also require adequate safeguards to be built in for the detection of unexpected adverse reactions and may have views as to whether a double-blind format, or a placebo control, are acceptable.

Many ambitious trials fail because insufficient numbers of patients are found to fulfil the criteria required for the study. Alternatively, the condition may be one (acute cystitis is a good example) in which the natural cure rate is so high, and the efficacy of standard treatment so good, that huge numbers would have to be examined to establish the superiority of a new agent, although it may be possible to establish efficacy. It is essential to be reasonably sure, before the trial starts, that sufficient patients can be accumulated to satisfy statistical requirements. During the conduct of the trial, regular checks of relevant microbiological, haematological, chemical, and radiological parameters should be made. All findings should be fully documented as soon as the information is available, rather than attempting to glean information from the patients' notes retrospectively, after the trial is completed.

DRUG LICENSING

Most countries have enacted some sort of legislation aimed at controlling the marketing of pharmaceutical products intended for use under medical supervision. In the USA, Federal regulations are administered by the Food and Drug Administration (FDA). Within the European Economic Community, a Committee on Proprietary Medical Products has been set up to produce guidelines for harmonizing regulatory requirements among member nations, although, at the time of writing, no binding agreements have been entered into.

In the UK, the Medicines Act of 1968 (implemented on 1st September 1971) invested executive powers in the government health and agriculture ministers, who constitute the British Drug Licensing Authority. This body, with the help of the Medicines Commission and its various specialist advisory committees, undertook a review of all pharmaceutical products intended for supervised medical or veterinary use, and this is still in progress.

Before clinical trials can be performed on a new drug in the UK, full toxicological data must be submitted to the Licensing Authority together with a full trial protocol and the names of the proposed investigators. Such applications are scrutinized by the Committee on Safety of Medicines (CSM), who must satisfy themselves that all reasonable criteria are met before recommending that a *Clinical Trial Certificate*, valid for two years, be issued.

Pharmaceutical manufacturers have long complained about the delays inherent in processing applications for a Clinical Trial Certificate and firms in the UK may now be granted a *Clinical Trial Exemption Certificate*, providing certain criteria are met. In particular, the holder of the exemption certificate must undertake to notify any adverse reaction arising during the trial, or any other matter which might reasonably cause the Licensing Authority to doubt the safety or quality of the product.

When sufficient clinical trial data have been accumulated, an application for a *Product Licence* may be made. All valid applications are again passed to the CSM for scrutiny. In some countries, licensing authorities require that new compounds should be shown to be superior to existing products, in an effort to reduce so-called 'me-too' products. However, in the UK the CSM judge new applications only on the grounds of safety, efficacy, and quality. If the CSM recommends refusal of a Product Licence, the application may be withdrawn or the applicant may elect to answer the objections raised, either in writing or in person before the CSM. Should the application still be refused, the applicant has the right of appeal to the Medicines Commission. Product Licences, once issued, are valid for five years.

Over the years, the requirements of licensing authorities worldwide (particularly for toxicological testing) have become progressively more stringent. Consequently, the cost of developing a new drug has escalated enormously. All the large pharmaceutical firms now have specialized departments to deal with licensing requirements and many attempt to circumvent the restrictions on clinical trials by conducting them in countries where regulations are more permissive. The period between the discovery and marketing of a new product is seldom less than five years. Shortening this period is important to the company marketing the new drug, since it maximizes the time during which it can recoup the cost of research and development (which may exceed £100 million) and profit from the discovery while enjoying patent protection.

DRUG MARKETING

During the 10 years from 1972 to 1981, over 200 compounds described as 'new chemical entities' were marketed in the UK for therapeutic use. Forty of these were antimicrobial agents; half of them β-lactam antibiotics.

Under the 1968 Medicines Act, all companies marketing products provided for the use of medical practitioners are required to produce data sheets giving a summary of relevant information about the drug, including the conditions for which its use is licensed, contraindications and known side-effects. Most pharmaceutical firms collaborate in producing an annual

Data Sheet Compendium, which is distributed free to registered medical practitioners.

Issue of a Product Licence is no guarantee that a compound is 100 per cent safe, not even that all adverse reactions have been detected before marketing. Because of this, the CSM issue postage-paid 'yellow cards' for the notification of adverse reactions, to all practitioners. Although the scheme is voluntary, it is important that prescribers collaborate fully with it. Such notifications are particularly important in the first few years in which a new compound is marketed. Copies of the notification form are routinely included with each issue of the British National Formulary.

The conduct of pharmaceutical companies in marketing their products is governed by a voluntary Code of Practice agreed between the members of the Association of the British Pharmaceutical Industry in consultation with the British Medical Association and the Department of Health and Social Security. The Code of Practice is published in the Data Sheet Compendium. It covers, among other things, the content and distribution of advertisements and other promotional literature; hospitality, gifts, and inducements to the medical and allied professions; marketing research; and relationships with the general public and lay communications media.

The subject of advertising is a perennial bone of contention between doctors and the pharmaceutical industry. The former complain that the industry tries to cloud their professional judgement under a deluge of irrelevant, mendacious, and uninterpretable gobbledegook; the latter claim their commercial right to exploit their products to their best advantage in the market place, and point to the factual data sheets and other information services that they place at the disposal of the medical profession.

The truth, as usual, inhabits the middle ground. Advertisements are subject to the usual advertising regulations and may not tell overt lies. Nonetheless, they are intended to sway the prescriber in favour of a particular product. Doctors cannot ignore advertisements and should be wary of claiming that they are uninfluenced by them. If they were not influenced, advertisements would not be so cost-effective as they clearly are.

Prescribers should therefore make a conscious effort to separate fact from fantasy in advertisements and cultivate a healthy critical attitude, especially towards new products. In particular, doctors should learn to distinguish between genuine advances and new products which, though effective, are no better than older, well tried, and cheaper remedies. They should also be wary of impressive claims ostensibly based on published independent assessments which turn out, in the small print, to refer to 'data on file' or dubious publications in obscure sources.

In the UK the *British National Formulary* and *Drug and Therapeutics*

Bulletin, published by the Consumers' Association, offer reliable sources of objective information to the medical practitioner. In the USA, the *National Formulary* and the *Medical Letter* provide a similar service. Many hospitals now produce therapeutic guides for the use of their medical staff. Pharmacies often offer a formal 'drug information service' to which general practitioners also have access, and most medical microbiology laboratories are able to offer accurate up-to-date advice on antimicrobial therapy.

It should be emphasized that, although the marketing of drugs is fairly well regulated throughout the industrially developed world, the same is not true of less favoured countries; in many nations of the world the standards of advertising and marketing often appear to overstep the bounds of what would be considered ethical in more developed countries.

DRUG NAMES

When a new antibiotic is first described in the scientific literature it usually appears under a number representing the manufacturer's laboratory code for the compound. This practice is to be discouraged, since the code is forgotten once a drug is named and, in later years, source references become difficult to locate. The reason for using a code is that names proposed by the manufacturer are not always subsequently accepted by the bodies controlling drug nomenclature. These are the British Pharmacopoeia Commission in the UK who recommend a British Approved Name (BAN) to the Medicines Commission and the United States Adopted Name (USAN) Council in the USA. International agreement is co-ordinated by the World Health Organization who specify the International Non-proprietary Name (INN). Once the *Approved Name* is introduced into the national Pharmacopoeia of a country, it becomes the *Official Name*. In addition to the Approved or Official Name, the drug may have various *proprietary names* under which it is marketed by the manufacturer(s) or his agents.

Approved Names try to avoid close nomenclatural similarities, but the profusion of 'sulpha-s', 'cefa-s', and '-cillins' still produces some confusion; when the same compound is marketed under different proprietary names, bewilderment is often complete.

There has been a good deal of debate as to whether doctors should use proprietary or non-proprietary names in writing prescriptions. On the one hand, it is pointed out that formulations differ so that the pharmacological properties of a drug may vary from product to product. Moreover, adverse reactions caused by a particular formulation may be more easily detected if the product is specified. On the other hand, non-proprietary names are less likely to cause confusion; they free the pharmacist from the necessity of keeping a large and varied stock of similar products and enable him to dispense the cheapest version of a particular drug.

The British National Formulary sensibly recommends prescribers to use non-proprietary names in all but those few instances where bioavailability problems are so important that the patient should always receive the same brand.

WHITHER ANTIBIOTICS?

The number of antimicrobial drugs available to the prescriber is now enormous and, at least as far as antibacterial compounds are concerned, the undoubted value of having a wide and varied choice has been overtaken by the confusion that is caused by the conflicting claims of so many agents with similar or overlapping indications. There is no dispute about the fact that we currently possess more antibacterial drugs than we need; most of the common infections can be adequately dealt with using a few well-tried agents. Indeed, most general practitioners rely on a few favourite antibiotics which they use to cover most bacterial infections. The WHO includes only a handful of antibacterial agents in its list of essential drugs (Table 32.2). The availability of antimicrobial drugs varies widely among different countries for reasons that must be commercial rather than therapeutic: for example, a total of 58 different β-lactam agents were available in Japan in 1987, and 40 were marketed in the UK; the comparative figure for Norway, where a restrictive licensing policy is in operation, was only 16, while the WHO essential drug list has a mere seven, all of which are penicillins.

Apart from the financial attractions of a share in a huge market, the main impetus for continuing research into antibacterial agents is the ever-present spectre of resistance. At no time has this reached the point where effective antibacterial treatment has become impossible, but it is difficult to assess how the continuing influx of new drugs has influenced the course of events (see Chapter 11).

The situation with the chemotherapy of non-bacterial infection is much less satisfactory. Although great strides have been made in the prevention of viral infection by immunization, chemotherapy for viral disease is extremely limited (see Chapters 6 and 28). Some sort of effective chemotherapy is available for most fungal, protozoal, and helminth infections, but the choice is very limited and, in many ways, unsatisfactory (see Chapters 4, 5 and 30). On a global scale, it is these conditions, rather than the traditional bacterial infectious diseases, which are responsible for the great majority of morbidity and mortality among humankind. The greatest

Table 32.2. Antimicrobial agents on the WHO list of essential drugs (fifth list, 1988)

Antibacterial agents	Antimycobacterial agents	Antifungal agents	Antiprotozoal agents	Anthelminthic agents
Ampicillin*	Clofazimine	Amphotericin B	Benznidazole	Diethylcarbamazine
Benzathine penicillin	Dapsone	Griseofulvin	Chloroquine*	Mebendazole*
Benzylpenicillin	Ethambutol	Ketoconazole	Diloxanide*	Metriphonate
Chloramphenicol*	Isoniazid	Nystatin	Meglumine antimoniate	Niclosamide
Cloxacillin*	Pyrazinamide	(Flucytosine)	Melarsoprol	Oxamniquine
Co-trimoxazole*	Rifampicin		Metronidazole*	Piperazine
Erythromycin*	Streptomycin		Nifurtimox	Praziquantel
Gentamicin*	Thiacetazone + isoniazid		Pentamidine	Pyrantel
Metronidazole*			Primaquine	Suramin
Phenoxymethylpenicillin			Proguanil	Thiabendazole
Piperacillin*			Quinine*	(Ivermectin)
Procaine penicillin			Sodium stibogluconate*	(Levamisole)
Spectinomycin			Suramin	
Sulphadimidine*			(Dihydroemetine)	
Tetracycline*			(Mefloquine)	
(Doxycycline)			(Sulfadoxine + pyrimethamine)*	
(Nitrofurantoin)			(Tetracycline)*	
(Trimethoprim)				

Drugs listed are on the main list, except those in brackets, which are on the complementary list. Asterisks indicate examples of a therapeutic group for which acceptable alternatives exist.

challenge for the future is to provide for these diseases the same sort of safe, effective chemotherapy that is now available for most bacterial infections, and to make effective therapy for all infections readily available for those who need it most.

Recommendations for further reading

A large number of books are available dealing with the practicalities of the use of antimicrobial agents. Since availability and usage differ considerably in different countries, no one book has universal applicability. The following are among the most authoritative texts in the English language.

Garrod, L. P., Lambert, H. P., and O'Grady, F. (1981). *Antibiotic and chemotherapy*, 5th edn. Churchill Livingstone, Edinburgh. (6th edn in press.)
Kagan, B. M. (ed.) (1980). *Antimicrobial therapy*, 3rd edn. W. B. Saunders, Philadelphia.
Kucers, A. and Bennett, N. McK. (1987). *The use of antibiotics*, 4th edn. Heinemann, London.

Excellent books dealing with the mode of action of antimicrobial agents and the principles underlying their use include:

Franklin, T. J. and Snow, G. A. (1989). *Biochemistry of antimicrobial action*, 4th edn. Chapman and Hall, London.
Gale, E. F., Cundliffe, E., Reynolds, P. E., Richmond, M. H., and Waring, M. J. (1981). *The molecular basis of antibiotic action*, 2nd edn. John Wiley & Sons, Chichester.
Greenwood, D. and O'Grady, F. (eds.) (1985). *The scientific basis of antimicrobial chemotherapy*. Cambridge University Press, Cambridge.
Pratt, W. B. and Fekety, R. (1986). *The antimicrobial drugs*. Oxford University Press, Oxford.

Laboratory aspects of antimicrobial therapy are dealt with in:

Lorian, V. (ed.) (1986) *Antibiotics in laboratory medicine*, 2nd edn. Williams & Wilkins, Baltimore.
Reeves, D. S., Phillips, I., Williams, J. D., and Wise, R. (1978). *Laboratory methods in antimicrobial chemotherapy*. Churchill Livingstone, Edinburgh. (New edition in preparation.)

An indispensable guide to the use of all therapeutic drugs for practitioners in the UK is provided by:

British National Formulary. British Medical Association and the Royal Pharmaceutical Society of Great Britain. (Revised at intervals of about 6 months.)

An excellent guide to the use of drugs specifically designed for the East African situation, but having a much wider applicability to developing nations of the world, is provided by:

Upunda, G., Yudkin, J., and Brown, G. (1980). *Therapeutic guidelines*. African Medical and Research Foundation, Nairobi.

This book has also been published in the Macmillan Tropical Community Health Manuals series as:

Guidelines to Drug Usage (1983). Macmillan, London.

Other books providing a valuable insight into the use and abuse of antimicrobial agents in the Third World include:

Melrose, D. (1982) *Bitter pills: medicines and the Third World poor*. Oxfam, Oxford.
World Health Organization (1988). *The world drug situation*. WHO, Geneva.
World Health Organization (1988). *The use of essential drugs*. 3rd report of WHO Expert Committee. WHO Technical Report Series, No. 770. WHO, Geneva.

Antimicrobial drugs are used so widely that papers dealing with aspects of their use appear in numerous journals. English language journals specifically devoted to antibiotics and antimicrobial therapy include:

   Antimicrobial Agents and Chemotherapy
   Chemotherapy (Basel)
   Journal of Antibiotics (Tokyo)
   Journal of Antimicrobial Chemotherapy

In addition, the *European Journal of Clinical Microbiology and Infectious Diseases* contains a 'New Antimicrobial Agents' section, in which pre-clinical data on new agents is presented.
   The *British Society for Antimicrobial Chemotherapy* periodically publishes authoritative reviews of aspects of antimicrobial therapy. Articles that have appeared so far are:

(1982). The antibiotic prophylaxis of infective endocarditis. *Lancet* ii, 1323-6.
(1985). Antibiotic treatment of streptococcal and staphylococcal endocarditis. *Lancet* ii, 815-17.
(1987). Diagnosis and management of peritonitis in continuous ambulatory peritoneal dialysis. *Lancet* i, 845-9.
(1988). Breakpoints in in-vitro antibiotic sensitivity testing. *Journal of Antimicrobial Chemotherapy* 21, 701-10.
(1989). The clinical evaluation of antibacterial drugs. *Journal of Antimicrobial Chemotherapy* 23 (Suppl. B), 1-42.

Index